Literary Lives

This classic and longstanding series has established itself making a major contribution to literary biography. The books in the series are thoroughly researched and comprehensive, covering the writer's complete oeuvre. The latest volumes trace the literary, professional, publishing, and social contexts that shaped influential authors—exploring the "why" behind writers' greatest works. In its thirtieth year, the series aims to publish on a diverse set of writers—both canonical and rediscovered—in an accessible and engaging way.

More information about this series at
http://www.palgrave.com/gp/series/14010

Kimberly J. Stern

Oscar Wilde

A Literary Life

palgrave
macmillan

Kimberly J. Stern
University of North Carolina
Chapel Hill, NC, USA

Literary Lives
ISBN 978-3-030-24603-7   ISBN 978-3-030-24604-4   (eBook)
https://doi.org/10.1007/978-3-030-24604-4

Cover illustration: Lordprice Collection / Alamy Stock Photo

This Palgrave Macmillan imprint is published by the registered company Springer Nature Switzerland AG.
The registered company address is: Gewerbestrasse 11, 6330 Cham, Switzerland

Acknowledgments

This book began in the classroom. Accordingly, I want to begin by thanking my students, who over the years have shared with me a love of the author treated in the following pages. The delight I have taken in writing this volume is owing, in large part, to the countless hours I have spent in enriching conversation with them.

I am also indebted to the many scholars of Oscar Wilde who have preceded me, especially those who feature within the pages of this book. These colleagues and mentors have offered me much food for thought and have been instrumental in refining my approach to Wilde and the intellectual traditions that shaped his work.

Several individuals and institutions have likewise contributed in substantial ways to this volume by providing me with access to vital manuscript material. These include the Board of Trinity College Dublin (Ireland); the William Andrews Cark Memorial Library at the University of California, Los Angeles (Los Angeles, California); Fogg Art Museum, Harvard University Museums (Cambridge, Massachusetts); and Merlin Holland, devoted executor of Wilde's literary estate. Certainly, none of this would have been possible without the support of my home institution, the University of North Carolina at Chapel Hill.

Finally, my deepest thanks to Phil and Felix, my joyful companions in this contemplative life.

Contents

About the Author

Kimberly J. Stern is Assistant Professor of English and Comparative Literature at the University of North Carolina at Chapel Hill. She is the editor of a Broadview edition of Oscar Wilde's *Salomé* (2015) and author of *The Social Life of Criticism: Gender, Criticism, and the Politics of Belonging* (University of Michigan Press, 2016).

List of Figures

1

The Biographer

It is always Judas who writes the biography.
Oscar Wilde, "The Critic as Artist"

In "The Critic as Artist" (1891), Oscar Wilde celebrates "the contemplative life, the life that has for its aim not *doing* but *being*, and not *being* merely, but *becoming*."[1] As a professional scholar, I have always been attracted by the idea that quiet reflection is not an isolating but rather a sociable endeavor, one that brings us into close proximity to the very stuff of life. It is a philosophy that I bring to the classroom, where I unfailingly encounter bright, curious faces just embarking upon their own intellectual journeys, some of them at the most transformative moment of their lives. Learning is an adventure—an unpredictable, messy, sometimes even perilous one, but an adventure nevertheless worth undertaking. "For what is mind," Wilde reminds us, "but motion in the intellectual sphere? The essence of thought, as the essence of life, is growth."[2]

Oscar Wilde: A Literary Life was inspired by my passion for learning and teaching. On the one hand, I longed to contemplate how Wilde, one of the most supple and complex minds I have ever encountered, approached the learning process. But I also sought to enhance the learning experience of my students, who had repeatedly approached me in search of an intellectual biography that would help them to navigate the mind of a writer they found energizing and provocative, if not always consistent. In this spirit, the following chapters presume that, as Lord Henry Wotton puts it in *The Picture of Dorian Gray* (1890/1), at least some of the "great events of the world take

© The Author(s) 2019
K. J. Stern, *Oscar Wilde*, Literary Lives,
https://doi.org/10.1007/978-3-030-24604-4_1

place in the brain," focusing less on what Wilde did than on what—and perhaps more importantly *how*—he thought.[3] This book is intended for all readers of Wilde, from those just embarking on the study of his work to seasoned readers who seek out a greater familiarity with the intellectual contexts that gave it shape. Most of all, however, I present this work as an aid to readers who, cognizant of the contradictions in Wilde's life and work, wish to understand his mind without abandoning what makes it so alluring in the first place.

Before embarking on this experiment, it is worth taking a moment to reflect upon what it means to write, let alone to read, an intellectual biography. There are few better starting points for such a discussion than Wilde himself. In the spirit of the chapters that follow, I begin by considering Wilde's own encounters with and responses to nineteenth-century biography. That he at once celebrated and disparaged the genre in his own work provides us with at least some insight into why an intellectual biography of Wilde is so necessary—and so difficult. Next, I consider how contemporary accounts of Wilde, though valuable in their own right, tend to suppress precisely those elements of intellectual biography that Wilde himself prized. Finally, I turn to the structure and methodologies I have deployed in this volume. I admit quite frankly that this is not a complete or definitive record of Wilde's life, for no record of such a writer can rightly claim to be complete or definitive. I have, however, endeavored to make sense of—and to celebrate—what remains incomplete and indefinite.

Wilde on Biography

In July 1876, at the age of 21, Oscar Wilde informed his friend William Ward that he had abandoned any prospect of competing for an Oxford scholarship. He planned instead "to edit an unfinished work of my father's, the Life of Gabriel Beranger, Artist."[4] His father, Sir William Wilde, had died in April of that year, having already seen the greater portion of the volume printed in the *Journal of the Royal Historical and Archaeological Association of Ireland* between 1871 and 1873. Wilde's mother, Lady Jane Francesca Wilde, was undertaking the very difficult task of completing the book, and Wilde, in one of his earliest forays into literary work, had volunteered his assistance.

Although the vast majority of William Wilde's works dealt with medical or archeological subject matter, in this volume he addressed a topic nearer to his son's heart: the life of an eighteenth-century Dutch artist who settled in Ireland in 1750 and became noted for his depictions of Irish antiquities. Standing at the intersection of art, science, and history, William Wilde was keenly aware of the methodological hurdles before him. He commences with a word on the challenges of biography:

> Every biographer who wishes to be impartial should, for the occasion at least, live among the scenes and during the period when and where the personage whose character he is limning resided. He ought to be well acquainted with the subject he has undertaken to describe, and, as far as possible, honestly identify himself with the pursuits, and exercise a fair critical discretion in reviewing the labours of the person who, for the time being, has become the chief actor in his drama. […] Men must be tried by the light of their own times, by the education they have received, and the circumstances by which they were surrounded, to afford them fair play in the history of any country.[5]

There are dangers, William Wilde reminds us, to life writing. Chief among these is the risk of mistaking oneself for one's subject and thereby measuring the figures of the past by the social and cultural standards of the present. Not only does such an approach risk eliding the personal and historical influences that color life events; it also risks drawing that life into the service of specific political or cultural ends. Although life may be (in the strictest sense) linear, it does not necessarily follow a logical or progressive sequence. If it does, one must remain aware that there were always other possible narratives and outcomes. To tell a life faithfully, in other words, the biographer must become a critic and historiographer as well, remembering always that stories are not found but rather made.

I cannot prove that William Wilde's musings on the challenges of biography inspired those of his son, who seems to have had little relish for fact-driven argument.[6] But it is certainly true that Wilde shared many of his father's concerns and took issue especially with the separation of the biographical subject from their cultural and aesthetic context. The risk was so apparent to Wilde that he made it a central dilemma in *The Picture of Dorian Gray*, in which a distressed Basil Hallward confesses of his famous portrait: "I felt, Dorian, that I had told too much, that I had put too much of myself into it."[7] Seen this way, the portrait does not merely reflect Dorian's sins: it also reflects the sins of the biographer. Like his father, Wilde was wary of any biography that attempted to align the life with specific political or cultural objectives; such an approach risked occluding what is truly valuable in life writing—the revelation of a singular personality. Yet Wilde also felt that attaining the kind of disinterested perspective recommended by his father required that the biographer avoid focusing unduly on mere events. Especially in the case of artists and thinkers, the best life writing would also constitute a kind of criticism.

Wilde was, to be sure, an avid consumer of biography. It is in this spirit that he recommended the reading of several intellectual lives in his 1886 piece "To Read or Not to Read."[8] Among the books Wilde insists everyone should peruse, he includes the letters of Marcus Cicero (BC 68–43), Giorgio Vasari's *Lives of the Most Excellent Painters, Sculptors, and Architects* (1550/68), Duc de St. Simon's *Memoirs* (1755), the *Autobiography of Benvenuto Cellini* (1887), and Suetonius's *The Lives of the Twelve Caesars* (121 AD). During his tenure as editor of the periodical *Woman's World* between 1887 and 1889, Wilde reviewed countless biographies, including Mabel Wotton's *Word-Portraits of Famous Writers* (1887), Lucy Bethia Walford's *Four Biographies from Blackwood* (1888), Bella Duffy's *Life of Madame de Stael* (1887), Frances Martin's *Life of Elizabeth Gilbert* (1887), the 1888 edition of John Evelyn's *Life of Mrs. Godolphin* (1847/1888), Phyllis Browne's *Life of Miss Mary Carpenter* (1888), and Janet Ross's *Three Generations of Englishwomen* (1888), to name only a few.[9] He reviewed countless other works for *The Pall Mall Gazette* during this period as well, including John Addington Symonds's *Ben Jonson* (1886) and Elme Marie Caro's *George Sand* (1887).[10]

The sheer number of essays Wilde wrote on biography at this time is suggestive. In an 1889 review of the *Dictionary of National Biography*, commenced only four years previously by Leslie Stephen, the *Edinburgh Review* proclaimed biography to be "at this moment the most popular form of Literature."[11] As Juliette Atkinson has observed, it is difficult to calculate precisely what proportion of works published during this period constitute biographical writing, in part owing to the plasticity of the genre itself, but it was without question comparable to the novel in its rate of publication and consumption at the bookstalls.[12] The preponderance of Victorian biographies in turn fostered a growing cynicism among critics, who frequently questioned the ethical value of exposing private events to public view and lamented the rapidity with which these often hackneyed accounts found their way to market.

Wilde contributed to this critical trend in his most sustained discussions of nineteenth-century biography, both of which appeared in *The Pall Mall Gazette* in 1887. The first was a review of Joseph Knight's *Life of Dante Gabriel Rossetti* (1887), suggestively titled "A Cheap Edition of a Great Man." One of Wilde's chief critiques in this essay was the author's inattention to the subtlety of Rossetti's literary output and failure to capture his real depth of character— what Wilde deems a "shallow and superficial" treatment of the biography's subject. Whereas his father had lamented the tendency to wrest biographical subjects from their proper historical context, Wilde maligns the author's tendency to focus solely on the events of a subject's life, to the exclusion of more speculative or critical overtures. He writes: "Rossetti's was a giant personality, and personalities such as his do not easily survive shilling primers."[13] To some extent, Wilde notes, any biographer must admit the impossibility of confining the mind and character of a person to words on a page—as powerful as words might be, they only (to invoke one of my favorite lines from *The Picture of Dorian Gray*) "give a plastic form to formless things" while omitting the more transcendent qualities of the subject.[14] Wilde elaborates:

> It is but a sorry task to rip the twisted ravel from the worn garment of life and to turn the grout in a drained cup. Better, after all, that we knew a painter only through his vision and poet through his song, than that the image of a great man should be marred and made mean for us by the clumsy geniality of good intentions. A true artist, and such Rossetti undoubtedly was, reveals himself so perfectly in his work, that unless a biographer has something more valuable to give us than idle anecdotes and unmeaning tales, his labour is misspent and his industry misdirected.[15]

For Wilde, the problem with life writing was quite simple. To understand art as a mere translation of the artist's lived experience is to elide its real value as something that is expansive, transcendent, or transformative. But to omit a discussion of creative work from the biography of an artist is to neglect the very wellspring of the artist's productive power: the mental life. "We sincerely hope," he concludes, "that there will soon be an end to all biographies of this kind. They rob life of much of its dignity and its wonder, add to death itself a new terror, and make one wish that all art were anonymous."[16]

A similar sentiment informs his review "Two Biographies of Keats," published just a few months later. In the case of William Rossetti's *Life of John Keats* (1887), Wilde perceived a dangerous attempt at "separating the man from the artist," a strategy that risked trading in the cultural myth of the poet for a demystified account that treated Keats as a thoroughly knowable subject.[17] Through an attempt to present a clear narrative account of Keats's life, Rossetti's work—like Sidney Colvin's *John Keats* (1887), which Wilde discusses in the same essay—divested the biography of everything that might give it real value, especially in the case of a writer like Keats, who famously celebrated placing the reader in "uncertainties, mysteries, doubts, without any irritable reaching after fact and reason."[18] In memorializing the life of such a man, it was essential to preserve and convey something of the intellectual vitality that made him a compelling subject in the first place. As Wilde puts it, "Part of Keats's charm as a man is his fascinating incompleteness. We do not want him reduced to a sand-paper smoothness or made perfect by the addition of popular virtues."[19]

Wilde's concerns about biographical writing thus extend and complicate his father's critique, placing them within the larger context of aesthetic philosophy and the Victorian literary market. The comprehensive biography—which fused narrative, correspondence, and anecdote—had become big business in the nineteenth century. As Ira Nadel observes, this form of life-writing, often spanning across multiple volumes and "inflated by lengthy excerpts from letters, reflects the importance of documents to validate a life, a defence as well as a justification of the biographical form. Undigested and often inaccurate, these facts were nonetheless assumed to be appropriate."[20] Wilde assuredly noted points of inaccuracy and misreading (not to mention infelicities of style) in his reviews of nineteenth-century biography, but his chief concern was that an excessive focus on the documentary account had divested biography of its generative properties. "We are overrun," Gilbert remarks in "The Critic as Artist,"

> by a set of people who, when poet or painter passes away, arrive at the house along with the undertaker, and forget that their one duty is to behave as mutes. But we won't talk about them. They are the mere body-snatchers of literature. The dust is given to one, and the ashes to another, and the soul is out of their reach.[21]

In this passage, biographers are treated as sinister figures who, like the "resurrection men" of the early nineteenth century, steal, dissect, and desecrate the deceased in pursuit of higher knowledge. Gilbert would go on to assert that these "industrious compilers of Lives and Recollections" are merely "the pest of the age, nothing more and nothing less."[22] In Wilde's view, the knowledge they convey is merely mechanical and often misleading. An overwhelming focus on the physical evidences of a life, then, curiously tended to contravene what Wilde regarded as the true value of biography: the revelation of a mind at work.

Wilde articulated this view with special sharpness in his treatment of a biographical series on British and American writers issued by London publishing house Walter Scott in 1887. Wilde was quick to offer his verdict. Focusing special attention on Eric Sutherland Robertson's *Life of Henry Wadsworth Longfellow* (1887) and Hall Caine's *Life of Samuel Taylor Coleridge* (1887), Wilde maintains that the best biographies attend less to life events than to the events of the mind:

> The real events of Coleridge's life are not his gig excursions and his walking tours; they are his thoughts, dreams and passions, his moments of creative

impulse, their source and secret, his moods of imaginative joy, their marvel and their meaning, and not his moods merely but the music and the melancholy that they brought him; the lyric loveliness of his voice when he sang, the sterile sorrow of the years when he was silent. [...] So mediocre is Mr. Caine's book that even accuracy could not make it better.[23]

Wilde's famous claim that "to reveal art and conceal the artist is art's true aim" might lead one to believe that he would resist any effort to comprehend the artist's personality.[24] Yet the aims of art are, assuredly, very different from the aims of biography. Hence, in life writing Wilde claims that one can only understand an artist by attending to his inner life in all of its mystery and chaos. To even approximate truth, the biographer must treat his task as a speculative and creative endeavor.

Wilde's approach to biography was hardly unique. As Atkinson notes, "throughout the nineteenth century, biographers found themselves in the awkward position of writing in a genre whose popularity and generally agreed social importance were as marked as its widespread denunciation."[25] Edmund Gosse reflected disparagingly on the "big-biography habit," which treated life writing as a merely perfunctory task. He writes: "we in England bury our dead under the monstrous catafalque of two volumes (crown octavo), and go forth refreshed, as those who have performed a rite which is not in itself beautiful, perhaps, but is inevitable and eminently decent."[26] Lytton Strachey would eventually offer a corrective to such approaches in *Eminent Victorians* (1918). Like Gosse, Strachey describes life writing as a morbid compulsion undertaken (often with an eye toward the literary market) immediately after the passing of the biographical subject:

> Those two fat volumes, with which it is our custom to commemorate the dead—who does not know them, with their ill-digested masses of material, their slipshod style, their tone of tedious panegyric, their lamentable lack of selection, of detachment, of design? They are as familiar as the cortege of the undertaker, and wear the same air of slow, funereal barbarism. One is tempted to suppose, of some of them, that they were composed by that functionary as the final item of his job.[27]

In his own work, Strachey accordingly resists the impulse to be exhaustive, seeking instead "to examine and elucidate certain fragments of the truth" in order to create a revealing portrait of the subject's personality—"to illustrate rather than to explain."[28] To this extent, Wilde was in keeping with a current

of biographical criticism that stretched from the 1880s well into the twentieth century.

But it is his precursor, Thomas Carlyle, who provides perhaps the most
illuminating touchstone for Wilde's understanding of life writing. Carlyle
famously argued in *On Heroes, Hero-Worship, and the Heroic in History* (1841)
for a "Great Man" theory of the past. Although such an idea might seem, on
the face of it, simply to treat biography as a tool for celebrating exemplary
individuals, in truth Carlyle describes biography as a reflective medium for
the reader.[29] Quoting loosely from Alexander Pope's "Essay on Man" (1744),
Carlyle remarks in "Biography" (1832): "Man is perennially interesting to
man; nay, if we look strictly to it, there is nothing else interesting."[30] It is not
biography's power to convey moral lessons that Carlyle celebrates here but
rather biography's capacity for addressing the innate egoism of man, an
impulse that is to be celebrated and nurtured. To record the life of a great man
is not merely to document heroic acts: it is to reflect upon a personality that
stood at the intersection of the intellectual and political currents of one's own
time. Seen this way, the biography becomes an object of meditation, a "mirror
both scientific and poetic" that inspires in the reader not idolatry but rather
self-knowledge.[31] To this extent, Carlyle's understanding of biography anticipates Wilde's remark in "The Critic as Artist" that "[i]n literature mere egoism
is delightful. [...] When people talk to us about others they are usually dull.
When they talk to us about themselves they are nearly always interesting [...]."[32]

Carlyle was a source of vital reflection for Wilde, who seems to have
appreciated his playful inversion of life and art.[33] As Giles Whiteley has
noted, the "Philosophy of Clothes" Carlyle articulates in *Sartor Resartus*
(1833–4/1836)—a work that is itself a kind of fictional biography—almost
certainly influenced Wilde's own attestations on the value of style and symbol.[34] It was a work Wilde would specifically request during his incarceration
in the 1890s. In his review of Crane's biography of Coleridge, however,
Wilde invokes Carlyle's views on biography more directly: "Carlyle once
proposed in jest to write a life of Michael Angelo without making any reference to his art."[35] Such an endeavor would, of course, be at once futile and
senseless; in omitting art and criticism, it would occlude precisely what qual-
ifies Michelangelo as a biographical subject in the first place. The punchline,
for Wilde, is that Crane's biography of Coleridge proved such a feat to be
"perfectly feasible," though by no means salutary.[36] Like Carlyle, then, Wilde
regards biography less as a record of events or exemplary lessons than as a
template for reflection about one's own life and history—a space where one
might witness the collision of multiple and sometimes incongruent strains
of thought.

Perhaps the strongest illustration of Wilde's investment in this approach emerges in his 1887 review of Walter Pater's *Imaginary Portraits* (1887). The essays contained in this volume provide biographical sketches of Jean-Antoine Watteau, Jean-Baptiste Pater, Sebastian van Storck, Denys L'Auxerrois, and Duke Carl of Rosenmold. So far from merely presenting narrative accounts or character sketches, Pater's portraits openly embrace the power of fiction and fantasy to bring the biographical subject to life. As James Eli Adams puts it, each portrait "focuses on an individual who is deeply solitary, an enigma to the world around him, yet inhabits a historical moment in which his peculiar desires become harbingers of epochal cultural transition," prompting the reader to speculate on his life, his context, and his cultural output.[37] *Imaginary Portraits* is, in short, an experiment in biography that seeks to capture less the documentary than the intellectual truth behind a life. To this extent, Wilde's description of the volume might well constitute his own definition of intellectual biography:

> a series of philosophic studies in which the philosophy is tempered by personality, and the thought shown under varying conditions of mood and manner, the very permanence of each principle gaining something through the change and colour of the life through which it finds expression.[38]

Refusing to pursue "any definite doctrine or seek to suit life to any formal creed," Pater instead proves himself to be an "intellectual impressionist," who does not merely recount events and anecdotes but tracks the creative and intellectual processes that distinguished his subjects. In Wilde's view, it is a sound approach, for "in matters of art, at any rate, thought is inevitably coloured by emotion, and so is fluid rather than fixed, and, recognizing its dependence upon moods and upon the passion of fine moments, will not accept the rigidity of a scientific formula or a theological dogma."[39]

These encounters with biographical writing raise important methodological questions for any intellectual biography—certainly for one seeking to capture the peculiar shifts and contradictions that characterized Wilde's mental history. How can one document a writer's inner life, which must always remain hidden from view and therefore, to some extent, a matter of interpretation? Is it possible to do so without succumbing to hagiography, exposé, or mere fiction? If one of the chief assets of the intellectual biography is its capacity as a vehicle for self-reflection, how does the biographer or reader avoid projecting themselves onto their subject? Above all, how does one narrate a mental life, which does not always follow a linear or progressive path? In order to answer these questions, we must first consider how existing biographies of Wilde have accounted for them.

Wilde as Biographical Subject

William Wilde had advised that the loyal biographer should walk "among the scenes and during the period" in which the subject lived. Yet proximity to the biographical subject also presents problems. The earliest biographies of Wilde were undertaken by his personal acquaintances, friends, and disciples. Of these, Robert Sherard's *Oscar Wilde: The Story of an Unhappy Friendship* (1902) and Frank Harris's *Oscar Wilde: His Life and Confessions* (1916) are perhaps the most frequently invoked in contemporary scholarship, although they are rife with inaccuracies, embellishments, and personal anecdote.[40] Lord Alfred Douglas, Wilde's lover at the time of his arrest and conviction for "acts of gross indecency" in 1895, produced two works offering assessments of Wilde's work and career.[41] In large part, as Douglas himself attests, these volumes served as a response to the "multitudinous gentlemen with ready pens who have not scrupled to decry and defame me."[42] While Douglas's effort at clarifying his personal role in the later years of Wilde's life need not be deemed inaccurate per se, his accounts are steeped in a defensive rhetoric and often colored by personal investments. As reflections of Wilde's mental development, they prove less than clarifying. Harris's volume, by the same token, amasses countless statements from Wilde's associates, thus relying upon sources whose accounts of Wilde are at once subjective and retrospective; in some cases, these sources recount second-hand anecdotes about Wilde which, while suggestive and colorful (often attempting to capture Wilde's idiosyncratic mannerisms and idiom), can hardly be taken as documentary fact. Recollected in the wake of Wilde's trial, conviction, and death, these sketches tell us much about the reception and reshaping of Wilde's legacy; they cannot be treated as an unmediated expression of his life or thought.

Arthur Ransome anticipated this problem in his 1912 volume *Oscar Wilde: A Critical Study*, noting that Wilde is "too near us to be seen without a blurring of perspectives."[43] Whereas Ransome had planned to write a volume focusing entirely on Wilde's literary output, he recognized that such "willful evasion" of Wilde's personality was futile.[44] To this extent, Ransome echoes Wilde's view that the successful biography must interweave the subject's experiences and creative work. He writes:

In the case of such a writer as Wilde, whose books are the by-products of a life more important than they in his own eyes, it is not only legitimate but necessary for understanding to look at books and life together as at a portrait of an artist by himself, and to read, as well as we may, between the touches of the brush. It is not that there is profit in trying to turn works of art into biographical data, though that may be a fascinating pastime. It is that biographical data cannot do other than assist us in our understanding of the works of art.[45]

When he wrote these lines, Ransome was attempting to justify the use of "biographical data" in his appraisal of Wilde's writing. Of course, one of the questions introduced by the early biographies of Wilde is whether private reminiscences can be rightly considered as "biographical data," not to mention whether it is even possible to verify the nominal "facts" of a life that has overlapped with one's own. In the present volume, these early biographies are not treated as incontrovertible accounts of Wilde's life. Still, they at times provide matter for speculation, particularly where they buttress or contradict "biographical data" that has been verified by documentary evidence. The accounts of Wilde's friends and associates—as well as the anecdotes about Wilde they contain—do play a role in the pages that follow. In the interest of transparency, however, I have made an effort to remind the reader to treat these accounts with circumspection, keeping in view always the vast distance between history and memory.

Wilde himself might well have questioned whether such a thing as "biographical data" exists in the first place. Scholars have recurred again and again to Wilde's famous claim in "The Decay of Lying" (1889/1891) that "Life imitates Art far more than Art imitates Life."[46] For some, this precept has justified drawing direct connections between the events of Wilde's life and his literary output. For others, it has provided a rationale for understanding "his own life as an evolving work of art," to borrow the words of Julia Prewitt Brown.[47] In this spirit, Regina Gagnier and Michèle Mendelssohn have suggested that Wilde's public personae were created—consciously and unconsciously—by the dynamic and very public discourse surrounding his identity from the commencement of his literary career.[48] These are invaluable works of scholarship, which have done much to place Wilde within the material and commercial contexts of the late nineteenth century; to a great extent, they also have helped to illuminate how deliberate efforts to market or mar Wilde's legacy may have precipitated the difficulties of contemporary biographers, who at times seem to be tracking the life of not one but of many men. If Wilde deliberately cultivated his status as celebrity, then the project of uncovering the "authentic" Wilde would seem to be a practically impossible feat, one rendered all the more vexing by his purposeful endeavors to blur the line between life and art.

Of course, Wilde's famous axiom did not merely endorse transferring the terms and techniques of art into life—infusing experience, as it were, with the contours and colors of a satisfying story. On the contrary, Wilde proposed that life mirrored art inevitably and often unwittingly. The argument he makes is informed by his engagement with German idealism and its proposition that knowledge of the world is dependent upon the activity of the percipient mind. Although Wilde was not strictly bound by an idealist view of the world (as I discuss at greater length in Chap. 5) it is clear that it shaped his aesthetic vision. In "The Decay of Lying," he goes on to explain:

> Nature is no great mother who has borne us. She is our creation. It is in our brain that she quickens to life. Things are because we see them, and what we see, and how we see it, depends on the Arts that have influenced us. To look at a thing is very different from seeing a thing. One does not see anything until one sees its beauty. Then, and then only, does it come into existence.[49]

Our experiences are of vital importance, but our understanding of the world can only transpire through subjective acts of perception and reflection. To this extent art serves not merely as a spectacle or expressive outlet: art is a medium through which mental development takes place. If life imitates art, then, it is because art transforms our capacity for seeing the world differently. A superficial engagement with art might lead one to simply reproduce the scenes and ideas one encounters there; a deeper engagement with art renders one more sensitive to higher forms of beauty and truth.

Inasmuch as art, perception, and experience are inseparable for Wilde, an intellectual biography must engage not merely with the subject's education, encounters, and objects of study. It must also consider the site of the subject's intellectual transformation—the work of art. In this volume, I have attempted to pair an attention to Wilde's intellectual encounters in this world—the interlocutors, source texts, and educational experiences that we find documented in his letters and journals—with an attention to his literary output. There are, assuredly, risks to such an approach. I readily acknowledge that what emerges here is only one facet of Wilde's personality, seen perhaps through the lens of my own intellectual investments. But my aim is not finally to answer the question of who Wilde was. I mean simply to illuminate that part of his life which has hitherto remained somewhat obscure: Wilde's view of the contemplative life and his adamant pursuit of it. In what follows, I want to explain precisely how such a project builds upon existing trends in

Wilde scholarship in order to demonstrate what an intellectual biography of Wilde can accomplish—as well as what it cannot.

In the case of Oscar Wilde, the enticement to focus on life events is especially strong. Wilde's conviction in 1895 for "acts of gross indecency," an event that transpired at the very peak of his professional success, was one of the most sensational and jarring events in the history of sexuality. If his conviction rendered him a pariah in the eyes of many during his lifetime, the twentieth century would recuperate him as a hero—"Saint Oscar" as Terry Eagleton would have it—a man whose works, even prior to the very public trial, speak to questions of identity, eros, and social transgression.[50] Wilde's sexuality occupies the very center of accounts by Christopher Nassar, Michael S. Foldy, Neil McKenna, and Gary Schmidgall, each of whom has clarified in distinct ways the relationship between Wilde's intimate life and the sexual mores of late-Victorian Britain.[51] It is little wonder that so many accounts tend to read Wilde's life and work retroactively as the life of a cultural revolutionary and gay icon, for his published writings likewise reflect what we now describe as a kind of "queer" politics: an effort to challenge the delineation of certain behaviors and identity categories as either normative or deviant. In this spirit, Ed Cohen has documented how the popular press transformed Wilde into an icon of alternative sexuality, while Alan Sinfield treats Wilde's plays as a site where he experimented with and elevated different forms of alterity.[52]

Such accounts are laudable for calling attention to the political, discursive, legal, and social challenges that forged the history of sexuality as we know it. In some cases, however, a focus on the dramatic events of Wilde's life has also generated a teleological challenge. If we retain the idea that Wilde was a gay man whose "rise and fall" was largely predetermined, then we may well overlook the intricate movements that defined his development. We see evidence of such an approach in Melissa Knox's *Oscar Wilde: A Long and Lovely Suicide* (1996) and Emer O'Sullivan's *The Fall of the House of Wilde: Oscar Wilde and his Family* (2016), both of which propose that Wilde's childhood experiences—for instance, the Mary Travers libel suit, during which his father's sexual infidelities were made public knowledge—precipitated the excesses of his own life.[53] Such accounts seek to present Wilde's life as a coherent history that was always moving inexorably toward his conviction for crimes of "gross indecency." Without question, the story of Wilde's famous trial constitutes an important part of his history, yet a focus on the public revelation of Wilde's sexuality has all too often led biographers to evaluate Wilde's career retrospectively, presupposing that he consistently inserted into his work (wittingly or not) the outlines of his evolving and presumably foreseeable tragedy.

A noteworthy corrective to this impulse appears in Nicholas Frankel's recent volume *Oscar Wilde: The Unrepentant Years* (2017), which rejects the claim that Wilde's imagination and literary output was on the decline at the end of his life. Focusing on the time just following Wilde's release from prison, Frankel demonstrates how a close attention to documentary evidence and a wariness of myth might yield alternative ways of understanding Wilde's life and work.[54] In like spirit, *Oscar Wilde: A Literary Life* resists, wherever possible, an understanding of his life that was destined to culminate in either tragedy or beatification. Although I track certain trajectories of influence and moments of synthesis, it is with an understanding that Wilde's personality and philosophy remain always somewhat out of view. Instead, I chart the intellectual movements of his life, which—like the movements of any mind—cannot be confined to a strict chronology. They combine, disintegrate, dance, stumble, vibrate, tremble, and at times linger uncertainly at the precipice.

To date, there exists no concise intellectual biography of Wilde for non-specialists. In his 1986 account, Edouard Roditi attempted to "indicate the central position that Wilde's works and ideas occupy in the thought and art of his age, and in the shift of English and American literature from established and aging Romanticism to what we now call modernism."[55] Roditi's account speculates on the nature of Wilde's religious and political reflections, though he typically reverts to Wilde's own literary output for his answers, rather than considering his education or readings in any substantial way. John Sloan's *Oscar Wilde* (2003) surveys Wilde's engagement with the social and intellectual contexts of his time, but these discussions are by design relatively concise and tend to conflate subjects (for instance, religion and ethics) that are well worth engaging on their own terms. Of the existing accounts of Wilde's life, then, Thomas Wright's *Built of Books: How Reading Defined the Life of Oscar Wilde* (2010) perhaps most closely approximates an intellectual biography. Wright focuses exclusively on Wilde's passion for books, noting that as "events in his biography, these readerly encounters were as significant as his first meetings with friends and lovers."[56] Wright's volume is extraordinarily helpful in terms of mapping out some of Wilde's most cherished volumes, and he is careful to note Wilde's attraction to books as material objects—travel companions, accessories, and sources of social interaction. Yet for Wright, books did not merely serve as tools for Wilde: they constituted the very foundation of his identity:

> [...] Wilde did not so much discover as create himself through his reading: he was a man who built himself out of books. He poured scorn on the notion that each of us has a fixed 'inner' self that represents our essential 'nature'—that self

was, he believed, a fiction invented by the political, economic and cultural powers that be. It could, therefore, be rewritten by the artist in life, with a little help from his favourite books. Wilde used these volumes as 'prompt books' for the various roles he assumed during the different phases of his life.[57]

The most obvious instance of this, Wright notes, is Wilde's adoption of the pseudonym "Sebastian Melmoth" after his release from prison. Whereas Wright regards Wilde's relationship to books as a process of mirroring, I propose that this relationship was far more complicated. Even in the case of this tragic moniker, Wilde did not merely imitate the character of Charles Maturin's *Melmoth the Wanderer* (1820); as I note in Chap. 3, he conflates this dark wanderer with the figure of Saint Sebastian, who himself reflects at once eros, spirituality, spectacle, and sacrifice. As in the case of most serious thinkers, Wilde did not appeal to books as scripts for the roles he self-consciously adopted over the course of his career; reading was an expansive, creative, and often disorganized endeavor. Indeed, it precisely the impulse to uncritically model one's life after a book that Wilde cautions against in *The Picture of Dorian Gray*, as I explain at greater length in Chap. 2. Wilde stood at the intersection of many different discourses and ideas; if he parroted them at times, he also proves a resistant, engaged, creative, and even perplexed reader. While Wright's research into Wilde's reading practices is invaluable, then, his account treats Wilde's intellectual life in a very different way, often mapping it onto the existing narrative of Wilde as a sort of cultural chameleon. The book does not pursue inquiries into specific areas of study or, indeed, sustained examination of the sources identified as Wilde's chief influences.

In the absence of an accessible intellectual biography, non-specialists have found themselves approaching questions about Wilde's intellectual life in one of two ways. On the one hand, a reader might divine an answer piecemeal by wading through more comprehensive biographical accounts, like those of Richard Ellmann or Barbara Belford.[58] Although there is much useful information to be gleaned from these studies, they tend to diffuse answers over the course of several hundred pages, understandably privileging chronology and scope over a sustained focus on specific intellectual topics. For the non-specialist reader, such accounts prove daunting in scope and do little to clarify Wilde's understanding of discrete fields of study. Even Ellmann's very engaging account, as George Sandulescu puts it, "is not an easy book for the general reader," precisely because it seeks to be narrative and comprehensive.[59]

On the other hand, one might turn to the scholarly monograph, which focuses on specific elements of Wilde's intellectual life. There are numerous such works currently available to readers and covering a range of topics. For instance, Davis Coakley and Jarlath Killeen have done much to reposition Wilde's work within the folkloric traditions of his native Ireland. In *The Unmasking of Oscar Wilde* (2015), Joseph Pearce examines Wilde's spiritual life, helpfully illuminating the role of both formal religion and a broader spiritual outlook played in Wilde's experience. And Iain Ross's masterful volume *Oscar Wilde and Ancient Greece* (2012) provides an extensive and rigorously researched account of Wilde's engagement with Hellenic culture, which Ross reveals to be a formative influence on his approach to cultural and aesthetic forms. I will not enumerate the countless works of invaluable scholarship to which I am indebted here, though I invite the reader to consult the notes for further discussion of them.

Yet if commencing with the scholarly monograph, which trains attention on only one area of Wilde's intellectual life, the reader will find that the dazzling range and complexity of his mental history remains inaccessible. In the spirit of the intellectual lives Wilde himself consumed and invoked in his own writing, *Oscar Wilde: A Literary Life* seeks to track Wilde's relationship to the intellectual currents of his day in a manner that will allow the non-specialist to gain specific knowledge about targeted areas of interest, while also understanding how layered and multifaceted his intellectual engagements truly were. Unlike the scholarly monograph or the narrative biography, this book does not seek to establish Wilde's development of a specific "philosophy," preferring instead to track his various—sometimes even inconsistent—responses to the works he read and appreciated. So far from serving as the last stop for readers of Wilde, this volume is meant to serve as a springboard for their own intellectual sallies. In this way, I hope to provide the non-specialist reader with an account that is rigorous while also empowering them to apply this knowledge in their own encounters with Wilde's writings.

Methodologies

What, then, is an intellectual biography? According to some, it tracks the emergence of a mind—one that has been judged by history to be at once singular and transformative. Joel Whitebook suggests in his life of Sigmund Freud that the intellectual biography is distinguished by an attempt to track "the relation between the unfolding of his thinking and crucial developments in his life history."[60] In like spirit, Fritz Ringer approaches the intellectual biography as akin to portraiture—the attempt to depict an *"intellectual personality"* through a reappraisal of the subject's writings.[61] Avrom Fleischman's intellectual biography of George Eliot is revealing in this respect. Fleischman's chief object was "to recreate in my own understanding the mind of the his-torical subject, to grasp the motivation, content, and action of that mind in her writing, both fictional and non-fictional."[62] He modestly adds: "This is, of course, an unattainable goal, not the less worth striving for."[63] Works that are explicitly labeled as intellectual biographies tend to reach beyond a strictly narrative account of the biographical subject in order to determine how the currents of mental life at a specific point in time shaped their subject's intel-lectual output. To this extent, the intellectual biography seeks to bridge the gap between historical and biographical argument, on the one hand, and criti-cal analysis on the other. It is, to be sure, a delicate balancing act.[64]

As I have established, Wilde himself confronted many of the questions that must inform the writing of an intellectual biography. Do documentary forms of evidence (letters, journals, and manuscripts) provide a reliable record of the subject's life, opinions, or aspirations? Is the more accurate account the one that is capacious or that scrupulously charts the subject's formative moments and milestones? Concerns regarding the relationship between speculation and fact have only mounted following the poststructuralist turn and a growing awareness that biographical subjects are to some extent constructed through discourse. When Roland Barthes announced the "death of the author" in 1967, he also proclaimed the failure of biography itself, since any attempt to understand the individual subject must also be limited by cultural, discursive, and interpretive constraints.[65] How can one recount a life story without imposing an artificial structure upon that life? How is the biographer to depict the mind of his subject without projecting upon it the expectations and preju-dices of the present moment? What is more, as Michael Benton has observed, intellectual biographies often "deal with subjects who stand apart from soci-ety's norms and whose intertwined lives and writings offer a critique of the world the rest of us inhabit."[66] In this way, the intellectual biography almost by definition examines a mind that is singular, refusing to follow prescribed paths and often existing in tension with the spirit of the age.

In "Rediscovering Intellectual Biography—and Its Limits," Malachi Hacohen is frank about the challenges that await the intellectual biographer. Biography tends, he observes, to "imply a linear narrative of life rather than plurality of directions, coherence of experience rather than multiplicity of contexts, teleology rather than contingency."[67] Such an approach reflects, as Hacohen points out, more a fidelity to the constraints of genre than a way to empirical truth. Wilde's critique of nineteenth-century biography centered upon precisely this problem: the constraints of a genre that must reduce life to a compendium of documentary facts, crudely amassed and stitched together in the fashion most likely to seduce the reading public. An insistence on narrative certainty risks eclipsing what is most fascinating about the intellectual biography: as Wilde himself puts it, "the life that has for its aim not *doing* but *being*, and not *being* merely, but *becoming*."[68]

In Wilde's vision of intellectual biography—and in mine—the objective is not to know the mind of the biographical subject but rather to track its movements and, as nearly as possible, to witness some of the collisions that may have kept it in motion. Like Fleischman, I prefer to treat my subject's life as "a work in progress, emphasizing not merely its transitional but its progressive character."[69] This is, I believe, a sensible approach to any intellectual biography. After all, even the most rational mind experiences its moments of disorder, rupture, vagrancy, and stasis. Although we can in hindsight construct a narrative that is linear, logical, and progressive, the reality is that most lives (and certainly most intellects) do not progress by such clearly measured steps. In the case of Oscar Wilde—who celebrated paradox, performance, and transformation—it is not only responsible but also appropriate that we should resist the temptation to impose a sense of coherence or fatalism. Accordingly, I approach the intellectual biography as an imperfect but illuminating medium, one that permits us to regard individual minds as "superb sites for analysis of discursive interaction."[70] In other words, the intellectual biography is distinguished by its focus on the evolution of a mind that is, of necessity, always evolving, frequently hidden, and almost never transparent. Like any work of scholarship, the intellectual biography is not a portrait but rather an impression. Rather than tracking what Wilde thought, this volume is far more interested in tracking *how* he thought. In so doing, it frees the reader to understand Wilde's life not as the rise and fall of a cultural icon but rather as a constellation of intersecting (and sometimes warring) impulses.

How, then, are we to make sense of a life that is so rife with contradiction? We cannot revert to mere narrative, for fear of imposing on life an artificial sense of coherence; nor can we dwell solely among Wilde's creative output, for to do so is to presume that art avails an unmediated reflection of life. In my treatment of Wilde, I have kept in view his own appraisal of biography, which is most illuminating when it moves between art and experience. But it is also vital, I think, that we consider how Wilde's mental life may have been shaped by the institutions and reading material that served as its springboard. John Gibbins suggests that the intellectual biography has increasingly come to describe an effort at placing a remarkable intellect within the context of events and places that we do not typically regard as the province of intellectual life: "great theories and thinkers," he proposes, "are generated from the less organized social and cultural milieu rather than as a result of curriculum, syllabus, set books, lectures, and examinations, delivered by more formal processes and procedures, albeit within a setting of congeniality."[71] On the one hand, Gibbons laments the tendency to reduce intellectual biography to little more than the subject's social milieu and experiences. On the other hand, this means leaving aside the equally important, if ostensibly less seductive matter of academic life. A true intellectual biography, Gibbons concludes, cannot skim over the institutional structures of learning that may have determined what and how the subject gained knowledge. It is in this spirit that the volume commences with a discussion of Wilde's approach to the contemplative life, considering both the educational institutions of the late nineteenth century and Wilde's occasional remarks upon the subject in his published and unpublished work.

My source base throughout this book ranges widely, spanning from Wilde's notebooks and correspondence to his treatment of discrete subjects in his published fiction, poetry, drama, and prose writing. There are challenges to working with such a source base, even (and perhaps especially) those non-literary documents that scholars have sometimes regarded as "biographical data." Owing in part to Wilde's careful attention to his aesthetic image, it can be difficult at times to determine whether his utterances are authentic—that is, reflect the true drift of his mind—or cultivated in the interest of promoting his persona as an aesthete. His 1895 prison letter, *De Profundis*, is an illuminating case in point. On the face of it, the document would seem to be the nearest thing we have to an autobiography of Wilde, since it details certain events of his life—perhaps most notably his relationship with Lord Alfred Douglas, his trial and conviction for "acts of gross indecency," and his experience of prison life—and reflects broadly on the spiritual, aesthetic, and pecuniary outcomes of those events. As Stephen Arata observes, however, it also seems to reflect Wilde's "attempt to write a gospel of his own" by retrospectively presenting the events of his life as precipitating his own "moment of climactic suffering," which in turn becomes meaningful and even inevitable.[72] Seen this way, one might well regard *De Profundis* as a rhetorical document that carefully cultivates a coherent and exalted narrative of the author. Although presented in a genre that purports to be private and authentic, the account nevertheless has been authored by a mind with specific aims and investments in view.

It is also a document that was produced under extraordinary circumstances. As Josephine Guy and Ian Small point out in their scrupulously researched discussion of *De Profundis*, the manuscript can hardly be regarded as an unmediated revelation of Wilde's experience and outlook. In most accounts, Wilde is believed to have composed the letter during short episodes of writing, owing to the dispensations of a prison warden who provided him with paper and ink late in 1896. It has been presumed that the brevity of these sessions required that Wilde compose impulsively and earnestly, with little opportunity for revision or reflection. But as Guy and Small observe, the version of the text most readers of Wilde encounter is typed and purged of any textual anomalies, despite the fact that several pages of the manuscript feature blots, suggestive erasures, scribblings, and amendments, all of which at least indicate that this dense and allusive piece of writing did not come into the world without a great deal of thought and revision. Indeed, despite the fact that it is often invoked as an authoritative account of Wilde's experience, scholars vary widely as to its generic assignation: is it an autobiography, confession, love letter, or a defense? Seen this way, we can only treat *De Profundis* as "a kind of *cento*, a composite document made up of several different pieces of work," produced under varying circumstances and reflecting many different modes of thought.[73] Like Arata, then, Guy and Small propose that the text testifies to Wilde's deliberate effort at self-fashioning. "The important lesson to take from this," they write, "is that the effectiveness of Wilde's prose is dependent not upon its 'truth,' but upon its artifice, its self-conscious manipulation of certain sorts of discourse. Then the most important question becomes whether that manipulation is appropriate to Wilde's purposes."[74] It is a question that cannot, they rightly observe, be answered by biography.

Yet perhaps it is not the only question one might ask. Even if we regard *De Profundis* as a kind of pastiche—a text in which Wilde makes several discrete sallies at the work of self-fashioning—we nevertheless must make certain presumptions about Wilde's intellectual, cultural, and personal priorities. In this volume, the most important question to ask is not whether Wilde's persona in *De Profundis* is rhetorically coherent or aligns with his efforts at self-fashioning at other points in his career, for even those purposes must remain subject to debate; the more pressing question is *how* he goes about this work. In other words, I am less concerned with determining whether or not Wilde's account serves any specific end than with reflecting upon the intellectual processes that informed his writing. My approach to those documents that are often seen as documenting Wilde's life—*De Profundis*, Wilde's correspondence, and the trial transcripts, to name a few—has thus been two-fold. First, I have attempted to put on display the conditions of their production, taking no single remark to reflect definitively upon the entirety of Wilde's career. While I highlight for the reader striking patterns of thought where they occur, I am far more interested in tracking recurrent questions than in asserting that Wilde endorsed any specific creed or métier. Second, I have sought less to verify the truth of Wilde's assertions about himself or others than to document how he makes these assertions. By attending to the movements of

Wilde's mind, we free ourselves to engage more responsibly with textual evidence and, I hope, to gain a new perspective on Wilde's intellectual life. Though we may not emerge with a definitive or indisputable narrative of Wilde's career, we should emerge with a better sense of what helped to shape it.

One of the distinguishing qualities of this volume is thus its attention to Wilde's source base. While several extant works have helped to locate and foreground Wilde's influences, few remark at length and in a manner accessible to the non-specialist on the original texts that helped to shape Wilde's intellectual development and literary output. Scrutinizing the works that most attracted Wilde—engaging not merely with the concepts they purvey but with their language and immediate contexts—helps to clarify why scholars have been so insistent on their significance. Perhaps more importantly, such a technique permits the reader to track the textual encounters and movements of Wilde's mind in a more direct and unmediated fashion. Some of the sources treated (for instance, John Henry Newman's 1870 *Grammar of Assent* or W.K. Clifford's 1879 *Lectures and Essays*) will be familiar to experts in the field, but they are presented here in a manner that is meant to enable the uninitiated reader to understand precisely why, how, and to what extent Wilde dwelled upon them.

I have also examined strains of influence that have not been sufficiently explored in popular biographies of Wilde. To offer just one of many possible examples, we might look to Wilde's father—doctor, archeologist, and folklorist Sir William Wilde. Assuredly, many studies mention William Wilde but very few provide the general reader with a clear and sustained understanding of how his writings may have informed Wilde's intellectual development. Even Gerard Hanberry's *More Lives Than One: The Remarkable Family of Oscar Wilde through the Generations* (2011) mentions William Wilde's works in passing, focusing instead on his life events and omitting sustained discussion of how his intellectual output may have informed Wilde's intellectual development.[75] By contrast, *Oscar Wilde: A Literary Life* includes readings of William Wilde's *Narrative of a Voyage to Madeira, Teneriffe, and Along the Shores of the Mediterranean* (1840), *Lough Corrib, its Shores and Islands* (1869), and *Irish Popular Superstitions* (1852), as well as his groundbreaking medical writings—including *Practical Observations on Aural Surgery* (1853) and *An Essay on the Malformations and Congenital Diseases of the Organs of Sight* (1862)—which have been seldom examined in the context of Wilde's career. This is not to suggest that my attention to William Wilde is wholly original. Hanberry's volume trains our attention resolutely and productively on how Wilde's family may have shaped his life and career. Yet by highlighting William Wilde's textual productions, I hope to demonstrate that even Wilde's most intimate connections may have exerted a powerful influence on his intellectual life.

In addition to these sources, this volume considers works infrequently invoked in Wilde biographies, such as Frank Granger's *Notes on the Psychological Basis of the Fine Arts* (1887) or the sermons of Cardinal Manning, to offer only two examples. One of the most striking omissions in existing Wilde scholarship, J. P Mahaffy's 1882 volume *The Decay of Modern Preaching*, is especially worthy of note, since it not only provides important context for Wilde's changing spiritual outlook but also constitutes an unacknowledged source for Wilde's famous essay "The Decay of Lying." Mahaffy's essay has been seldom mentioned in the context of Wilde's career (for example, in Emer O'Sullivan's *The Fall of the House of Wilde*, which acknowledges the connection in a single sentence). By making explicit the textual connections that scholars of Wilde sometimes leave unspoken, I hope to put readers in a better position to draw their own conclusions about Wilde's life and career. In other words, I am less concerned here with presenting a monolithic view of Wilde's philosophy than I am with highlighting how his ideas converged with, chafed against, and responded to the intellectual currents of his time. To this extent, the reader should treat this life as "part of a larger project, which biography alone cannot address."[76] If the life is to be treated as a work of art, we would do well to remember that Wilde felt that all art should be engaged on its own terms, unfettered by prescriptive lessons. *Oscar Wilde: A Literary Life* invites readers to engage with Wilde's intellectual biography in just this spirit—not as a complete work of art but rather as a constellation of ideas, contradictions, and possibilities.

The chapters that follow are not arranged chronologically, though they are arranged with purpose. I commence by discussing Wilde's education and his evolving understanding of the learning process. By considering Wilde's own experiences, as well as his published and unpublished reflections on education, I clarify Wilde's vision of the "contemplative life" as mobile, dynamic, and recursive. To this extent, Chap. 2 provides a methodological springboard for later discussions about Wilde's more targeted intellectual ventures. There is perhaps an irony in my adoption of chapter titles that neatly apportion Wilde's mental life into familiar fields of study: education, religion, science, philosophy, and reform, respectively. To be sure, such an approach risks replicating anachronistic and potentially confining disciplinary boundaries. In the nineteenth century, fields of study were hardly as clearly demarcated as they are today. It was largely owing to institutional and social changes over the course of the nineteenth century that knowledge came to be appraised, differentiated, and organized into fields that today seem fixed and unassailable.[77]

Accordingly, there are countless points of intersection and overlap across these chapters. As I discuss in Chap. 4, for example, Wilde's approach to the empirical sciences was colored by his interest in the philosophical methods of empiricists like David Hume, as well as the theological reflections of writers like Ernest Renan. Despite such points of connection—to an extent, because of them—I have chosen to align each chapter with a familiar subject area or discipline, while providing cross-references in the text at moments of especially provocative intersection. It is my hope that this approach will make the nineteenth-century intellectual landscape more navigable to contemporary readers of Wilde, while also allowing them to perceive that landscape as vast, layered, and shifting.

If Wilde's ideas sometimes seem to transgress disciplinary boundaries, then, it is at times because those boundaries were themselves still relatively new and permeable. In this spirit, I argue in Chap. 3 that theology was not an occasional but rather a central influence on Wilde's worldview. Whereas extant accounts frame Wilde's interest in religion as primarily aesthetic, devotional, or political, this chapter recommends treating Wilde's evolving investment in theology as an intellectual project. Neither atheist nor true convert, Wilde emerges here as an earnest scholar of religion, whose spiritual inquiries challenged the very categories of nineteenth-century religious thought. Chapter 4 considers Wilde's interest in science as a means of illuminating the secrets of the natural world through the combined efforts of empirical observation and imagination. Resisting the urge to treat science as either a model or a foil for Wilde's literary experiments, I propose that Wilde engaged with science as a mode of imaginative and speculative thought. In Chap. 5, I track Wilde's engagement with philosophy, ranging from Plato and Aristotle to Continental influences like Georg Friedrich Hegel and Arthur Schopenhauer. Rather than aligning Wilde clearly with any specific school of thought, this account proposes that Wilde was a skeptical, if engaged reader of philosophy, treating it less as a means of advancing toward truth than as a medium (albeit imperfect) for reflecting upon the *process* of truth-seeking. In Chap. 6, I observe that Wilde's political disposition has been difficult for contemporary readers to navigate precisely owing to shifting connotations of the term "reform" in the nineteenth century. In the end, Wilde would come to acknowledge the importance of material and even programmatic reform efforts, while insisting that such measures must be complemented by critical reflection and the sympathetic imagination—namely, by a universal commitment to the contemplative life.

One of my central claims in this volume, then, is that Wilde was the product of a time when intellectual disciplines were in the process of being consolidated but were still in many ways diffuse and subject to interpretation. Admittedly, there are limits to such an approach. There is, quite simply, not enough room here to fully account for the endless minutiae and subtleties of the Victorian intellectual landscape. While I cannot provide a complete account of every historical development that shaped Wilde's experience, I have attempted to provide faithful overviews and to provide readers with immediate access to the historical context through the source material itself. For readers who wish to enrich and complicate their understanding of these areas and of Wilde's participation in them, I have appended to this volume a list of "Further Reading," which I hope will compensate for what remains beyond the scope of an intellectual biography that openly invites speculation.

Beginning

Let us then return to Wilde's vision of the contemplative life: "the life that has for its aim not *doing* but *being*, and not *being* merely, but *becoming*."[78] It is an idea built on ancient foundations. When he wrote this line, Wilde may well have been thinking of Plato, who had proposed that the universe consisted of material reality (the world of becoming, which was always in flux) and ideas (the world of being). As we have already seen, Wilde would invert this formula, treating the world of ideas as endlessly fluid, mobile, and generative. Yet even in these few lines of text, we might well detect the traces of other thinkers and, by extension, the movements of Wilde's mind. His vision of the "calm and self-centered" thinker, who looks out from "the high tower of Thought [...]" recalls Aristotle's claim that only the gods can truly enjoy the contemplative life (what he calls the *bios theoretikos*) unfettered by worldly concerns.[79] "We, too," Gilbert avers, "might live like them." There are echoes too of Plotinus, who remarked in the *Enneads* that at the most advanced stage of contemplation there is "no distinction existing between being and knowing, contemplation and its object constituting a living thing, a life, two inextricably one."[80] And even as Wilde invokes Plotinus's vision of perfect knowledge as a divine attribute, he also likens the philosopher to Persephone, the Greek goddess of the underworld who enacts the curses placed by the living upon departed souls. Seen this way, the contemplative life permits one, like Persephone, to "look out upon the world and know its secret."[81] Contemplation brings one to the greatest heights and into the very depths; it may be divine but not always a comfort. Oscar Wilde was thinking of all three figures at the time of writing his essay. Indeed, all three are invoked in the dialogue on more than one occasion. But their coexistence in Wilde's essay does not merely reflect his penchant for particular philosophers or schools of thought: it at once articulates and enacts what the contemplative life meant for Wilde.

There is no direct and intelligible line of influence that will lead us to Oscar Wilde. We must instead treat his intellectual life as a convergence of ideas. I make no effort to demonstrate how they may have been synthesized into a coherent worldview. Such a project is, in my view, inconsistent with Wilde's understanding of a contemplative life that is always evolving. It is, at any rate, beyond the scope of this book; and it is a project I wish to leave to my readers. In "The Critic as Artist," Gilbert sagely reminds us that the foundation of all knowledge is self-reflection, and that "[t]o know anything about oneself one must know all about others."[82] The aim of this volume is to place Wilde's life and work within the context of his intellectual pursuits in order to understand not who Wilde was but rather how he undertook this quest for self-discovery. By placing him within the community of thinkers that most attracted his attention, I seek to provide readers with a platform for inaugurating their own inquiries into the work of this fascinating writer. I hope, moreover, that confronting the complexity of Wilde's mental life provides some good matter for self-reflection—that readers will learn something of themselves and their own learning process along the way. It is in this spirit that I have written *Oscar Wilde: A Literary Life*. Custom would have us call it an "intellectual biography"—but we might do well also to refer to it as "a contemplative life."

Notes

1. Oscar Wilde, "The Critic as Artist," in *Criticism*, ed. Josephine M. Guy, vol. 4 of *The Complete Works of Oscar Wilde* (Oxford: Oxford University Press, 2007): 123–206, 178.
2. Wilde, "The Critic as Artist," 189.
3. Oscar Wilde, *The Picture of Dorian Gray* (1891), in *The Picture of Dorian Gray: The 1890 and 1891 Texts*, ed. Joseph Bristow, vol. 3 of *The Complete Works of Oscar Wilde* (Oxford: Oxford University Press, 2005), 21.
4. Oscar Wilde, *Complete Letters of Oscar Wilde*, ed. Merlin Holland and Rupert Hart-Davis (New York: Henry Holt and Company, 2000), 25.
5. William Wilde, *Memoir of Gabriel Beranger: And His Labours in the Cause of Irish Art and Antiquities* (Dublin: M.H. Gill and Son, 1880), 1. The passage in question was first published in the *Journal of the Royal Historical and Archaeological Association of Ireland* 1 (1870/1871): 33–64, 33.
6. Like Simon Reader, I recognize that Wilde was fascinated by empiricism and at times demonstrates a greater investment in fact than has sometimes been supposed. What I mean to suggest here is that Wilde resisted the value of facts

alone as the foundation for historical knowledge. See Simon Reader, "Wilde at Oxford: A Truce with Facts," *Philosophy and Oscar Wilde*, ed. Michael Y. Bennett (New York: Palgrave Macmillan, 2018): 9–28.

7. Wilde, *Dorian Gray*, 265.

8. Oscar Wilde, "To Read or Not to Read," in *Journalism I*, ed. John Stokes and Mark Turner, vol. 6 of *The Complete Works of Oscar Wilde* (Oxford: Oxford University Press, 2013): 62–63.

9. The references to these works can be found in the reviews listed here, respectively: Oscar Wilde, "Some Literary Notes," In *Journalism 2*, ed. John Stokes and Mark Turner, vol. 7 of *The Complete Works of Oscar Wilde* (Oxford: Oxford University Press, 2013):175–84, 183–4, 181–2; "Literary and Other Notes," in *Journalism 2*, ed. John Stokes and Mark Turner, vol. 7 of *The Complete Works of Oscar Wilde* (Oxford: Oxford University Press, 2013): 56–65, 61–2, 58–60, 62–3; "Literary and Other Notes," in *Journalism 2*, ed. John Stokes and Mark Turner, vol. 7 of *The Complete Works of Oscar Wilde* (Oxford: Oxford University Press, 2013): 22–33, 25–6; "Some Literary Notes," in *Journalism 2*, ed. John Stokes and Mark Turner, vol. 7 of *The Complete Works of Oscar Wilde* (Oxford: Oxford University Press, 2013): 138–49.

10. See Oscar Wilde, "Ben Johnson on English Worthies," in *Journalism 2*, ed. John Stokes and Mark Turner, vol. 7 of *The Complete Works of Oscar Wilde* (Oxford: Oxford University Press, 2013): 92–5; "M. Caro on George Sand," in *Journalism 2*, ed. John Stokes and Mark Turner, vol. 7 of *The Complete Works of Oscar Wilde* (Oxford: Oxford University Press, 2013): 82–4.

11. "The Literature and Language of the Age," *The Edinburgh Review* 169.346 (April 1889): 328–50, 329.

12. Juliette Atkinson, *Victorian Biography Reconsidered: A Study of Nineteenth-Century 'Hidden' Lives* (Oxford: Oxford University Press, 2010).

13. Oscar Wilde, "A Cheap Edition of a Great Man," in *Journalism I*, ed. John Stokes and Mark Turner, vol. 6 of *The Complete Works of Oscar Wilde* (Oxford: Oxford University Press, 2013): 146–49, 146.

14. Wilde, *Dorian Gray*, 22,184.

15. Wilde, "A Cheap Edition," 147.

16. Wilde, "A Cheap Edition," 148.

17. Wilde, "Two Biographies of Keats," in *Journalism I*, ed. John Stokes and Mark Turner, vol. 6 of *The Complete Works of Oscar Wilde* (Oxford: Oxford University Press, 2013): 187–89, 187.

18. John Keats's concept of "negative capability" was first articulated in his Letter to George and Thomas Keats (22 December, 1817) in *The Complete Poetical Works and Letters of John Keats*, ed. Horace E. Scudder (Boston: Houghton, Mifflin, and Company, 1899): 276–277, 277.

19. Wilde, "Two Biographies of Keats," 187.

20. Ira Nadel, *Biography: Fiction, Fact, and Form* (New York: Palgrave, 1984), 6.

21. Wilde, "The Critic as Artist," 127.

22. Wilde, "The Critic as Artist," 126.

23. Oscar Wilde, "Great Writers by Little Men," in *Journalism I*, ed. John Stokes and Mark Turner, vol. 6 of *The Complete Works of Oscar Wilde* (Oxford: Oxford University Press, 2013): 134–37, 136.

24. Wilde, *Dorian Gray*, 167.

25. Atkinson, *Victorian Biography Reconsidered*, 17.

26. Edmund Gosse, "The Custom of Biography," *Anglo-Saxon Review* 8 (March 1901):195–208, 195.

27. Lytton Strachey, *Eminent Victorians* (London: G.P. Putnam's Sons, 1918), vi–vii.

28. Strachey, vi.

29. Josephine M. Guy suggests that Wilde was familiar with *Heroes and Hero-worship*, pointing to his invocation of Carlyle in "Pen, Pencil, and Poison" as evidence of the fact. See Josephine M. Guy, ed. *Criticism: Historical Criticism, Intentions, The Soul of Man*, vol. 4 of *The Complete Works of Oscar Wilde* (Oxford: Oxford University Press, 2007), 574n.

30. Thomas Carlyle, "Biography," *Fraser's Magazine* 5. 27 (April 1832): 253–60, 253.

31. Carlyle, "Biography," 253.

32. Wilde, "Critic as Artist," 126.

33. Wilde wryly referred to *The French Revolution* (1837), for instance, as "one of the most fascinating historical novels ever written." Though the remark might seem to be derogatory, Carlyle's objective in that volume had been to inter-weave historical fact and the imagination, thus reaching beyond the docu-mentary to access a higher truth about the past. Wilde, "The Decay of Lying," in *Criticism*, ed. Josephine M. Guy, vol. 4 of *The Complete Works of Oscar Wilde* (Oxford: Oxford University Press, 2007): 72–103, 87.

34. Wilde seems to have relished *Sartor Resartus*, despite what he describes in "The Truth of Masks" as its "grotesque wisdom and somewhat mouthing metaphysics." See Oscar Wilde, "The Truth of Masks," in *Criticism*, ed. Josephine M. Guy, vol. 4 of *The Complete Works of Oscar Wilde* (Oxford: Oxford University Press, 2007): 208–28, 213. A fictional biography of a fic-tional German philosopher—one who reflects at length upon the power of clothing, symbols, and fiction itself—*Sartor Resartus* is a work that would have natural appeal to a writer known for blurring the distinction between life and art. Wilde would refer directly to his reading of *Sartor Resartus* in an 1899 letter to Frank Harris (*Complete Letters*, 1162), but allusions to Carlyle also abound in his letters and published writings, as several scholars have noted. See for instance: Rebecca Mitchell, "'Cultivated Idleness': Carlyle, Wilde, and Victorian representations of Creative Labour," *Word and Image* 32.1 (2016): 104–115; Marylu Hill, "A Tale of a Table: Oscar Wilde, Virginia Woolf, and the Legacy of Thomas Carlyle," *Carlyle Studies Annual* 29 (2013): 137–154.

See also Giles Whiteley, *Oscar Wilde and the Simulacrum: The Truth of Masks* (Cambridge: Cambridge University Press, 2013), 149–53.

35. Wilde, "Great Writers," 136. Wilde must have encountered this in Richard Garnett's 1887 biography of Carlyle, the only known source for the anecdote. It too was issued by Walter Scott. See Richard Garnett, *Life of Thomas Carlyle* (London: Walter Scott, 1887), 103.

36. Wilde, "Great Writers," 136.

37. James Eli Adams, "Pater's Imaginary Portraits," *English Literature in Transition* 59.1 (2016): 105–108, 106.

38. Oscar Wilde, "Mr Pater's Imaginary Portraits," in *Journalism I*, ed. John Stokes and Mark Turner, vol. 6 of *The Complete Works of Oscar Wilde* (Oxford: Oxford University Press, 2013): 178–80, 178–79.

39. Wilde, "Mr Pater's Imaginary Portraits," 243.

40. Guy and Small provide a scrupulous analysis of early Wilde biographies in *Studying Oscar Wilde: History, Criticism, and Myth* (Greensboro, NC: ELT Press, 2006), 13–20.

41. See especially Lord Alfred Douglas, *Oscar Wilde and Myself* (New York: Duffield and Company, 1914) and *Oscar Wilde: A Summing-Up* (London: Duckworth, 1940).

42. Douglas, *Oscar Wilde and Myself*, 5.

43. Arthur Ransome, *Oscar Wilde: A Critical Study* (New York: Mitchell Kennerley, 1912), 10. An echo of this sentiment famously appears in Wilde's "Pen, Pencil, and Poison," in which we are told of the poisoner Thomas Griffiths Wainewright: "Of course, he is far too close to our own time for us to be able to form any purely artistic judgement about him. It is impossible not to be feel a strong prejudice against a man who might have poisoned Lord Tennyson, or Mr. Gladstone, or the Master of Balliol." Oscar Wilde, "Pen, Pencil, and Poison," in *Criticism*, ed. Josephine M. Guy, vol. 4 of *The Complete Works of Oscar Wilde* (Oxford: Oxford University Press, 2007): 104–122, 121.

44. Ransome, 10.

45. Ransome, 12–13.

46. Wilde, "Decay of Lying," 90.

47. Julia Prewitt Brown, *Cosmopolitan Criticism: Oscar Wilde's Philosophy of Art* (Charlottesville: University of Virginia Press, 1997), 6.

48. See Regina Gagnier, *Idylls of the Marketplace: Oscar Wilde and the Victorian Public* (Palo Alto: Stanford University Press, 1986); Michèle Mendelssohn, *Making Oscar Wilde* (Oxford: Oxford University Press, 2018).

49. Wilde, "Decay of Lying," 95.

50. Terry Eagleton, *Saint Oscar and Other Plays* (Oxford: Blackwell, 1997).

51. See Christopher Nassar, *Into the Demon Universe: A Literary Exploration of Oscar Wilde* (New Haven: Yale University Press, 1974); Michael S. Foldy, The Trials of *Oscar Wilde: Deviance, Morality, and Late Victorian Society* (New Haven: Yale University Press, 1997); Neil McKenna, *The Secret Life of Oscar*

Wilde: An Intimate Biography (New York: Basic Books, 2009); and Gary Schmidgall, *The Stranger Wilde: Interpreting Oscar* (New York: Dutton, 1994).

52. See Ed Cohen, *Talk on the Wilde Side: Toward a Genealogy of a Discourse on Male Sexualities* (New York: Routledge, 2013); Alan Sinfield, *The Wilde Century: Effeminacy, Oscar Wilde, and the Queer Moment* (New York: Columbia University Press, 1994).

53. See Melissa Knox, *Oscar Wilde: A Long and Lovely Suicide* (New Haven: Yale University Press, 1996); Emer O'Sullivan, *The Fall of the House of Wilde: Oscar Wilde and his Family* (New York: Bloomsbury, 2016).

54. Nicholas Frankel, *Oscar Wilde: The Unrepentant Years* (Cambridge: Harvard University Press, 2017). One might regard this caution against mythologizing the author in light of Wilde's "Portrait of Mr. W.H.," in which Erskine is misled by a forged portrait to endorse the theory that Shakespeare's sonnets were written for a boy, Willie Hughes. Erskin's friend, Cecil Graham, refuses to abandon the theory and shoots himself in order to prove its validity. Later, the narrator hears of Erskine's death and presumes that he too has committed suicide. In fact, Erskine has been ill for some time and dies of natural causes. To this extent, the narrator finds that he too has been seduced by the prospect of a coherent and romantic life story.

55. Edouard Roditi, *Oscar Wilde* (New York: New Directions, 1986), 5.

56. Thomas Wright, *Built of Books: How Reading Defined the Life of Oscar Wilde* (New York: Henry Holt, 2008), 5.

57. Wright, 5–6.

58. Richard Ellmann, *Oscar Wilde* (New York: Alfred A. Knopf, 1987); Barbara Belford, *Oscar Wilde: A Certain Genius* (New York: Random House, 2000).

59. C. George Sandulescu, *Rediscovering Oscar Wilde* (Gerrards Cross: C. Smyth, 1994), 196. It has by now been well-established that Richard Ellmann's volume contains several documentary errors, though it remains the most comprehensive volume available and continues to be of inestimable value to readers of Wilde. Readers of Ellmann's volume may wish to consult the revised edition of Horst Schroder's *Additions and Corrections to Richard Ellmann's Oscar Wilde* (Braunschweig: H. Schroeder, 2002).

60. Joel Whitebook, *Freud: An Intellectual Biography* (Cambridge: Cambridge UP, 2017), 1–16, 16.

61. Fritz Ringer, *Max Weber: An Intellectual Biography* (Chicago: Chicago University Press, 2010), 5.

62. Avrom Fleischman, *George Eliot's Intellectual Life* (Cambridge: Cambridge University Press, 2010), ix.

63. Fleischman, ix.

64. Michael Benton notes that the intersection of fiction and nonfiction has been a concern in literary biography almost from its inception: "The concurrent rise of the novel and biography meant that fictions incorporated quasi-documentary items like letters and diary entries more commonly found in

biographies, whereas biographies presented scenes and people with the creative eye of the novelist." Michael Benton, *Literary Biography* (Oxford: Wiley Blackwell, 2009, 5). See also Elinor Shaffer, "Shaping Victorian Biography," in *Mapping Lives: The Uses of Biography*, ed. Peter France and William St. Clair (Oxford: Oxford University Press, 2002): 115–34.

65. Roland Barthes, "The Death of the Author," in *Image-Music-Text* (New York: Hill and Wang, 1977): 142–48.
66. Benton, 2.
67. Malachi Hacohen, "Rediscovering Intellectual Biography—and Its Limits," *History of Political Economy* 39 (2007): 9–29. 17.
68. Oscar Wilde, "The Critic as Artist," 178.
69. Fleischman, x.
70. Hacohen, 22.
71. John R. Gibbons, "'Old Studies and New': The Organisation of Knowledge in University Curriculum," in *The Organisation of Knowledge in Victorian Britain*, ed. Martin Daunton (Oxford: Oxford University Press, 2005): 235–62, 235.
72. Stephen Arata, "Oscar Wilde and Jesus Christ," in *Wilde Writings: Contextual Conditions*, ed. Joseph Bristow (Toronto: University of Toronto Press, 2003): 254–72, 263–4.
73. Guy and Small, *Studying Oscar Wilde*, 54.
74. Guy and Small, *Studying Oscar Wilde*, 74.
75. One of the more detailed considerations of William Wilde's written work appears in Iain Ross's *Oscar Wilde and Ancient Greece* (2012), though the volume's focus on Hellenism perforce restricts his treatment of William Wilde to select works, omitting his writings on medicine, religion, and philosophy. See Ross, 9–18.
76. Hacohen, 27.
77. See for instance: Martin Daunton, ed., *The Organisation of Knowledge in Victorian Britain* (Oxford: Oxford University Press, 2005).
78. Oscar Wilde, "The Critic as Artist," 178.
79. Wilde, "Critic as Artist," 179. According to Aristotle: "[…] the activity of God being preeminently blissful will be speculative, and if so then the human activity which is most nearly related to it will be most capable of happiness […] for while the whole life of the Gods is fortunate or blessed, the life of men is blessed in so far as it possesses a certain resemblance to their speculative activity." Aristotle, *The Nicomachean Ethics*, ed. Lesley Brown (New York: Oxford, 2009), 10.8.341.
80. Plotinus, *The Essence of Plotinus: Extracts from the Six Enneads and Porphyry's Life of Plotinus* (Eugene: Wipf and Stock, 2007), 114.
81. Wilde, "Critic as Artist," 205.
82. Wilde, "Critic as Artist," 176.

Bibliography

Adams, James Eli Adams. 2016. Pater's Imaginary Portraits. *English Literature in Transition* 59 (1): 105–108.

Arata, Stephen. 2003. Oscar Wilde and Jesus Christ. In *Wilde Writings: Contextual Conditions*, ed. Joseph Bristow, 254–272. Toronto: University of Toronto Press.

Aristotle. 2009. *The Nicomachean Ethics*, ed. Lesley Brown. New York: Oxford.

Atkinson, Juliette. 2010. *Victorian Biography Reconsidered: A Study of Nineteenth-Century 'Hidden' Lives*. Oxford: Oxford University Press.

Barthes, Roland. 1977. The Death of the Author. In *Image-Music-Text*, 142–148. New York: Hill and Wang.

Belford, Barbara. 2000. *Oscar Wilde: A Certain Genius*. New York: Random House.

Benton, Michael. 2009. *Literary Biography*. Oxford: Wiley Blackwell.

Brown, Julia Prewitt. 1997. *Cosmopolitan Criticism: Oscar Wilde's Philosophy of Art*. Charlottesville: University of Virginia Press.

Carlyle, Thomas. 1832. Biography. *Fraser's Magazine* 5 (27/April): 253–260.

Cohen, Ed. 2013. *Talk on the Wilde Side: Toward a Genealogy of a Discourse on Male Sexualities*. New York: Routledge.

Daunton, Marton. 2005. *The Organisation of Knowledge in Victorian Britain*. Oxford: Oxford University Press.

Douglas, Lord Alfred. 1914. *Oscar Wilde and Myself*. New York: Duffield and Company.

———. 1940. *Oscar Wilde: A Summing-Up*. London: Duckworth.

Eagleton, Terry. 1997. *Saint Oscar and Other Plays*. Oxford: Blackwell.

Ellmann, Richard. 1987. *Oscar Wilde*. New York: Alfred A. Knopf.

Fleischman, Avrom. 2010. *George Eliot's Intellectual Life*. Cambridge: Cambridge University Press.

Foldy, Michael S. 1997. *The Trials of Oscar Wilde: Deviance, Morality, and Late Victorian Society*. New Haven: Yale University Press.

Frankel, Nicholas. 2017. *Oscar Wilde: The Unrepentant Years*. Cambridge: Harvard University Press.

Gagnier, Regina. 1986. *Idylls of the Marketplace: Oscar Wilde and the Victorian Public*. Palo Alto: Stanford University Press.

Garnett, Richard. 1887. *Life of Thomas Carlyle*. London: Walter Scott.

Gibbons, John R. 2005. 'Old Studies and New': The Organisation of Knowledge in University Curriculum. In *The Organisation of Knowledge in Victorian Britain*, ed. Martin Daunton, 235–262. Oxford: Oxford University Press.

Gosse, Edmund. 1901. The Custom of Biography. *Anglo-Saxon Review* 8 (March): 195–208.

Guy, Josephine M., and Ian Small. 2006. *Studying Oscar Wilde: History, Criticism, and Myth*. Greensboro: ELT Press.

Hacohen, Malachi. 2007. Rediscovering Intellectual Biography—And Its Limits. *History of Political Economy* 39: 9–29.

Hill, Marylu. 2013. A Tale of a Table: Oscar Wilde, Virginia Woolf, and the Legacy of Thomas Carlyle. *Carlyle Studies Annual* 29: 137–154.

Keats, John. 1899. *The Complete Poetical Works and Letters of John Keats*, ed. Horace E. Scudde. Boston: Houghton, Mifflin, and Company.

Knox, Melissa. 1996. *Oscar Wilde: A Long and Lovely Suicide*. New Haven: Yale University Press.

McKenna, Neil. 2009. *The Secret Life of Oscar Wilde: An Intimate Biography*. New York: Basic Books.

Mendelssohn, Michèle. 2018. *Making Oscar Wilde*. Oxford: Oxford University Press.

Mitchell, Rebecca. 2016. 'Cultivated Idleness': Carlyle, Wilde, and Victorian Representations of Creative Labour. *Word and Image* 32 (1): 104–115.

Nadel, Ira. 1984. *Biography: Fiction, Fact, and Form*. New York: Palgrave.

Nassar, Christopher. 1974. *Into the Demon Universe: A Literary Exploration of Oscar Wilde*. New Haven: Yale University Press.

O'Sullivan, Emer. 2016. *The Fall of the House of Wilde: Oscar Wilde and His Family*. New York: Bloomsbury.

Plotinus. 2007. *The Essence of Plotinus: Extracts from the Six Enneads and Porphyry's Life of Plotinus*. Eugene: Wipf and Stock.

Ransome, Arthur. 1912. *Oscar Wilde: A Critical Study*. New York: Mitchell Kennerley.

Reader, Simon. 2018. Wilde at Oxford: A Truce with Facts. In *Philosophy and Oscar Wilde*, ed. Michael Y. Bennett, 9–28. New York: Palgrave Macmillan.

Ringer, Fritz. 2010. *Max Weber: An Intellectual Biography*. Chicago: Chicago University Press.

Roditi, Edouard. 1986. *Oscar Wilde*. New York: New Directions.

Sandulescu, C. George. 1994. *Rediscovering Oscar Wilde*. Gerrards Cross: C. Smyth.

Schmidgall, Gary. 1994. *The Stranger Wilde: Interpreting Oscar*. New York: Dutton.

Schroder, Horst. 2002. *Additions and Corrections to Richard Ellmann's Oscar Wilde*. Braunschweig: H. Schroeder.

Shaffer, Elinor. 2002. Shaping Victorian Biography. In *Mapping Lives: The Uses of Biography*, ed. Peter France and William St. Clair, 115–134. Oxford: Oxford University Press.

Sinfield, Alan. 1994. *The Wilde Century: Effeminacy, Oscar Wilde, and the Queer Moment*. New York: Columbia University Press.

Strachey, Lytton. 1918. *Eminent Victorians*. London: G.P. Putnam's Sons.

The Literature and Language of the Age. 1889. *The Edinburgh Review* 169 (346/April): 328–350.

Whitebook, Joel. 2017. *Freud: An Intellectual Biography*. Cambridge: Cambridge University Press.

Whiteley, Giles. 2013. *Oscar Wilde and the Simulacrum: The Truth of Masks*. Cambridge: Cambridge University Press.

Wilde, William. 1880. *Memoir of Gabriel Beranger: And His Labours in the Cause of Irish Art and Antiquities*. Dublin: M.H. Gill and Son.

Wilde, Oscar. 2000. *Complete Letters of Oscar Wilde*, ed. Merlin Holland and Rupert Hart-Davis. New York: Henry Holt and Company.

———. 2005. *The Picture of Dorian Gray* (1891). In *The Picture of Dorian Gray: The 1890 and 1891 Texts*, ed. Joseph Bristow. Vol. 3 of *The Complete Works of Oscar Wilde*. Oxford: Oxford University Press.

———. 2007a. The Critic as Artist. In *Criticism*, ed. Josephine M. Guy, 123–206, 178. Vol. 4 of *The Complete Works of Oscar Wilde*. Oxford: Oxford University Press.

———. 2007b. The Decay of Lying. In *Criticism*, ed. Josephine M. Guy, 72–103. Vol. 4 of *The Complete Works of Oscar Wilde*. Oxford: Oxford University Press.

———. 2007c. Pen, Pencil, and Poison. In *Criticism*, ed. Josephine M. Guy, 104–122. Vol. 4 of *The Complete Works of Oscar Wilde*. Oxford: Oxford University Press.

———. 2013a. Ben Johnson on English Worthies. In *Journalism 2*, ed. John Stokes and Mark Turner, 92–95. Vol. 7 of *The Complete Works of Oscar Wilde*. Oxford: Oxford University Press.

———. 2013b. A Cheap Edition of a Great Man. In *Journalism 1*, ed. John Stokes and Mark Turner, 146–149. Vol. 6 of *The Complete Works of Oscar Wilde*. Oxford: Oxford University Press.

———. 2013c. Great Writers by Little Men. In *Journalism 1*, ed. John Stokes and Mark Turner, 134–137. Vol. 6 of *The Complete Works of Oscar Wilde*. Oxford: Oxford University Press.

———. 2013d. Mr Pater's Imaginary Portraits. In *Journalism 1*, ed. John Stokes and Mark Turner, 178–180. Vol. 6 of *The Complete Works of Oscar Wilde*. Oxford: Oxford University Press.

———. 2013e. Literary and Other Notes. In *Journalism 2*, ed. John Stokes and Mark Turner, 22–33. Vol. 7 of *The Complete Works of Oscar Wilde*. Oxford: Oxford University Press.

———. 2013f. Literary and Other Notes. In *Journalism 2*, ed. John Stokes and Mark Turner, 56–65. Vol. 7 of *The Complete Works of Oscar Wilde*. Oxford: Oxford University Press.

———. 2013g. Some Literary Notes. In *Journalism 2*, ed. John Stokes and Mark Turner, 138–49. Vol. 7 of *The Complete Works of Oscar Wilde*. Oxford: Oxford University Press.

———. 2013h. Some Literary Notes. In *Journalism 2*, ed. John Stokes and Mark Turner, 175–84. Vol. 7 of *The Complete Works of Oscar Wilde*. Oxford: Oxford University Press.

———. 2013i. M. Caro on George Sand. In *Journalism 2*, ed. John Stokes and Mark Turner, 82–84. Vol. 7 of *The Complete Works of Oscar Wilde*. Oxford: Oxford University Press.

————. 2013j. To Read or Not to Read. In *Journalism I*, ed. John Stokes and Mark Turner, 62–63. Vol. 6 of *The Complete Works of Oscar Wilde*. Oxford: Oxford University Press.

————. 2013k. Two Biographies of Keats. In *Journalism I*, ed. John Stokes and Mark Turner, 187–89. Vol. 6 of *The Complete Works of Oscar Wilde*. Oxford: Oxford University Press.

Wright, Thomas. 2008. *Built of Books: How Reading Defined the Life of Oscar Wilde*. New York: Henry Holt.

2

The Teacher

Education is an admirable thing,
but it is well to remember from time to time
that nothing that is worth knowing can be taught
Oscar Wilde, "The Critic as Artist"

Oscar Wilde's bold pronouncement seems unequivocal.[1] The lessons of the classroom can never rival the wisdom acquired through experience. It is a literary gloss on the old bumper sticker maxim: those who can, do; those who can't, teach.[2] Certainly, Wilde's forays in higher education would seem to confirm his commitment to such a philosophy. In 1877, while studying at Oxford, Wilde absconded to Greece with his former Trinity College tutor, J. P. Mahaffy, and failed to return for the beginning of the term. In a letter to H. R. Bramley, then a fellow and tutor at Magdalen College, Wilde presented his case: "I hope you will not mind if I miss ten days at the beginning: seeing Greece is really a great education for anyone and will I think benefit me greatly, and Mr. Mahaffy is such a clever man that it is quite as good as going to lectures to be in his company."[3] When he finally did return to the university, Wilde was promptly suspended for the remainder of the term. "I was sent down from Oxford," he remarked, "for being the first undergraduate to visit Olympia."[4]

Wilde's response reflects a decided preference for the informal terms of his "study abroad" experience over the rigid requirements of his academic pursuits at Oxford. In Wilde's view, it was perfectly ludicrous that the dons should rank his desire for a direct engagement with Hellenic culture as subsidiary to the Literae Humaniores program at Oxford, the study of "Greats" which, appropriately, focused on Greek history and culture.[5] This wariness of formal

© The Author(s) 2019
K. J. Stern, *Oscar Wilde*, Literary Lives,
https://doi.org/10.1007/978-3-030-24604-4_2

education would surface time and again in Wilde's published work—for instance, in *An Ideal Husband* (1895) when the profligate Mrs. Cheveley remarks: "I have forgotten all about my schooldays. I have a vague impression that they were detestable."[6] While at times seeming to share Mrs. Cheveley's cynicism, Wilde's attitude toward his own education was deeply ambivalent. After all, his claim that the streets of Greece might constitute "really a great education"—as enriching if not more so than the lectures halls of Oxford—was a controversial one. As Iain Ross notes: "any assertion of the value of a trip to Greece, particularly one undertaken in preference to attending lectures, carried combative implications" at the time, highlighting as it did a growing tension between a humanistic model of learning and more empirical methods.[7] Benjamin Jowett, then Master of Balliol College, had revived an interest in the Greeks not only as a vital part of the university curriculum but also as a model for the tutorial system, which he treated as the very foundation of a productive, virtuous, and civic-minded education. When Heinrich Schliemann's discoveries at Mycenae raised interest in a more empirical approach to studying the past, Jowett expressed deep skepticism, concerned that a focus on material knowledge might detract from the value of philosophy and reflective dialogue.[8] At Oxford, Wilde thus found himself confronted by two very different pedagogies: one emphasizing the power of application and experience, the other celebrating abstract thought and textual study.

Moreover, Wilde seems to have taken genuine pleasure in his formal academic successes. Even as he seemed to malign the imparting of traditional "lessons," he won the Newdigate Prize for "Ravenna" (a poem composed in 1878, after his Mediterranean tour with Mahaffy), earned a rare double first in Greats, and often spoke fondly of his time at Oxford.[9] Despite his truancy, academic achievement plainly mattered to Wilde, and his first instinct upon graduation from Oxford was to pursue a career in education. After unsuccessfully seeking a position as a tutorial fellow at Magdalen College, Wilde applied for a post as Her Majesty's Inspector of Schools (HMI). Had he obtained the position, Wilde would have traveled throughout the country surveying and assessing educational practices in state institutions, as well as select independent schools. Wilde wrote to educational reformer Oscar Browning for support, noting somewhat emphatically: "any Education work would be very congenial to me."[10] In 1885, Wilde again expressed interest in the position, exclaiming to George Curzon: "I want to be one of Her Majesty's Inspectors of Schools! This is ambition—however, I want it, and want it very much, and I hope you will help me."[11] Committed to this aspiration, he wrote to Mahaffy the following year with yet another request for a testimonial that might secure him the post.[12]

Although Wilde was not appointed to the position, an interest in education—whether in the schoolroom, the lecture hall, or the Oxford tutorial—would inform almost everything he wrote from this time forward. The examples are virtually endless: his mock Socratic dialogues, Lord Henry Wotton's strange "teachings" in *The Picture of Dorian Gray* (1890/1), the hapless Miss Prism's admonishments in *The Importance of Being Earnest* (1895), his biblical parables, and so on. Given Wilde's status as one of the great public intellectuals of the fin de siècle—a man notorious for parading his learning in lecture halls as much as in parlors—it is striking that his views on education are so frequently overlooked.[13] Indeed, the consistency with which Wilde returned to teaching as a philosophical problem over the course of his career suggests less a refusal of pedagogy than an ambitious desire to reflect critically upon it. If Wilde persistently derides the value of formal schooling, his writings invite readers to imagine an alternative pedagogical model: one in which the pronouncements of the dry-as-dust schoolmaster might be replaced by a more dynamic and immersive learning experience.

If we intend to navigate Wilde's intellectual development over the next several chapters, we would do well to consider first how he approached the learning process itself. In this spirit, the following pages track Wilde's reflections on education and his evolving understanding of a learning style that, in its resistance to utility or certitude, would determine the sometimes whimsical course of his own intellectual journey. To this extent, they provide a methodological springboard for subsequent chapters, which explore how Wilde pursued knowledge in a range of disciplinary areas. Wilde's views on education in many ways dovetail with those of critic and poet Matthew Arnold, who served as HMI in England from 1851 to 1883. Arnold had helped to popularize the idea that education should seek to promote "sweetness and light"—beauty and intelligence—rather than the cultivation of practical skills. So far from being "made a mere ladder with 'information,'" Arnold had reasoned, a pupil should instead be trained to a "sense of pleasurable activity and of creation."[14] Wilde seems to have embraced a similar outlook, claiming that the true purpose of education was to cultivate the intellectual faculty: in a word, to promote learning for learning's sake. But whereas Arnold and his contemporaries often appraised education as a means of securing political and social welfare, Wilde set little value on concrete aims. Wilde's approach to learning was informed by his reading of ancient literature and took shape within the context of an educational system that was increasingly defined by institutional discipline and practical learning outcomes. As we shall see, however, one of the most striking outcomes of Wilde's education was a belief that shirking one's lessons was, paradoxically, the best way to learn them.

School Days

Wilde claimed on multiple occasions that he had never attended public school, having received the lion's share of his education at home. In 1880, the *Biograph and Review* reported that Wilde's early education was entirely informal: "He considers that the best of his education in boyhood was obtained from [...] association with his father and mother and their remarkable friends. He went to no public school, but had tutors at home and was given that finest of all educators, the best literature of the day."[15] Certainly, his family home at Merrion Square in Dublin would have been a lively enough education for the young Wilde, and as a boy, he was given unusual access to his parents' dinners and soirees. Yet Wilde was by no means a self-educated man. Although observing to Irish biographer D.J. O'Donoghue that he had spent "about a year" at public school, in reality he spent some 7 years in residence there.[16]

Wilde briefly attended St. Columba's College, Dublin in 1863, but the following year joined his brother William ("Willie") at Portora Royal School, Enniskillen, a reputable institution that prepared many of its students for matriculation to Trinity College, Dublin. What we know of Wilde's time at Portora is admittedly sparse, since Wilde himself neglected ever to comment at length on his time there. What remains are the accounts of his schoolfellows; the writings of the Reverend William Steele, who served as headmaster during Wilde's tenure at Portora; and documents pertaining to the history of the school itself (the yearly register, prospectus, memoranda, and coverage of the school in local newspapers).[17] While we cannot say with absolute certainty how Wilde viewed his experience at Portora, we can speculate on what kind of educational program he experienced there and how it dovetails with or departs from his later reflections on education. At Portora, Wilde would find himself immersed in a characteristically Victorian model of instruction, one dependent upon the modeling of virtue, the value of competition, and the recitation of received wisdom.

Portora was in a state of productive flux at the time of Wilde's arrival in 1864, in part owing to the guidance of Reverend William Steele. Steele's approach to school governance was inspired in part by the monitorial system of Thomas Arnold, who served as headmaster of Rugby School from 1828 to 1841. Arnold had recommended a departure from an older model of authoritarian discipline, preferring to promote a spirit of self-governance among students. Rather than being regarded as subordinates in need of discipline, pupils were to be treated as gentlemen capable of participating in the management of the school and spurred on by a healthy spirit of competition.[18] By deliberately avoiding the unnecessary use of disciplinary measures, Steele won a loyal following among the Portora students. One pupil, Maurice Dockrell, noted that Steele's "gentlemanly, kindly bearing, his avoidance of all trickery in dealing with us, made him a universal favorite."[19] Graves Atkinson Leech, who attended at the same time as Wilde, praised Steele as "honest and fearless, straightforward and candid, frank and manly [...] the mirror of a genial winning courtesy."[20] While such accounts testify to Steele's affability, they also serve as a testimony to his managerial strategies at Portora. The very year of Wilde's advent, Steele reflected:

> I have always thought that school boys ought to be dealt with as rational and moral creatures, not forgetting, however, that their understanding is as yet immature, and their conscience but partially developed [...] It appears, therefore, to me evident that the moral sentiments should be submitted to trial, moderated by an authority, firm but gentle [...][21]

In his approach to educational discipline, Steele was in keeping with some of the major trends in mid-Victorian pedagogy. In his 1859 *Teacher's Assistant*, Charles Northend insisted that "perfect discipline" consists not in "rigid and upright positions, in exact and undeviating movements, nor in constrained looks."[22] On the contrary, the most effective school room is one in which "the pupils attend to all their duties, perform all their movements, and regard all the requirements of the school with cheerful alacrity, and with an evident and constant desire to co-operate with the teacher."[23]

In Steele's view, the best tool for cultivating this spirit of self-discipline was the public examination.[24] Certainly, Portora was more progressive in its approach to assessment than other schools at the time. As Iain Ross has demonstrated, examination records "confirm that the approach taken to the classics at Portora ranged far beyond the narrowly grammatical."[25] Translation exercises were often accompanied by questions of historical and literary interpretation, so it would be misleading to suggest that the focus on examinations was ever merely a matter of "cramming." It is also clear, however, that the Portora curriculum was designed specifically to facilitate admission to and success at the major universities. Students were expected to demonstrate a mastery of Greek and Latin grammar through formal exercises, recitations, and public reviews. In a word, the Portora curriculum continued to depend resolutely upon the students' ability to follow a predetermined course of study—not an open-ended quest for knowledge so much as the cultivation of specific skill sets.

As an added incentive, Steele honored those who were most successful in their examinations at lavish public ceremonies, believing that "a judicious distribution of prizes is one of the most effective means of exciting zeal and diligence in the boys of a public school": many of the victors would receive cash prizes.[26] By all accounts, Steele's strategy worked. Having examined students on the Greek of the Acts of the Apostles, Reverend Greer doubted "if any one within the county had a better knowledge of the original Greek than those to whom the premiums had been awarded."[27] An 1867 article in the *Impartial Reporter* notes further:

> This year those who have just left the class-room to enter on their collegiate course are determined to uphold the prestige of Portora as *facile princeps* of the public schools in Ireland. On Thursday last sixty two young men entered Trinity College, Dublin, from various places of education, of these nineteenth obtained honors at entrance. The Rev. Mr Steele sent up six young gentlemen—Messrs McCartie, Clarke, Haughton, Stubbs, Gordon, and Boxwell, every one of whom obtained entrance honors, that is to say, not only did all who left Portora obtain honors, but a third of the entire number of places were taken by the pupils sent up from Enniskillen alone.[28]

The numbers are certainly striking, and they seem to be representative of a larger trend: under Steele's leadership, Portora was to become the most revered public school in Ireland, its chief function advertised boldly in the 1868 issue of *Our Schools and Colleges*: it "prepares [boys] for Universities and for public Competitive Examinations."[29]

There were practical benefits, as well as measurable defects, to arranging the Portora curriculum around the public examination. In 1862 the Revised Code for elementary education had instituted a system of "payment by results," which rewarded high examination scores with financial subsidies. With a renewed focus on the material rewards of academic achievement, many students found themselves cramming for examinations from the moment they arrived at Portora. In 1878, funds from the disestablished Church of Ireland were directed toward an endowment that made funds available to all Intermediate schools on a competitive basis. As the incomes of instructors depended upon the results of these competitive examinations, "teaching to the test" became common practice. By 1886, Portora no longer housed any boarders (compared to the 120 boarders it had boasted two decades earlier) and provided lessons to only twenty-three day boys. In the case of the Royal Schools, the chief cause of decline was an unremitting focus on the examination. "It is true," a writer for the *Journal of Education* reported that year, "that, when this is undertaken as a supplement to other studies, no harm need ensue; but where, as in some of the institutions which have advanced claims to a share in the endowments, the Intermediate programme constitutes the whole work of the school, a system of unmitigated and concentrated cramming is the inevitable result."[30]

Existing accounts of Portora during the time of Wilde's attendance describe the school as well-ordered and largely successful—an institutional model that produced scholars of a high caliber who excelled in academic endeavors. It was not, however, a system that impressed Wilde even as a child. To be sure, Wilde had the makings of a good scholar from the start. An anonymous source remembers him as being "very good on the literary scholarship, with a special leaning to poetry," a boy who set himself apart by liking "to have editions of the classics that were of stately size with large print," and Frank Harris recalls that Wilde was a "wide reader" who could imbibe text at an alarming rate.[31] Nevertheless, Wilde failed to adopt the forms of mental discipline advocated by Steele, except when it aligned with his own interests. By every existing account, Wilde initially failed to distinguish himself at Portora and was known for his desultory study habits. According to Richard Ellmann, "the more studious pupils assumed that he was a skimmer rather than a scholar," noting that he "did not cram for examinations, and read the prescribed texts for pleasure, along with much that was unprescribed, neglecting what he found boring."[32] Robert Sherard, a former master of Portora reported: "Oscar Wilde was never looked upon as a formidable competitor by the boys who went in for examinations in Portora school."[33] And according to Harris, Wilde himself was keenly aware of his perceived shortcomings, reportedly observing: "Until the last year of my school life at Portora [...] I had nothing like the reputation of my brother Willie. I read too many English novels, too much poetry, dreamed away too much time to master the school tasks."[34]

Such accounts must be treated with some degree of skepticism, though Wilde's record at Portora would seem to confirm that Wilde was not, at this point in time, particularly diligent in his studies. An exceptional thinker, Wilde was far from an exceptional student. It was only when Wilde distinguished himself in the *viva voce* of *The Agamemnon* that he began to attract notice as a serious scholar. Indeed, it was apparently the discovery of the classics that motivated much of Wilde's intellectual fervor in his final years at Portora.[35] In 1866 he was a prizeman in the Junior School. In 1869, he won third prize for Scripture, earning a copy of Bishop Joseph Butler's *Analogy* (1736) as his reward. The following year he won the Carpenter Prize for Greek Testament, and in 1871 he was one of three students to earn a Royal School scholarship to Trinity College (Fig. 2.1). Wilde's later successes at Portora do

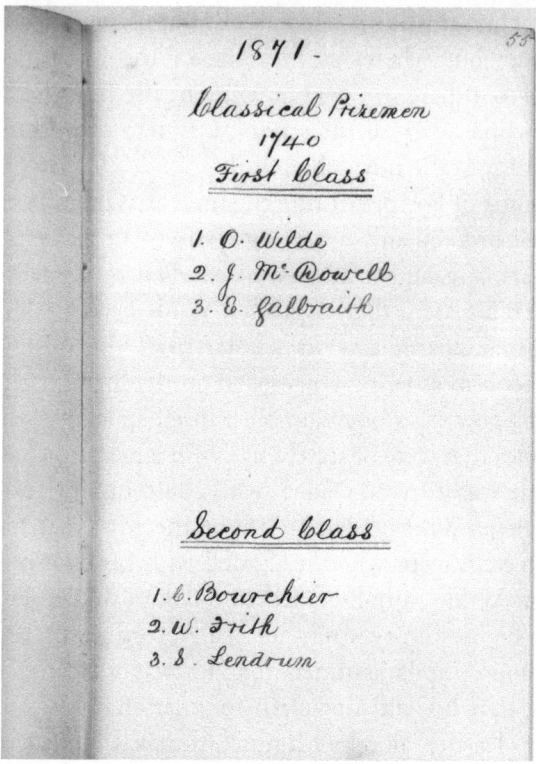

Fig. 2.1 Page from the Portora School prize book, 1871. (Courtesy of the Merlin Holland Picture Archive)

not reflect his conversion to the public school work ethic. On the contrary, they help to highlight the vast distance between Steele's vision of mental discipline and that of the young Wilde. When Steele informed Wilde of his Trinity scholarship, he reputedly praised the young scholar for his hard work over the preceding year. Wilde is said to have reflected upon this moment in later years: "The 'hard' work had been very interesting to me, or I would not have done much of it."[36] Wilde's remark, like his performance at Portora, would seem to reflect a certain disdain for the prescriptions of formal education. Wilde had little interest in learning what did not give pleasure, and in this, he may seem to resemble so many other pupils of his background. Still, it is precisely because Wilde's experience of and resistance to his education is so typical that it is worthy of further consideration. After all, Wilde's performance at Portora suggests an aversion to mental discipline that was curiously paired with a love of private study. In other words, Wilde seems to have shunned one set of disciplinary behaviors in favor of another.

Plato's Classroom

Wilde's resistance to formal academic study seems to have persisted at Trinity College where, as Sherard recalls, he continued to be regarded as "an average sort of man."[37] One don reported that he "was plainly not the man for the δόλιχος [dolichos, long struggle], though first-rate for a short examination."[38] The latter remark suggests that Wilde's intellectual capacities—his ability to read quickly, his retentive memory, and his talent for synthesizing an argument—were well-suited to "cramming" when it pleased him, though he remained averse to anything approaching real intellectual labor. For Wilde, the chief value of the university experience was the liberty it afforded him to avoid adopting any single mode of thought: free to "loiter in the grey cloisters at Magdalen, and listen to some flute-like voice singing in Waynfleete's chapel or lie in the green meadow," as he put it, the Oxford undergraduate could luxuriate in a culture of learning that was not confined to the walls of the schoolroom or lecture hall.[39] In his essay "Primavera" (1890), Wilde opens by underscoring the intellectual rewards of summer vacation: "In the summer term Oxford teaches the exquisite art of idleness, one of the most important things that any University can teach."[40] Such a remark helps to explain why Wilde was so resistant to conventional spaces and systems of learning: the structure of formal education in many ways restricted the natural movement and flexibility of thought. The implication is that real learning takes place only when the mind is not preoccupied by deadlines, examinations, or the pursuit of academic status. While Wilde was tremendously proud of his Oxford degree, he seems to have most relished the culture of idle curiosity the university cultivated.

Wilde's interest in learning for learning's sake, while not exactly new, constituted a significant departure from the focus on practical education that had dominated English culture for much of the last century. Throughout the eighteenth and nineteenth centuries, the desire for a more liberal approach to learning collided with what many perceived to be the practical aims of education. Swiss reformer Johann Heinrich Pestalozzi claimed in his 1827 *Letters on the Education of Infancy* that education ought to accommodate the unique inclinations and interests of the pupil, who should determine the pace and focus of his own lessons. For Pestalozzi, this student-centered approach was to be balanced by an attention to preparing pupils for the challenges of civic life through the cultivation of practical skills and experiences.[41] In like manner, Maria and Richard Lovell Edgeworth emphasized the importance of applied learning in *Practical Education* (1798), arguing that the best forms of recreation are those suited to a specific purpose; by this logic, imaginative play is less important (and theoretically less appealing to a child) than play directed toward some predetermined goal. Perhaps the most notorious early proponent of a goal-oriented "practical education," was Jeremy Bentham, who treated education as resolutely utilitarian. "Education," he writes, "is a series of conduct directed to an end: before any directions can properly be given for the education of any person, the end of his education must be settled."[42] This end, Bentham insists, must work toward the greater happiness of the community, so that education, whatever its immediate practical aim, ultimately becomes a building block for civic leadership and public virtue. If progressive approaches to pedagogy in the late eighteenth and early nineteenth centuries framed education as experimental, comprehensive, and student-centered, they also tended to focus on practical outcomes: the development of vocational skills, good citizenship, or spiritual advancement.

The limitations of the Benthamite model were laid bare in the 1873 *Autobiography* of John Stuart Mill. Having been educated by his father according to Bentham's dictates, Mill found himself disillusioned when he began to question the utilitarian ends toward which his entire education had been directed: "All my happiness was to have been found in the continual pursuit of this end. The end had ceased to charm, and how could there ever again be any interest in the means?"[43] For his own part, Wilde suspected that Mill never entirely escaped his father's influence, observing that to the end of his life "the pendulum of thought and developement [sic] of the dialectical idea" bore little interest to Mill.[44] It is precisely on this point—the resolute focus on practical outcomes—that Wilde differed from so many of his contemporaries.

Wilde's resistance to the concept of practical education originated in his reading of Greek and Roman philosophy during this period. A partial record of Wilde's encounters with the Classics can be gleaned from his Commonplace Book, kept between 1874 and 1879. To be sure, as Josephine Guy and Ian Small have observed, Wilde's notebook entries typically consist of extended transcriptions or paraphrases of Wilde's readings, a fact that tends to obfuscate Wilde's agency and rhetorical intent. Nevertheless, it is suggestive that his thoughts turn repeatedly in these journals to classical models of education.

Reflecting on Theodor Mommsen's *The History of Rome* (1868), for instance, Wilde writes:

> The Roman was educated for the family and the state: to be a pater familias and a civis: the refinement of Greek culture coming through the romantic medium of impassioned friendships, the freedom and gladness of the palaestra [gymnasium], were unknown to the boy whose early recollections were those of the senate house and the farm. So [to] one gravitas was the ideal, to the other "ευτραπελια" [eutrapelia; acuity][45]

The stoic pedagogy of the Romans was, by this account, all too grounded in a desire for social stability and rule of law: education was instead a means of establishing and maintaining a civic ideal that prized institutions above individuals. Wilde underscores his contempt for such a view, noting that a sheer love of wisdom "had no place in the narrow conservative education of a race who gave up art to their slaves and made it a handicraft and expelled the philosopher from Rome."[46]

The Greeks, by contrast, came to be aligned for Wilde with the cultivation of intellect for its own sake, as in a later entry where he directly invokes Plato's *Republic*:

> As it is the crown and prize of life—the flower which fadeth not, the joy which never disappoints—so it [is] the aim of early education.
> Let a boy says Plato from his childhood find things of beauty a delight (ευθυς παιζοι εν τοις καλοις): and in another place he says the end of music is the love of beauty (δει γαρ τελευταντα μουσικα εις του καλου ερωτικα) and these expressions come in a scheme of the noblest education.[47]

It is here, in Wilde's paraphrasing of Plato's educational schema that we begin to see signs of his budding investment in educational theory and, more specifically, in treating pleasure as both the catalyst and outcome of true learning. In *The Republic* of Plato, Socrates posits that all pleasure signals the fulfillment of a natural appetite. Juxtaposing the "class of foods, drinks, and relishes and nourishment generally" to the class of "true opinion, knowledge and reason," Socrates concludes that the highest form of pleasure is the pursuit of wisdom, since it is more directly aligned with true and enduring things. To this extent, pleasure becomes a measure of one's proximity to higher knowledge:

> And if there be a pleasure in being filled with that which is according to nature, that which is more really filled with more real being will more really and truly enjoy true pleasure; whereas that which participates in less real being will be less

truly and surely satisfied, and will participate in an illusory and less real pleasure?[48]

Only for the mind that "follows the philosophical principle" is the highest form of pleasure possible, for such a mind is not under the stress of containing its baser impulses.[49] By contrast, those who "know not wisdom and virtue, and are always busy with gluttony and sensuality," will inevitably suffer a sense of loss after the cessation of sensory delight.[50] The pursuit of knowledge is, for Plato, equivalent to the pursuit of the beautiful and the good; if sensory pleasure reflects evidence of one's proximity to beauty, then the greatest pleasure is to be achieved through the love of ideas.[51] In other words, Plato treats the pursuit of knowledge as the highest end and the surest mode of realizing beauty, truth, and pleasure, a sentiment Wilde echoes throughout his Oxford notebooks.

Wilde encountered a similar argument at work in Aristotle.[52] He was especially attracted by Aristotle's investment in the "idealism of reason"—his claim that the greatest good consists in the rational soul acting in conformity with virtue.[53] In his notebooks, Wilde highlights Aristotle's treatment of learning not as a means of securing happiness but rather as a pleasure unto itself:

> So in Aristotle the philosophers [sic] life is the contemplative life: he expressly disavows any philanthropic aim to Σοφια [sophia; knowledge]
>   "η μεν γαρ σοφια ουδεν θεωρει εξ ων εσται ευδαιμων ανθρωπος" ["For wisdom does not consider because of what things a man will be happy"]. (Eth. 6. 13). It is good says Aristotle for it's [sic] own sake because it is an "αρετη [arete; virtue] of the soul": the fact of it's [sic] existence is the reason for its existence.[54]

In this passage, Wilde echoes the insights he had already gleaned from Plato. True wisdom does "not consider because of what things a man will be happy": it is not motivated by a desire to produce happiness, for wisdom is a "virtue of the soul" that transcends utility. In Aristotle, then, discipline and pleasure are treated less as rivals than as complements to one another, "for the pleasures arising from thinking and learning will make us think and learn all the more."[55] Wilde's recurrence to the educational models of Aristotle and Plato suggests an investment in education as the pleasurable pursuit of wisdom undertaken for its own sake and with no particular end in mind. An attention to the learning process—as opposed to learning outcomes—would henceforth become a cornerstone of Wilde's approach to education.

The most direct expression of Wilde's investment in a Platonic model of learning would appear several years later in Wilde's mock-Socratic dialogue. "The Critic as Artist" (1891). Presented as a conversation between two men on "the importance of doing nothing," Wilde presents the dialogue as evidence of the kind of thought process such an immersive, Platonic education might make possible. The most explicit reference to educational theory emerges approximately midway through the text when Gilbert directly invokes Plato's description of knowledge acquisition in *The Republic*. The passage foregrounds Wilde's belief in the centrality of the arts to both mental and moral development:

> You remember that lovely passage in which Plato describes how a young Greek should be educated, and with what insistence he dwells upon the importance of surroundings, telling us how the lad is to be brought up in the midst of fair sights and sounds, so that the beauty of material things may prepare his soul for the reception of the beauty that is spiritual. Insensibly, and without knowing the reason why, he is to develop that real love of beauty which, as Plato is never weary of reminding us, is the true aim of education.[56]

At first glance, Gilbert's claim that the "true aim of education" is to cultivate a "real love of beauty" might strike the Victorian (and perhaps the contemporary) reader as a playful gesture meant simply to reinforce the primacy of artistic expression. In this spirit, Gilbert wryly observes: "I can imagine the smile that would illuminate the glossy face of the Philistine if one ventured to suggest to him that the true aim of education was the love of beauty."[57] Yet the "love of beauty" invoked here by Wilde, an astute scholar of the Classics, is also perforce the love of wisdom. If this might seem to be one of Gilbert's more subversive moments, he is in many ways merely ventriloquizing Plato. He continues:

> By slow degrees there is to be engendered in him such a temperament as will lead him naturally and simply to choose the good in preference to the bad, and, rejecting what is vulgar and discordant, to follow by fine instinctive taste all that possesses grace and charm and loveliness. Ultimately, in its due course, this taste is to become critical and self-conscious, but at first it is to exist purely as a cultivated instinct, and 'he who has receive this true culture of the inner man will with clear and certain vision perceive the omissions and faults in art or nature, and with a taste that cannot err, while he praises, and finds his pleasure in what is good, and receives it into his soul, and so becomes good and noble, he will rightly blame and hate the bad, now in the days of his youth, even before he is able to know the reason why:' and so, when, later on, the critical and

self-conscious spirit develops in him, he 'will recognize and salute it as a friend with whom his education has made him long familiar.'[58]

So far, Gilbert's argument seems to follow Plato precisely, describing the experience of true beauty as one of the highest pleasures, a sign of the soul's responsiveness to the harmonies it perceives in the world. For Wilde, the best education is one in which the student is continually surrounded by and engaging with beauty. By studying and reflecting upon the beauty he sees before him, the pupil becomes more keenly attuned to the fineness and delicacy of his fellow creatures: he enlarges the scope of his own feelings and perceptions, becoming at once more sympathetic and more self-determined.

This model of education is evidently one that Wilde had treasured for many years. During his 1881–1882 lecture tour of America, Wilde had repeatedly invoked Plato's image of the young Greek. Having visited Charles Leland's Public School of Industrial Art in Philadelphia, Wilde brought to his lectures handicrafts produced by some of the schoolchildren: "It is a practical school of morals," he observes in his 1882 lecture "House Decoration." Wilde continues: "No better way is there to learn to love Nature than to understand Art. It dignifies every flower of the field. And, the boy who sees the thing of beauty which a bird on the wing becomes when transferred to wood or canvas will probably not throw the customary stone."[59] In an interview the same year, Wilde suggested to a *Tribune* reporter: "the knowledge of the beautiful is personal and can only be acquired by one's own eyes and ears. This truth was the origin of the theory of beautiful surroundings. A child should have around him from his infancy beautiful things."[60] For Wilde, a familiarity with what is pleasurable does not breed hedonism or indifference to the evils of the world but rather an intimacy with the highest forms of virtue. The student learns to make beauty the very object of his studies and, by admiring the beauty he sees in "a bird on the wing," is drawn into direct sympathy with all living creatures. This immersive school of aesthetics is more than a source of pleasure; it becomes a source of moral enrichment. The student learns not only what is beautiful but also to embrace, without need of formal prescriptions or "lessons," what is true and good.

Wilde's former Trinity tutor, J.P. Mahaffy—the man Wilde would call his "first and greatest teacher"—echoed this sentiment in his volume *Old Greek Education* (1881).[61] In Mahaffy's view, drawing and music were incorporated into the Greek curriculum for two reasons: "first and most obviously for critical purposes, that men might better judge and appreciate works of art; secondly, for that aesthetical effect which is so forgotten by us, the unconscious moulding of the mind to beauty by the close an accurate study of beautiful forms."[62] Mahaffy's analysis of the Greek system is not merely appreciative—

here, as elsewhere in the volume, he finds the stark contrast between Victorian and Hellenic approaches to arts education deeply troubling. Whereas his contemporaries regard the arts chiefly as a "humanizing" influence that serves to distract boys from "coarse and harmful pursuits," Mahaffy insists that the Greeks recognized in the arts a far greater power to shape individual character and social life.[63] Hence, martial music not only inspires the soldier who is departing for battle; it actually, he avers, can make a culture more violent. Wilde, a careful reader of Mahaffy's work who famously "made improvements and corrections all through" his 1874 volume *Social Life in Greece*, seems to have agreed with his assessment that a departure from conventional disciplinary forms might help to revitalize nineteenth-century educational programs.[64]

Mahaffy also shared Wilde's belief in the intellectual value of leisure, observing that the Greeks were "far better educated than we are" chiefly because "Greek life afforded proper leisure for thorough intellectual training."[65] As we have already established, Wilde too regarded "doing nothing" chiefly as a mode of reflection, for to be idle is at times to have a profoundly busy mental life. Gilbert's celebration of idleness is thus part of a larger critique of Victorian educational reform, serving as a counterpoint to the "learned conversation" Gilbert associates with the Victorian pedagogue. Gilbert, after all, has no "desire to talk learnedly. Learned conversation is either the affectation of the ignorant or the profession of the mentally unemployed."[66] What passes for "learning," in other words, is little more than the repetition of received wisdom. This, in Wilde's view, would seem to be the chief failing of modern education—its insistence on transmitting established lessons that are "tested" and reinforced through institutional custom. Gilbert's lampoon of the Victorian pedagogue is striking:

> If you meet at dinner a man who has spent his life in educating himself—a rare type in our time, I admit, but still one occasionally to be met with—you rise from table richer, and conscious that a high ideal has for a moment touched and sanctified your days. But oh! my dear Ernest, to sit next to a man who has spent his life in trying to educate others! What a dreadful experience that is! How appalling is that ignorance which is the inevitable result of the fatal habit of imparting opinions! How limited in range the creature's mind proves to be! How it wearies us, and must weary himself, with its endless repetitions and sickly reiteration! How lacking it is in any element of intellectual growth! In what a vicious circle it always moves![67]

Whereas the man of true education enriches his fellows through unconscious influence and conversation, the pedagogue oppresses them. Rather than promoting "intellectual growth," he disciplines the mind through "endless repetitions and sickly reiteration," a move calculated not only to bore his companions but actually to arrest the quest for knowledge.

To be sure, repetition can be a powerful tool for the teacher, and Gilbert readily acknowledges as much. The practice of recitation elevates the status of an utterance, helping to single out ideas that are worthy of repetition: "The Creeds," Gilbert observes, "are believed, not because they are rational, but because they are repeated."[68] Victorian reformers articulated similar ideas about the educational value of recitation and repetition. In his volume, *The Discipline of the Physical and Intellectual Powers* (1847), William Gordon argued that repetition "produces facility of action," whether in physical or intellectual pursuits.[69] Such practices not only make it possible for students to reproduce received wisdom; they also, he argues, help to cultivate a habit of mind that is temperate, virtuous, and attuned to the pleasures of learning. "The culture and discipline of the mind," he continues, "produce the most important results on our well-being as rational and moral creatures. The diligent cultivation of our faculties secures at once our usefulness and our happiness, and in the conquest and control of our passions consists the highest dignity of our nature."[70] Such an approach dovetails with Catherine Robson's recent caution against viewing the Victorian focus on recitation "in a cynical manner" and her reminder that "the mind's secure possession of a literary work is self-evidently a highly desirable and multivalent good," one that does not necessarily imply indifference or passivity on the part of the student.[71]

For Wilde, however, this particular form of pleasure may come at the expense of cultivating in the student true intellectual growth. If the custom of reciting a passage from a favorite poem might prove enjoyable, the Victorian schoolmaster relied upon repetition as proof of the student's mastery, treating learning less as a pleasurable process than as a "dim, dull abyss of facts."[72] In one of the more earnest moments of the dialogue, Gilbert observes:

> We, in our educational system, have burdened the memory with a load of unconnected facts, and laboriously striven to impart our laboriously-acquired knowledge. We teach people how to remember, we never teach them how to grow. It has never occurred to us to try and develop in the mind a more subtle quality of apprehension and discernment.[73]

To reduce the pursuit of knowledge to a foreseeable program of facts and rehearsed truisms is hardly, Wilde suggests, a test of true learning. The best students will instead capitalize on the power of repetition without reverting to those disciplinary practices that might render formal education laborious and burdensome. Repetition has real value, Gilbert avers: "Form is everything. It is the secret of life. Find expression for a sorrow, and it will become dear to you. Find expression for a joy, and you intensify its ecstasy. Do you wish to love? Use Love's Litany, and the words will create the yearning from which the world fancies that they spring."[74] If the repetition of received wisdom renders the student a passive recipient of knowledge, then, Wilde concedes that recitation might be replaced by an attention to aesthetic form itself. To copy the forms of beauty one finds in Nature is quite a different thing from conjugating Latin verbs or transcribing passages from Scripture. Hence, the boy who traces "a bird on the wing" makes his chief object of study aesthetic form rather than content, thus becoming more attuned to what is good and beautiful in the world.

It is in this spirit that we can begin to understand Gilbert's aversion to "learned conversation." If Gilbert shrugs off "learning" as the mere performance of academic scripts, it is clear that his conversation is informed by a very different kind of learning, one that takes the form of aesthetic engagement. Hence, while he dismisses "improving conversation" as a "foolish method," Gilbert returns us to an immersive, Platonic model of education that literally surrounds the reader with beautiful things:

> Through the parted curtains of the window I see the moon like a clipped piece of silver. Like gilded bees the stars cluster round her. The sky is a hard hollow sapphire. Let us go out into the night. Thought is wonderful, but adventure is more wonderful still. Who knows but we may meet Prince Florizel of Bohemia, and hear the fair Cuban tell us that she is not what she seems?[75]

Gilbert's final words confirm that the best intellectual inquiries are tentative rather than fact-finding, aesthetic rather than empirical. Seen this way, his claim that "nothing that is worth knowing can be taught" does not so much undermine the importance of education as resist the mode of "sickly reiteration" Wilde associates with the figure of the Victorian schoolmaster. Gilbert's "theory of education," as Ernest calls it, is thus predicated on a resistance to the institutional forms that were quite typical of the period.[76]

The Schoolmaster

In his own experience, Wilde felt that the most effective teachers were those who did not merely possess knowledge but actually modeled the passionate pursuit of wisdom through the utterance itself, seeking to multiply and extend rather than to affix truth. Wilde proclaimed that his "first and [...] best teacher" was Mahaffy, the classics scholar at Trinity College who sparked his lifelong passion for the Greeks.[77] Wilde wrote of Mahaffy: "[H]e took deliberately the artistic standpoint towards everything, which was coming more and more to be my standpoint. He was a delightful talker, too, a really great talker in a certain way—an artist in vivid words and eloquent pauses."[78] What Wilde found appealing about Mahaffy was not his possession of concrete knowledge but rather his ability to radiate, by means of "vivid words and eloquent pauses," the process of reflection itself. Mahaffy communicated his knowledge not as a lecturer or scientist but rather as an "artist" and virtuoso. By Wilde's account at least, Mahaffy did not put knowledge on display but instead performed an intellectual fluidity that his students were invited to share, emulate, and pursue.

It is noteworthy that when Wilde eventually quarreled with Mahaffy, it was because his former tutor had, in Wilde's eyes, betrayed his most effective attribute as a teacher: his style.[79] In a review of Mahaffy's, *The Principles of the Art of Conversation* (1887), Wilde critiqued his mentor on the grounds that, despite endorsing sound rhetorical principles, he had adopted the posture of a pedagogue rather than that of an artist. Initially, Wilde expresses his objections in terms of Mahaffy's methodology:

> In discussing this important subject, of conversation, he has not merely followed the scientific method of Aristotle which is, perhaps, excusable, but he has adopted the literary style of Aristotle for which no excuse is possible. There is, also, hardly a single anecdote, hardly a single illustration, and the reader is left to put the Professor's abstract rules into practice, without either the examples or the warnings of history to encourage or to dissuade him in his reckless career.[80]

All of the artistry Wilde had ascribed to Mahaffy's pedagogy suddenly vanished as his dynamic style assumed the form of "abstract rules" to be imbibed by the passive student. Wilde admits that the book "pleases in spite of its pedantry, and is the nearest approach, that we know of, in modern literature to meeting Aristotle at an afternoon tea."[81] But even as Wilde's use of this epithet honors his teacher's intellect, it also indicts him for the empirical methods he had adopted. While the Platonic dialogue reflected Wilde's understanding of education as dialogic and recursive, the Aristotelian treatise was far more structured and prescriptive. If Mahaffy's work is empirically sound, Wilde observes, it also displays a fundamental lack of style. The same arguments emerge in relation to Wilde's other instructors at Trinity. According to Frank Harris, Wilde described one of his tutors at Trinity, Robert Yelverton

Tyrrell, as being "very kind to me—intensely sympathetic and crammed with knowledge," noting with some regret that "'[i]f he had known less he would have been a poet.'"[82] Tyrrell's intellectual surplus, however impressive, rendered him less suited in Wilde's view to the kind of boundless conversation that was so essential to good teaching.

Wilde seems to have held a similar view of John Ruskin, whom he describes as vacillating between the mode of the schoolmaster and the more organic methods of the artist. Although Wilde was initially impressed by Ruskin after attending his 1874 lectures on Florentine art, it was in Ruskin's conversation that Wilde detected evidence of a great teacher. Wilde reportedly noted: "He was a great poet and teacher [...] and therefore of course a most preposterous professor; he bored you to death when he taught, but was an inspiration when he sang."[83] The insinuation here is that Ruskin was at his best when he traded the posture of the pedagogue—the professor standing at the lectern—for the more speculative mode of the poet. Years later, writing from prison, Wilde would observe that his "dearest memories" of Oxford were of his walks with Ruskin, who revealed himself in such moments to be something of a "prophet, of priest, and of poet," a man whose eloquence reflected the "fire of passion, and the marvel of music, making the deaf to hear, and the blind to see."[84] Again, Wilde's assessment celebrates the almost mystical qualities of his teacher's language. More aesthetic than didactic, Ruskin's words do not exert authority but rather instill power in his students, "making the deaf to hear, and the blind to see." Ruskin's real pedagogical power, by this logic, was reflected in the aesthetic quality of his words; reflecting the grace and vitality of a mind at work, his utterances inspired students to reflection rather than merely professing knowledge.

The most effective teachers, then, do not deliver fully formed philosophies to their pupils; rather, they model the importance of pursuing knowledge for its own sake, abandoning utility and intellectual certainty for a more mobile and recursive learning experience. This idea too originates in the work of the Greek philosophers that constituted the focus of Wilde's Oxford education.[85] In *Theaetetus* (ca. BC 369), a dialogue that focuses pointedly on the nature and value of true knowledge, Socrates prompts his student to acts of independent thought by continually shifting the focus of conversation, seeking to prolong rather than to resolve the dialogic process.[86] Socrates has a reputation, as he himself admits, for being "the strangest of mortals" who "drive[s] men to their wits' end."[87] Bobbing and weaving his way through the dialogue, Socrates actually *performs* the answer that eludes articulation. In other words, these evasive maneuvers and attempts to view a question from different perspectives reflect Socrates's claim that the practice of truth-seeking is every bit as important as the attainment of truth. Of his own students, Socrates remarks: "[i]t is quite clear that they never learned anything from me; the many fine discoveries to which they cling are of their own making."[88] Education, by this logic, does not consist of a catechism, a litany of fixed truths possessed by the master and transmitted fully formed to the student. It instead derives strength and momentum from the vital, unpredictable, and often recalcitrant spirit of conversation. The "Socratic method" of inquiry does not lead students to discover the knowledge already possessed by their teachers or even by themselves. It is, on the contrary, a method that luxuriates in highly stylized and deliberately open-ended communication.[89] Knowledge is not to be discovered but rather pursued.

It is suggestive that Socrates himself rejected outright the designation of *teacher* on the grounds that it implies the transmission rather than the cultivation of knowledge. In *The Apology* (ca. BC 360), Socrates announces plainly of any man who claims him as a teacher: "I never taught or professed to teach him anything. And if he says he has ever learned or heard anything from me in private which all the world has not heard, let me tell you that he is lying."[90] Although Socrates may seem to speak in riddles, his argument about the role of the teacher reflects a careful attention to the term itself. The Greek word that is often translated as *teacher* in this passage, *didaskalos*, also signifies *master*, a hierarchical connotation that is preserved in the English term *didacticism*. By declining the title of *didaskalos*, Socrates refuses to assume the role of master or pedagogue, preferring instead to frame himself as a kind of philosophical midwife whose chief objective is the "delivery" of new insights from the mind of the student.[91] The suggestion, then, is that the dialogic process modeled by Socrates of necessity resists the master-disciple relationship, which presumes that the teacher's role is simply to transplant factual knowledge into the student's mind. Socrates refuses the terms of formal education in order to promote a model of learning that is dialogic without being hierarchical, productive without being resolute.

It, therefore, should come as little surprise that, drawing on his formal training in Greats at Oxford, Wilde's mock-Socratic dialogues would present the schoolmaster as a kind of intellectual and social parasite. In "The Critic as Artist," Gilbert objects strenuously to the figure of the teacher, framing him as a "dominating" and ultimately oppressive presence. "People say that the schoolmaster is abroad," Gilbert observes: "I wish to goodness he were. But the type of which, after all, he is only one, and certainly the least important, of the representatives, seems to me to be really dominating our lives; and just as the philanthropist is the nuisance of the ethical sphere, so the nuisance of the intellectual sphere is the man who is so occupied in trying to educate others, that he has never had any time to educate himself."[92] For Gilbert, to treat knowledge in this way is to refuse the potential for true innovation both within the mind of the schoolmaster, who ceases to engage with new ideas, and in the mind of the student, who never learns to ask the vital questions. Thus, we see at work in Wilde's dialogue a Greek understanding of the term *teacher*: the "school*master*" is suspect precisely because he takes part in an intellectual hierarchy that values the transmission rather than the genesis of ideas. Accustomed to an educational program that prioritizes facts and learning by rote, the master yields passively to a process of intellectual mirroring and regurgitation: the man "who has spent his life in trying to educate others" possesses a mind "limited in range" and able to produce only "endless repetitions and sickly reiteration."[93] Such an educational program is, for Wilde, the end of thought itself.

To some extent, such a power dynamic might seem to recommend a departure from all forms of organized, institutional learning. Peter Bailey has considered how nineteenth-century texts present the autodidact "as a defensive alternative from the interpersonal processes of education," proposing that self-education was for Wilde the only course of study capable of freeing both student and teacher from the despotic relations of the master-disciple contract. The student does not acquire new knowledge, Bailey maintains, so much as rediscover within himself knowledge already possessed although perhaps only dimly perceived, through a process akin to Plato's theory of *anamnesis* (recollection). Liberated from the mediating influence of a teacher, the student is able to develop his capacity for independent thought, thereby facilitating a more personal and immediate apprehension of knowledge. Bailey is right to suggest that Wilde was wary of any pedagogical mode that depended on the unilateral transmission of knowledge from teacher to student. It is precisely such a master-disciple relationship that constitutes the dramatic crux of *The Picture of Dorian Gray*. For Lord Henry Wotton, the world of thought is preeminently flexible, liberating, and divorced from praxis. He treats thought chiefly as a process or "improvisation," peppered with paradox, riddles, and irresolution. On more than one occasion, Lord Henry mesmerizes his interlocutors by pursuing provocative and even volatile lines of inquiry: "He played with the idea, and grew wilful; tossed it into the air and transformed it; let it escape and recaptured it; made it iridescent with fancy, and winged it with paradox."[94] Although his utterances frequently take the form of aphorisms, Lord Henry himself does not profess any particular philosophical system ("no theory of life seemed to him to be of any importance compared with life itself"), and his companions are continually left in doubt as to his true convictions.[95] As Lady Agatha puts it, "'He never means anything that he says.'"[96] This "Prince Paradox" seems to luxuriate in intellectual loose ends and to exemplify in explicit terms the pedagogical style that Wilde had explored in his earlier writings.[97]

Dorian, in all his "rose-red youth and [...] rose-white boyhood," lacks such an understanding.[98] Not having come to knowledge on his own terms, Dorian assumes the role of Lord Henry's disciple and treats his aphorisms as practical edicts to guide his conduct in and experience of the world. Lord Henry's chief role in determining the young man's fate consists, then, in exposing Dorian to philosophical ideas with which the youth is not yet prepared to engage. Understood as intellectual experiments, Lord Henry's utterances provide a platform for discussion, debate, and reflection; understood as lessons, they become misguided and dangerous. Such an argument has deeply political connotations, as Michel Foucault explains in *The Government of Self and Others*. Whereas empirical knowledge (*mathemata*), can be conferred on or transmitted to students by means of propositions or formulae, in the cultivation of philosophical knowledge, Foucault observes, "[t]here is no learning of a formula, but an abrupt and sudden coming on of the light within the soul. And there is no inscription and depositing of ready made formulae in the soul, but the perpetual feeding of philosophy by the secret oil of the soul."[99] The transmission of philosophical knowledge to the student is "either pointless or dangerous," potentially leading those who fail to understand "that philosophy has no other reality than its own practices" to become overpowering and resistant to the dialogic process that fosters intellectual growth.[100] In other words, Lord Henry does precisely what Foucault would later warn against: rather than encouraging Dorian to work toward philosophical revelation, he presents his musings to Dorian as formulae: "He had made him premature."[101] Dorian's epicurean education is directed not by intellectual passion but rather by the strange "yellow book" given to him by Lord Henry. Detecting in the book's hero a "prefiguring type of himself," Dorian patterns his behavior after the fictional character, systematically studying perfumes, music, jewels, embroideries, and sensations, consulting the yellow book as one might consult a playbook.[102] While the extent to which Lord Henry actively seduces Dorian is open to speculation, there is little question that Wilde's novel underscores the risks of an education predicated on the transmission of static truths from teacher to student.[103]

Thus, while Wilde's suspicion of traditional pedagogy proceeds from a fear that students might become "disciples" who uncritically adopt the worldview of their "masters," this concern should not lead us to align him with the opposite extreme: a solipsistic model of learning in which the claims of individuality trump the potential rewards of sociability. Coinciding with Wilde's

principle of self-education—those long, idle hours spent meditating or reading a book on the sofa—is a highly cooperative, multivocal, and socialized
form of discourse. In this regard, the tutorial system Wilde encountered at
Oxford significantly shaped his understanding of the learning process. Linda
Dowling has established the importance of "tutor worship" to the Oxford
experience starting from the time of Jowett, noting that the relationship
between tutor and pupil was meant to "become part of an ethos in which
intellectual growth was to merge with religious awakening, and instruction
would verge on intimacy."[104] Although Dowling places this dynamic within
the context of an emerging institutional "code" that would align the Hellenic
ideal with homosexuality, in a much broader sense the intimacy of the Oxford
tutorial promised to treat the student as more a fellow seeker than a mere
receptacle for knowledge. As Montagu Burrows observes in *Pass and Class: An
Oxford Guide-Book* (1860), the "confidential relations between Tutor and
pupil here advised are not advantageous only in an intellectual point of view";
it also, Burrows goes on to explain, established an "intimate connection
between the intellectual and the moral life."[105] This ideal would inform Wilde's
belief in learning as a dialogic, social, and pleasurable exercise capable of
changing not merely one's opinion but one's way of existing in the world. For
Wilde, the most effective education is an ongoing discursive project in which
the individual (whether student or teacher) is continually asking questions
and testing new theories through alternating moments of social engagement
and solitary reflection.

A similar suspicion of the didactic mode informs Wilde's other critical dialogue, "The Decay of Lying" (1889). The value of intellectual loose ends is
underscored when Cyril points out that Vivian's desire to remain indoors cor-
recting proofs would seem to defy his staunch insistence on the virtues of
living in the world. As Vivian puts it: "Who wants to be consistent? The
dullard and the doctrinaire, the tedious people who carry out their principles
to the bitter end of action, to the *reductio ad absurdum* of practice. Not I. Like
Emerson, I write over the door of my library the word 'Whim.'"[106] From its
very outset, then, we are to understand that the exchange between Vivian and
Cyril will not end in any definitive outcome or "end of action." The best form
of education, in Vivian's view, is one that luxuriates in untested hypotheses
and imaginative digressions. In other words, if Plato suggests that the process
is as important as the attainment of truth, Wilde proclaims in this dialogue
that only process matters.[107] "Many a young man," Vivian observes, "starts in
life with a natural gift for exaggeration which, if nurtured in congenial and
sympathetic surroundings, or by the imitation of the best models, might grow
into something really great and wonderful. But, as a rule, he comes to noth-

ing. He either falls into careless habits of accuracy [...] or takes to frequenting the society of the aged and the well-informed." For Vivian, the young person's vast potential for creative and intellectual growth is something to be nurtured by a course of "study" that prioritizes encounters with the dissenter and the eccentric. If he fails to do so, this "morbid and unhealthy faculty of truth-telling" threatens to diminish his capacity for independent thought. Possessed by a "monstrous worship of facts," the mind's capacity for growth atrophies and real learning becomes impossible.[108] By promoting "lying" as an art form, Vivian thus advances two vital elements of Wilde's pedagogical style. First, he provokes readers into questioning their most deeply held convictions, thus instantiating a process of intellectual reflection that demands active engagement. Vivian performs, that is to say, precisely the speculative mode of inquiry he wishes to promote.[109] Second, he inverts the Platonic claim regarding the truth-telling power of art itself. Plato had claimed that artists provide us with mere representations of beauty—they do not provide that higher form of Beauty that is indistinguishable from truth. Wilde, however, proposes that accessing truth is always of less importance than the process of seeking after it. Accordingly, the very best teachers do not convey lessons but instead practice a stylized discourse that promotes the pupil's sensitivity to beauty: the best teachers are, in a word, artists.[110]

Professor of Aesthetics

Wilde would attempt to adopt this ethos when he assumed the role of lecturer during his American tour. Arriving in New York on 2 January 1882, Wilde faced a largely skeptical audience, their fascination and ridicule fueled to some extent by W. S. Gilbert and Arthur Sullivan's aesthetic spoof *Patience* (1881), which was then running at the Standard Theater. It was hoped that Wilde's presence would help to popularize the operetta, and American audiences were certainly quick to associate Wilde with the "aesthetic sham," Reginald Bunthorne. Wilde was lampooned widely in the press as the "Apostle of the Utter," whose claim to aesthetic knowledge was a mere pose.[111] His lectures, at least at first, were described as no more than "a precious curiosity in a side show"—more sensational than educational.[112]

Keenly attuned to the importance of pedagogical style, Wilde put a great deal of effort into preparing for his lecture tour. His very attire—the famous velvet waistcoat and knee-breeches featured in countless nineteenth-century visual satires—reflected a living engagement with the aesthetic philosophy that his lectures sought to promote (Fig. 2.2). Scholars have often regarded Wilde's

Fig. 2.2 Oscar Wilde on the platform. *The National Police Gazette* (28 January 1882), 1

apparel as a visual display of his subversive rhetoric, a costume that "attacked the accepted conventions of Victorian style" and exposed its preoccupation with social artifice.[113] Within the context of Wilde's interest in aesthetic education, however, we might also view the costume as a deliberate study in pedagogical style. By approaching the task of lecturing as a kind of performance, Wilde wished to do more than simply profess truths about art: inspired by the examples of Mahaffy and Ruskin, he visibly embodied the figure of teacher as artist.[114] His audiences would not merely imbibe his lessons; they would see those ideas manifested in the flesh. In "The Relation of Dress to Art," Wilde thus observes: "Art is not to be taught in Academies. It is what one looks at, not what one listens to, that makes the artist. The real schools should be the streets."[115] Or, put even more succinctly in his lecture "The Decorative Arts" (1882): "True art in dress will make our attire an instructor, an educator."[116] If Wilde assumed the position of the pedagogue at the lectern, the substance of his lectures reflected a desire that everyone should live by art, pursuing an aesthetic education in daily life. As one American reviewer noted of his performance at the McDonald's Opera House in Montgomery, Alabama, "Mr. Wilde himself graced the occasion with his presence and showed that grace in practice which he so beautifully teaches in the principle."[117] Wilde admitted in an interview with the *Salt Lake Herald* that one of the chief reasons for his eccentric dress was that "live poets have principles, and that is that one should do as one preaches."[118]

To be sure, Wilde's costume became a favorite target for his critics, yet attempts at ridicule seem only to have presented him with further opportunities to innovate on his newly acquired status as teacher. Confronted by a row of Harvard undergraduates mockingly costumed in aesthetic garb, Wilde reportedly addressed them prior to the lecture: "I see about me certain signs of an aesthetic movement. I see certain young men who are, no doubt, sincere; but I can assure them that they are no more than caricatures." As he surveyed the audience, Wilde added: "Save me from my disciples!"[119] With this exclamation, Wilde effectively issued to the Harvard undergraduates a "lesson" in discipleship. If they intended to lampoon Wilde's celebrity status and the devotion of his followers, it was a joke that Wilde himself was willing to endorse: satire was perhaps a greater tribute to his philosophy than emulation and allegiance. Wilde proceeded to regale the students with stories of his own undergraduate experience. In particular, he described how Ruskin persuaded Wilde and his classmates to build a road between North and South Hinksey in order to demonstrate the virtues of physical labor. "And what became of the road?" Wilde interjected. "Well, like a bad lecture it ended abruptly—in the middle of the swamp." Having abandoned the project between terms, the students returned to find Ruskin departed for Venice and no one overseeing the project. For Wilde, the building project served as a model for his own aesthetic movement: "So I sought them out—leader they would call me—but there was no leader: we were all searchers only and we were bound to each other by noble friendship and by noble art."[120] In the end, Wilde's address to these undergraduate critics framed the ideal learning experience as one that moves away from the master-disciple model, becoming instead an inborn impulse to labor for the sake of art, fellowship, and personal growth. Wilde's stint as lecturer, it is true, garnered mixed reviews; in some ways, much like Ruskin, Wilde was more successful off stage than as a professor of aesthetics.[121] Yet, his efforts to tailor his public image to the lecture hall—to adopt a voice, gesture, and dress appropriate to his subject matter—suggest an ongoing attempt to move beyond the didactic mode of the pedagogue and to embrace a teaching style that would demand audience engagement.

For Wilde, costume was more than merely a question of captivating the attention of his listeners. His appearance helped to convey how the "lessons" he preached might find their way into everyday practice. In his lectures, Wilde discussed the importance of an aesthetic education at length, emphasizing the dangers of treating a lesson as something to be accomplished rather than as an integral part of everyday life. "The art systems of the past," he observes, "have been devised by philosophers who looked upon human beings as obstructions. They have tried to educate boys' minds before they had any."[122] Ideally, education would not instill in a student's mind an understanding of aesthetic principles, but would, instead, cultivate a sensitivity to the beautiful wherever it is to be found. To that end, Wilde recommended that all students, rather than pursuing the abstract study of art, be provided with workshops devoted to the production of handicrafts. Wilde had marveled at the art produced by students at Charles Leland's Public School of Industrial Art in Philadelphia. He toted samples of their work to his lectures, exhibiting them as evidence that this new mode of education might help to revive both the aesthetic and moral sensibilities of the rising generation: "In every school I would have a workshop, and I would have an hour a day set apart when boys could learn something practically of art. [...] This would be a golden hour to the children, and they would enjoy that hour most, learn more of the lessons of life and of the morality of art than in years of book study. And you would soon raise up a race of handicraftsmen who would transform the face of your country."[123] Leland insisted that art was an indispensable part of every child's education. In the production of art, he reasoned, one learns only by doing; in effect, the study of art teaches one *how* to learn. In *Practical Education* (1888), Leland explains this connection at length:

> Now it is a very good habit for a boy in the beginning of his education to learn *how to learn* his lessons, and I believe this could be done by making him feel at first that the manner in which he gets his lesson, and the perfection of it, is the end aimed at. As it is he thinks naturally enough that to *understand* the lesson in hand is all he has to do. To get through it with the teacher is, as he believes, sufficient. Now if he knew that to commit it perfectly as well as to understand it is *inevitable*, I believe that the dullest boy would soon take a different view of it.[124]

Paradoxically, Leland views the most "practical education" as one that sets aside all practical objectives in favor of cultivating in the student a desire and ability to learn. The point is not to relinquish the real world altogether but rather to recognize that one can best achieve specific learning outcomes—the cultivation of memory, critical thinking, and power of expression—by treating learning as an art that must be continually practiced.

For Wilde, as for Leland, then, the most effective education provides students with access to an environment and community that prioritizes experience and process above the acquisition of facts or learning by rote. Assuming that the "true aim of education" is that "love of beauty" which ensures the individual's ability to see the world in proper cultural, ethical, and social proportion, it was absolutely vital that students become fluent in the language of aesthetics from an early age. Education was not, in Wilde's view, something to be reserved for the elite but was instead something to be sought out by every man in every context. It is not "merely at Oxford, or Cambridge," Gilbert remarks, "that the sense of beauty can be formed and trained and perfected."[125] In his lecture "The English Renaissance of Art" (1882), Wilde argues that the aesthetic improvement of English culture depends upon the proper education of the country's artisans and workers, noting that "[a]ll the teaching in the world is of no avail if you do not surround your workman with happy influences and with beautiful things."[126] Such a direct and ongoing encounter with the aesthetic is not, for Wilde, merely a question of improving worker morale; aesthetic education is essential to the cultivation and dissemination of beauty throughout human society. One cannot "have right ideas about colour unless he sees the lovely colours of Nature unspoiled; impossible for him to supply beautiful incident and action unless he sees beautiful incident and action in the world about him."[127] Living by art—in other words, integrating the pursuit of beauty into one's life rather than making it a mere object of study—is the only way of improving the individual's perception of the beautiful, whether it is a question of objects ("beautiful things" and the "lovely colors of Nature") or ideas ("beautiful incident and action").

This outlook was doubtless informed by Wilde's extensive reading of Cardinal John Henry Newman.[128] In his *Idea of a University* (1854), Newman contends that the university is not a forum for the promotion of specific religious or political ideas but rather a space for the development of intellectual culture in its own right. What sets Newman's educational theory apart is its insistence that, although education may ultimately reap practical or moral benefits, the cultivation of the intellect is an end valuable in and of itself. Newman's definition of knowledge and, by extension, his understanding of education, aligns it more closely with philosophy than with the acquisition of scientific fact. He writes:

> When I speak of Knowledge, I mean something intellectual, something which grasps what it perceives through the senses; something which takes a view of

things; which sees more than the senses convey; which reasons upon what it sees, and while it sees; which invests it with an idea.[…] The principle of real dignity in Knowledge, its worth, its desirableness, considered irrespectively of its results, is this germ within it of a scientific or a philosophical process. This is how it comes to be an end in itself; this is why it admits of being called Liberal.[129]

In Newman's view, it is process itself—the ability of the mind to imaginatively generate new links between the seen and the unseen—that makes knowledge valuable. Indeed, Newman is reticent about any form of "particular and practical" knowledge, believing that this belongs more to the "useful or mechanical arts" than to education as such: "Knowledge," he writes, "in proportion as it tends more and more to be particular, ceases to be Knowledge."[130] In effect, Newman proposes that the most valuable knowledge is that which has no practical application but instead luxuriates in process, always bearing within it the potential for future discussion and deliberation.

Newman seems to have anticipated the potential problems with such an argument: "Now, when I say that Knowledge is, not merely a means to something beyond it, or the preliminary of certain arts into which it naturally resolves, but an end sufficient to rest in and to pursue for its own sake, surely I am *uttering no paradox*."[131] It is a claim that Newman makes several times over the course of *An Idea for a University*, and he no doubt was right to guard himself against the claims of more pragmatic educators.[132] The idea that education was meant to teach one *how* to learn arguably did not catch fire until Leonard Nelson proclaimed decades later that the best teacher will "lead the student to think for himself, and thereby to win a calm certainty of judgment."[133] Although pupils were not universally subjected to the method of Mr. Gradgrind—the schoolmaster in Charles Dickens's *Hard Times* (1854) who treats students as "little pitchers […] to be filled so full of *facts*"—educational institutions at all levels continued to stress the importance of acquired skills, achievement, and breadth of knowledge.[134] To move away from this model of practical education to one that, in Wilde's words, actively sought after "'useless information'" bordered on heresy.[135] Wilde—a lifelong admirer of Newman who sent him a copy of his poem "Rome Unvisited" (1881) as a young man, read all of his works in the 1870s, and reread them during his prison term—ultimately embraced the paradox that Newman so carefully avoided.[136] For Wilde, paradox itself was the stylistic performance of a pedagogical method that both he and Newman endorsed. After all, a paradox constitutes a hermeneutic loop, an irresolvable puzzle that invites the reader continually to revolve a thought over and over in their head. If, as Newman himself would have it, "style is a thinking out into language," paradox reflects what was, for Wilde, the ideal mode of reflection: a stylized mobility of thought.[137]

Final Examination

As early as 1880, while still in residence at Oxford, Wilde wrote to Rennell Rodd that the university was "the only sphere of thought where one can be, simultaneously, brilliant and unreasonable, speculative and well-informed, creative as well as critical, and write with all the passion of youth about the truths which belong to the august serenity of old age."[138] Years later, he would seek to recreate precisely such an atmosphere of idle learning at his home at Babbacombe Cliff. In a letter to Lady Mount-Temple, Wilde elaborated on the academic regimen of Lord Alfred Douglas, who was then studying for exams with his tutor, Campbell Dodgson.[139] Wilde observed that his home had "become a kind of college or school, for Cyril studies French in the nursery, and I write my new play in Wonderland, and in the drawing-room Lord Alfred Douglas—one of Lady Queensberry's sons—studies Plato with his tutor for his degree at Oxford in June."[140] Wilde drew up a list of rules for the school:

Babbacombe School

Headmaster – Mr Oscar Wilde
Second Master – Mr Campbell Dodgson
Boys – Lord Alfred Douglas

Rules.
Tea for master and boy at 9.30 a.m.
Breakfast at 10.30.
Work. 11.30–12.30.
At 12.30 Sherry and biscuits for headmaster and boys (the second master objects to this).
12.40–1.30. Work.
1.30. Lunch.
2.30–4.30. Compulsory hide-and-seek for headmaster.
5. Tea for headmaster and second master, brandy and sodas (not to exceed seven) for boys.
6–7. Work.
7.30. Dinner, with compulsory champagne.
8.30–12. Écarté, limited to five-guinea points.
12–1.30. Compulsory reading in bed. Any boy found disobeying this rule will be immediately woken up.[141]

There is no mistaking the joke. Wilde's regimented system of education, so far from restricting students to "compulsory" lessons, is no system at all. That Wilde's account of the Babbacombe school includes a *dramatis personae* and behavioral script is highly suggestive. Wilde adamantly resisted the idea that learning should follow a script, and the rigid schedule he presents here reflects his insistence on a more flexible approach to learning. In a characteristic move, he parodies the "roles" students and teachers are expected to play, ultimately forsaking the script in favor of a more dynamic learning process. In this, he confessed to Dodgson that he believed they had "succeeded in combining the advantages of a public school with those of a private lunatic asylum."[142] Dodgson himself confirmed that this "lazy and luxurious" life at Babbacombe mingled pleasure with serious intellectual endeavor, noting: "We argue for hours in favour of different interpretations of Platonism."[143] What Wilde's set of "rules" tells us, then, is that real learning took place precisely when work did not.[144]

Wilde once famously noted: "It is a very sad thing, that nowadays there is so little useless information."[145] If, as Wilde suggests, it is the dynamic movement of thought that drives men and ideas, then useless information—knowledge pursued with no particular end in mind—is precisely what the world so desperately needs. Consider one of Wilde's most famous witticisms: "In examinations," he commented, "the foolish ask questions that the wise cannot answer."[146] On the surface, the aphorism seems merely to reject the examination as a measure of knowledge, since it relies on the student's recitation of answers that are deemed either right or wrong. On a deeper level, though, Wilde's maxim implies that the best teachers by definition must defy resolution, for to answer a question is to arrest the hermeneutic through which intellectual beauty reveals itself. As Lord Goring puts it in *An Ideal Husband*: "It is always worth while asking a question, though it is not always worth while answering one."[147]

Where, then, does this leave the reader who is eager to follow in Wilde's intellectual footsteps? Is it even possible to track the intellectual biography of a thinker who deliberately refuses to treat the learning process as linear or coherent? I would argue that it is precisely such an intellectual life—curious, digressive, and protean—that is most worthy of examination. In the following chapters, our task is not to determine what Wilde thought but rather *how* he thought about religion, science, philosophy, and social reform. These are fields of study that ostensibly seek to provide clear answers to the questions that matter most—questions of the spirit, the physical universe, the nature of existence, and the future of our world. Although we may detect hypotheses and suggestive patterns of thought in Wilde's public and private writings, he seldom provides us with clear answers. We can, however, develop a sense of how Wilde approached these questions. If his penchant for contradiction and obfuscation may at times prove bewildering, there is in his process both sincerity and pleasure. I invite the reader to luxuriate in this process and, perhaps, to find pleasure here as well.

Notes

1. Oscar Wilde, "The Critic as Artist," in *Criticism*, ed. Josephine M. Guy, vol. 4 of *The Complete Works of Oscar Wilde* (Oxford: Oxford University Press, 2007): 123–206, 136.
2. The original quip was coined by George Bernard Shaw: "He who can, does. He who cannot, teaches." "Maxims for Revolutionists," in *Man and Superman* (New York: Brentano's, 1922): 227–44, 230.
3. Oscar Wilde, *Complete Letters of Oscar Wilde*, ed. Merlin Holland and Rupert Hart-Davis (New York: Henry Holt and Company, 2000), 45.
4. Charles Ricketts, *Oscar Wilde: Recollections* (London: Pallas Athene, 1932), 35.
5. Iain Ross has impressively tracked Wilde's lifelong engagement with Hellenism in *Oscar Wilde and Ancient Greece* (Cambridge: Cambridge University Press, 2012).
6. Oscar Wilde, *An Ideal Husband*, in *The Major Works*, ed. Isobel Murray (New York: Oxford University Press, 2000): 389–476, 394.
7. Iain Ross, "Oscar Wilde in Greece: Topography and the Hellenist Imagination," *International Journal of the Classical Tradition* 16.2 (June 2009): 176–96, 178.
8. An excellent discussion of this transitional moment appears in M.L. Clarke's *Classical Education in Britain, 1500–1900* (Cambridge: Cambridge University Press, 1959). See also Linda Dowling, *Hellenism and Homosexuality in Victorian Oxford* (Ithaca: Cornell University Press, 1994).
9. Wilde once referred to his Oxford days in a letter to Louis Wilkinson as "the most flower-like time" in his life (*Complete Letters*, 1113).
10. Wilde, *Complete Letters*, 87.
11. Wilde, *Complete Letters*, 264.
12. Wilde, *Complete Letters*, 280.
13. Notable exceptions to this rule include Peter Bailey, "Aestheticism and the Erotics of Pedagogy" (Ph.D. diss., Cornell University, Department of English, 2009) and the insightful essay by William Shuter, "Pater, Wilde, Douglas and the Impact of 'Greats,'" *English Literature in Transition* 46, no. 3 (2003): 250–78. See also Kimberly J. Stern, "'At Wits' End': Oscar Wilde's Aesthetic Pedagogy," *Nineteenth Century Studies* 28 (2018): 127–45. Brief

passages from this chapter appeared previously in the latter piece and are reproduced here courtesy of *Nineteenth Century Studies*.

14. Matthew Arnold, *Report of the Committee of Council on Education* (London: Eyre and Spottiswoode, 1883), 229, 258.
15. "Oscar Wilde," *The Biograph and Review* 4 (1880): 130–35, 131.
16. *The Poets of Ireland: A Biographical and Bibliographical Dictionary of Irish Writers of English Verse* (Dublin: H. Figgis, 1912), 87.
17. Reports documenting Wilde's life at Portora (such those offered by Frank Harris and Robert Sherard) are not unassailable, since they often document utterances and conversations years and even decades after they may have taken place. As Iain Ross points out, "there is no way to verify them," though they often confirm more direct and authoritative accounts of Wilde's life (Ross, *Oscar Wilde and Ancient Greece*, 19). I have attempted to indicate in the text where I am drawing on these texts and, for the most part, have turned to them to complement rather than to replace more authoritative primary documents.
18. See, for example, Thomas Arnold, "Discipline of Public Schools," *Miscellaneous Works* (New York: D. Appleton and Co., 1846).
19. Qtd. in Davis Coakley, *Oscar Wilde: The Importance of Being Irish* (Dublin: Town House and Country House, 1994), 79.
20. Qtd. in Coakley 80. Such recollections of Steele might well remind readers of Doctor Strong in Charles Dickens's *David Copperfield*: "[…] the Doctor himself was the idol of the whole school; and it must have been a badly composed school if he had been anything else, for he was the kindest of men, with a simple faith in him that might have touched the stone hearts of the very urns upon the wall." Charles Dickens, *David Copperfield* (New York: W.W. Norton, 1989), 243.
21. Heather White, *"Forgotten Schooldays": Oscar Wilde at Portora Royal School* (Gortnaree: Principia Press, 2001), 93–4. Like so many nineteenth-century educational reformers, Steele's emphasis on the process of knowledge acquisition takes its cue from John Locke's *Essay Concerning Human Understanding*: "Let us then suppose the Mind to be, as we say, white Paper, void of all Characters, without any *Ideas*; How comes it to be furnished? Whence comes it by that vast Store, which the busy and boundless Fancy of Man has painted on it, with an almost endless [sic] Variety? Whence has it all the Materials of Reason and Knowledge? To this I answer, in one Word, from Experience: In that, all our Knowledge is founded; and from that it ultimately derives itself." John Locke, *Essay Concerning Human Understanding* (London: R. Griffin and Co., 1836), 51.
22. Charles Northend, *Teacher's Assistant, or Hints and Methods in School Discipline and Instruction* (Boston: Crosby, Nichols, and Company, 1859), 43–4.

23. Northend, 43–4. The idea was reinforced by thinkers like William Ross, who maintained that the schoolmaster should be an "autocrat" and yet "studiously endeavor to avoid rather than to create occasions for the exhibition of his power," behaving always "in a friendly, open, and straightforward manner" in order to command the confidence of his pupils. William Ross, *The Teacher's Manual of Method; or, general principles of teaching and school-keeping* (London: Longman, Brown, Green, Longmans, and Roberts, 1858), 140.

24. Cathy Shuman has ably demonstrated the relationship between the university examination and the formation of social (especially economic) identity in *Pedagogical Economies: The Examination and the Victorian Literary Man* (Palo Alto: Stanford University Press, 2000).

25. Iain Ross, *Oscar Wilde and Ancient Greece*, 20.

26. Steele notes: "as proof of the high importance I attach to this matter, I may add that I have been in the habit of expending upwards of £70 a year on Prizes and Examination Papers" (qtd. in White 41).

27. Qtd. in White, 92.

28. Qtd. in White, 96.

29. Herbert Fry, *Our Schools and Colleges. Containing the principal particulars respecting endowed Grammar Schools* (London: Robert Hardwicke, 1868), 99.

30. "Ireland," *Journal of Education* (1 November 1886): 468–9, 469.

31. Frank Harris, *Oscar Wilde: His Life and Confessions* (New York, 1916), 28.

32. Richard Ellmann, *Oscar Wilde* (New York: Alfred A. Knopf, 1987), 54.

33. Robert Sherard, *The Life of Oscar Wilde* (New York: Mitchell Kennerly, 1906), 110.

34. Harris, 29.

35. As Richard Ellmann puts it, "What distinguished him was his excitement over the literary qualities of Greek and Latin texts, and his disinclination to enter into textual minutiae" (55). Having already cultivated a taste for historical study through his father, an amateur archaeologist who published multiple volumes on the subject, Wilde seems to have been captivated by the Classics at Portora. Although J.P. Mahaffy would later fuel his interest in the Greeks at Trinity College, it was at Portora that Wilde began to study Greek literature in a serious way. Sir Edward Sullivan reports that "the classics absorbed almost his whole attention in his later school days, and the flowing beauty of his oral translations in class, whether of Thucydides, Plato or Virgil, was a thing not easily to be forgotten" (Harris, 28).

36. Harris, 32. As Iain Ross observes, "[f]or Wilde, the ancient world was a resource for play, not work. The classical texts were absorbed constituents of his developing self rather than instruments of academic advancement, though if advancement might be accomplished through performance—

play—there could be no objection to the bonus" (*Oscar Wilde and Ancient Greece*, 21).

37. Sherard, 117.

38. Harris, 28.

39. Wilde, "The Critic as Artist," 192. Vacation was a principal part of the Oxford experience. Montagu Burrows notes that although the greater part of the year was taken up by vacation, it was hardly a time of idle luxury: "It must then be taken as a postulate that this, the greater portion of the year, must on no account be treated as Vacation by the reading man. Each of course must judge for himself how much he really requires for relaxation. The student proper will probably take only a small portion of the Long Vacation, say the beginning and the end; he will take by no means all of the shorter ones. The rest he will find absolutely necessary for his private reading, and for working up the many subjects which in the short and hurried period of Term he has been obliged to put aside." Montagu Burrows, *Pass and Class: An Oxford Guidebook* (Oxford: Parker, 1860), 33.

40. Oscar Wilde, "Primavera," in *Journalism 2*, ed. John Stokes and Mark Turner, vol. 7 of *The Complete Works of Oscar Wilde* (Oxford: Oxford University Press, 2013): 249–52, 249.

41. For further information regarding the work of Pestalozzi, see Daniel Tröhler, *Pestalozzi and the Educationalization of the World* (New York: Palgrave, 2013); and Johann Heinrich Pestalozzi, *Letters of Pestalozzi on the Education of Infancy* [1827] (Boston: Carter and Hendee, 1830).

42. Jeremy Bentham, "Principles of Education," in vol. 3 of *The Works of Jeremy Bentham*, ed. John Bowring (Edinburgh: William Tait, 1843), 10:71.

43. John Stuart Mill, *Autobiography*, ed. Jack Stillinger (Boston: Houghton Mifflin, 1969), 81.

44. Oscar Wilde, Commonplace Book, in *Oscar Wilde's Oxford Notebooks: A Portrait of Mind in the Making*, ed. Philip E. Smith II and Michael Helfand (Oxford: Oxford University Press, 1989): 107–52, 120 [61]. For all references to Wilde's Notebook Kept at Oxford and Commonplace Book, I have included the pagination from Smith and Helfand's edition, followed by the manuscript pagination in brackets (as shown).

45. Wilde, Commonplace Book, 115 [40].

46. Wilde, Commonplace Book, 115 [40].

47. Wilde, Commonplace Book, 145[185]. Wilde quotes here, with slight deviations from the original, from Plato's *Republic* 558B and 403C.

48. Plato, *The Republic*, in vol. 3 of *The Dialogues of Plato*, trans. Benjamin Jowett (New York: Oxford University, 1892): 1–338, 298 [585e].

49. Plato, *The Republic*, 300 [586e].

50. Plato, *The Republic*, 298 [586a].

51. In *The Symposium*, the female philosopher Diotima presents the highest form of love as love of wisdom: "For wisdom is a most beautiful thing, and

Love is of the beautiful." Plato, "The Symposium," in vol. 1 of *The Dialogues of Plato*, trans. Benjamin Jowett (New York: Scribner, 1874): 449–514, 496 [204b].

52. Wilde classifies Aristotle as a "mystic" who "wd. [would] have defined philosophy as a 'knowledge of being or of essence'" (Commonplace Book, 127 [100]).

53. Wilde, Commonplace Book, 149 [201].

54. Wilde, Commonplace Book, 145 [189].

55. Aristotle, *The Nicomachean Ethics*, ed. Lesley Brown (New York: Oxford, 2009), 137 [1152b].

56. Wilde, "The Critic as Artist," 191.

57. Wilde, "The Critic as Artist," 191.

58. Wilde, "The Critic as Artist" 191.

59. Oscar Wilde, "House Decoration," *Miscellanies*, ed. Robert Ross (London: Methuen and Company, 1908): 279–90, 290.

60. "The Theories of a Poet," *New York Tribune* (8 January 1882): 7. Wilde echoes this idea in another interview: "My theory is that you cannot teach anybody what is really beautiful. The true spirit of a painting or a poem cannot by any method be taught—it must be gradually revealed. A schoolboy, for instance, can arrive at an understanding of a scientific truth under a competent teacher, but the only way in which anybody can come to a knowledge of the beautiful is by being thrown among beautiful surroundings. I think if you desire a cultured society, you must put the youth of the land into beautiful homes and let them gradually come to feel a necessity for such surroundings. A young man reared among such surroundings has not got to make a distinct effort to appreciate the beautiful. He will, if reading, come at once into sympathy with his author in his description of the true and the beautiful." "The Science of the Beautiful," *New York World* (8 January 1882), 2.

61. Wilde, *Complete Letters*, 127n.1.

62. J.P. Mahaffy, *Old Greek Education* (New York: Harper and Brothers, 1882), 58.

63. Mahaffy, *Old Greek Education*, 60.

64. J.P. Mahaffy, *Social Life in Greece* (London: Macmillan, 1874), viii. Mahaffy's study is largely descriptive, with brief interjections suggesting that education is not quite what it used to be. Although Wilde left no record indicating how he responded to this volume, we do know that he regarded Mahaffy's other attempt at politicizing the Hellenic past—his 1887 volume *Greek Life and Thought*—as heavy-handed and polemical. "He might," Wilde said of this work, "have made his book a work of solid and enduring interest, but he has chosen to give it a merely ephemeral value, and to substitute for the scientific temper of the true historian the prejudice, the flippancy, and the violence of the platform partisan." Oscar Wilde, "Mr. Mahaffy's New Book,"

in Journalism 2, ed. John Stokes and Mark Turner, vol. 7 of *The Complete Works of Oscar Wilde* (Oxford: Oxford University Press, 2013): 12–14, 12.

65. Wilde, "Mr. Mahaffy's New Book," 12.
66. Wilde, "The Critic as Artist," 135.
67. Wilde, "The Critic as Artist," 182.
68. Wilde, "The Critic as Artist," 196.
69. William Gordon, *The Discipline of the Physical and Intellectual Powers* (London: Charles H. Law, 1847), 26.
70. Gordon, 27.
71. Catherine Robson, *Heart Beats: Everyday Life and the Memorized Poem* (Princeton: Princeton University Press, 2012), 2.
72. Wilde, "The Critic as Artist," 142.
73. Wilde, "The Critic as Artist," 201.
74. Wilde, "Critic as Artist," 196.
75. Wilde, "Critic as Artist," 136.
76. Wilde, "Critic as Artist," 196.
77. Wilde, *Complete Letters*, 562.
78. Qtd. in Harris, 41. Harris's account is, admittedly, suspect in many respects and relies extensively on anecdotal evidence. Still, the record of Wilde's regard for Mahaffy's approach to conversation is buttressed by Wilde's published account of his mentor in "Aristotle at Afternoon Tea," in which he lauds Mahaffy's conversational technique, while deploring his turn to pedantry.
79. Wilde also broke with Mahaffy on political grounds, noting his former mentor's tendency to read Greek history through the lens of Unionism ("Mr Mahaffy's New Book," 12–14). Mahaffy's biographers, William Stanford and Robert McDowell, speculate that Wilde's critique of Mahaffy may been motivated by his mentor's failure to secure him the post of HMI, though their argument is based strictly on the timing of the review's publication. There remains no evidence suggesting that Mahaffy either did or did not attempt to assist Wilde in securing the position. See Stanford and McDowell, Mahaffy: *Biography of an Anglo-Irishman* (New York: Routledge, 1971), 79–83.
80. Oscar Wilde, "Aristotle at Afternoon Tea," in *Journalism 2*, ed. John Stokes and Mark Turner, vol. 6 of *The Complete Works of Oscar Wilde* (Oxford: Oxford University Press, 2013): 35–37, 35.
81. Wilde, "Aristotle at Afternoon Tea," 35. See also J. P. Mahaffy, *The Principles of the Art of Conversation* (London: Macmillan, 1887). It is worth noting that, as in the case of Mahaffy, Wilde critiqued Aristotle's style while remaining deeply impressed by the philosopher's approach to knowledge. In his Commonplace Book, Wilde remarked that "in Aristotle the philosopher's life is the contemplative life: he expressly disavows any philanthropic aim to *Sophia*." He continues: "[I]t is good says Aristotle for it's [sic] own sake

because it is an '[*arete*] of the soul': the fact of its existence is the reason of its existence" (Commonplace Book, 145 [189]).

82. Qtd. in Harris, *Oscar Wilde*, 41.

83. Qtd. in Harris, *Oscar Wilde*, 48.

84. Wilde, *Complete Letters*, 349.

85. As previous scholars have demonstrated, much of Wilde's work can be understood as an attempt to revise Platonic idealism. See, for instance, Edward A. Watson, "Wilde's Iconoclastic Classicism: 'The Critic as Artist,'" *English Literature in Transition* 27, no. 3 (1984): 225–35; Kelly Comfort, "The Critic as Artist and Liar: The Reuse and Abuse of Plato and Aristotle by Wilde," *Wildean* 32 (January 2008): 57–70; and Eva Thienpont, "'To Play Gracefully with Ideas': Oscar Wilde's Personal Platonism in Poetics," *Wildean* 20 (January 2002): 37–48.

86. Although the pages of *Theaetetus* remained uncut in Wilde's copy of Jowett's *Dialogues of Plato*, he quotes from Jowett's introduction to *Theaetetus* in his Commonplace Book. See Wilde, Commonplace Book, 133 [133].

87. Plato, *Theaetetus*, in vol. 3 of *The Dialogues of Plato*, ed. and trans. Benjamin Jowett (London: Oxford University Press, 1871), 301–420, 354. Cornford's translation conveys the point even more powerfully: "[S]o the ignorant world describes me in other terms as an eccentric person who reduces people to hopeless perplexity." *Theaetetus*, trans. F. M. Cornford, in *Collected Dialogues*, ed. Edith Hamilton and Huntington Cairns (Princeton, NJ.: Princeton University Press, 1961): 845–919, 854.

88. Plato, *Theaetetus*, in vol. 3 of *The Dialogues of Plato*, 350.

89. Victorino Tejera suggests that the treatment of Plato's dialogues as treatises was an historical development and does not reflect the original design of the works. He notes that the "doctrinal interpretations of the dialogues are antidialogical misreadings that have avoided being called misreadings by the tacit denial-in-practice that what they are misreading are not only dialogues but works of literary art." "The Hellenistic Obliteration of Plato's Dialogism," *Plato's Dialogues: New Studies and Interpretations*, ed. Gerald A. Press (Lanham, MD: Rowman and Littlefield, 1993): 129–44, 137.

90. Plato, *The Apology*, in vol. 1 of *The Dialogues of Plato*, trans. Benjamin Jowett (New York: Scribner, 1874): 303–40, 331.

91. Plato, *Theaetetus*, in vol. 3 of *The Dialogues of Plato*, 350.

92. Wilde, "The Critic as Artist," 181.

93. Wilde, "The Critic as Artist," 181.

94. Oscar Wilde, *The Picture of Dorian Gray* (1891), in *The Picture of Dorian Gray: The 1890 and 1891 Texts*, ed. Joseph Bristow, vol. 3 of *The Complete Works of Oscar Wilde* (Oxford: Oxford University Press, 2005), 204.

95. Wilde, *The Picture of Dorian Gray* (1890), 111; (1891), 281. In the same chapter, Lord Henry's zeal for the "New Hedonism," which is to value "experience itself, and not the fruits of experience" (109), echoes Walter Pater's

insistence on the value of sensory experience in *Studies in the History of the Renaissance* (1873). Since Lord Henry neglects to provide a larger philosophical context for this argument, however, such an epicurean world-view becomes ethically suspect. As Pater himself noted in his review of the novel: "Clever always, this book, however, seems intended to set forth anything but a homely philosophy of life for the middle-class—a kind of dainty Epicurean theory, rather—yet fails, to some degree, in this; and one can see why. A true Epicureanism aims at a complete though harmonious development of man's entire organism. To lose the moral sense therefore, for instance, the sense of sin and righteousness, as Mr. Wilde's hero—his heroes are bent on doing as speedily, as completely as they can, is to lose, or lower, organization, to become less complex, to pass from a higher to a lower degree of development." Walter Pater, "A Novel by Mr. Oscar Wilde," *The Bookman* (November 1891): 59–60, 59.

96. Wilde, *The Picture of Dorian Gray*, 201.
97. Wilde, *The Picture of Dorian Gray*, 192.
98. Wilde, *The Picture of Dorian Gray*, 184.
99. Michel Foucault, *The Government of Self and Others: Lectures at the Collège de France, 1982–1983*, ed. Frédéric Gros, trans. Graham Burchell (New York: Palgrave, 2011), 248, 249.
100. Wilde, *The Picture of Dorian Gray*, 48, 219.
101. Wilde, *The Picture of Dorian Gray*, 48, 219.
102. Wilde, *The Picture of Dorian Gray*, 105, 276. As Matthew Potolsky observes in his discussion of Pater's *Marius the Epicurean* (1885), "literary pedagogy becomes a dangerous stunt, the teacher a circus master who seduces his students and promptly vanishes from the scene, leaving them to find their footing alone. So decisive is the teacher's force that he need not even be present for his ideas to have an effect." Matthew Potolsky, "Fear of Falling: Walter Pater's *Marius the Epicurean* as a Dangerous Influence," *English Literary History* 65, no. 3 [1998]: 701–29, 702.
103. For instance, whereas Jonathan Freedman and Joseph Bristow have written eloquently on Lord Henry's rhetorical and "verbal seduction" of Dorian, Esther Rathkin suggests "Lord Henry does not influence Dorian or instill in him any despicable proclivities or wishes." Esther Rathkin, *Unspeakable Secrets and the Psychoanalysis of Culture* (Albany: State University of New York Press, 2008), 166. See, however, Jonathan Freedman, *Professions of Taste: Henry James, British Aestheticism and Commodity Culture* (Stanford: Stanford University Press, 1993), 44; and Joseph Bristow, "Wilde, Dorian Gray, and Gross Indecency," in *Sexual Sameness: Textual Differences in Lesbian and Gay Writing*, ed. Joseph Bristow (New York: Routledge, 1992), 44–63.
104. Dowling, *Hellenism and Homosexuality*, 33, 35.
105. Burrows, *Pass and Class*, 53.

106. Oscar Wilde, "The Decay of Lying," in *Criticism*, ed. Josephine M. Guy, vol. 4 of *The Complete Works of Oscar Wilde* (Oxford: Oxford University Press, 2007): 72–103, 74. Wilde alludes to Ralph Waldo Emerson's essay "Self-Reliance" (1841), in which Emerson writes: "I am ashamed to think how easily we capitulate to badges and names, to large societies and dead institutions. Every decent and well-spoken individual affects and sways me more than is right. I ought to go upright and vital, and speak the rude truth in all ways." Ralph Waldo Emerson, "Self-Reliance," in *Self-Reliance, the Over-Soul, and Other Essays* (Claremont, CA: Canyon Coyote Press, 2010): 19–40, 22.

107. Wilde would undoubtedly have attended Pater's Oxford lectures on Plato, which stressed that, despite the importance of process to the Platonic dialogue, Plato seems to have regarded change and mobility as something to be resisted. There was, in short, a clear distinction between Plato's theory of how thought works and nineteenth-century responses to that theory on the part of aesthetes such as Pater and Wilde. Pater notes, in an essay based on these lectures: "It is something in this way that, for Plato, motion and the philosophy of motion identify themselves with the vicious tendency in things and thought. [...] Change, he protests, through the power of a true philosophy, shall not be the law of our being; and it is curious to note the way in which, consciously or unconsciously, that philosophic purpose shapes his treatment, even in minute detail, of education, of art, of daily life, his very vocabulary, in which such pleasant or innocent words, as 'manifold,' 'embroidered,' 'changeful,' become the synonymes [sic] of what is evil." Walter Pater, "A Chapter on Plato," *Macmillan's Magazine* 66 (May 1892): 31–38, 38.

108. Wilde, "The Decay of Lying," 76–77.

109. As Shuter astutely observes, "what Wilde's critical dialogues actually display is the 'Oxford temper,' which Wilde defined as the ability and willingness 'to play gracefully with ideas'" in a manner specifically crafted after the model of Greats ("Pater, Wilde, Douglas and the Impact of 'Greats,'" 261).

110. As Iain Ross suggests, for Wilde "the Forms or Archetypes or Ideas that in Plato's philosophy exist beyond the sensible world might be located instead in the *psuchê*, 'soul,' of the artist, thus rescuing art from Plato's charge of an uncomprehending mimicry of shadows" (*Oscar Wilde and Ancient Greece*, 150).

111. John T. Flanagan, "Oscar Wilde's Twin City Appearances," *Minnesota Historical Society* (March 1936): 38–48, 41.

112. "The Apotheosis of Snobbery," *Columbus Sunday Morning News*, 7 May 1882, 1.

113. Mary Warner Blanchard, *Oscar Wilde's America: Counterculture in the Gilded Age* (New Haven, Conn.: Yale University Press, 1998), 137.

114. Following his lecture tour, Wilde took lessons in "elocution and gesture" from Hermann Vezin, an actor and drama critic who had worked with such noted actors as Charles Kean, John Hare, William Hunter Kendal, and Dame Madge Kendal. Wilde remarked: "With Mr. Vezin, grace of gesture is an unconscious result—not a conscious effort. It has become nature, because it was once art." "Helena in Troas," *Journalism 1*, ed. John Stokes and Mark Turner, vol. 6 of *The Complete Works of Oscar Wilde* (Oxford: Oxford University Press, 2013): 78–80. Like Wilde's earlier mentors, Vezin seems to have privileged a pedagogy that embraces process above the attainment of a definitive end (Sherard, 239).

115. Oscar Wilde, "The Relation of Dress to Art," in vol. 6 of *The Complete Works of Oscar Wilde* (Oxford: Oxford University Press, 2013): 36–38, 37.

116. Oscar Wilde, "The Decorative Arts," in Kevin O'Brien, *Oscar Wilde in Canada: An Apostle for the Arts* (Toronto, Ont.: Personal Library, 1982): 151–64, 157.

117. "Oscar Wilde," *Montgomery Daily Advertiser*, 30 June 1882, 4.

118. Oscar Wilde, interview by *Salt Lake Herald*, 12 April 1882, in *Oscar Wilde in America: The Interviews*, ed. Michael Hofer (Urbana-Champaign: University of Illinois Press, 2013): 128–29, 129.

119. "Freshmen at Oscar Wilde's Lecture," *Harvard Crimson*, 1 February 1882, 4.

120. Oscar Wilde, "Art and the Handicraftsman," in *Miscellanies*, ed. Robert Ross (London: Methuen and Company, 1908): 291–308, 307.

121. For a comprehensive account of the public responses to Wilde's lecture tour, see *Oscar Wilde in America*; and Roy Morris Jr., *Declaring His Genius: Oscar Wilde in North America* (Cambridge, Mass.: Harvard University Press, 2013).

122. Wilde, "House Decoration," 289.

123. Wilde, "The Decorative Arts," 163.

124. Charles Leland, *Practical Education* (London: Whittaker, 1888), 128–29. To be sure, Leland was more ambivalent about such exhortations to live by art. He takes great pains to differentiate his "practical education" in the arts from the efforts of the British Aesthetes, which he refers to as "'aesthetic trifling,' 'sunflower nonsense,' and 'playing at art'" (20). Yet he also seems to defend the Aesthetes as the harbingers of a modern age in which aesthetic knowledge would prove absolutely vital to success in practical life: "Those who talk about the sunflower mania and 'art craze' as something temporary, and who mistake the aesthetes for the main army yet to come, are like the ambassadors sent by an African king to visit London, and who at the first small Arab village thought themselves at the end of their journey" (90).

125. Wilde, "The Critic as Artist," 192.

126. "The English Renaissance of Art," in *Miscellanies*, ed. Robert Ross (London: Methuen and Company, 1908): 241–77, 275.

127. Wilde, "The English Renaissance of Art," 275.

128. Shuter rightly observes that Wilde's fascination with the movement of thought may, in addition, have been informed by his reading of Friedrich Hegel, who insisted that "'[t]ruth lies in a movement or process: not in isolation and rest'" (262–63). See Friedrich Hegel, *The Logic of Hegel*, trans. William Wallace (New York: Clarendon Press, 1874), cxxxv.

129. John Henry Newman, *The Idea of a University*, 3rd ed. (London: Basil Montagu Pickering, 1873), 113 (discourse 5, sect. 6).

130. Newman, *The Idea of a University*, 112 (discourse 5, sect. 6).

131. Newman, *Idea of a University*, 103 (discourse 5, sect. 2; emphasis added).

132. Newman defends his argument against being labeled a "paradox" multiple times throughout *The Idea of a University*. The frequency of these qualifications would seem to indicate some rhetorical anxiety on Newman's part about espousing paradox as the foundation for his argument. See *The Idea of a University*, 103 (discourse 5, sect. 2); 111 (discourse 5, sect. 5); 145 (discourse 6, sect. 9); 390 ("A Form of Infidelity of the Day: Its Sentiments," sect. 4); and 474 ("Christianity and Scientific Investigation," sect. 7).

133. Leonard Nelson, *Politics and Education*, trans. W. Lansdell (London: George Allen and Unwin, 1928), 195.

134. Charles Dickens, *Hard Times*, ed. Kate Flint (New York: Penguin, 1995), 10.

135. Wilde, *The Picture of Dorian Gray* (1891), 195.

136. To my knowledge, Wilde's letter to Newman accompanying "Rome Unvisited" does not survive but is mentioned in both primary and secondary accounts of Wilde's life. See Sherard, 146 and Ellmann, 57. In a letter to William Ward on 26 July 1876, Wilde mentioned having "bought a lot of [Newman's] books before leaving Oxford" (*Complete Letters*, 25). The following year, Wilde expressed a wish to visit Newman, although there is no evidence that this encounter ever took place (*Complete Letters*, 41). Newman's works appear on a list of books Wilde requested during his prison term and, following his release, Arthur Clifton observed to Carlos Blacker on 8 October 1895: "He has been reading Pater and Newman lately, one book a week" (*Complete Letters*, 665n).

137. Newman, *The Idea of a University*, 276.

138. Wilde, *Complete Letters*, 102–3.

139. Dodgson was a distant cousin of Charles Dodgson, author of *Alice's Adventures in Wonderland*; hence, Wilde alludes to Wonderland in the following passage.

140. Wilde, *Complete Letters*, 547.

141. Wilde, *Complete Letters*, 556.

142. Wilde, *Complete Letters*, 555.

143. Wilde, *Complete Letters*, 868.

144. Thus, Wilde seems to reject what Burrows calls "[t]he old school-boy adage, 'Work while you work and play while you play.'" Burrows continues: "The

general rule seems to be that the mind should be thoroughly unbent during the periods of recreation. If some of the usual amusements are not preferred, at least as much as possible of the free open air of heaven should be drunk in; long walks rather than short ones; out of the city rather than in it: but better still, if used in subordination to the rules for time already laid down, the river, the gymnasium, the rifle-ground, the racket-court, and the cricket-field. If any one of these (or other recreations of the same sort) is found on experience to interfere with such rules, it will be well to give it up at once and take to one that does not, rather than drive off the evening's work to late hours" (40).

145. Oscar Wilde, "A Few Maxims for the Instruction of the Over-Educated," in *The Major Works*, ed. Isobel Murray (New York: Oxford University Press, 2000): 570–71, 570.

146. Oscar Wilde, "Phrases and Philosophies for Use by the Young," in *The Major Works*, ed. Isobel Murray (New York: Oxford University Press, 2000): 572–73, 573.

147. Wilde, *An Ideal Husband*, 423.

Bibliography

Aristotle. 2009. *The Nicomachean Ethics*, ed. Lesley Brown. New York: Oxford.

Arnold, Thomas. 1846. Discipline of Public Schools. In *Miscellaneous Works*. New York: D. Appleton and Company.

Arnold, Matthew. 1883. *Report of the Committee of Council on Education*. London: Eyre and Spottiswoode.

Bailey, Peter. 2009. Aestheticism and the Erotics of Pedagogy. Ph.D. diss., Cornell University, Department of English.

Bentham, Jeremy. 1843. Principles of Education. Vol. 3 of *The Works of Jeremy Bentham*. Ed. John Bowring. Edinburgh: William Tait.

Blanchard, Mary Warner. 1998. *Oscar Wilde's America: Counterculture in the Gilded Age*. New Haven: Yale University Press.

Bristow, Joseph. 1992. Wilde, Dorian Gray, and Gross Indecency. In *Sexual Sameness: Textual Differences in Lesbian and Gay Writing*, ed. Joseph Bristow, 44–63. New York: Routledge.

Burrows, Montagu. 1860. *Pass and Class: An Oxford Guidebook*. Oxford: Parker.

Clarke, M.L. 1959. *Classical Education in Britain, 1500–1900*. Cambridge: Cambridge University Press.

Coakley, Davis. 1994. *Oscar Wilde: The Importance of Being Irish*. Dublin: Town House and Country House.

Comfort, Kelly. 2008. The Critic as Artist and Liar: The Reuse and Abuse of Plato and Aristotle by Wilde. *Wildean* 32 (January): 57–70.

Dickens, Charles. 1989. *David Copperfield*. New York: W.W. Norton.

———. 1995. *Hard Times*, ed. Kate Flint. New York: Penguin.

Dowling, Linda. 1994. *Hellenism and Homosexuality in Victorian Oxford*. Ithaca: Cornell University Press.

Ellmann, Richard. 1987. *Oscar Wilde*. New York: Alfred A. Knopf.

Emerson, Ralph Waldo. 2010. Self-Reliance. In *Self-Reliance, the Over-Soul, and Other Essays*, 19–40. Claremont: Canyon Coyote Press.

Flanagan, John T. 1936. Oscar Wilde's Twin City Appearances. *Minnesota Historical Society* 17 (March): 38–48.

Foucault, Michel. 2011. *The Government of Self and Others: Lectures at the Collège de France, 1982–1983*, ed. Frédéric Gros. Trans. Graham Burchell. New York: Palgrave.

Freedman, Jonathan. 1993. *Professions of Taste: Henry James, British Aestheticism and Commodity Culture*. Stanford: Stanford University Press.

Freshmen at Oscar Wilde's Lecture. 1882. *Harvard Crimson*, February 1, 4.

Fry, Herbert. 1868. *Our Schools and Colleges. Containing the Principal Particulars Respecting Endowed Grammar Schools*. London: Robert Hardwicke.

Gordon, William. 1847. *The Discipline of the Physical and Intellectual Powers*. London: Charles H. Law.

Harris, Frank. 1916. *Oscar Wilde: His Life and Confessions*. New York.

Hegel, Friedrich. 1874. *The Logic of Hegel*. Trans. William Wallace. New York: Clarendon Press.

Ireland. 1886. *Journal of Education* (November 1): 468–469.

Leland, Charles. 1888. *Practical Education*. London: Whittaker.

Locke, John. 1836. *Essay Concerning Human Understanding*. London: R. Griffin and Company.

Mahaffy, John Pentland (J.P.). 1874. *Social Life in Greece*. London: Macmillan.

———. 1882. *Old Greek Education*. New York: Harper and Brothers.

———. 1887. *The Principles of the Art of Conversation*. London: Macmillan.

Mill, John Stuart. 1969. *Autobiography*, ed. Jack Stillinger. Boston: Houghton Mifflin.

Morris, Roy. 2013. *Declaring His Genius: Oscar Wilde in North America*. Cambridge: Harvard University Press.

Nelson, Leonard. 1928. *Politics and Education*. Trans. W. Lansdell. London: George Allen and Unwin.

Newman, John Henry. 1873. *The Idea of a University*. London: Basil Montagu Pickering.

Northend, Charles. 1859. *Teacher's Assistant, or Hints and Methods in School Discipline and Instruction*. Boston: Crosby, Nichols, and Company.

Pater, Walter. 1891. A Novel by Mr. Oscar Wilde. *The Bookman* (November): 59–60.

———. 1892. A Chapter on Plato. *Macmillan's Magazine* 66 (May): 31–38.

Pestalozzi, Johann Heinrich. 1830. *Letters of Pestalozzi on the Education of Infancy*. Boston: Carter and Hendee.

Plato. 1871. *Theaetetus*. In Vol. 3 of *The Dialogues of Plato*. Trans. Benjamin Jowett. London: Oxford University Press, 301–420.

———. 1874a. *The Apology*. In Vol. 1 of *The Dialogues of Plato*. Trans. Benjamin Jowett. New York: Scribner, 303–340.

———. 1874b. *The Symposium*. In Vol. 1 of *The Dialogues of Plato*. Trans. Benjamin Jowett. New York: Scribner, 449–514.

———. 1892. *The Republic*. In Vol. 3 of *The Dialogues of Plato*. Trans. Benjamin Jowett. New York: Oxford University, 1–338.

———. 1961. *Theaetetus*. In *Collected Dialogues*. Trans. F.M. Cornford. Princeton: Princeton University Press, 845–919.

Potolsky, Matthew. 1998. Fear of Falling: Walter Pater's *Marius the Epicurean* as a Dangerous Influence. *English Literary History* 65 (3): 701–729.

Rathkin, Esther. 2008. *Unspeakable Secrets and the Psychoanalysis of Culture*. Albany: State University of New York Press.

Ricketts, Charles. 1932. *Oscar Wilde: Recollections*. London: Pallas Athene.

Robson, Catherine. 2012. *Heart Beats: Everyday Life and the Memorized Poem*. Princeton: Princeton University Press.

Ross, William. 1858. *The Teacher's Manual of Method; or, General Principles of Teaching and Schoolkeeping*. London: Longman, Brown, Green, Longmans, and Roberts.

Ross, Iain. 2009. Oscar Wilde in Greece: Topography and the Hellenist Imagination. *International Journal of the Classical Tradition* 16 (2): 176–196.

———. 2012. *Oscar Wilde and Ancient Greece*. Cambridge: Cambridge University Press.

Shaw, Bernard. 1922. Maxims for Revolutionists. In *Man and Superman*, 227–244. New York: Brentano's.

Sherard, Robert. 1906. *The Life of Oscar Wilde*. New York: Mitchell Kennerly.

Shuman, Cathy. 2000. *Pedagogical Economies: The Examination and the Victorian Literary Man*. Palo Alto: Stanford University Press.

Shuter, William. 2003. Pater, Wilde, Douglas and the Impact of 'Greats'. *English Literature in Transition* 46 (3): 250–278.

Stanford, William, and Robert McDowell. 1971. *Mahaffy: Biography of an Anglo-Irishman*. New York: Routledge.

Stern, Kimberly J. 2018. 'At Wits' End': Oscar Wilde's Aesthetic Pedagogy. *Nineteenth Century Studies* 28: 127–145.

Tejera, Victorino. 1993. *Plato's Dialogues: New Studies and Interpretations*, ed. Gerald A. Press, 129–144. Lanham: Rowman and Littlefield.

The Apotheosis of Snobbery. 1882. *Columbus Sunday Morning News*, May 7, 1.

The Poets of Ireland: A Biographical and Bibliographical Dictionary of Irish Writers of English Verse. 1912. Dublin: H. Figgis.

The Science of the Beautiful. 1882. *New York World*, January 8, 2.

The Theories of a Poet. 1882. *New York Tribune*, January 8, 7.

Thienpont, Eva. 2002. 'To Play Gracefully with Ideas': Oscar Wilde's Personal Platonism in Poetics. *Wildean* 20 (January): 37–48.

Tröhler, Daniel. 2013. *Pestalozzi and the Educationalization of the World*. New York: Palgrave.

Watson, Edward A. 1984. Wilde's Iconoclastic Classicism: 'The Critic as Artist'. *English Literature in Transition* 27 (3): 225–235.

White, Heather. 2001. *"Forgotten Schooldays": Oscar Wilde at Portora Royal School*. Gortnaree: Principia Press.

Whitely, Giles. 2013. *Oscar Wilde and the Simulacrum: The Truth of Masks*. Cambridge: Cambridge University Press.

Wilde, Oscar. 1880. *The Biograph and Review* 4: 130–135.

———. 1908a. Art and the Handicraftsman. In *Miscellanies*, ed. Robert Ross, 291–308. London: Methuen and Company.

———. 1908b. The English Renaissance of Art. In *Miscellanies*, ed. Robert Ross, 241–277. London: Methuen and Company.

———. 1908c. House Decoration. In *Miscellanies*, ed. Robert Ross, 279–290. London: Methuen and Company.

———. 1982. The Decorative Arts. In *Oscar Wilde in Canada: An Apostle for the Arts*, ed. Kevin O'Brien, 151–164. Toronto: Personal Library.

———. 1989. Commonplace Book. In *Oscar Wilde's Oxford Notebooks: A Portrait of Mind in the Making*, ed. Philip E. Smith II and Michael Helfand, 107–152. Oxford: Oxford University Press.

———. 2000. A Few Maxims for the Instruction of the Over-Educated. In *The Major Works*, ed. Isobel Murray, 570–571. New York: Oxford University Press.

———. 2000a. *Complete Letters of Oscar Wilde*, ed. Merlin Holland and Rupert Hart-Davis. New York: Henry Holt and Company.

———. 2000b. An Ideal Husband. In *The Major Works*, ed. Isobel Murray, 389–476. New York: Oxford University Press.

———. 2000c. Phrases and Philosophies for Use by the Young. In *The Major Works*, ed. Isobel Murray, 572–573. New York: Oxford University Press.

———. 2005. The Picture of Dorian Gray (1891). In *The Picture of Dorian Gray: The 1890 and 1891 Texts*, ed. Joseph Bristow. Vol. 3 of *The Complete Works of Oscar Wilde*. Oxford: Oxford University Press.

———. 2007a. The Critic as Artist. In *Criticism*, ed. Josephine M. Guy, 123–206. Vol. 4 of *The Complete Works of Oscar Wilde*. Oxford: Oxford University Press.

———. 2007b. The Decay of Lying. In *Criticism*, ed. Josephine M. Guy. Vol. 4 of *The Complete Works of Oscar Wilde*. Oxford: Oxford University Press.

———. 2013a. *Salt Lake Herald* (12 April 1882). In *Oscar Wilde in America: The Interviews*, ed. Michael Hofer, 128–129. Urbana-Champaign: University of Illinois Press.

———. 2013b. Aristotle at Afternoon Tea. In *Journalism 2*, ed. John Stokes and Mark Turner, 35–37. Vol. 6 of *The Complete Works of Oscar Wilde*. Oxford: Oxford University Press.

———. 2013c. Helena in Troas. In *Journalism 1*, ed. John Stokes and Mark Turner, 78–80. Vol. 6 of *The Complete Works of Oscar Wilde*. Oxford: Oxford University Press.

———. 2013d. Mr. Mahaffy's New Book. In *Journalism 2*, ed. John Stokes and Mark Turner, 12–14. Vol. 7 of *The Complete Works of Oscar Wilde*. Oxford: Oxford University Press.

———. 2013e. Primavera. In *Journalism 2*, ed. John Stokes and Mark Turner, 249–252. Vol. 7 of *The Complete Works of Oscar Wilde*. Oxford: Oxford University Press.

———. 2013f. The Relation of Dress to Art. In *Journalism 1*, ed. John Stokes and Mark Turner, 36–38. Vol. 6 of *The Complete Works of Oscar Wilde*. Oxford: Oxford University Press.

3

The Priest

It is the confession, not the priest, that gives us absolution.
Oscar Wilde, *The Picture of Dorian Gray*

In 1897, from a cell in Reading Gaol, Oscar Wilde mused: "When I think about religion at all, I feel as if I would like to found an order for those who *cannot* believe: the Confraternity of the Fatherless, one might call it, where on an altar, on which no taper burned, a priest, in whose heart peace had no dwelling, might celebrate with unblessed bread and a chalice empty of wine."[1] On the face of it, Wilde's fantasy of a church for the skeptic seems in keeping with his resistance to all forms of institutional authority. Here, as elsewhere in his writings, Wilde voices a decidedly secular impulse, openly avowing that his is a profane—if not actually a godless—worldview.

That Wilde has often been treated as a heretical thinker is understandable. Douglas Sladen, Wilde's classmate at Oxford, reported that when they sat for the Divinity examination on the same day, Wilde was determined to defy religious authority. The Divinity was, Sladen recalls, "simply a qualifying exam, to show that we had sufficient knowledge of the rudiments of the religion of the Church of England to be graduates of a religious university." Arriving thirty minutes late, Wilde allegedly announced "You must excuse me; I have no experience of these pass examinations," a remark apparently meant to suggest that such exercises were beneath him. The examiners, Sladen notes, were appalled at Wilde's arrogance and accordingly

gave him a Bible, and told him to copy out the long twenty-seventh chapter of the Acts. He copied it out so industriously in his exquisite handwriting that

© The Author(s) 2019
K. J. Stern, *Oscar Wilde*, Literary Lives,
https://doi.org/10.1007/978-3-030-24604-4_3

their hearts relented, and they told him that he need not write out any more. Half-an-hour afterwards they noticed that he was copying it out as hard as ever, and they called him up to say, "Didn't you hear us tell you, Mr. Wilde, that you needn't copy out any more?"

"Oh yes," he said, "I heard you, but I was so interested in what I was copying, that I could not leave off. It was all about a man named Paul, who went on a voyage, and was caught in a terrible storm, and I was afraid that he would be drowned, but, do you know, Mr. Spooner, he was saved, and when I found that he was saved, I thought of coming to tell you."[2]

Sladen's account was composed many years after Wilde's death and must, therefore, like so many anecdotes relating to the author's life, be regarded with an appropriate degree of skepticism. Nevertheless, such stories have helped to reinforce Wilde's reputation as an opponent of religion, a reputation that was only reinforced by the moral and political subversion of his later writings.[3]

Yet to regard Wilde's wry commentaries on religious dogma as the expressions of a man who simply valued this world over the next, is to overlook an absolutely vital aspect of his intellectual life. Wilde's interest in religious thought (and Catholicism in particular) has been noted by several biographers and scholars.[4] In his important 1987 biography, Richard Ellmann insists that Wilde's attraction to religious ritual was primarily aesthetic, noting that he was "more Protestant heresiarch than Catholic zealot."[5] According to Ellmann, Wilde saw in Catholic ritual a spiritualization of the aesthetic principles he sought to convey through his writing, invoking as evidence of this fact Dorian Gray's passion for clerical vestments, censers, and pageantry.[6] Since then, others have demonstrated that Wilde's understanding of religion may have been more nuanced, bearing a direct relation to the aesthetic principles that defined his career. Guy Willoughby, for instance, proposes that Wilde regarded Christ as a model for "an expanded organic view of self and society that derives from aesthetic appreciation, rather than moral instinct."[7] Ellis Hanson has likewise claimed that Wilde's investment in religious practice was closely tied to his framing of Christ as a "romantic artist" and "god of love," a reading that finds compelling echoes in the work of Stephen Arata, Terry Eagleton, Patrick R. O'Malley, and others.[8] By contrast, Joseph Pearce focuses his attention primarily on Wilde's spiritual biography, largely as a way of combatting a tendency to regard Wilde's life and career through the "lens of either puritan or prurient motives."[9] Pearce's account tracks Wilde's spiritual evolution, taking seriously what some might consider to be Wilde's unexpected penchant for traditional religious values. Nevertheless, even Pearce suggests that Wilde ultimately "argued for the Church purely from an aesthetic perspective."[10]

Religious thought was indeed a vital source of aesthetic reflection and inspiration for Wilde. But it is precisely for this reason that we must consider Wilde's deep and abiding investment in religion, not as cultural ornament but rather as devotional and intellectual practice. Wilde's religious views vacillated over the years, and it is virtually impossible to ascribe any stable religious identity to the man who would remark to Scottish writer William Sharp in 1885: "Art and Liberty seem to me more vital and more religious than any Creed."[11] In this chapter, my aim is not to align Wilde with any particular theology or to demonstrate how he finally leveraged faith in the service of his art. Wilde's Trinity College tutor J.P. Mahaffy once remarked that theology is "broad and has many sides," noting somewhat provocatively: "it is even better to do it inconsistently as regards the various sides."[12] In this spirit, the following pages document how Wilde engaged with religion as a broad and many-sided problem, highlighting important moments in his religious development alongside the theological writings that helped to shape that process. Placed within the context of theological discourses that were themselves fluctuating over the course of the second half of the nineteenth century, we can begin to see Wilde's relationship to faith as at once typical, for they reflect the questions and impulses shared by his contemporaries, and singular, for he gives to them a distinct and illuminating form. If Wilde read and thought widely on theological matters, he certainly did so "inconsistently." Yet these inconsistencies do not reveal a lack of seriousness but rather a sincere and unremitting attention to matters of faith. Neither atheist nor true convert, Wilde emerges here as an earnest scholar of theology, whose spiritual inquiries challenged the very categories of nineteenth-century religious thought.

The Origins of Faith

Oscar Wilde was christened by his uncle, the Reverend Ralph Wilde on 26 April 1855, in St. Mark's Church, historically a seat for the Church of Ireland. His parents, Sir William and Lady Jane Francesca Wilde, were both members of the Protestant Ascendancy, an elite body of landowning Anglo-Irish Protestants who first came to power in Ireland in the seventeenth century. William Wilde's family was, in the words of Jarleth Killeen "resolutely Protestant."[13] His brothers, John and Ralph Wilde, both became clergymen for the Church of Ireland. Lady Wilde's grandfather John Elgee had been Archdeacon of Leighlin. Her uncle, Richard Waddy Elgee, followed him as Rector of Wexford, and her father, Charles Elgee, though preferring a career in law, retained, and practiced the faith of his upbringing. Wilde's immediate family circle was, on the face of it, staunchly devoted to the Protestant tradition.

Perhaps the most unequivocally Protestant voice in Lady Wilde's immediate acquaintance was her uncle by marriage, the clergyman and novelist Reverend Charles Maturin, whose work both Lady Wilde and her son admired.[14] Maturin is said to have been vehemently anti-Catholic, and his 1820 novel *Melmoth the Wanderer* is unsparing in its critique of the Church, which it represents as celebrating preferment and power at the expense of affective bonds. The novel relates the story of a man, Alonza Monçada, who is forcibly confined to a monastery where he is denied "all the enjoyments of life."[15] Reflecting on the experience, Monçada relates the account of a young man who was thought to have become too intimate with a fellow monk. When the young man's love is exposed, he is severely punished:

> The executioners were pitiless. They compelled him to quit his bed, and applied the scourge with such outrageous severity, that at last, mad with shame, rage and pain, he burst from them, and ran through the corridor calling for assistance or for mercy. The monks were in their cells, none dared to stir,—they shuddered, and turned on their straw pallets. [...] A more perfect human form never existed than that of this unfortunate youth. He stood in an attitude of despair—he was streaming with blood. The monks, with their lights, their scourges, and their dark habits, seemed like a groupe of demons who had made prey of a wandering angel,—the groupe resembled the infernal furies pursuing a mad Orestes.[16]

It is naturally suggestive, in light of Wilde's own sexual history, that one of the most horrific scenes in *Melmoth the Wanderer* centers on the persecution of a monk who is suspected of loving another man. The description of the suffering, beautiful young monk might well have been conflated for Wilde in later years with the image of Guido Reni's *St. Sebastian* (c. 1616), which he saw at Genoa's Palazzo Rosso in 1873.[17] Following his release from prison, a destitute Wilde would adopt the suggestive pseudonym "Sebastian Melmoth," thus conflating the image of the beautiful young martyr with the oppressive moral climate of Maturin's novel.[18] Scholars have since proposed that Wilde saw in St. Sebastian a figure for the suffering homosexual, who martyrs himself in the service of love.[19]

While the example of the young monk is striking, however, it is by no means clear that either Maturin or Wilde would have understood this figure solely in light of the Catholic prohibition against homosexuality. Wilde's understanding of the link between religion and sexuality was complicated, as it was for his friend Robert Ross and other members of the Anglo-Catholic community. In the nineteenth century, William Sachs observes, Anglo-Catholicism was a distinct cultural movement, a "network of people and organizations within which one could cultivate a sharpened religious sensibility and find freedom from ordinary public scrutiny and expectations."[20] While neither Anglican nor Catholic doctrine openly supported alternative sexual practices, Anglo-Catholic circles did provide a space for alterity, and some churches were especially welcoming to gay parishioners. In this way, Sachs continues, "[g]ay life found an Anglican niche," one that was crucially informed by the seeming alterity of Catholicism itself.[21] The violent scenes Wilde encountered in Maturin's novel clearly did not, then, inspire a wholesale repudiation of the Catholic faith. As we shall see, Wilde would come to disparage the institutional forms that Maturin critiques in *Melmoth the Wanderer*, while also finding in Catholicism strains of affective, aesthetic, and even political thought that were anything but restrictive.

William Wilde too was reputed to have harbored anti-Catholic sentiments. In a letter to David Hunter-Blair, Wilde confessed that he had "incurred his father's grave displeasure by certain leanings he showed towards the Catholic Church," indicating that he would be disinherited should he formally convert.[22] In the 1870s, William Wilde's half-brother, Henry Wilson, was similarly perturbed by Wilde's Catholic sympathies and his religious poems (which had been published in the *Irish Monthly*, a Catholic publication). When he died in 1877, Wilson left only £100 to Wilde (in contrast to the £2000 bequeathed to Wilde's brother) on the condition that he remains loyal to the Protestant faith.[23] Wilde noted in a letter to Reginald ("Kitten") Harding that Wilson was "bigotedly intolerant of the Catholics and seeing me 'on the brink' struck me out of his will. It is a terrible disappointment to me; you see I suffer a good deal from my Romish leanings, in pocket and mind. [...] Fancy a man going before 'God and the Eternal Silences' with his wretched Protestant prejudices and bigotry clinging still to him."[24]

One might well presume, based on such biographical details, that Wilde's fascination with Catholicism signaled a rejection of the largely Protestant world of his upbringing. There is nothing straightforward, however, about Oscar Wilde or his religious origins. As Killeen has pointed out, Wilde's religious sensibility cannot be reduced to a simple distinction between Protestant and Catholic practices and must instead be considered within the context of his unique position as an Irishman at the intersection of the Protestant Ascendancy, the folkloric traditions of Ireland, and Roman Catholicism.[25] To complicate matters further, the Wilde household was replete with a spirit of political and religious dissent during Wilde's boyhood. That his identification with Catholicism should be contingent and sometimes idiosyncratic may well be attributed to the fact that his cultural and familial origins were themselves somewhat contingent and idiosyncratic on matters of faith.

Although emerging from a Protestant background, both of Wilde's parents were known for holding more broad-minded views on theology. Despite apparent misgivings about his son's conversion, William Wilde was a medical practitioner who frequented the homes of Irish Catholics and dissenters alike, and he spoke of these acquaintances with sympathy and affection. If he worried about his son's doctrinal affinities, it can at least be said that William Wilde expressed tolerance of other religions and was fascinated by the historical and archeological evidences of religious thought. In his youth William Wilde was acquainted with Gideon Ouseley, the Methodist preacher sometimes referred to as "apostle to the Irish" owing to his practice of preaching in the Irish tongue.[26] He had also been befriended by Father Patrick Prendergast, a Catholic priest, and antiquarian who possessed numerous ancient relics (including the Cross of Cong and the shrine of St. Patrick's tooth).[27] Prendergast inspired a lifelong passion for religious artifacts in William Wilde, who would repeatedly speak of these relics in years to come. Reverberations of his passion for the subject can be found in Wilde's review of Margaret Stokes's volume *Early Christian Art in Ireland* (1887), a piece in which Wilde singles out the shrine of St. Patrick's tooth and the "processional cross of Cong Abbey" for special praise: "Beautiful this cross certainly is with its delicate intricacy of ornamentation, its grace of proportion, and its marvel of mere workmanship, nor is there any doubt about its history."[28] Indeed, the history to which Wilde alludes appears in William Wilde's *Lough Corrib, its shores and islands* (1867), a work inspired by the archeological ventures he undertook in the company of his sons near the family's summer home, Moytura house.

William Wilde's interest in religious history is perhaps best discerned, however, in his *Narrative of a Voyage to Madeira, Teneriffe, and Along the Shores of the Mediterranean* (1840). Having undertaken the voyage as personal physician to an invalid traveling to the Holy Land, the doctor diverted himself by comparing Biblical and historical accounts against modern topographical and archeological discoveries. His discussion of Tyre, in particular, is characterized by frequent Scriptural references, and in 1840 he read a paper before the British Association, "On the Topography of Ancient Tyre," claiming that scientific evidence confirmed Biblical reports that the port city had been submerged in water gradually over time.[29] William Wilde's interest in Scripture seems, nevertheless, to have been more cultural than doctrinal in nature. He repeatedly expressed frustration at the extent to which doctrinal differences generated cultural and political instability. Over the course of his *Narrative*, he several times touches upon the question of religious tolerance, often expressing concern about the bigotry he perceived among his fellow Christians abroad. He writes:

> For my own part, I only wonder that a Jew resident in Jerusalem ever becomes a Christian; for, perhaps, in no other place upon the globe is Christianity presented to him in a more *unchristian* spirit; the character and conduct of those who generally profess it is neither calculated to gain his confidence nor respect. [...] I am sure that if any of my enlightened Roman Catholic fellow-countrymen were to witness the scenes, and to know the real state of Christianity among those persons belonging to their church in Jerusalem, they would blush for their superstitious practices and be ashamed to acknowledge them as fellow worshippers.[30]

In this passage, his most explicit condemnation of the Church, William Wilde objects not to Roman Catholic theology but rather to the manner in which Jews and Muslims were treated by Catholics in Jerusalem. As in the case of Maturin's novel, it was evidence of unchristian sentiment—a sense of hierarchy and exclusion—that sparked his disapprobation. If William Wilde was reputed to have rejected his own son's turn to Catholicism, then, one should not necessarily conclude that his outlook or the Wilde household itself was unwaveringly Protestant. We would do better to acknowledge that Wilde was raised by parents for whom religion was intertwined with historical, political, and social institutions that were not exclusively spiritual in nature.

This was especially true in the case of Lady Wilde, who brought her son to an awareness of Catholicism early in life. Just a few years following Wilde's christening, the Reverend L.C. Prideaux Fox, a chaplain at the Glencree Reformatory, reported that Wilde's mother "had asked me to instruct two of her children, one of them being that future erratic genius, Oscar Wilde. After a few weeks I baptized these two children, Lady Wilde herself being present on the occasion."[31] Fox's account indicates that Lady Wilde wished for her sons to be received into the Catholic faith.[32] The story of this clandestine baptism, undertaken when Wilde would have been eight or nine years old, is illustrative of Wilde's relationship with religion over the course of his life. An Irish Protestant brought to Catholicism on qualified terms—in private and without the knowledge even of his father—would be echoed in Wilde's tendency to waver between true conversion and a renunciation of religious dogma.[33]

Lady Wilde was similarly elusive in her religious leanings. Traditionally, she has been treated as a dissenter, yet she emerged from a more traditional religious background. As Karen Sasha Anthony Tipper has observed, Lady Wilde's Anglican upbringing was challenged by "her reading about other

cultures and other religions, especially those of classical Greece, and her travels to Scandinavia in 1859 prompted her to eschew the dogma of any
church."[34] Perhaps unsurprisingly, then, Lady Wilde's writings present a curious commingling of secular and religious impulses. In her verse, she presents
political events as matters of Biblical scope and frequently conflates the political and social struggles of the Irish with the plight of Christian martyrs. In
"The Exodus," she denounces the government for failing to adequately miti-
gate the hunger and destitution wrought by the potato famine of 1845–49,
which had reportedly elevated forced emigration to "a million a decade" (a
line that serves as a haunting refrain throughout the poem). A committed
nationalist, Lady Wilde suggests that those in power must consider not only
their political but also their religious duty:

> Ye stand at the Judgment-bar to-day —
>   The Angels are counting the dead-roll, too;
> Have ye trod in the pure and perfect way,
>   And ruled for God as the crowned should do?[35]

It is a theme Lady Wilde would repeat several times across her *oeuvre*, for
instance in "The Faithless Shepherds," in which she again observes that English
leaders, whose economic policies had decimated working-class Ireland, remain
blind to "The writing of God on the wall— / 'Ye are weighed, and found
wanting'—Oh, shame!"[36]

Despite her tendency to link this world and the next, however, Lady Wilde
was hardly what one would term a "secular" thinker. While she carefully studied the works of the German higher critics, she always remained committed
to the existence of an unseen, spiritual reality. As she wrote in her Introduction
to *Ancient Legends, Mystic Charms, and Superstitions of Ireland* (1888), "it
would be impossible to make the Irish a nation of sceptics [sic], even if a
whole legion of German Rationalists came amongst them to preach a crusade
against all belief in the spiritual and the unseen."[37] A proud Irishwoman, Lady
Wilde relished the work of Friedrich Schleiermacher, Immanuel Kant, and
Arthur Schopenhauer, but never allowed them to eclipse her spiritual affinities. Although by no means consistent or systematic in her religious practices,
Lady Wilde might well be said to have embraced a kind of religious humanism, one that treats the divine spirit as coextensive with the self. It is an idea
to which she recurred throughout her life but which is articulated with special
clarity in her 1891 essay on the poetry of Philip James Bailey. Reflecting on
the poet's two signature works—the revised 1845 edition of *Festus* (1839/1845)
and *The Angel World* (1850)—Lady Wilde summarizes Bailey's outlook

concisely as "the identity of all spirit with God's spirit."[38] All souls, according to Bailey, are at once unique and yet connected to an eternal spirit; accordingly, the soul can never be destroyed, only improved. Lady Wilde seems to have sympathized with this understanding of divinity, setting aside the poem itself for a time to remark upon the merits of Bailey's theology:

> Revelation teaches that even here God dwells in humanity, as in a living temple. Yet each soul has a distinctive existence, though, being a portion of the divine essence, it is ever aspiring to blend again with the infinite. We are prisoned angels; gods, shrouded in clay; Man, Angel, Deity in one mysterious combination; and the highest aim of all noble life is the perfect manifestation of this mystic triad.[39]

Lady Wilde had encountered the same concept in the work of Emanuel Swedenborg, whose *Of Heaven and Hell* (1758) she is reported to have been translating for a new English edition in the 1850s.[40] One of Swedenborg's most striking claims is that the Bible describes the transformation of humanity from a physical to a spiritual being through a process known as "regeneration," a process Lady Wilde aptly likens to the Hindu concept of reincarnation.[41] She had voiced the same idea in her 1877 essay "The Destiny of Humanity," speculating on the possibility that all human beings (alive and dead) partake of a common spirit. The universe is, she avers, like "an infinite harp—strike one chord, and all vibrate in unison—and we feel that man was not brought into this wondrous sphere of conscious being merely for this world and for this one brief life; the whole planet system is his kingdom, and the whole universe is to him a consecrated temple, where, by right of his deathless intellect, he holds an eternal place."[42]

Thus, although Lady Wilde is often understood to be a Protestant with Catholic leanings, in truth her spiritual vision was far more eclectic in scope. Her investigations into Irish mythology commence with a comparative history of world religions, suggesting that most systems of belief are just that—*systems* that seek to translate and codify how human beings understand their place in relation to a larger cosmic order. The Greeks, she notes, were renowned for espousing such a "sublime Pantheism [...] that sees gods in everything, yet with one Supreme God overall."[43] In Lady Wilde's view, "all the sublime creations of human genius, the lofty deeds of heroism and self-sacrifice, are true theophanisms—manifestations of God in beauty, harmony, love, or holiness."[44] In short, Lady Wilde's understanding of divinity was far from conservative. It transcended national and denominational statutes, insisting somewhat paradoxically that faith was an experience both subjective and universal. It is an idea her son would later explore in his poem "Panthea," which features two lovers who "shall be / Part of the mighty universal whole, / And through all æons mix and mingle with the Kosmic Soul!"[45]

Seen this way, Lady Wilde's poetry does not simply articulate a fear of judgment in the next world; to seek divine judgment one need only look within. In "The Parable of Life," for instance, Lady Wilde presents what may well have been her own struggle against worldly ambition in decidedly Christian terms. At the outset, the poem features a soul wandering through a "fiery desert plain" bereft of companionship or even the basic necessities of life.[46] The faithful spirit, she reflects, has never drunk from "the desert springs; / For the soul that is filled with the Spirit of God, Recks little of earthly things."[47] Lady Wilde's appeal to a typically anti-materialist Christian worldview comes to a head when the soul is confronted by earthly temptation and ambition:

> Woe to the soul that ascends the mount
> Of pomp, and power, and pride,
> With the glories of earth within his reach,
> And the Demon at his side.[48]

It is a striking reflection, delivered by a poet who by all accounts was both conscientious and personally ambitious. Lady Wilde had, without question, longed for literary fame and she routinely admitted a proclivity for self-indulgence, remarking once that her professional success stemmed largely from her ability to make higher ideals accessible to the common man: "alas how few I meet who make my soul ascend to their higher level. *Mais je suis vraiment égoiste.*"[49]

Still, Lady Wilde's egoism was not always, strictly speaking, at odds with her spiritual aspirations. Wilde once wrote of his mother: "she rejects all forms of superstition and dogma, particularly any notion of priest and sacrament standing between her and God. She has a very strong faith in that aspect of God *we* call the Holy Ghost—the divine intelligence of which we on earth partake."[50] Although rejection of "priest and sacrament" would seem to align her explicitly with Protestantism, Lady Wilde's interest in a direct experience of divinity in this world more closely aligns her with the pantheistic traditions she describes with such eloquence in *Ancient Legends*. If she deplores the soul who "ascends the mount / Of pomp, and power, and pride," she celebrates the soul that recognizes its own divinity. Rejecting one form of self-aggrandizement, Lady Wilde seems paradoxically to embrace another. In her poem "Salvation," she accordingly writes:

Thou art lord in thine own kingdom;
      Rule thyself—thou rulest all!
Smile, when from its proud dominion
      Earthly joy will rudely fall.
Be true unto thyself and hear not
Evil thoughts, that would enslave thee.
God is in thee! Mortal fear not;
Trust in Him, and He will save thee![51]

The caution against "Earthly joy" and "Evil thoughts" might seem strikingly moralistic for a woman who clearly did appreciate the things of this world. Certainly, the proclamation that one must "Rule thyself," with its emphasis on personal restraint, would seem to chafe against her own bohemian proclivities. The dictum would later be echoed in *De Profundis*, where Wilde remarks: "I ceased to be lord over myself. I was no longer the captain of my soul, and did not know it."[52] Juxtaposed to Lady Wilde's celebration of self-discipline, however, is the revelation that "God is in thee," a remark that risks sounding dangerously like self-apotheosis.[53] By this account, the virtuous individual is neither saintly nor self-effacing. Instead, Lady Wilde proclaims, it is only by being "true unto thyself" that one acquires spiritual clarity and power. To recognize the divinity within oneself is less a matter of seeking preferment (in this world or the next) than it is of acquiring self-knowledge.

Such an outlook might well lead readers to regard Lady Wilde and her son as secular thinkers. For many years, historians of the Victorian period emphasized a turn from belief to unbelief, claiming that the rise of modernity coincided with a waning of conventional religious attitudes and practices. More recently, however, this narrative of secularization has been called into question, with many noting how purportedly "modern" ways of seeing the world were also intertwined with spiritual and theological inquiry.[54] It is beyond question that the higher criticism—not to mention the 1859 publication of Charles Darwin's *On the Origin of Species*—led many Victorians to question longstanding religious beliefs; but it is also true that for many, like Lady Wilde, these texts prompted a renewed interest in theology. As Charles La Porte puts it in *Victorian Poets and the Changing Bible* (2011), Biblical criticism was responsible not simply for a "crisis of faith;" in the case of the most celebrated poets (including Alfred Lord Tennyson, Robert Browning, and Elizabeth Barrett Browning) it precipitated a new attention to the religious possibilities of literary production, so that many Victorian writers would come to treat literature as inspired text, capable of prompting spiritual reflection and transformation.[55]

To be sure, the opposition between secular and religious was largely forged in the twentieth century and does not categorically align with nineteenth-century theories of faith. George Jacob Holyoake, the British writer, and editor who first coined the term "secularist" in 1851 was careful to differentiate between secularism and atheism:

> Secularism is not an argument against Christianity, it is one independent of it. It does not question the pretensions of Christianity; it advances others. Secularism does not say there is no light or guidance elsewhere, but maintains that there is light and guidance in secular truth, whose conditions and sanctions exist independently, and act forever.[56]

To this extent, those narratives that align the period with a decline in religious belief tend to adopt an anachronistic understanding of theological discourse, occluding the real complexity and fluidity of Victorian faith practices.[57] It would be misguided, then, to understand the period strictly in terms of devotion or atheism—piety or doubt. Nevertheless, readings of Wilde have often been informed by the idea that to be "modern" he must also have renounced piety and the institutions of faith. As we track the evolution of Wilde's spiritual life, we would do well to remain wary of such stark doctrinal divisions. Wilde's modernity is more truly expressed, I would propose, through his spiritual curiosity and cultivated efforts at bridging the gap between the secular and divine.

Early Teachers

Wilde's experience of religion at Portora Royal School, where he attended from 1864 to 1871, has been more or less undocumented.[58] Certainly, the public face of the school was strongly Anglican. At the time of Wilde's advent in February 1864 only three Presbyterian and three Catholic boys boarded at the school.[59] The headmaster, Reverend William Steele, was a minister in the Church of Ireland, and the Board of Education was thoroughly Protestant. Regardless of whether or not religious tolerance flourished at Portora, it is certain that Wilde would have been routinely exposed to doctrinal sermons that chafed against the more heterodox proclivities of his home life. Within a year of Wilde's arrival, Steele preached a sermon in which he argued that a complete education required cultivating among his pupils their "duty as Christian boys."[60] To this end, Steele's words reflected a fidelity to Scriptural authority and the Word of God:

He requires all who would be His disciples indeed to come out from the world, and to separate themselves from its evil practices and corrupt ways; He requires us to hate and abhor the impure desire, the unholy thought, which are so apt to stir within our evil hearts; He requires us to keep the door of our lips, that we offend not with our tongues, to suffer no filthy or profane expression to pass the barrier of our mouths; He requires that our conduct and conversation in the world should be as becometh the Gospel of Christ—that we shrink from every sinful act, and forbidden indulgence, and mean or questionable proceeding. This is to be a Christian indeed [...][61]

By this account, to be truly Christian is to resist temptation and to avoid "questionable" pursuits. The Christ Wilde encountered in Steele's sermons was an icon of silence, acquiescence, and restraint. While the religious disposition of the young Wilde remains somewhat obscure, then, we can speculate that his later works reflect an interest in at least revising the liturgy he found rehearsed before him every Sunday. Sir Edward Sullivan reported that during his own tenure at Portora, Wilde "would frequently vary the entertainment by giving us extremely quaint illustrations of holy people in stained-glass attitudes: his power of twisting his limbs into weird contortions being very great."[62] If Sullivan's anecdote be taken for truth, Wilde would seem to have had at least a capacity for appreciating the more dramatic elements of religious narrative, though Sullivan was careful to remark that there was never "any suggestion of irreverence in the exhibition."[63]

Indeed, there is at least some concrete evidence that Wilde embraced and even found comfort in religious ritual as a child. Perhaps one of the most striking evidences of the young Wilde's religious sentiment stemmed from the early death of his sister Isola, while he was in residence at Portora. Only twelve years old at the time, Wilde was reportedly devastated by the loss. Meeting Wilde when he returned to Dublin, the attending physician described him as "an affectionate, gentle, retiring, dreamy boy whose lonely and inscrutable grief found its outward expression in long and frequent visits to his sister's grave in the village cemetery."[64] The young Wilde seemed to have found some solace in a portable memento mori, which he crafted at the time—an envelope decorated with crosses and containing strands of Isola's hair (Fig. 3.1). At the center, Wilde inscribed "My Isola's Hair," followed by the date of her passing, 23 February. The paper is peppered with inscriptions one might expect to find upon a tombstone: "Thy will be done," "God is love," "Resurgam [I shall rise again]," "She rests in peace." At the very center, placed above a decorative crown is a quotation from Mark V:39—"She is not dead but sleepeth"—an allusion to the twelve-year-old daughter of Jairus, whom Christ is said to have

Fig. 3.1 Envelope containing strands of Isola Wilde's hair. (Courtesy of the Merlin Holland Picture Archive)

resurrected from the dead. Serving as a kind of portable shrine to his lost sibling, the envelope was found among Wilde's scant possessions after his death in Paris in 1900. He had retained the relic for over three decades. Certainly, it would seem to suggest that Wilde was not altogether dismissive of religion: at the very least, religious symbols and text played an important role in his emotional life.

If Wilde's early religious experiences are somewhat difficult to document, they become far more legible after his matriculation to Trinity College, Dublin in 1871. Here, Wilde was mentored by J.P. Mahaffy, who has sometimes been labeled as vehemently anti-Catholic. Wilde biographer Boris Brasol suggests that "the extravagances of [Mahaffy's] atheistic catechism used to shock even his agnostic co-religionists."[65] Hunter-Blair, who converted to Catholicism in 1875, insisted that Wilde's turn away from Catholicism was hastened by the interference of Mahaffy.[66] His suspicions were, to be sure, well-founded. In 1877, having diverted Wilde from his much anticipated trip to Rome in order to show him the wonders of Greece, Mahaffy reported to his wife that Wilde had "come round under the influence of the moment from Popery to Paganism, but what his Jesuit friends will say, who supplied the money to land him in Rome, it is not hard to guess. I think it is a fair case of cheating the devil."[67] While Mahaffy's religious views may well have deviated from the mainstream, however, it is by no means clear that he was either atheistic or intolerant in his outlook. In his written work, Mahaffy demonstrates a deliberate comingling of religious devotion and humanism that would later also distinguish the work of his disciple.[68]

Perhaps the most striking evidence of this is Mahaffy's 1882 volume, *The Decay of Modern Preaching*. At the outset of this provocative piece, Mahaffy proposes that the nineteenth-century crisis in faith stems from the supposition that Christianity had remained largely unaltered since its inception, dependent upon the stability and infallibility of all cultural forms and rituals attached to it. "Nothing is more marked in most Christian preachers," he writes,

> than the firmness with which they hold and declare that their form of faith was established once for all by its Founder, and that no change or modification whatever is to be tolerated by the orthodox. This rigid adherence to the doctrines of Christianity is extended even to the very *form* in which it is preached, and nothing is thought better or more profitable than to repeat the old watchwords of those who once stirred the world to its depths.[69]

The preachers of early Christianity, in Mahaffy's view, were cultural revolutionaries. Advocating for a single theology in a pantheistic world, these innovators were driven to argue passionately for their ideas: "They were to hate father and mother and brethren for His sake; they were to quarrel with the whole civilised world, and set themselves apart as a peculiar society."[70] If Mahaffy's prose reflects an admiration for the religious tolerance of the pagan world, it also conveys an appreciation for the earliest Christian preachers, whom he presents as provocative and daring. In the nineteenth century, Mahaffy continues, matters of doctrinal variance were generally passed over. The preacher's office was merely to reinforce the incontrovertible truth of Christian dogma through the repetition and reiteration of old ideas. In Mahaffy's view, it was this refusal to engage actively with the challenges of the present that constituted the greatest obstacle for modern preachers. Because theology is by its very nature "a science full of mystery," the man of the deepest faith and greatest capacity for guiding others must eschew simple answers and, on occasion, invite challenges to tradition. The modern preacher must "feel that his subject is broad and has many sides, and that each deserves to be put forward strongly and clearly—it is even better to do it inconsistently as regards the various sides—but each in its turn."[71]

Mahaffy's book may be one of the most surprisingly overlooked sources for Wilde's suggestively titled "The Decay of Lying," a Socratic dialogue published in an 1889 issue of *The Nineteenth Century* and revised for inclusion in his 1891 collection *Intentions*.[72] Deliberately provocative and often strategically sophistic, Wilde's essay stages a defense of Romanticism against the ravages of nineteenth-century realism. Famously, Wilde's chief provocateur, Vivian, proclaims that "Life imitates Art far more than Art imitates Life."[73] Wilde's defense of aestheticism would seem a far cry from Mahaffy's critique of religious doctrine, yet at several points, he explicitly grounds his argument in theological claims, as if to demonstrate that to reinterpret our relationship to Nature is perforce to reinterpret our relationship to God. Vivian reflects, for instance:

> A cultured Mahomedan once remarked to us, "You Christians are so occupied in misinterpreting the fourth commandment that you have never thought of making an artistic application of the second" He was perfectly right, and the whole truth of the matter is this: The proper school to learn art in is not Life but art.[74]

The Muslim's invocation of the fourth commandment in Deuteronomy 5:12—"Keep the Sabbath day, to sanctify it"—highlights the doctrinal questions at the heart of the Sabbatarian controversy. Wilde suggests here that the debate about whether Scripture permits either work or worship on the Sabbath is perhaps less significant than the question of how man might most productively cultivate a personal relationship with the divine. For the Muslim, art presents a possible answer to this problem. Deuteronomy 5:8 states: "Thou shalt not make thee any graven image, or any likeness of any thing that is in heaven above, or that is in the earth beneath, or that is in the water beneath the earth." The Muslim of Vivian's anecdote would have taken this prescription very seriously. The Koran, after all, prohibits the representation of living creatures, hence the non-representational nature of so much Islamic art. Wilde had touched upon this idea once before in a review of Ernest Lefebvre's *Embroidery and Lace* (1888) where he observes: "The triumph of the Mussulman gave the decorative art of Europe a new departure—that very principle of their religion that forbade the actual representation of any object in nature being of the greatest artistic service to them."[75] Ultimately, the Muslim becomes the mouthpiece for Wilde's claim that the best art does not seek to reproduce life. Instead, it seeks to reach beyond this world and to serve as a kind of spiritual conduit for the willing participant.[76]

Indeed, Vivian ultimately claims in "The Decay of Lying" that religion and art are not merely compatible but actually mutually dependent impulses. The Catholic clergy, he asserts, are in truth the guardians of the imagination. "As for the Church," he remarks, "I cannot conceive anything better for the culture of a country than the presence in it of a body of men whose duty it is to believe in the supernatural, to perform daily miracles, and to keep alive that mythopoeic faculty which is so essential for the imagination."[77] By this logic, the clergy work to preserve that part of human culture that cannot be directed or explained by reason. If Vivian's remark seems to undermine the theological value of clerical work, it also presents religion as an institution that is at once comprehensible and transcendent, human and divine.

By contrast, Vivian invokes the Church of England as a site of gross realism, where the clergy all too often debate the finer points of doctrine and exegesis, rather than aspiring to higher ideals. He laments: "it is sufficient for some shallow uneducated passman out of either University to get up in his pulpit and express his doubts about Noah's ark, or Balaam's ass, or Jonah and the whale, for half of London to flock to hear him, and to sit open-mouthed in rapt admiration of his superb intellect."[78] Reading this passage, we might well recall Wilde's frustration that the Divinity was a "pass examination," requiring the mere recitation of established religious principles. Wilde's apparent resistance to organized religion increasingly reflected less a heretical impulse than a genuine desire to promote among his readers a more vital and personal relationship with the divine.

Wilde's Oxford Movement

Wilde's tutelage under Mahaffy perhaps reinforced what he had learned from his mother—that the secular was not necessarily at odds with the spiritual life, although institutional practice sometimes insisted upon such a division. But it was while at Oxford that Wilde would most openly express the challenges of reconciling these two very important components of his spiritual life. At Oxford, Wilde quickly found himself befriended by men of different religious persuasions, and he was visibly taken with Catholicism. Lord Ronald Gower, a sculptor, and politician who is sometimes cited as a model for Lord Henry Wotton in *The Picture of Dorian Gray* (1890/1), described Wilde in his journals as: "A pleasant cheery fellow, but with his long-haired head full of nonsense regarding the Church of Rome. His room filled with photographs of the Pope and of Cardinal Manning."[79] Hunter-Blair confirmed this account, remarking upon "the religious pictures and other objects of Catholic devotion with which at this period he began to adorn his rooms."[80] Other sources report that Wilde surrounded himself in the 1870s with images of Cardinal John Henry Newman, and that he numbered among his possessions a plaster bust

Fig. 3.2 Edward Burne-Jones, The Days of Creation: The Sixth Day, 1870–1876. Watercolor, gouache, shell gold, and platinum paint on linen-covered panel prepared with zinc white ground; 102.3 × 36 cm (40 1/4 × 14 3/16 in.) Harvard Art Museums/Fogg Museum, Bequest of Grenville L. Winthrop, 1943.459. (Photo: Imaging Department © President and Fellows of Harvard College)

of the Madonna. When he shared rooms with William Ward after December 1876, his décor would also include photographs of Edward Burne-Jones's *The Days of the Creation* and *Christ and Magdalen* (Fig. 3.2), both works that illustrate the emergence of the spiritual into the material world.[81]

Wilde discussed the former work in a review of the Grosvenor Gallery in 1877, observing that the crystal in the fourth panel "glows like a heated opal," a line that perhaps recalls Walter Pater's recommendation in *Studies in the History of the Renaissance* (1873) that every life should glow with "that hard gem-like flame."[82] Pater had recommended valuing sensory experience for its own sake, though a few years later in *Marius the Epicurean* (1885) he would highlight the positive role that sensory experience plays in religious ritual. Wilde's review suggests that he saw in the work of Burne-Jones a similar impulse to translate sensory experience into a form of devotion. Wilde writes: "The faces of the angels are pale and oval-shaped, in their eyes is the light of Wisdom and Love, and their lips seem as if they would speak to us; and strength and beauty are in their wings. They stand with naked feet, some on the shell-strewn sands whereon tide has never washed nor storm broken, others it seems on pools of water, others on strange flowers; and their hair is like the bright glory round a saint's head."[83] To be sure, it would be misguided to read Wilde's review as a statement of his personal views on religion, yet it is suggestive that he praises the work less for its Pre-Raphaelite subversions than for its ability to give bodily form to the spirit, presenting angels "as if they would speak to us."

Wilde's penchant for religious art was not, however, purely aesthetic. Indeed, Hunter-Blair (who would later become a Benedictine abbot) recalled that the "constant trend of his conversation" toward religious matters was so inexorable at the time that it "considerably bored those of his acquaintances who were not in the slightest degree interested in such matters."[84] Whether or not this accurately represents how his companions responded to Wilde's ruminations on faith, Hunter-Blair was impressed by Wilde's apparent interest in the possibility of conversion. After being received into the Catholic Church on 25 March 1875, Hunter-Blair felt that Wilde became enthralled by the possibility of conversion: "Oscar was greatly interested in the step I had taken, asked me many questions, and shewed me what I had not known before, how deep, and I am sure genuine, was his own sympathy with Catholicism, and how much moved he was by my having taken the step which I did."[85]

Wilde's correspondence from this period without question reflects his fascination with Catholicism, and he frequently expressed this interest in aesthetic terms. Traveling through Italy in 1875, he described to his mother in lavish detail the splendor of Giotto's work at the Scrovegni Church (Padua), "[…] the walls covered entirely with frescoes by him; one wall the life of Mary, the other the life of Christ; the ceiling blue with gold stars and medallion pictures; the west wall a great picture of Heaven and Hell suggested to him by Dante […]"[86] For Wilde, Giotto's azure sky invoked the narratives of Christ and Dante alike—a reasonable though in this case suggestive combination. While both present visions of spiritual transport, the first invokes the incontestable narrative of Scripture passed from God to man, the second a poet's vision of man passing into the afterlife. Even as Wilde is transfixed by the aesthetic splendor of the church at Padua, his reflections on the scene belie an interest in comparing scriptural and secular manifestations of divinity. In other words, Wilde's reception of Catholic art was neither cosmetic nor reflective of unwavering belief; if anything, these works provided him with a testing ground for exploring a range of theological problems, including the challenge of querying tradition and the prospect of finding divinity in man.

Almost precisely a year later, Wilde found himself visiting his friend and future artist Frank Miles, whose father Robert Henry William Miles was rector of the Church of St. Mary and All Angels at Bingham, Nottinghamshire. Wilde described the Reverend Miles as "a very advanced Anglican and a great friend of Newman, [Edward] Pusey, [Cardinal Henry Edward] Manning, [John Hall] Gladstone and all English theologians. He is very clever and interesting: I have learned a lot from him."[87] Wilde's description of the Bingham rectory presents a striking point of comparison to his rendering of Giotto's frescoes:

> A wonderful garden with such white lilies and rose walks; only that there are no serpents or apples it would be quite Paradise. The church is very fine indeed. Frank and his mother, a very good artist, have painted wonderful windows, and frescoed angels on the walls, and one of his sisters has carved the screen and altar. It is simply beautiful and everything done by themselves.[88]

Once again, Wilde's description of the church juxtaposes the divine and the profane. Though wrought by human hands, Bingham rectory seems curiously more pristine than Eden itself. What is more, Wilde's chief interest at Bingham rectory is the familial and familiar source of the religious spectacle he witnessed there. The paintings are all the more beautiful for the fact that Miles and his mother have produced them together, manifesting a shared and deeply personal connection to the divine. If Wilde was attracted by religious ritual, it was not merely owing to his penchant for visual extravagance; it was because art, however simple, constitutes a bridge between this world and the next.

If religion, like art, provides man with a way of transcending material reality, then for Wilde the most valuable religious experiences seem to have been imaginative rather than analytical, mystifying rather than coherent. The very year he visited Bingham Rectory, Wilde would write a telling letter to William Ward, which moves between theologies within a space of just a few lines. Wilde commences by commenting on the solemn declaration of papal infallibility by Vatican I in 1870:

> If you want an interesting book get *Pomponio Leto* [1876]—an account of the last Vatican Council—a really wonderfully dramatic book. How strange that on the day of the Pope publicly declaring that his Infallibility and that of the Church were identical a fearful storm broke over Rome *and two thunderbolts fell from heaven*. It reads like the talkative ox of Livy (*bos locutus est*) and the rain of blood, that were always happening.[89]

Noting that the announcement of papal infallibility coincided with a "fearful storm"—a tempest of almost Biblical proportions—Wilde seems at first to side with the Anglican Church. The Thirty-Nine Articles officially reject the Infallibility of the Church on the grounds that while God may be unerring, men are not. Wilde openly articulates his perplexity on the matter: "I don't know what to think myself, I wish you would come to Rome with me and test the whole matter. I am afraid to go alone."[90] Only a few lines later, however, Wilde speculates again on the Anglican penchant for reason, observing, "I think it is a mere dream, and very strange that they should be so anxious to believe the Blessed Virgin conceived in sin."[91] Although this might at first seem to be a wry commentary on the role sexuality plays in Biblical narrative and exegesis, Wilde also seems to offer an approving nod in the direction of the Immaculate Conception precisely because it defies logic and feeds the imagination. As in "The Decay of Lying," Wilde's remarks betray frustration at the rationalism he aligns with Anglican practice. As if to confirm this stance, he admits to Ward in another letter from this period: "I confess not to be a worshipper at the Temple of Reason. I think man's reason the most misleading and thwarting guide that the sun looks upon [...] Faith is, I think, a bright lantern for the feet, though of course an exotic plant in man's mind, and requiring continual cultivation."[92]

Wilde's constant vacillation between Anglican and Catholic precepts, often within the space of a single page, suggests a desire to seek out a unique spiritual identity that might align with his understanding of art and society. At times, Wilde's ruminations on Catholic doctrine dovetail with the efforts of the German higher critics—men like Ludwig Feuerbach and David Friedrich Strauss, who advocated for a more historical and philological approach to Scripture. Wilde wrote, again to Ward, in very decided terms regarding the incarnation and atonement of Christ:

I wonder you don't see the beauty and necessity for the *incarnation* of God into man to help us to grasp at the skirts of the Infinite. The atonement is I admit hard to grasp. But I think since Christ the dead world has woke up from sleep. Since him we have lived. I think the greatest proof of the Incarnation aspect of Christianity is its whole career of noble men and thoughts and not the mere narration of unauthenticated histories.[93]

While he does not concede the literal truth of the incarnation, Wilde affirms that it provides a useful model for envisioning humanity in its most elevated state. Rather than treating Christ as the Word made flesh, Wilde sees in Christ the transformative power of ideas. By this logic, the power of religion does not reside in the revering and reiterating of sacred narratives, a practice that encourages the individual always to look elsewhere for absolution. Instead, Wilde suggests that Christ lives on through the ideas and narratives of mankind itself.

This approach to Christianity was doubtless informed by John Ruskin, whom Wilde first encountered at Oxford.[94] Until 1848, Ruskin had lived his life according to the Evangelical doctrines of his childhood. He once reflected that his mother's "unquestioning evangelical faith in the literal truth of the Bible placed me, as soon as I could conceive or think, in the presence of an unseen world."[95] This focus on literal truth increasingly weighed on Ruskin, and by 1858 he had experienced a sharp break with his religious upbringing. He records the moment of his conversion at length in his autobiographical narrative, *Praeterita* (1885). Hearing a "consolatory discourse on the wickedness of the wide world" at a church in Turin, Ruskin found it difficult to engage this "languid form of prayer."[96] He writes:

> Myself neither cheered nor greatly alarmed by this doctrine, I walked back into the condemned city, and up into the gallery where Paul Veronese's Solomon and the Queen of Sheba glowed in full afternoon light. The gallery windows being opened, there came in with the warm air, floating swells and falls of military music which seemed to me more devotional, in their perfect art, tune, and discipline, than anything I remembered of evangelical hymns. And as the perfect color and sound gradually asserted their power on me, they seemed finally to fasten me in the old Jewish faith, that things done delightfully and rightly, were always done by the help and in the spirit of God.[97]

This event would be succeeded by decades of agnosticism. It was finally in a monastery in Assisi, where Ruskin spent several months in 1874, that he came to develop his own critique of organized religion: "But the more I loved or envied the monks and the more I despised the modern commercial and fashionable barbaric tribes, the more acutely also I felt that the Catholic political hierarchies, and isolated remnants of celestial enthusiasm were hopelessly at fault in their dealing with these adversaries: having also elements of corruption in themselves."[98] Echoing the critiques once leveled by Maturin, Ruskin came increasingly to think that the best religion must be more subjective and democratic in scope, eschewing the doctrinal severity that had marred his own Evangelical upbringing. Strikingly, Wilde attended Oxford from 1874 to 1878—at precisely the time Ruskin was moving from a position of agnosticism to belief. His awakening faith was perhaps not unseen by Wilde, who would note in an 1888 letter to Ruskin: "There is in you something of prophet, of priest, and of poet, and to you the gods gave eloquence such as they have given to none other, so that your message might come to us with the fire of passion, and the marvel of music, making the deaf to hear, and the blind to see."[99]

All too often, it has been presumed that Wilde's aestheticism contrasts sharply to Ruskin's insistence on the social value of religious art. According to

Norbert Kohl, for instance, Ruskin's belief in the didactic power of art was a key point of departure from the work of Wilde. "Unlike adherents of the Aesthetic Movement," he writes, Ruskin

> maintained an image of man and society that integrated the aesthetic into the moral and religious world order. [...] For Ruskin, the artist was not an outsider seeking an elite status on the fringes of society by means of his autonomous art, but he was a responsible member of the community, making his contribution to it by means of his talent and the tools of his trade.[100]

It may well be true that Ruskin's view of the social order was more traditional and utilitarian than that of Wilde. Certainly, Ruskin's manner of articulating his aesthetic philosophy was more conservative and has sometimes earned him a reputation as a moralist and pedant. Yet the two thinkers were in truth closer in spiritual outlook than Kohl suggests. Great works of art, as Ruskin avers in *Queen of the Air* (1869), "are not conceived didactically, but are didactic in their essence, as all good art is."[101] The line has frequently been understood as testifying to Ruskin's belief that all art must teach good lessons. On the contrary, Ruskin speaks of art's didactic function as working "in the purest way, indirectly and occultly": it is "didactic chiefly by being beautiful."[102] If Ruskin pronounced more openly upon the value of the lessons we can learn from art, he agreed with Wilde in adopting a Platonic view of education: art is edifying because whatever is beautiful is, by its very nature, also good. As George Landow has established, Ruskin believed that great art was an emanation of man's desire to connect with the divine, and Wilde, who had already written extensively about the relationship between aesthetic production and faith, seemed very much to share this view.[103]

One of the hallmarks of Ruskin's work, from the time of his spiritual crisis to the end of his life, was a tendency to see God in nature and in the works of men. In "The Nature of the Gothic" (1851), for instance, Ruskin famously proposes that the history of art might be understood as progressing through three distinct phases: the Byzantine, the Gothic, and the Renaissance. Contradicting the view that art was always progressing to greater levels of skill and attainment, Ruskin proposed that the Gothic style was preferable to the Renaissance because, despite its imperfections and signature excess, it expressed man's humility before God. Where Renaissance artists reveled in technical perfection and a turn to mimesis, Gothic architecture reflected man's laborious efforts to honor and comprehend divinity. In later years, Wilde would revise this idea, noting to Robert Ross in 1900: "By the way, I suppose the great revival of architecture, Gothic and Renaissance, as due simply to the fact that God found he could only live in temples made by hands: in the heart of man he could not live, he was not the first."[104] Wilde's remark perhaps reflects a despairing view of nineteenth-century theology, one informed by Ruskin who noted in volume 2 of *Modern Painters* that the decline of art was fostered by a tendency to dispense with "unlikelihoods" in preference to "an apparently closer following of nature and probability."[105] With the celebration of human achievement and secular values, Ruskin averred, came a corresponding decline in mysticism and religious devotion: "the painter had no longer any religious passion to express."[106] While Wilde was in many ways a champion of humanism, it is also clear that he was enthralled by mysticism. Having grasped from Mahaffy a belief that religion could be transformative, innovative, and even rebellious, Wilde too prioritized inconsistencies and "unlikelihoods" above technical attainments.

Wilde's preference for mysticism over certainty—for speculation over dogma—also finds its roots in his reading of John Henry Newman (a figure treated more extensively in Chap. 2). Wilde's admiration for Newman has been well-established. Having read his works as an undergraduate at Oxford, he reportedly sent a copy of his poem "Rome Unvisited" to Newman and received warm praise in response.[107] In a letter to William Ward in 1876, he noted that he "bought a lot of [Newman's] books before leaving Oxford."[108] The following year, after leaving Oxford, Wilde expressed a wish to visit Newman "to burn my fingers a little more," presumably alluding to his flirtations with Catholic conversion.[109] Wilde transported his collection of Newman's works across America during his 1882 tour, and he would revisit his *Apologia Pro Vita Sua* (1864) during his incarceration in the 1890s. Following Wilde's release from prison, in 1895, Arthur Clifton wrote to Carlos Blacker: "He has been reading Pater and Newman lately, one book a week."[110] All of this is to say that the doctrinal differences between Wilde and Newman, however profound, never effaced Wilde's attraction to the man's work.

At times Newman seems curiously to echo Mahaffy's insistence on the reconciliation of faith and intellect. As he observes in *An Idea for a University* (1852), the truly religious man "rejoices in the widest and most philosophical systems of intellectual education, from an intimate conviction that Truth is his real ally, as it is his profession; and that Knowledge and Reason are sure ministers to Faith."[111] In Newman's view, the true object of the university was to cultivate an intellect which, rather than specializing in a particular field of knowledge, "is disciplined for its own sake, for the perception of its own proper object, and for its own highest culture."[112] Only through a comprehensive and contemplative view of the world could one attain a meaningful relationship with God or one's fellow man. But the contemplative view was also, for Newman, directly related to aesthetic sensibility, thus aligning him more closely with a Platonic sense of beauty: the pleasure one takes in the perception of beauty is, therefore, for Newman, consistent with the aims of philosophy and theology. In his *Essay in Aid of a Grammar of Assent* (1870), Newman accordingly argues that conscience "corresponds to our perception of the beautiful and the deformed. As we have naturally a sense of the beautiful and graceful in nature and art, though tastes proverbially differ, so we have a sense of duty and obligation, whether we all associate it with the same particular actions or not."[113] While Newman distinguishes between "taste" and "conscience" on the grounds that the latter is chiefly concerned with one's treatment of others, he notes that the basis for moral sentiment is an awareness of beauty that is both innate and cultivated.

This was in direct contrast to Cardinal Manning, whose sermon on the university motto "Dominus Illuminatio Mea," Wilde had attended with Hunter-Blair upon the opening of the new church at St. Giles's in 1875. The sermon suggested that Catholicism, with its insistence upon the infallibility of the "Divine Teacher," was fundamentally at odds with the modern university, which seemed to luxuriate in doubt. Manning opined: "Rationalism, like 'the moth that fretteth a garment,' or like the cankerworm that eats away the leaves of the vine, has overspread the pages of Holy Writ. 'Dominus illuminatio mea' is still emblazoned upon the open Book of Scripture: but what response does it now give back to those who interpret it according to the individual criticism of the individual mind?"[114] In reinforcing the primacy of divine judgment, Manning had denounced the spirit of independent thought that Wilde, especially under the influence of Pater, would come to value as the cornerstone of aesthetic criticism. The distinction Manning drew between the seminary and the secular university effectively set faith in opposition to intellect. The sentiment is perhaps most powerfully articulated in his closing reflection: "The Divine Method like God himself is changeless. 'Fides ex auditu,' 'Faith cometh by hearing'—not by books."[115] Hunter-Blair recalls that Wilde, who enthusiastically accompanied him to this and other Catholic events at Oxford, was disheartened by what he had heard: "As [...] the discourse consisted in large part of a fierce denunciation of the tone and teaching of the University which Oscar and I both loved with all our hearts, we both came away feeling rather depressed."[116]

At times, Wilde's quest for spiritual clarity has been represented as in tension with his interest in achieving literary fame. Frequently, scholars have referred to Wilde's own words as evidence that he found himself at a crossroads in the 1870s, posed with a choice between worldly success and spiritual clarity: "If I *could hope* that the Church would wake in me some earnestness and purity," he wrote in 1877, "I would go over as a *luxury*, if for no better reason. But I can hardly hope it would, and to go over to Rome would be to sacrifice and give up my two great gods 'Money and Ambition.'"[117] As we have seen, however, Wilde's understanding of art, even at this early date, was already shaped by a belief in the divine. For this reason, it is quite telling that in the same letter, Wilde appends a postscript that again presents religious contemplation as an exercise at once pleasurable, sympathetic, subversive, and personal:

> *I have a vacant page.*
> I won't write to you theology, but I only say that for *you* to feel the fascination of Rome would to me be the greatest of pleasures: I think it would *settle me*. And really to go to Rome with the bugbear of formal logic on one's mind is quite as bad as to have the 'Protestant jumps'.
> But I know you are keenly alive to beauty, and do try and see in the Church not man's hand only but also a little of God's. Wilde, *Complete Letters*, 40.

Wilde characteristically wrote in a dense, fluid scrawl, his missives often filling every inch of every sheet. Availed of a rare "vacant page," Wilde uses the space to differentiate between "theology," which he refuses to discuss, and a personal encounter with divinity. It is, he suggests here, an experience that does not abide by "formal logic," an argument he had made on many earlier occasions and would make again in the future. Perhaps most strikingly, however, Wilde's understanding of the "beauty" to be seen in sites of worship is not strictly humanist or theological. Instead, Wilde elegantly articulates the point he repeatedly reverts to over the course of the 1870s and 1880s: that the aesthetic spectacle must be seen as a coalescence of the profane and divine, "not man's hand only but also a little of God's."

New Theologies

In a letter to Harding only a few weeks later, Wilde would refer to this period as "an era in my life, a crisis."[118] It was indeed: he was on the eve of his first visit to Rome, a visit that would bring him into the very presence of Pope Pius IX. For some biographers, Wilde's visit to Rome has been seen as a spiritual failure. Wilde was reportedly silent in the presence of the Pope but proclaimed the grave of John Keats to be "the holiest place in Rome."[119] Transposing the religious and the secular, Wilde noted at the time that "he *too* was a Martyr, and worthy to lie in the City of Martyrs."[120] Such a statement might well seem to indicate that Wilde had chosen to revere his fellow man and their aesthetic productions as worthier objects of devotion. Yet the vision of Keats as Saint Sebastian, the beautiful young martyr standing as a conduit between this world and the next, does not so much refute as reinforce the kind of theology Wilde had long been in the process of cultivating. The essence of religion, for Wilde, was its capacity for stirring the imagination and thus forging a conduit between this world and the next. Wilde's new theology would seek to demonstrate the fluidity between the things men craft—through a discipline that is itself a form of devotional practice—and the unseen world to which such artifacts might transport us.

One of the most striking details of Wilde's correspondence following his visit to Rome is the frequency with which he encloses drafts of his work to acquaintances. The poems he wrote and circulated at this time (for instance, "Rome Unvisited," "Easter Day," and "On the Recent Massacre of the Christians in Bulgaria") were decidedly religious in theme, and it is suggestive that Wilde's emergence as a poet coincided with what he had termed his "spiritual crisis."[121] Having received reports that the poem was popular among Catholic clergy, Wilde remarked to the Reverend Matthew Russell that he was "surprised at the way it has touched the hearts of the Catholic priests I have met. It was recited nine times at the Glencree Reformatory the day it arrived there!"[122] Significantly, these readings took place at the very site of Wilde's first Catholic baptism over a decade earlier. His surprise may have stemmed from the fact that the poem does not reflect the confidence of an unquestioning soul but rather one troubled with indecision, enticed by but not yet fully committed to the Catholic Church. Attempting to bridge the gap between the institutions of this world and the spiritual sanctuary of the next would become a hallmark of Wilde's prose works from this time forward.

Wilde's unique brand of Christology would ultimately find its most explicit outlet in his 1891 essay, "The Soul of Man Under Socialism" (which is discussed at greater length in Chap. 6). Inspired by his reading of Peter Kropotkin, an anarchist whom Wilde described as "a man of that soul of that beautiful white Christ which seems coming out of Russia," the essay presents Christ as a template for a new social order predicated paradoxically on leveling social difference in order to maximize individuality.[123] According to Kropotkin, capitalism and an undue focus on legislating behavior had diverted human society away from its natural evolutionary course, which was made less arduous through mutual aid and cooperation. In *Law and Authority* (1886), Kropotkin writes:

In existing States a fresh law is looked upon as a remedy for evil. Instead of themselves altering what is bad, people begin by demanding a *law* to alter it. [...] In short, a law everywhere and for everything! A law about fashions, a law about mad dogs, a law about virtue, a law to put a stop to all the vices and all the evils which result from human indolence and cowardice.[124]

In such a passage, it becomes readily apparent how Kropotkin's anarchism might have resonated with Wilde, who insists throughout "The Soul of Man Under Socialism" that "The Ideals that we owe to Christ are the ideals of the man who abandons society entirely, or of the man who resists society absolutely."[125] In Wilde's view, laws do not reflect innate or enduring social values but rather the attempts of a historically situated society to regulate and delimit individual liberty. It is a stipulation that would be echoed in the dictum uttered by Lord Henry Wotton in *The Picture of Dorian Gray*: "The only way to get rid of temptation is to yield to it."[126] If Wilde's contemporaries sometimes took this to reflect a kind of libertinism, it is worth recalling that Wilde's understanding of sin in the 1890s was largely based on a wariness of social restrictions he regarded as arbitrary and unnatural. For Lord Henry, abiding strictly by ethical laws *forged* by society and custom runs the risk of actually atrophying one's spirit: "[...] your soul grows sick with longing for the things it has forbidden to itself, with desire for what its monstrous laws have *made* monstrous and unlawful."[127]

Rather than reverting to Christ as a symbol of restraint, then, Wilde instead presents in "The Soul of Man Under Socialism" a vision of Christ as a kind of nonconformist, who values individual liberty as a key to salvation and spiritual peace. In Wilde's view, Christ's asceticism was less about self-denial than it was about acknowledging that the greatest value is the personality itself, for "man reaches his perfection, not through what he has, not even through what he does, but entirely through what he is."[128] Such a celebration of the self is strongly reminiscent of Lady Wilde's claim that "God is in thee;" even more telling, however, is Wilde's determination to dissolve the boundaries between religious and political philosophy by suggesting that Christ was himself a sort of antinomian, a thinker who valued individuality as the only sure way of sustaining community. "'Know thyself!' was written over the portal of the antique world. Over the portal of the new world, 'Be thyself' shall be written. And the message of Christ to man was simply 'Be thyself.' That is the secret of Christ."[129] Ellis Hanson has astutely noted that Wilde's attraction to Catholicism is inseparable from his attraction to art as a way of understanding the world. He writes: "Christ's divinity is apparent not in his pedigree but in his perfection, just as his truth is neither historical accuracy nor moral righteousness but the poetic truth of art—that is to say, the truth of lies."[130] Seen this way, Wilde was drawn to Christ because he embodies the perfection of form—and fiction—Wilde felt was essential to an understanding of this world. "For Wilde," Hanson elegantly notes, "the truth of Christ lay in his beauty as a poetic lie."[131]

Such an approach to the figure of Christ also sets Wilde in opposition to thinkers like Thomas à Kempis, whose *Imitation of Christ* (1418–27) Wilde devoured in 1877, upon his departure from Oxford. If Wilde appreciated the "Christocentric Catholicism" of Thomas à Kempis, as Joseph Pearce puts it, the work's doctrinal focus would seem to have been less appealing to him. Where Pearce notes Wilde's admiration for the figure of Christ encountered here, Wilde also remarked to William Ward that he had made a habit of reading Kempis at bedtime: "I think half-an-hour's warping of the inner man daily is greatly conducive to holiness."[132] This concern for the religious strictures of Kempis would find articulation in the "Soul of Man Under Socialism," where he would identify the emulation of moral exemplars as a decidedly un-Christian mode of being. "All imitation," Wilde noted, "in morals and in life is wrong."[133]

Wilde may well have cultivated this argument through his reading of Ernest Renan's *Vie de Jésus* (1863). In "The Critic as Artist" (1891), Wilde would suggest that the nineteenth century was a "turning point in history, simply on account of the work of two men, Darwin and Renan, the one the critic of the Book of Nature, the other the critic of the books of God."[134] Seeking to provide an authentic account of the origins of Christianity, Renan presents Christ as an historical personage, focusing more on his intellectual development than on his divinity. To this end, Renan's Christ emerges as "a man of supreme personality, who, by his bold originality, and by the love which he was able to inspire, became the object, and settled the direction, of the future faith of mankind."[135] Christ was, Renan asserts, an "indomitable revolutionary," an "anarchist" who sought to "revolt against paternal authority."[136] At bottom, Christ promoted a "pure worship, a religion without priests and external observances, resting wholly on the feelings of the heart, on the imitation of God, on the close communion of the conscience with the heavenly Father, were the results of these principles."[137] Such a vision of religious devotion carries strong echoes of Wilde's own fantasy of founding a "Confraternity of the Fatherless"—a worship that is not to be bound by dogma or hierarchy.

Perhaps more strikingly, however, Renan's understanding of Christ as a "supreme personality" helps to shed light on Wilde's remarks on the subject in *De Profundis*.[138] Directly invoking Renan's work as "that gracious fifth Gospel," Wilde reminds his reader that for Renan Christ's greatest feat was the cultivation of his own image: "[…] he made himself as much loved after his death as he had been during his lifetime. And certainly, if his place is among the poets, he is the leader of all the lovers."[139] For Renan, Christ's power resided in his profound sense of self-determination and sympathy:

> He did not argue with his disciples; he exacted from them no effort of attention. He did not preach his opinions; he preached himself. Very great and highly disinterested minds often present, associated with much loftiness, those characteristics of perpetual attention to themselves and extreme personal susceptibility which, in general, are peculiar to women. Their conviction that God is in them and perpetually occupies himself with them, is so strong that they have no dread of imposing themselves upon others; our reserve, and our respect for the opinion of others, which is a part of our weakness, could not belong to them. This exaltation of personality is not egoism; for such men, possessed by their idea, gladly give their lives to consummate their work; it is the identification of self with the object it has embraced, carried to its farthest point.[140]

Such a connection between the self and the divine, Renan suggests, found a unique outlet in Christ's language, his "vivid images" and "the pointed terseness, which we call wit, [which] adorned his aphorisms."[141] Indeed, the power of Christ's parables and lessons, such as Renan presents them to be, rely less upon their dogmatic underpinnings than on their capacity to arouse the imagination of his listener. The original Christian theology, as represented by Renan, becomes a curiously antinomian one: an "absolute religion, excluding nothing" and defined not by "rigid dogmas, but images susceptible of endless interpretations."[142]

Despite the echoes of Renan across *De Profundis*, Jan Gordon has noted that Wilde favored the confessional mode in prison, reading St. Augustine's *Confessions* and *De Civitate Dei*, Pascal's *Provincial Letters*, and Newman's *Apologia Pro Vita Sua*, among others. "Not unlike Newman," she writes, "who used his retreat to Littlemore as a metaphoric mental and emotional imprisonment from which to write a pastoral letter both to the faithful and to his accusers, Oscar Wilde uses the confessional overtones of the epistolary form to detail his 'conversion' to the new faith of hedonism."[143] Such a claim certainly makes sense within the context of Wilde's other writings—perhaps most obviously, Lord Henry Wotton's exuberant defense of "New Hedonism" in *The Picture of Dorian Gray*. Yet his prison writings suggest that Wilde's interest in the confessional genre was in fact a genuine work of spiritual reflection, one that had less to do with justifying his love of the material world than with returning to the spiritual quandaries of his youth. Admittedly, Wilde's words in *De Profundis* seem to belie an authentically religious experience. He writes:

> Religion does not help me. The faith that others give to what is unseen, I give to what one can touch, and look at. My gods dwell in temples made with hands; and within the circle of actual experience is my creed made perfect and complete: too complete, it may be, for like many or all of those who have placed their heaven in this earth, I have found in it not merely the beauty of heaven, but the horror of hell also.[144]

Admitting that he finds no succor in worship, Wilde might well seem to be without religion. His insistence upon worshiping "what one can touch, and look at" would seem to reinforce Wilde's reputation as a man of fashion who, as he noted to Oscar Browning "is perhaps a better judge of neckties than of bibles."[145] One might well recall that Wilde once regarded conversion as embattled with "two great gods, 'Money and Ambition.'"

In the context of Wilde's intellectual development, however, his invocation of gods that "dwell in temples made with hands" instead reminds us that Wilde did not wish to banish religion from this world but rather to see it manifested everywhere around us. When Wilde describes himself as "agnostic," then, we should understand this term in its nineteenth-century sense, as a rare acknowledgment that he did not and could not know everything about God:

> Every thing to be true must become a religion. And agnosticism should have its ritual no less than faith. It has sown its martyrs, it should reap its saints, and praise God daily for having hidden Himself from man. But whether it be faith or agnosticism, it must be nothing external to me. Its symbols must be of my own creating.[146]

To be an agnostic, even in the nineteenth century, was not quite the same as being a skeptic. An agnostic believes that true and complete knowledge of the divine is impossible and, believing the authority of religious dogma to be illusory, refuses to abide by any single set of theological doctrines. The agnostic does not necessarily doubt the existence of God or spirit; he doubts only that unerring knowledge of God or spirit is within our grasp. As Leslie Stephen put it in 1884, "[t]he Agnostic is one who asserts—what no one denies—that there are limits to the sphere of human intelligence."[147]

Following his release from prison, Wilde lived for a time in Rome, invited to travel with Harold Mellor and hoping to reunite with Robert Ross. When reporting his imminent arrival to Ross, he announced his intention to finally convert to Catholicism, though he characteristically admitted his misgivings on the subject: "I fear that if I went before the Holy Father with a blossoming rod it would turn at once into an umbrella or something dreadful of that kind. It is absurd to say that the age of miracles is past. It has not yet begun."[148] On the one hand, Wilde seems to recoil from the possibility of true conversion, perhaps fearing that he was too heretical to find a home in the Church. On the other hand, his speculation on the "age of miracles" reminds us that the formality of conversion may have been far less important to Wilde than spiritual *feeling*. Was the greater miracle a blossoming rod, Wilde seems to ask, or the prospect of a man like himself formally converting?

In Rome, Wilde's interest in Catholicism seems to have been rekindled. On Easter Day in 1900, he received the blessing of Pope Leo XIII and was apparently overcome by the Pope's charisma and presence: "He was wonderful as he was carried past me on his throne, not of flesh and blood, but a white soul robed in white, and an artist as well as a saint—the only instance in History, if the newspapers are to be believed."[149] Wilde's interest the Pope's physical appearance persisted over subsequent weeks. In May, Wilde informed Ross that he had "again seen the Holy Father. Each time he dresses differently; it is most delightful. Today over his white and purple a velvet cape edged with ermine, and a huge scarlet and gold stole. I was deeply moved as usual."[150] If it is tempting to view Wilde's fascination with the Pope's garments as further evidence of his attraction to visual ornament, it is surely significant that Wilde identifies the experience of these audiences as "moving"—so moving, in fact, that he would repeat these visits several times over the course of just two months. He confessed to More Adey: "I do nothing but see the Pope: I have already been blessed many times, once in the private Chapel of the Vatican. […] I spend all my money in getting tickets."[151]

Yet Wilde's experience of religious spectacle, while informed by aesthetic principles, was not strictly aesthetic in nature. On Easter Day, following his initial audience with Pope Leo XIII, Wilde describes glimpsing a bishop: "He was swarthy, and wore a yellow mitre. A sinister mediaeval man, but superbly Gothic, just like the Bishops carved on stalls or on portals. And when one thinks that once people mocked at stained-glass attitudes! They are the only attitudes for the clothed. The sight of this Bishop, whom I watched with fascination, filled me with the sense of the great realism of Gothic art."[152] In such a passage, Wilde seems to recall Ruskin's appraisal of the Gothic style (and perhaps his own juvenile impersonations of stained-glass figures). If Ruskin suggested that the Gothic conveyed man's religious passion at the expense of realism, Wilde reveals that certain elements of religious pageantry might access and invigorate the religious fervor that men really feel. Much as it might seem to belong to another, different world, spiritual experience was for Wilde very real and immediate. His interest in clerical vestments, seen this way, is less about a persistent fascination with visual spectacle than about the possibility that such spectacles might help us to recapture a dwindling capacity for divine reflection.

It is unsurprising, then, that Wilde was especially disappointed by some of the less inspiring forms of aesthetic devotion he witnessed at Rome. At one point, he laments that the Pope had "approved of a dreadful handkerchief, with a portrait of himself in the middle, and basilicas at the corners. Where I see the Pope I admire Bernini: but Bernini had a certain dash and life and assertion—theatrical life, but life for all that: the handkerchief is a dead thing."[153] Gian Lorenzo Bernini was an extraordinary seventeenth-century architect and sculpture, known especially for his work at St. Peter's Basilica, where the ornate *Baldachin* serves at once as a marker of human achievement and submission to a higher power. Bernini's work is renowned for its baroque style, fine detail, and religious fervor. Wilde's mention of Bernini here sharpens the contrast between the grandeur of the papacy as a religious spectacle and its reduction to a commercial and utilitarian object. The handkerchief was too much of this world to constitute a meaningful tribute to the Church Wilde had so long admired for its mysticism and extravagance. It is perhaps for this reason that, despite Wilde's fascination with Pope Leo XIII, he also warned that "there is danger in Popes."[154] As a divine incarnation, the Pope serves as a stirring object for the imagination, helping the soul to speculate upon the connection between the secular and the divine. As a man, however, the Pope became simply another participant in the world of political and economic competition. Reflecting on the incarceration of sixteenth-century Italian artist Benvenuto Cellini, Wilde reflected: "It was a Pope who said of Cellini to a conclave of Cardinals that common laws and common authority were not made for men such as he; but it was a Pope who thrust Cellini into prison, and kept him there till he sickened with rage."[155]

Confessional

It has been said that Wilde longed for Catholic conversion in his final days, and that may well be the case.[156] It is striking, however, that he more than once shrugged off suggestions that he might actually subscribe to Catholic doctrines. To More Adey, he wrote: "My position is curious: I am not a Catholic: I am simply a violent Papist. No one could be more 'black' than I am. I have given up bowing to the King. I need say no more."[157] Wilde's fidelity, in this passage at least, belongs to Catholic iconography rather than to any doctrinal system. This is not to suggest that Wilde merely appreciated the visual spectacle of Catholic ritual or that his interest in religion was leveraged principally in the service of art. For Wilde, iconography provided an immediate and personal (as opposed to liturgical or institutional) connection to the divine. While in Rome, at precisely the time he was repeatedly seeking an audience with the Pope, Wilde wrote to Robert Ross of his uncertainty as to how he might best classify his religious identity. "It is a curious and therefore natural thing," he writes, "but I cannot stand Christians because they are never Catholics, and I cannot stand Catholics because they are never Christians. Otherwise I am at one with the Indivisible Church."[158] As Wilde became more vocal about his desire to convert, he seems also to have more frankly confessed his fraught relationship to the Church. His remark that he "cannot stand Christians because they are never Catholics" certainly echoes his father's frustrating encounters with Christians abroad, whose doctrinal loyalties seemed ironically to negate the Christian spirit of benevolence and kinship.

Wilde himself remained, to the end, deeply attracted to a model of Christianity that would cultivate sympathy among men. It was in this spirit that he proclaimed himself to be in strict violation of Church doctrine regarding the atonement in a letter to Robert Ross: "Christ did not die to save people, but to teach people how to save each other. This is, I have no doubt, a grave heresy, but it is also a fact."[159] For Wilde, the spirit of Christ was perforce the spirit of communal feeling. If Christ was preeminently an individualist—an embodiment of the personal liberty Wilde repeatedly celebrated over the course of his life—that individualism could only thrive in a world that embraced human ties and rejected the institutional or doctrinal barriers that might rend them asunder. In *De Profundis*, Wilde thus writes: "But while Christ did not say to men, 'Live for others,' he pointed out that there was no difference at all between the lives of others and one's own life."[160] Like his mother, he embraced an understanding of the soul that was at once subjective and universal.

On 14 December 1900, Robert Ross wrote to More Adey, anticipating Wilde's passing. At the center of his account is a description of Wilde's formal conversion to Catholicism:

> They informed me that Oscar could not live for more than two days. His appearance was very painful, he had become quite thin, the flesh was livid, his breathing heavy. He was trying to speak. He was conscious that people were in the

room, and raised his hand when I asked him whether he understood. He pressed our hands. I then went in search of a priest, and after great difficulty found Father Cuthbert Dunne, of the Passionists, who came with me at once and administered Baptism and Extreme Unction—Oscar could not take the Eucharist. You know I had always promised to bring a priest to Oscar when he was dying, and I felt rather guilty that I had so often dissuaded him from becoming a Catholic, but you know my reasons for doing so.[161]

Scholars have suggested that Ross remained convinced that no conversion could prevent Wilde from returning to a life of indulgence and transgression, sexual, or otherwise.[162] One might also speculate that Ross recognized in Wilde an affinity for Catholicism that did not amount to true acceptance. After all, Wilde's confessions to Ross regarding his desire to convert more or less consistently reveal a man for whom spiritual reflection—not doctrinal faith—was the surest route to salvation.

It is impossible to state with any degree of certainty how Wilde understood his relationship to God. Such matters are, after all, variable, delicate, complicated, and deeply personal. We can, however, draw a few meaningful conclusions about Wilde's manner of engaging religion as an intellectual subject. Wilde's "Confraternity of the Fatherless" is not merely a sanctuary for decadents and aesthetes. Indeed, the rituals of this order feature "unblessed bread and a chalice empty of wine," a seeming departure from the appetitive luxuries with which Wilde is so often aligned. It is a church for those who struggle to bridge this world and the next, and unlike Matthew Arnold, who had lamented the Victorian "crisis of faith," Wilde at times seems to find beauty in that struggle. One of Wilde's most overtly religious poems, "Rome Unvisited"—the poem that was reportedly lauded by Newman himself—is revealing on this point. In this poem, which was read and reread by the Catholic priests at Glencree Reformatory, Wilde does not provide a declaration of faith but rather a statement of his own spiritual perplexity. As he reflects joyfully on the prospect of seeing "The only God-anointed King" in his own lifetime, the speaker only betrays the faintest hope of calling "upon the holy name / Of Him who now doth hide His face."[163] If Wilde is often aligned with the celebration of masks, performance, and even duplicity, it is worth noting that this proclivity extends even to his religious life. The challenge of conversion was, for Wilde, somewhat paradoxically rooted by his deep appreciation for divine mystery. It is the moment of suspended belief that captivates Wilde's attention.

Such a moment is depicted, I think, with special beauty in Wilde's "Santa Decca." Wilde's poem invokes a still and silent place, stripped bare by the knowledge that divinity no longer has a place in this world: "The Gods are dead." In the second and final stanza, however, the speaker calls upon his companion to speculate on the possibility that new deities will come to take their place. The mystification and suspense of these final lines might well apply to Wilde's own faltering encounters with faith:

> And yet—perchance in this sea-trancèd isle,
> Chewing the bitter fruit of memory,
> Some God lies hidden in the asphodel.
> Ah Love! If such there be then it were well
> For us to fly his anger: nay, but see
> The leaves are stirring: let us watch a while.[164]

Notes

1. Oscar Wilde, *Complete Letters of Oscar Wilde*, ed. Merlin Holland and Rupert Hart-Davis (New York: Henry Holt and Company, 2000), 732.
2. Douglas Sladen, *Twenty Years of My Life* (New York: E.P. Dutton and Company, 1913), 109–100. G.T. Atkinson offered a similar account in 1929. According to this report, the proctor asked Wilde: "Are you taking Divinity or Substituted Matter?" The examination on Divinity typically focused on Anglican doctrine, but non-Anglicans were permitted to substitute material more germane to their own faith. Wilde reportedly replied: "Oh, the Forty-Nine Articles." When the proctor reminded him that it was the Thirty-Nine Articles that defined the Anglican faith, Wilde is said to have replied: "Oh, is it really?" G.T Atkinson, "Oscar Wilde at Oxford," *Cornhill Magazine* 66 (May 1929), 562.
3. It is an oft-repeated biographical detail that Wilde failed the Divinity and was compelled to repeat it again two years later. See for instance Merlin Holland, *Oscar Wilde: A Life in Letters* (New York: Fourth Estate, 2003), 37.
4. See for instance Richard Ellmann, *Oscar Wilde* (New York: Random House, 1984), 53–4; Joseph Pearce astutely notes that Wilde occasionally rejects or questions religious ritual as well, as in his "Sonnet on Hearing the Dies Irae Sung in the Sistine Chapel." See Joseph Pearce, *The Unmasking of Oscar Wilde* (San Francisco: Ignatius Press, 2000), 135.
5. Ellmann, 53–54.
6. Ellmann, 54. Ronald Schuchard offers a compelling counterpoint to Ellmann's account, noting that Wilde's fascination with Karl de Huysmans's *À Rebours*—that volume sometimes suspected as a source for Dorian Gray's sensory education—is less a sign of hedonism than of spiritual struggle. The

hero of Huysmans's novel, Des Esseintes, was raised by Jesuits, and his narrative is arguably the story of a prodigal son who abandons his faith only to rediscover and redefine it. Schuchard writes: "Wilde clearly found in Huysmans [...] the syndrome of his own spiritual condition, and for the rest of his life he was to follow the spiritual progress of the French revivalists and to employ them as models for his own life." Ronald Schuchard, "Wilde's Dark Angel and the Spell of Decadent Catholicism," in *Rediscovering Oscar Wilde*, ed. C. George Sandulescu (Gerrards Cross: Colin Smythe, 1994): 371–96, 381.

7. Guy Willoughby, *Art and Christhood: The Aesthetics of Oscar Wilde* (Rutherford: Farleigh Dickinson University Press, 1993), 15.

8. Ellis Hanson, *Decadence and Catholicism* (Cambridge: Harvard University Press, 1997), 95. See also Terry Eagleton, *Saint Oscar* (Bloomington: Indiana University, 2004); Patrick R. O'Malley, "Religion," *Palgrave Studies in Oscar Wilde*, ed. Frederick S. Roden (London: Palgrave, 2004): 167–88. Stephen Arata elegantly outlines Wilde's complex appraisal of Christ as an "incarnate image"—a body whose power is "finally indistinguishable from the power of an ideal art." Stephen Arata, "Oscar Wilde and Jesus Christ," in *Wilde Writings: Contextual Conditions*, ed. Joseph Bristow (Toronto: University of Toronto Press, 2003): 254–72, 265.

9. Pearce, 16.

10. Pearce, 91.

11. Wilde, *Complete Letters*, 270.

12. J.P. Mahaffy, *The Decay of Preaching*, (London: Macmillan, 1882), 134.

13. Jarlath Killeen, *The Faiths of Oscar Wilde: Catholicism, Folklore, and Ireland* (London: Palgrave, 2005), 5.

14. The influence of Maturin on Lady Wilde's understanding of poetic genius has been noted in passing by several biographers and scholars. See Karen Sasha Anthony Tipper, *A Critical Biography of Lady Jane Wilde, 1821?–1896, Irish Revolutionist, Humanist, Scholar and Poet* (Lewiston: The Edwin Mellen Press, 2002), 420; Terence de Vere White, *The Parents of Oscar Wilde: Sir William and Lady Wilde* (London: Hodder and Stoughton, 1967), 276; Eric Lambert, *Mad With Much Heart: A Life of the Parents of Oscar Wilde* (London: Frederick Muller, 1967), 55–7; and Joy Melville, *Mother of Oscar* (London: John Murray, 1994), 10.

15. Charles Robert Maturin, *Melmoth the Wanderer* (New York: Penguin, 2000), 126.

16. Maturin, 119–120. It is worth noting, however, that Maturin also produced writings that more closely approximate social criticism, as in his novel *Women; or, Pour et contre* (1818), a pointed satire of religious extremism. Thus, while Joy Melville has detailed the many ways in which Lady Wilde emulated Maturin's posture as an eccentric man of letters—for instance, in her preference to keep the shutters drawn during the day to cultivate a more

dramatic atmosphere—Maturin may also have informed Lady Wilde's impulse to unite social action, literary taste, and religious sentiment.

17. Terry Eagleton proposes a more erotic charge to the image of St. Sebastian, conflating it with the destructive power of love itself. In Eagleton's play *Saint Oscar*, Wilde proclaims: "I love him [Lord Alfred Douglas] as the torturer's victim loves the knife that will put him out of his agony; as Saint Sebastian loved the arrows" (19).

18. In a letter to Lord Houghton that same year, Wilde compared John Keats to "a Priest of Beauty slain before his time, a lovely Sebastian killed by the arrows of a lying and unjust tongue" (*Complete Letters*, 49). Wilde may well have conflated this image with those he viewed only two years earlier at the Etruscan Museum in the monastery of San Onofrio. At the time, Wilde described to his father the following: "You come first to a big tomb, transplanted lintel, roof slightly conical, walls covered with wonderfully beautiful frescoes, representing first the soul in the shape of a young man naked, led by a beautifully winged angel or genius to the two-horsed chariot which is to convey them to Elysium—and then represents the banquet which awaits him" (*Complete Letters*, 8).

19. In his fascinating essay "Wilde's Exquisite Pain," for example, Ellis Hanson refers in passing to the figure of St. Sebastian as a "favorite classical emblem of gay male masochism." See Ellis Hanson, "Wilde's Exquisite Pain," in *Wilde Writings: Contextual Conditions*, ed. Joseph Bristow (Toronto: University of Toronto Press, 2003): 101–23, 119.

20. William Sachs, *Homosexuality and the Crisis of Anglicanism* (Cambridge: Cambridge University Press, 2009), 184. See also James Eli Adams, *Dandies and Desert Saints: Styles of Victorian Masculinity* (Ithaca: Cornell University Press, 1995).

21. Sachs, 184.

22. David Hunter Blair, "Oscar Wilde as I Knew Him," in *Victorian Days and Other Papers* (Freeport, NY: Books for Libraries Press, 1939): 115–43, 125–6.

23. Additionally, the will stipulated that Wilson would only cede his share of a fishing lodge in Connemara to Wilde provided that he not convert for at least five years.

24. Wilde, *Complete Letters*, 54. Wilde would recycle this sentiment in a letter to William Ward just a few weeks later: "I have suffered very much for my Roman fever in mind and *pocket* and happiness" (*Complete Letters*, 57). Killeen claims that Wilde's religious identity was also inseparable from his support of Irish nationalism, thus suggesting that Wilde's interest in matters of religious doctrine were as much secular as they were spiritual.

25. See Killeen, for instance.

26. According to T.G. Wilson, Oscar Wilde "retailed many of his father's stories" about Ousley and, impressed by the name itself, "recommended a

friend of his to write a book with the title 'Gideon Ouseley.'" T.G. Wilson, *Victorian Doctor: Being the Life of Sir William Wilde* (New York: L.B. Fischer, 1946), 7.

27. Wilson, 5–6. See also Lambert, 6–7; White, 37.
28. Oscar Wilde, "Early Christian Art in Ireland" [1887], in *Journalism 2*, ed. John Stokes and Mark Turner, vol. 7 of *The Complete Works of Oscar Wilde* (Oxford: Oxford University Press, 2013): 38–39, 38.
29. William Wilde, *Narrative of a Voyage to Madeira, Teneriffe, and Along the Shores of the Mediterranean* (Dublin, William Curry Jun. and Company, 1840), 153. The Scriptural account appears, for instance, in Ezekiel 26:19–21: "For thus saith the Lord God; When I shall make thee a desolate city, like the cities that are not inhabited; when I shall bring up the deep upon thee, and great waters shall cover thee; / When I shall bring thee down with them that descend into the pit, with the people of old time, and shall set thee in the low parts of the earth, in places desolate of old, with them that go down to the pit, that thou be not inhabited; and I shall set glory in the land of the living; / I will make thee a terror, and thou shalt be no more: though thou be sought for, yet shalt thou ne'er be found again, saith the Lord God."
30. William Wilde, *Narrative*, 378.
31. L.C.P. Fox, "People I have met," *Donahoe's Magazine* 53:4 (1905): 465–78, 472.
32. As Richard Ellmann rightly notes, private baptisms often remained unregistered, so the absence of any record of the event is unsurprising (19–20). Still, it is important to note that this event, like so many in Wilde's life, remain open to speculation.
33. Fox did eventually report the baptism to William Wilde, who is rumored to have replied: "he did not care what they were so long as they became as good as their mother" (Fox, 472).
34. Tipper, 13.
35. Lady Wilde, "The Exodus," in *Poems by Speranza* (Glasgow: Cameron and Ferguson, 1871): 43–45, 45 [lines 62–65].
36. Lady Wilde, "The Faithless Shepherds," in *Poems by Speranza* (Glasgow: Cameron and Ferguson, 1871): 45–47, 47 [lines 78–79].
37. Lady Wilde, *Ancient Legends, Mystic Charms, and Superstitions of Ireland* (London: Ward and Downey, 1888), 8.
38. Lady Wilde, "Philip James Bailey," in *Notes on Men, Women, and Books* (London: Ward and Downey, 1891): 261–85, 282.
39. Lady Wilde, "Bailey," 282–3.
40. It is a matter of some dispute whether or not she ever completed this work. Joy Melville suggests the changes to the new edition were quite minor, so that any work Lady Wilde may have done to correct the translation were practically negligible. See Melville, 56.

41. Lady Wilde, "Bailey," 263.
42. Lady Wilde, "Divinity of Humanity," in *Essays and Stories* (Boston: C.T. Brainard, 1909), 126–127.
43. Lady Wilde, *Ancient Legends*, 3.
44. Lady Wilde, "Bailey," 283.
45. Oscar Wilde, "Panthea," in *Poems and Poems in Prose*, ed. Bobby Fong and Karl Beckson, vol. 1 of *The Complete Works of Oscar Wilde* (Oxford: Oxford University Press, 2000), 10–15, 15 [lines 172–4].
46. Lady Wilde, "The Parable of Life," in *Poems by Speranza* (Glasgow: Cameron and Ferguson, 1871): 75–80, 75 [line 2].
47. Lady Wilde, "The Parable of Life," 75 [lines 38–40].
48. Lady Wilde, "The Parable of Life," 78 [lines 117–120].
49. The French phrase translates literally as: "… *but I am truly an egoist*" (my translation). Qtd. in Melville, 41.
50. Wilde, *Complete Letters*, 25.
51. Lady Jane Wilde, "Salvation," in *Poems by Speranza* (Glasgow: Cameron and Ferguson, 1871): 108–109, 109 [lines 19–26].
52. Wilde, *De Profundis*, in *De Profundis. "Epistola: In Carcere Et Vinculis,"* ed. Russell Jackson and Ian Small, vol. 2 of *The Complete Works of Oscar Wilde* II (Oxford: Oxford University Press, 2007), 96.
53. Suggestively, Walter Kenilworth would note in 1912 that Wilde's understanding of spiritual life celebrated "the consciousness of divinity within one's own nature." Walter Winston Kenilworth, *A Study of Oscar Wilde* (New York: R.F. Fenno, 1912), 97.
54. One of the most famous challenges to the secularization thesis appears in Charles Taylor's *A Secular Age* (Cambridge: Harvard University Press, 2007).
55. Charles LaPorte, *Victorian Poets and the Changing Bible* (Charlottesville: University of Virginia Press, 2011).
56. George Jacob Holyoake, *The Logic of Life* (London: Austin and Company, 1870), 16.
57. As Michael Rectenwald notes, the secular is itself "far from being merely a space devoid of religion, is never neutral or content-free; rather, the secular always contains substantive elements, including social, political, economic, and other content and meaning." Michael Rectenwald, *Nineteenth Century British Secularism: Science, Religion, and Literature* (New York: Palgrave, 2016), 5.
58. The most comprehensive discussion of Wilde's life at Portora remains Heather White's *"Forgotten Schooldays:" Oscar Wilde at Portora Royal School, Iniskillen, County Fermanagh, Ireland, 1864 to 1871* (Fermanagh: Principia Press, 2002). See also Ellmann, 21–4; Iain Ross, *Oscar Wilde and Ancient Greece* (Cambridge: Cambridge University Press, 2012), 18–25.
59. White, 34–5.

60. William Steele, *A sermon preached at Portora Royal School, on Sunday, June 14, 1864* (Dublin: M.H. Gill, 1864), 10.

61. Steele, *A sermon*, 11.

62. Qtd. in Frank Harris, *Oscar Wilde: His Life and Confessions* (New York, 1916), 25.

63. Harris, 25.

64. Stuart Mason, *Bibliography of Oscar Wilde* (London: T.W. Laurie, Ltd., 1906), 295.

65. Boris Brasol, *Oscar Wilde: The Man, The Artist* (London: Williams and Norgate Ltd., 1938), 23.

66. Hunter-Blair, "Oscar Wilde as I Knew Him," 135–36.

67. William Bedell Stanford and Robert Brendan McDowell, *Mahaffy: A Biography of an Anglo-Irishman* (New York: Routledge and Kegan Paul, 1971), 41.

68. For further background on Mahaffy's extensive religious education, see Kimberly J. Stern, "On the Publication of J.P. Mahaffy's *The Decay of Modern Preaching*," BRANCH [http://www.branchcollective.org]

69. Mahaffy, *Decay*, 13–4.

70. Mahaffy, *Decay*, 15.

71. Mahaffy, *Decay*, 134.

72. The essay has only been mentioned only once before in the context of Wilde's career, in Emer O'Sullivan's *The Fall of the House of Wilde* (New York: Bloomsbury Press, 2016), 148. O'Sullivan notes chiefly that Mahaffy's book highlights the value of rhetoric and intelligence in preaching.

73. Oscar Wilde, "The Decay of Lying," *Criticism*, ed. Josephine M. Guy, vol. 4 of *The Complete Works of Oscar Wilde* (Oxford: Oxford University Press, 2007): 73–103, 94.

74. Oscar Wilde, "The Critic as Artist," *Criticism*, ed. Josephine M. Guy, vol. 4 of *The Complete Works of Oscar Wilde* (Oxford: Oxford University Press, 2007): 123–206, 186.

75. Oscar Wilde, "A Fascinating Book" in *Journalism 2*, ed. John Stokes and Mark Turner, vol. 7 of *The Complete Works* of Oscar Wilde (Oxford: Oxford University Press, 2013): 88–96, 90.

76. By contrast, Wilde's other noteworthy treatment of Islam came in the form of a sonnet, "On the Massacre of the Christians in Bulgaria," a poem that draws a stark binary between the Christian and Muslim and proclaims: "Come down, O Son of God! incestuous gloom / Curtains the land, and through the starless night / Over thy Cross a Crescent moon I see!" Oscar Wilde, "On the Massacre of the Christians in Bulgaria," in *Poems and Poems in Prose*, ed. Bobby Fong and Karl Beckson, vol. 1 of *The Complete Works of Oscar Wilde* (Oxford: Oxford University Press, 2000), 36–7 [lines 9–11]. Wilde sent the sonnet to William Gladstone, inquiring if he might assist in getting the poem published (*Complete Letters*, 46–7). Gladstone had recently

written *The Bulgarian Horrors and the Question of the East* (1876), which often reverts to inflammatory and racially charged language.

77. Wilde, "The Critic as Artist," 99.

78. Wilde, "The Critic as Artist," 100.

79. Lord Ronald Gower, *My Reminiscences* (London: Kegan Paul, 1883), 134. A Catholic priest observed around the same time: "Behind his superficial veneer of vanity and foolish talk there is, I am convinced, something deeper and more sincere, including a genuine attraction toward Catholic belief and practice. But the time has not come. The finger of God has not yet touched him." Qtd. in E.H. Mikhail, ed., *Oscar Wilde: Interviews and Recollections*, vol. 1 (New York: Barnes and Noble, 1979), 7.

80. Hunter-Blair, "Oscar Wilde as I Knew Him," 128.

81. See Ellmann, 69. Ellmann identifies painting in question as "Christ and Magdalen," though to my knowledge the work by Burne-Jones best fitting this description (and also available to Wilde in the 1870s) would have been *Noli me Tangere*, a stained-glass piece designed by Burne-Jones and executed by William Morris for Jesus Church (Troutbeck) in 1873.

82. Oscar Wilde, "The Grosvenor Gallery," in *Journalism I*, ed. John Stokes and Mark Turner, vol. 6 of *The Complete Works of Oscar Wilde* (Oxford: Oxford University Press, 2013): 1–11, 7. Walter Pater, *Studies in the History of the Renaissance* (London: Macmillan, 1873), 210.

83. Wilde, "The Grosvenor Gallery," 7.

84. Hunter-Blair, "Oscar Wilde as I Knew Him," 128.

85. Hunter-Blair, "Oscar Wilde as I Knew Him," 125.

86. Wilde, *Complete Letters*, 11.

87. Wilde, *Complete Letters*, 22.

88. Wilde, *Complete Letters*, 21.

89. Wilde, *Complete Letters*, 22–23.

90. Wilde, *Complete Letters*, 23.

91. Wilde, *Complete Letters*, 23.

92. Wilde, *Complete Letters*, 25.

93. Wilde, *Complete Letters*, 26.

94. Like Wilde, Walter Pater admired the aesthetic quality of Catholic churches, a sentiment he repeatedly expresses in his novel of spiritual development, *Marius the Epicurean* (1885). Thomas Wright characterizes Pater as being a "great lover of hymns" and reports that he once remarked: "The Church of England is nothing to me apart from its ornate services." Qtd. in Thomas Wright, vol. 2 of *The Life of Walter Pater* (London: Everett and Co., 1907), 38. This impulse has led many scholars to conclude that Wilde too valued religion chiefly for the aesthetic spectacles it sometimes made possible, though it is worth noting that in later years Pater regarded his lack of faith as a predicament rather than as a choice, describing theology as a "great house,

scored all over with hieroglyphics by perished hands." Walter Pater, "Coleridge's Writings," *Westminster Review* (January 1866): 48–60. 58.

95. John Ruskin, *Praeterita* (London: George Allen, 1908), 128.

96. Ruskin, *Praeterita*, 495.

97. Ruskin, *Praeterita*, 495–6.

98. Ruskin, *Praeterita*, 480.

99. Wilde, *Complete Letters*, 349.

100. Norbert Kohl, *Oscar Wilde: The Works of a Conformist Rebel* (Cambridge: Cambridge University Press, 2011), 78.

101. John Ruskin, *Queen of the Air*, vol. 9 of *The Works of John Ruskin* (Sunnyside: George Allen, 1874), 18.

102. Ruskin, *Queen*, 19, 31.

103. George P. Landow, *Ruskin* (New York: Routledge, 1985).

104. Wilde, *Complete Letters*, 1191.

105. John Ruskin, *Modern Painters* 2 (New York: John Wiley, 1862), 50.

106. Ruskin, *Modern Painters* 51.

107. To my knowledge, Wilde's letter to Newman does not survive but is frequently mentioned, for instance, in Sherard, 146 and Ellmann, 57.

108. Wilde, *Complete Letters*, 25.

109. Wilde, *Complete Letters*, 41.

110. Wilde, *Complete Letters*, 665n.

111. John Henry Newman, *The Idea of a University* (London: Longmans, Green, and Company, 1891), xi.

112. Newman, *Idea*, 152.

113. John Henry Newman, *An Essay in Aid of a Grammar of Assent* (London: Burns, Oates, and Company, 1870), 103–104.

114. Henry Edward Cardinal Manning, *Dominus Illuminatio Mea*, (London: Longmans, Green, and Company, 1875), 19.

115. Manning, 21.

116. Hunter-Blair, "Oscar Wilde as I Knew Him," 127. Both Richard Ellmann and Joseph Pearce have understood Wilde's remark that he found Manning "fascinating" on an earlier occasion (having seen him preach on 9 July 1876 at The Church of Our lady of Victories in High Street Kensington) to mean that he was attracted by his theology. His later responses to both Newman and Manning suggest that he took issue with both theological approaches but ultimately found the former to be a source of greater intellectual insight. See Ellmann, 59 and Pearce, 85.

117. Wilde would go on to suggest that the Church provided merely a source of consolation in troubled times: "Still I get so wretched and low and troubled that in some desperate mood I will seek the shelter of a Church which simply enthralls me by its fascination. I hope that now in the Sacred City you are wakened up from the Egyptian darkness that has blinded you. *Do* be touched by it, *feel* the awful fascination of the Church, its extreme beauty

and sentiment, and let every part of your nature have play and room" (*Complete Letters*, 38–39).

118. Wilde, *Complete Letters,* 43.

119. Wilde, *Complete Letters,* 247. Wilde's quip about the grave of Keats was not made until January 1885 in a letter to the Reverend J. Page Hopps. The sentiment, however, was made plain on multiple occasions immediately following Wilde's visit to that site.

120. Wilde, *Complete Letters,* 49.

121. See Wilde, *Complete Letters,* 16; 49, 56–57; 46. Some of these poems ("San Minato," "E Tenebris," or "Vita Nuova," for instance) seem to articulate a familiar tension between faith covert sin—a struggle biographers have often interpreted as early evidence of Wilde's struggle to accept his own sexual identity.

122. Wilde, *Complete Letters,* 53.

123. Wilde, *De Profundis,* 124.

124. Peter Kropotkin, *Law and Authority: An Anarchist Essay* (London: International Publishing Company, 1886), 1–2.

125. Oscar Wilde, "The Soul of Man Under Socialism," in *Criticism*, ed. Josephine M. Guy, vol. 4 of *The Complete Works of Oscar Wilde* IV (Oxford: Oxford University Press, 2007): 231–68, 265.

126. Oscar Wilde, *The Picture of Dorian Gray* (1891), in *The Picture of Dorian Gray: The 1890 and 1891 Texts,* ed. Joseph Bristow, vol. 3 of *The Complete Works of Oscar Wilde* (Oxford: Oxford University Press, 2005), 21.

127. Wilde, *Dorian Gray,* 21. Emphasis added. As Jeff Nunokawa has put it, Wilde's penchant for the "forbidden indulgence" is thus curiously ethical at its center. In order to discipline "questionable" desires, one must first embrace it, "rather like the martial art by which one exhausts and confuses the enemy force by first yielding to it." Jeff Nunokawa, *Tame Passions of Wilde: The Styles of Manageable Desire* (Princeton: Princeton University Press, 2003), 6.

128. Wilde, "Soul of Man," 241.

129. Wilde, "Soul of Man," 240.

130. Hanson, *Decadence and Catholicism,* 238.

131. Hanson, *Decadence and Catholicism,* 241.

132. Wilde, *Complete Letters,* 21.

133. Wilde, "Soul of Man," 241.

134. Wilde, "Critic as Artist," 205. See Arata for an especially detailed examination of Wilde's engagement with Renan.

135. Ernest Renan, *Life of Jesus* (London: W. Scott, 1897), 1.

136. Renan, *Life of Jesus,* 50, 81, 27.

137. Renan, *Life of Jesus,* 58.

138. Stephen Arata describes *De Profundis* as Wilde's attempt to write a gospel of his own, thereby not only invoking but actually following the model of

Christ whose moment of climactic suffering served as an essential narrative function: "In Wilde's view, the crucifixion confers meaning retrospectively on all Christ's actions by binding those actions into a narrative whole" (Arata, 263–4). Arata too notes the influence of Renan upon Wilde's language and treatment of Christ in *De Profundis*.

139. Renan, *Life of Jesus*, 50.
140. Renan, *Life of Jesus*, 50.
141. Renan, *Life of Jesus*. 58.
142. Renan, *Life of Jesus*, 279–80.
143. Jan B. Gordon, "Wilde and Newman: the Confessional Mode," *Renascence* 22. 4 (Summer 1970): 183–91, 183.
144. Wilde, *De Profundis*, 165.
145. Wilde, *Complete Letters*, 80. Wilde was responding to Oscar Browning's request that he should procure for him a specific edition of a bible and prayer book. It is worth noting that Wilde follows this remark by noting: "but I shall not fail to enquire about the latter."
146. Wilde, *De Profundis*, 165.
147. Leslie Stephen, *An Agnostic's Apology and Other Essays* (London: Smith, Elder, and Co., 1893), 1.
148. Wilde, *Complete Letters*, 1177.
149. Wilde, *Complete Letters*, 1181–82.
150. Wilde, *Complete Letters*, 1186.
151. Wilde, *Complete Letters*, 1184.
152. Wilde, *Complete Letters*, 1179–80. The language closely parallels Wilde's 1881 poem "Easter Day," in which he describes the Pope in these terms: "Priest-like, he wore a robe more white than foam, / And, king-like, swathed himself in royal red, / Three crowns of gold rise high upon his head." In the poem, the spectacle of the Pope—dressed in elaborate raiment and surrounded by throngs of people—paradoxically calls to the speaker's mind the image of Christ "who wandered by a lonely sea, / And sought in vain for any place of rest." Oscar Wilde, "Easter Day," in *Poems and Poems in Prose*, ed. Bobby Fong and Karl Beckson, vol. 1 of *The Complete Works of Oscar Wilde* (Oxford: Oxford University Press, 2000): 34 [lines 5–7, 10–11].
153. Wilde, *Complete Letters*, 1181–82.
154. Wilde, "Soul of Man Under Socialism," 261.
155. Wilde, "Soul of Man Under Socialism," 261.
156. Nicholas Frankel rightly notes that it would be a mistake to understand Wilde's enduring fascination with the Church as reflecting a renewed interest in conversion. See Nicholas Frankel, *Oscar Wilde: The Unrepentant Years* (Cambridge: Harvard University Press, 2017), 267.
157. Wilde, *Complete Letters*, 1184.
158. Wilde, *Complete Letters*, 1191.
159. Wilde, *Complete Letters*, 709.

160. Wilde, *De Profundis* 114.
161. Wilde, *Complete Letters*, 1219–1220.
162. This approach may find its origins in Hesketh Pearson's second-hand account of Wilde's conversion: "Somehow I had got the impression that Ross was a very keen Catholic, and was amazed when he told me that he was a confirmed Atheist. 'But weren't you responsible for Wilde's deathbed conversion?' I asked. 'Oh, I was a Catholic in those days right enough,' he replied, 'though I most certainly was not responsible for Wilde's conversion—in fact, I wasn't a bit keen on it, as it wouldn't have suited his constitution and no priest could possibly have listened to his confessions in a becoming frame of mind. No, he made me promise to bring a priest when he was no longer in a fit condition to shock one, which I did.'" Hesketh Pearson, *Modern Man and Mummers* (New York: Harcourt, Brace and Company, 1922), 156. By contrast, Giles Whiteley suggests that Ross took a leading role in Wilde's deathbed conversion: "Wilde's actual conversion was orchestrated by Robert Ross, if not against his wishes, then at least without his knowledge, and seems to have been more to do with Ross's guilt, as he incorrectly thought, over having introduced Wilde to homosexuality, than any real desire on Wilde's part." Giles Whitely, *Oscar Wilde and the Simulacrum: The Truth of Masks* (Cambridge: Cambridge University Press, 2013), 170.
163. Oscar Wilde, "Rome Unvisited," in *Poems and Poems in Prose*, ed. Bobby Fong and Karl Beckson, vol. 1 of *The Complete Works of Oscar Wilde* (Oxford: Oxford University Press, 2000): 7–10, 10 [lines 55–6].
164. Oscar Wilde, "Santa Decca," in *Poems and Poems in Prose*, ed. Bobby Fong and Karl Beckson, vol. 1 of *The Complete Works of Oscar Wilde* (Oxford: Oxford University Press, 2000),: 43–4. 44 [lines 9–14].

Bibliography

Adams, James Eli. 1995. *Dandies and Desert Saints: Styles of Victorian Masculinity*. Ithaca: Cornell University Press.

Arata, Stephen. 2003. Oscar Wilde and Jesus Christ. In *Wilde Writings: Contextual Conditions*, ed. Joseph Bristow, 254–272. Toronto: University of Toronto Press.

Atkinson, G.T. 1929. Oscar Wilde at Oxford. *Cornhill Magazine* 66 (May): 562.

The Bible. Authorized King James Version. 1998. Oxford: Oxford University Press.

Brasol, Boris. 1938. *Oscar Wilde: The Man, the Artist*. London: Williams and Norgate.

Eagleton, Terry. 2004. *Saint Oscar*. Bloomington: Indiana University.

Ellmann, Richard. 1987. *Oscar Wilde*. New York: Alfred A. Knopf.

Fox, L.C.P. 1905. People I have met. *Donahoe's Magazine* 53 (4): 465–478.

Frankel, Nicholas. 2017. *Oscar Wilde: The Unrepentant Years*. Cambridge: Harvard University Press.

Gordon, Jan B. 1970. Wilde and Newman: The Confessional Mode. *Renascence* 22 (4): 183–191.

Gower, Lord Ronald. 1883. *My Reminiscences*. London: Kegan Paul.

Hanson, Ellis. 1997. *Decadence and Catholicism*. Cambridge: Harvard University Press.

———. 2003. Wilde's Exquisite Pain. In *Wilde Writings: Contextual Conditions*, ed. Joseph Bristow, 101–123. Toronto: University of Toronto Press.

Harris, Frank. 1916. *Oscar Wilde: His Life and Confessions*. New York.

Holland, Merlin. 2003. *Oscar Wilde: A Life in Letters*. New York: Fourth Estate.

Holyoake, George Jacob. 1870. *The Logic of Life*. London: Austin.

Hunter-Blair, David. 1939. Oscar Wilde as I Knew him. In *Victorian Days and Other Papers*, 115–143. Freeport: Books for Libraries Press.

Kenilworth, Walter Winston. 1912. *A Study of Oscar Wilde*. New York: R.F. Fenno.

Killeen, Jarlath. 2005. *The Faiths of Oscar Wilde: Catholicism, Folklore, and Ireland*. London: Palgrave.

Kohl, Norbert. 2011. *Oscar Wilde: The Works of a Conformist Rebel*. Cambridge: Cambridge University Press.

Kropotkin, Peter. 1886. *Law and Authority: An Anarchist Essay*. London: International Publishing Company.

Lambert, Eric. 1967. *Mad with Much Heart: A Life of the Parents of Oscar Wilde*. London: Frederick Muller.

Landow, George P. 1985. *Ruskin*. New York: Routledge.

Manning, Henry Edward Cardinal. 1875. *Dominus Illuminatio Mea*. London: Longmans, Green, and Company.

Mason, Stuart. 1906. *Bibliography of Oscar Wilde*. London: T.W. Laurie.

Maturin, Charles Robert. 2000. *Melmoth the Wanderer*. New York: Penguin.

Melville, Joy. 1994. *Mother of Oscar*. London: John Murray.

Mikhail, E. H., ed. Oscar Wilde: Interviews and Recollections. Vol. 1. New York: Barnes and Noble, 1979.

Newman, John Henry Cardinal. 1870. *An Essay in Aid of a Grammar of Assent*. London: Burns, Oates, and Company.

———. 1878. *Adapted to the Seasons of the Ecclesiastical Year from Parochial and Plain Sermons*. London: Rivingtons.

———. 1891. *The Idea of a University*. London: Longmans, Green, and Company.

Nunokawa, Jeff. 2003. *Tame Passions of Wilde: The Styles of Manageable Desire*. Princeton: Princeton University Press.

O'Malley, Patrick R. 2004. Religion. In *Palgrave Studies in Oscar Wilde*, ed. Frederick S. Roden, 167–188. London: Palgrave.

O'Sullivan, Emer. 2016. *The Fall of the House of Wilde*. New York: Bloomsbury Press.

Pater, Walter. 1866. Coleridge's Writings. *Westminster Review* (January): 48–60.

———. 1873. *Studies in the History of the Renaissance*. London: Macmillan.

Pearce, Joseph. 2000. *The Unmasking of Oscar Wilde*. San Francisco: Ignatius Press.

Pearson, Hesketh. 1922. *Modern Man and Mummers*. New York: Harcourt, Brace and Company.

Rectenwald, Michael. 2016. *Nineteenth Century British Secularism: Science, Religion, and Literature*. New York: Palgrave.

Renan, Ernest. 1897. *Life of Jesus*. London: W. Scott.

Ruskin, John. 1862. *Modern Painters*. Vol. 2. New York: John Wiley.

———. 1874. Queen of the Air. In *Vol. 9 of The Works of John Ruskin*. Sunnyside: George Allen.

———. 1908. *Praeterita*. London: George Allen.

Sachs, William. 2009. *Homosexuality and the Crisis of Anglicanism*. Cambridge: Cambridge University Press.

Schuchard, Ronald. "Wilde's Dark Angel and the Spell of Decadent Catholicism." In Rediscovering Oscar Wilde, ed. C. George Sandulescu. Gerrards Cross: Colin Smythe, 1994, 371–396.

Sladen, Douglas. 1913. *Twenty Years of My Life*. New York: E.P. Dutton.

Stanford, William, and Robert McDowell. 1971. *Mahaffy: Biography of an Anglo-Irishman*. New York: Routledge.

Steele, William. 1864. *A Sermon Preached at Portora Royal School, on Sunday, June 14, 1864*, 10. Dublin: M.H. Gill.

Stephen, Leslie. 1893. *An Agnostic's Apology and Other Essays*. London: Smith, Elder, and Company.

Stern, Kimberly J. 2019. The Publication of John Pentland Mahaffy's *The Decay of Modern Preaching* (1882). *BRANCH: Britain, Representation and Nineteenth-Century History*. In Extension of *Romanticism and Victorianism on the Net*, ed. Dino Franco Felluga. Web. 31 March 2019.

Taylor, Charles. 2007. *A Secular Age*. Cambridge: Harvard University Press.

Tipper, Karen Sasha Anthony. 2002. *A Critical Biography of Lady Jane Wilde, 1821?–1896, Irish Revolutionist, Humanist, Scholar and Poet*. Lewiston: The Edwin Mellen Press.

White, Terence de Vere. 1967. *The Parents of Oscar Wilde: Sir William and Lady Wilde*. London: Hodder and Stoughton.

White, Heather. 2001. *Forgotten Schooldays: Oscar Wilde at Portora Royal School*. Gortnaree: Principia Press.

Wilde, William. 1840. *Narrative of a Voyage to Madeira, Teneriffe, and Along the Shores of the Mediterranean*. Dublin: William Curry Jun. and Company.

Wilde, Lady Jane Francesca. 1871a. The Exodus. In *Poems by Speranza*, 43–45. Glasgow: Cameron and Ferguson.

———. 1871b. The Faithless Shepherds. In *Poems by Speranza*, 45–47. Glasgow: Cameron and Ferguson.

———. 1871c. The Parable of Life. In *Poems by Speranza*, 75–80. Glasgow: Cameron and Ferguson.

———. 1871d. Salvation. In *Poems by Speranza*, 108–109. Glasgow: Cameron and Ferguson.

———. 1888. *Ancient Legends, Mystic Charms, and Superstitions of Ireland*. London: Ward and Downey.

———. 1891. Philip James Bailey. In *Notes on Men, Women, and Books*, 261–285. London: Ward and Downey.

———. 1909. Divinity of Humanity. In *Essays and Stories*. Boston: C.T. Brainard.

Wilde, Oscar. 2000a. *Complete Letters of Oscar Wilde*, ed. Merlin Holland and Rupert Hart-Davis. New York: Henry Holt.

———. 2000b. Easter Day. In *Poems and Poems in Prose*, ed. Bobby Fong and Karl Beckson, 34. Vol. 1 of *The Complete Works of Oscar Wilde*. Oxford: Oxford University Press.

———. 2000c. On the Massacre of the Christians in Bulgaria. In *Poems and Poems in Prose*, ed. Bobby Fong and Karl Beckson, 36–37. Vol. 1 of *The Complete Works of Oscar Wilde*. Oxford: Oxford University Press.

———. 2000d. Panthea. In *Poems and Poems in Prose*, ed. Bobby Fong and Karl Beckson, 10–15. Vol. 1 of *The Complete Works of Oscar Wilde*. Oxford: Oxford University Press.

———. 2000e. Rome Unvisited. In *Poems and Poems in Prose*, ed. Bobby Fong and Karl Beckson, 7–10. Vol. 1 of *The Complete Works of Oscar Wilde*. Oxford: Oxford University Press.

———. 2000f. Santa Decca. In *Poems and Poems in Prose*, ed. Bobby Fong and Karl Beckson, 43–44. Vol. 1 of *The Complete Works of Oscar Wilde*. Oxford: Oxford University Press.

———. 2005. *The Picture of Dorian Gray* (1891). In *The Picture of Dorian Gray: The 1890 and 1891 Texts*, ed. Joseph Bristow. Vol. 3 of *The Complete Works of Oscar Wilde*. Oxford: Oxford University Press.

———. 2007a. The Critic as Artist. In *Criticism*, ed. Josephine M. Guy, 123–206, 187. Vol. 4 of *The Complete Works of Oscar Wilde*. Oxford: Oxford University Press.

———. 2007b. De Profundis. In *De Profundis. Epistola: In Carcere Et Vinculis*, ed. Russell Jackson and Ian Small. Vol. 2 of *The Complete Works of Oscar Wilde*. Oxford: Oxford University Press.

———. 2007c. The Decay of Lying. In *Criticism*, ed. Josephine M. Guy, 72–103. Vol. 4 of *The Complete Works of Oscar Wilde*. Oxford: Oxford University Press.

———. 2007d. The Soul of Man Under Socialism. In *Criticism*, ed. Josephine M. Guy, 231–268. Vol. 4 of *The Complete Works of Oscar Wilde*. Oxford: Oxford University Press.

———. 2013a. Early Christian Art in Ireland. In *Journalism 2*, ed. John Stokes and Mark Turner, 38–39. Vol. 7 of *The Complete Works of Oscar Wilde*. Oxford: Oxford University Press.

———. 2013b. A Fascinating Book. In *Journalism 2*, ed. John Stokes and Mark Turner, 88–96. Vol. 7 of *The Complete Works of Oscar Wilde*. Oxford: Oxford University Press.

———. 2013c. The Grosvenor Gallery. In *Journalism I*, ed. John Stokes and Mark Turner, 1–11. Vol. 6 of *The Complete Works of Oscar Wilde*. Oxford: Oxford University Press.

Willoughby, Guy. 1993. *Art and Christhood: The Aesthetics of Oscar Wilde*. Rutherford: Farleigh Dickinson University Press.

Wilson, T.G. 1946. *Victorian Doctor: Being the Life of Sir William Wilde*. New York: L.B. Fischer.

Wright, Thomas. 1907. *The Life of Walter Pater*. Vol. 2. London: Everett and Co.

4

The Scientist

Is all human sorrow as meaningless as sea sickness?
Is the voice of one crying in the wilderness merely the result
of the molecular action of locusts and wild honey?
Oscar Wilde, Commonplace Book

In 1885, Oscar Wilde reviewed Mark Andre Raffalovich's volume of poems, *Tuberose, and Meadowsweet* (1885), for the *Pall Mall Gazette*. With characteristic wit, he took the poet to task for "making 'tuberose' a trisyllable always, as if it were a potato blossom and not a flower shaped like a tiny trumpet of ivory."[1] Shortly thereafter, Raffalovich publicly responded to the review in a letter provocatively titled "The Root of the Matter." In it, he addressed Wilde's judgments point for point, hoping to defeat his critic by asserting his greater claim to scientific knowledge. The word "tuberose" was a trisyllable, Raffalovich averred, if "properly derived from the Latin *tuberosus*, the lumpy flower."[2] Wilde lost no time in offering his rebuttal:

> Henceforth there really must be two derivations for every word, one for the poet and one for the scientist. And in the present case the poet will dwell on the tiny trumpets of ivory into which the white flower breaks, and leave to the man of science horrid allusions to its supposed lumpiness and indiscreet revelations of its private life below ground. In fact, tuber as a derivation is disgraceful. On the roots of verbs Philology may be allowed to speak, but on the roots of flowers she must keep silence. We cannot allow her to dig up Parnassus.[3]

© The Author(s) 2019
K. J. Stern, *Oscar Wilde*, Literary Lives,
https://doi.org/10.1007/978-3-030-24604-4_4

Disparaging Raffalovich's appeal to systems of scientific classification, Wilde seems to propose that science has no place in literature. The "man of science" is to deal chiefly in matters of fact, literally dirtying his hands as he excavates the very roots of the world we inhabit. Poetry, by contrast, must elevate this world and our perception of it by dispensing with such taxonomies. One might well presume, on the basis of such an anecdote, that Wilde deplored the methods of the scientist. Even as a boy, Wilde was said to have preferred philosophy to physics. At Portora Royal School, he reportedly owned "editions of the classics that were of stately size with large print," as if proclaiming to all that, even at a young age, a passion for the written word left little room for other pursuits.[4] By comparison, Sir Edward Sullivan, who attended Portora at the same time, claims that Wilde "laughed at science and never had a good word for a mathematical or science master."[5]

Only a few years later, however, Wilde's notebooks suggest either that Sullivan was mistaken or that his understanding of the sciences may have matured. In addition to invoking some of the most renowned names in science (such as Johann Kepler, Nicolas Copernicus, Francis Bacon, Sir Isaac Newton, Thomas Huxley, and Charles Darwin), Wilde's correspondence and journals discuss a range of less familiar figures. These include William Cullen, physician and renowned professor at Edinburgh Medical School; mathematician William K. Clifford; Pierre Flaurens, a pioneer in neuroscience; famed anatomist William Hunter; Philippe Pinel, a key figure in the history of psychiatry; physiologist Claude Bernard; zoologist Henry Milne-Edwards; mathematician Nikolai Lobachevski; anthropologist Edward Tylor; physician William Harvey; and others. As Giles Whiteley has established, Wilde was an avid reader of *Popular Science Monthly*, where he likely encountered the work of naturalist G.J. Allman and German physiologist Emil du Bois-Reymond.[6] Intersecting with philosophical ruminations on Plato and Aristotle, we find in Wilde's writings frequent references to evolution, the scientific method, materialism, physics, chemistry, and scientific technology. If he is better known as a student of classical literature, it is worth noting that Wilde's inquiries into the Greeks were inseparable from investigations into the most urgent scientific questions of the day.

Much of the existing scholarship on Wilde has treated science as indistinguishable from philosophy, and understandably so.[7] After all, at the time of Wilde's matriculation at Oxford in 1874 the curriculum for the Literae Humaniores continued to be grounded in textual study. According to N.A. Rupke, scientific lectures were given prior to 1850, but the material presented at these lectures was not included in examinations: "Thus Oxford's formal requirements contained hardly any science, and the little that there was centered on mathematics [...] the sort of science that could be learned from books rather than from the experimental or observational study of nature."[8] The most explicitly scientific work Wilde was required to read at Oxford would have been Francis Bacon's *Novum Organon* (1620), which according to Montagu Burrows held "a sort of midway position between Logic and Philosophy," serving more as an historical artifact than a scientific treatise.[9] Although students might pursue more detailed inquiries into mineralogy, botany, physiology, paleontology, and other fields in the School of Natural Sciences, Wilde's course of study required only a passing acquaintance with contemporary advances in science. Given that Wilde's formal engagement with scientific thought would have been somewhat limited, it is all the more striking that his college notebooks so prominently feature more specialized works of science.

To date, scholars have tended to explain Wilde's interest in scientific discourse by linking it to his longstanding investment in aesthetic theory: science, in other words, avails concrete laws that can be compared or applied to the "laws" of beauty. In this spirit, Philip E. Smith and William Helfand chart in the notebooks a dialogic process whereby Wilde gradually came to develop his own understanding of cultural evolution, one we see reiterated in works like "The Rise of Historical Criticism" (1879) and, years later, *The Picture of Dorian Gray* (1890/91).[10] Taking a slightly different tack, Suzanne Raitt has suggested that Wilde treats art as "a kind of science—but not one on which we should depend." The "implicit analogy he draws between the scientist and artist," Raitt explains, is one that cautions against the dehumanizing impulses of the intellect (whether scientific or aesthetic) whose utilitarian aims coldly anatomize their subject.[11] By contrast, Carolyn Lesjak proposes that atomic theory provided a model for Wilde's aesthetic method, which was governed by an associative logic. In his notebooks, Lesjak proposes, Wilde establishes "proximate" relations among a range of scientific and cultural lexicons: intellectual links that are as suggestive and sometimes paradoxical as his published work.[12] While I am largely persuaded by Lesjak's argument, which productively resists ascribing to Wilde's work a synthetic or linear logic, even here an attention to Wilde's aesthetic method occludes the diligence—and difficulty—with which he navigated scientific discourse.[13] In Wilde's time, scientific discourse was itself hardly as clearly delineated as it is today. The motion of atoms was, to offer one example, a principle Wilde approached with some skepticism, carefully noting in his Commonplace Book that scientists were "obliged to postulate" their existence in attempting the "impossible" task of explaining the "nature of matter and force."[14] The concepts we now align with scientific thought—empiricism, classification, and the primacy of factual knowledge—were contested categories in the nineteenth century. To treat Wilde's engagements with scientific thought primarily as efforts at systematizing his emergent views on art, then, would be to overlook the very crucial fact that he may not have understood the category of "science" precisely as we do.

Placing Wilde in direct dialogue with the thinkers he so often invoked in his public and private writings, this chapter proposes that Wilde's view of scientific inquiry was far more capacious. I have elected to treat science as distinct from philosophy here, in the main because Wilde himself treats their forms and objects as distinct. To be sure, Wilde frequently moves between the work of philosophers and scientists as he reflects on the nature of induction or empiricism; ultimately, however, he also differentiates between the philosopher, who luxuriates in the sphere of thought, and the scientist, who seeks to explain the world in which we live. In the following pages, I seek to highlight what is distinct about Wilde's approach to science, even as I explore his own troubled efforts to reflect upon its disciplinary scope. Rather than insisting that Wilde deployed scientific thought in any deliberate or consistent manner, the following pages track the recurrence of select scientific questions in Wilde's writings, taking note of strong resonances and apertures among the sources he invokes most frequently (for instance, Herbert Spencer or John Tyndall). If these ideas at times dovetail with the "science of aesthetics," this is not merely because Wilde sought to view art in a systematic way; of equal importance is Wilde's tendency to view science as an imaginative and speculative endeavor. Scientific inquiry was not, for Wilde, merely analogous to imaginative work, nor should we assume that it was only ever absorbed instrumentally into his writings on art; on the contrary, Wilde regarded it as a vital expression of man's curiosity about the world and, in the best instances, as practically indistinguishable from the work of the poet.

Early Excavations

The term "science" was far more flexible in the nineteenth century than it is today, for it was at precisely this time that hitherto distinct subjects and methodologies—from chemistry and zoology to astronomy and medicine—were being consolidated under the common *aegis* of scientific knowledge. In the words of John Pickstone, "Science, as a supposedly unitary body of knowledge, was invented in an England that was newly disparate, cognitively as well as geographically."[15] This process was ushered along in part by the efforts of research universities, museums, voluntary associations, and political agents, for whom the "unity" of the sciences helped to buttress arguments for funding and promoting research in specific areas. Significantly, Wilde's encounters with science were abetted by a growing institutional attention to certain fields of study, taking place at a time when disparate subjects were coming to be seen as connected, even though they did not necessarily share a common understanding of scientific "truth." When I refer to "science" in this chapter, I thus use the term as Wilde did, to describe a range of analytical methods that were deployed to understand the processes of the natural world. Some wonderful extant work examining Wilde's relationship to very specific scientific concepts (such as heredity or contamination) has emerged in recent years.[16] Here, however, I am more interested in how Wilde engaged with science as a set of intellectual concerns that, as encountered in his formal and informal education, was not nearly as coherent or consistent as we might expect.

Wilde's earliest exposure to the sciences almost surely came to him through his father. William Wilde was a doctor by trade, a specialist in ophthalmology who studied surgery at Steevens' Hospital and at the Park Street School in Lincoln Place, Dublin. In 1837, he became a Licentiate of the Royal College of Surgeons, following a brilliant performance in the midwifery examination at Rotunda Hospital. Suffering in health (reportedly due to long hours of study in preparation for the exam), he was advised to serve as personal physician to Robert Meiklam, an ailing member of the Royal Yacht Squadron who had planned a tour of the Mediterranean. The health of both patient and doctor, it was hoped, would be reclaimed by the change in environment. The result of this journey was his 1840 work *The Narrative of a Voyage to Madeira, Teneriffe, and Along the Shores of the Mediterranean*, which combined archaeological research, travelogue, and historical writing. In 1846, William Wilde was appointed editor of the *Dublin Quarterly Journal of Medical Science*, contributing two articles in particular—"Epidemic Ophthalmia" (1851) and "Aural Surgery" (1853)—that would transform the field. Soon after, he published *Practical Observations on Aural Surgery and the Nature and Treatment of Diseases of the Ear* (1853), and the same year was appointed surgeon-oculist in ordinary to the queen in Ireland. Inspired by an inquiry from Scottish oculist William Mackenzie, he also published a series of essays about the medical decline of Jonathan Swift. When compiled into a single volume, *The Closing Years in the Life of Dean Swift* (1849) proved to be an idiosyncratic but popular combination of biography, literary history, and medical mystery. The record of William Wilde's achievements is, in short, that of a successful, prolific, and well-established man of science.[17]

Given such a record of accomplishments, it is perhaps unsurprising that his writings convey a keen attention to the ethical responsibilities and privileges of the professionally trained scientist. William Wilde repeatedly spoke out against what he deemed to be outdated and often harmful medical practices, a trend he attributed to the rise of print media and consumer culture. In "Medical Epidemics—Glaucoma and Iridectomy" (1860), he warns readers against "quack advertisers," echoing a caution he had issued just a few years earlier in *Irish Popular Superstitions* (1852):

> Of all superstitions, the medical lingers longest, perhaps, because the incentive to its existence must remain, while disease, real or imaginary—either that capable of relief, or totally incurable—continues to afflict mankind, and, therefore, in every country, no matter how civilized, the quack, the mountebank, the charm-worker, and the medico-religious impostor and nostrum-vendor, will find a gullible, *payable* public to prey upon.[18]

William Wilde's solution to the problem was twofold. First, he insisted that scientists must be familiar with the history of scientific thought, including theories, treatments, and mythologies that might well seem obsolete. The true man of science needed not merely to retain a fixed set of diagnostic facts but to understand the processes through which that knowledge had been produced, treating science itself as an historical discourse still in the process of unfolding. Engaging critically with such a history, he observes, "not only becomes interesting, but practically instructive" for the student who wishes to cultivate a more comprehensive knowledge of the human body.[19] To this extent, William Wilde promoted an understanding of science that was textual, historical, and even speculative—not principally a matter of *fact*.

He also, and perhaps somewhat surprisingly, recommended a departure from strict empiricism, that philosophical technique (treated more fully in Chap. 5) which draws upon sensory experience and observation as the source of all knowledge. In *Practical Observations*, William Wilde surveys the history of aural surgery in detail, noting that it is "an art but just emerging from darkness, ignorance, empiricism, prejudice, and superstition."[20] While the term "empiricism" today may connote scientific rigor—an effort to discern through experiment the physical laws of the natural world—in nineteenth-century medicine it was more closely aligned, as this passage suggests, with quackery. The empiric was characterized by a primary focus on observing and treating the symptoms of disease, to the exclusion of a broader theoretical or historical knowledge. As Craig Ashley Hanson notes, "the empiric belonged to the company of non-licensed healers that included practitioners (of both sexes) ranging from the barber and bonesetter to the quack, all of whom focused on treating symptoms and alleviating pain or discomfort."[21] William Wilde's attack on empiricism by no means reflects a categorical aversion to experience and observation in the treatment of disease. Experience was an essential component of the scientific method; however, if the scientist relied *only* upon what one could perceive, then he was obliged to discount what might be happening on a smaller—for instance, vascular or even cellular—scale.

William Wilde was hardly alone in refusing to align scientific inquiry with empirical observation. As Alex Warwick points out, the very term "science" was hotly contested in the nineteenth century. If the contemporary reader is guided by "a notion of Science as a neutral realm beyond the vagaries of human existence," this is a concept that was deliberately cultivated —through a variety of political, intellectual, and social interests—over the course of Wilde's lifetime.[22] Take, for instance, Bacon's *Novum Organum*, the only scientific volume Wilde was required to study at Oxford. At precisely the moment when Wilde was matriculating, Bacon's work was falling under general suspicion, not because it was outdated or speculative but rather because it was too dependent upon inductive logic. As Jonathan Smith puts it, the 1870s saw a "revision if not [...] the outright repudiation" of Baconian science and its methodological principles: "[p]ure objectivity, absolute certainty, avoidance of hypotheses, gradually widening generalization, systematic elimination of possible explanations."[23] At the same time, the primacy of induction was contested by a growing emphasis on imagination, experiment, and speculative thinking. Perhaps the loudest voice in this movement was Irish physicist John Tyndall. In "On the Scientific Use of the Imagination" (1870), Tyndall insisted that the imagination was not at war with the sciences. On the contrary, the work of the scientist was always creative, possibly even oracular in scope, so that even "Newton's passage from a falling apple to a falling moon was, at the outset, a leap of the repaired imagination."[24] Tyndall's representation of the scientist as a kind of hierophant of the natural world was echoed by countless others: chemist George Gore, mineralogist Robert Hunt, logician William Stanley Jevons, Henry Buckle (whose work is discussed in greater detail below), and, of course, William Wilde.

The period between the 1820s and the 1870s has sometimes, as James McGeachie observes, been regarded as a "heyday of the Dublin clinical school," a time when innovative European methods of "clinical, diagnostic, and teaching methods" came to be widely discussed and implemented.[25] William Wilde was a key figure in this historical moment, and his writings— reflecting the knowledge he gleaned as census commissioner for Ireland (1845–1875) as much as the speculative register of his work as amateur ethnographer—reveal the striking ways in which scientific innovation depended upon a much larger network of political, cultural, and historical concerns.[26]

Though a polymath, then, William Wilde was hardly exceptional, for his wide-ranging interests reflect a popular movement within the Dublin medical community to reappraise the analytical and observational methods of science.

Wilde's father was insistent that the real man of science must balance an attention to acquired knowledge against contingency—those deviations from scientific "fact" which might serve as a platform for new knowledge. His work as an amateur archaeologist may well have fueled his understanding of science as an historical and speculative endeavor, but his outlook was also informed by his extensive experience as a medical practitioner. If his published work articulates a passionate interest in compiling medical data, he consistently presents his own "case studies" as idiosyncratic and warns against treating them as exemplars. In *Practical Observations* he accordingly does "not profess to invent or introduce new remedies," insisting that the study is not "a complete system of Aural Surgery, giving a full description of all the diseases of the Ear which have been recorded by authors." Openly proclaiming that his work resists the impulse to be inductive, empirical, or comprehensive, William Wilde seeks instead to "supply the reader with a practical treatise" based on his own professional experiences and to "be regarded somewhat in the light of a monograph, a form of publication peculiar to the School, and one generally containing more useful and practical information than either a large systematic work or a manual."[27] In short, William Wilde felt that advancements in the diagnosis and treatment of illness depended less upon objective and inductive reasoning than on the professional chronicle, which is by nature subjective, deductive, and often inconclusive.

In this spirit, William Wilde's most celebrated works serve less as definitive guides to diagnosis than as professional touchstones—vignettes that yield different conclusions to the clinician depending upon the specific case in question. We can see this illustrated in *Practical Observations*, where William Wilde presents a series of short chronicles, detailing the manifestation and progress of ailments that have often eluded diagnosis. In a section on the treatment of myringitis (infection of the middle ear), he tells the story of Master J_, a twelve-year-old who after swimming in the ocean began exhibiting a high fever and extreme pain on both sides of his head, "as if something was bursting out through the ear."[28] The boy's illness is then recounted in minute detail as it comes and goes over the course of a month. So far from documenting his progress toward a cure or new treatment, William Wilde instead describes experimenting with a variety of remedies: leeches, blistering, dietary changes, iodine, laudanum, mercury, potash, to name only a few.[29] The effect is not merely to document his understanding of the "facts" of the case, which resolves somewhat mysteriously after prolonged illness; instead, William

Fig. 4.1 From William R. Wilde, *An Essay on the Malformations and Congenital Diseases of the Organs of Sight* (London: John Churchill, 1862), 88

Wilde documents his process as a doctor experimenting with different treatment options. It is his method rather than the discovery of scientific fact that his narrative reveals.

His *Essay on the Malformation and Congenital Diseases of the Organs of Sight* (1862) applies a similar narrative approach to diagnostic medicine. In a discussion of *corectopia* (displacement of the pupil), for instance, he notes that visible symptoms do not coincide consistently with the expected symptoms or manifestations of disease. In an accompanying illustration, the patient's eyes appear only slightly distorted (Fig. 4.1). He remarks that "at first view" one might expect the deficiency to be structural in nature, as "the edges of both [sides of the iris] appear to be irregular and fringed, but this, by careful examination with a lens, we find to arise from the turning over of the pigment round the pupillary edge."[30] A diagnosis based strictly upon an external examination yields, in this case, only a cursory understanding of the eye's structure. Indeed, even an assessment of symptoms proves unfruitful: "The subject of this peculiarity never suffered from disease of the eyes of any description, and none of his family have been similarly affected. Although at present rather near-sighted, he has been able to shoot snipe, and to follow his profession, that of an officer, without any inconvenience."[31]

It is worth noting that the drawings and diagrams included in this volume, many of them executed by the author himself, at once testify to the importance and limitations of empirical study. William Wilde had lamented the presumption among physicians that the organs of sight and hearing were too intricate to adequately examine or represent. In response, his works complement minute verbal descriptions of his subjects with detailed illustrations that capture both typical and atypical manifestations of disease. If these sketches reveal seldom documented physiological details, at times they also reveal how challenging a strictly empirical approach to diagnosis can be. Hence, in his discussion of the aforementioned military officer, the accompanying illustration demonstrates the challenges of perceiving slight variations in the structures of the eye and the necessity of considering the *unseen* in all forms of scientific inquiry.

His deployment of this methodology is perhaps even more discernible in his writings on ethnography, natural history, and archaeology. As T.G. Wilson, Terence de Vere White, and other biographers have noted, William Wilde was captivated by the idea that scientific study might help to illuminate one's cultural inheritance and the hidden meaning of the very soil beneath our feet.[32] He cultivated a lifelong passion for archaeology, which he pursued by taking part in archaeological digs. As Eric Lambert puts it, William Wilde "literally immersed himself in archaeological exploration [...] plunged into caves, delved into tumuli" and made several important discoveries about the topography and cultural history of his native land.[33] In the course of doing so, he brought his knowledge of the human body immediately to bear on the excavation of the past. During his exploration of the catacombs of Sackara, for instance, he discovered the remains of a young man, whose arms "presented an appearance so truly abnormal, and so different from any thing the effect of disease, or any known congenital malformation" that he removed it from the site for further study.[34] The fragment, of which he provides a detailed illustration (Fig. 4.2), is described at length, and William Wilde deduces from it and the surrounding relics that it belonged to a man "above the lower caste" who seems to have suffered from "original malformation," rather than any accident or disease "subsequent to birth."[35] The text features similar speculations throughout, as he seeks to reconstruct partial histories from the broken bodies of the past. His description of this process in both his medical and archaeological writings assuredly inspired his son's appreciation for the visionary scientist who could, as Oscar Wilde would put it in "The Rise of Historical Criticism" (1879), reconstruct the past "from a single bone, or tooth even."[36]

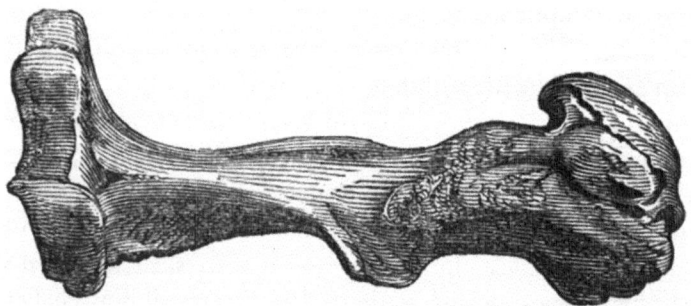

Fig. 4.2 From William R. Wilde, *A Narrative of a Voyage to Medeira, Teneriffe, and Along the Shores of the Mediterranean* (Dublin: William Curry, 1844), 256

The same approach is apparent in Lady Wilde's reflections on archaeological research in *Ancient Legends, Mystic Charms, and Superstitions of Ireland* (1888). Whereas cultural traditions are always colored by the specific historical and cultural contexts in which they were forged, Lady Wilde explains, "the scientific mythographic student knows how to eliminate the accidental addition from the true primal basis, which remains fixed and unchangeable."[37] Upon this foundation, the scientific mind is able to "reconstruct the first articles of belief in the creed of humanity, and to pronounce almost with certainty upon the primal source of the lines of human life that now traverse the globe in all directions."[38] Lady Wilde might well be describing the methodology adopted by her husband in essays like "The Ancient Races of Ireland," which was included as a supplemental chapter in *Ancient Legends*. Based on excavations of his native soil, William Wilde's essay reconstructs in dramatic detail not merely the history but also the physical appearance, language, religious rituals, lodgings, tools, and farming practices of ancient peoples.

Importantly, William Wilde was often accompanied on archaeological digs by both of his sons. While scholars have been unable to prove definitively that Wilde studied his father's works, he undoubtedly observed and understood his manner of pursuing scientific research by participating in these excursions. An illustration from Lough Corrib, executed by Wilde's brother, features two figures engaged in such a venture. The figures in question are presumably Sir William Wilde and Oscar Wilde (Fig. 4.3). As Iain Ross puts it, these outings inspired in Wilde a tendency to regard "the country of his birth, with its Homeric bards and monuments, a second Greece."[39] Certainly, Wilde's sense of his own national identity would have been elevated and enriched by the experience of actually digging up the past with his father, and he remembered these outings fondly in later years. These memories were enough to inspire in

Fig. 4.3 Illustration of Hag's Castle on Lough Mask, from a drawing by "Master [Willie] Wilde": William R. Wilde, *Lough Corrib: Its Shores and Islands* (Dublin: McGlashan and Gill, 1867), 261

him a desire to pursue further archaeological studies while at Oxford. In 1879, Wilde sought an archaeological studentship and wrote to A.H. Sayce for his assistance, noting "I think it would suit me very well as I have done a good deal of travelling already, and from my boyhood have been accustomed, through my father, to visiting and reporting on ancient sites, taking rubbings and measurements, and all the techniques of ordinary *open air* archaeologia."[40]

During Wilde's time at Oxford an interest in scientific study, and especially in geology, was mounting. Between 1851 and 1875, no students focused their studies on chemistry or physiology; only five focused on mathematics; and 32 focused on the natural sciences. Between 1876 and 1900, those numbers escalated dramatically: 14 students studied chemistry, 14 studied physiology, 10 studied mathematics, and a staggering 86 focused their undergraduate work on the natural sciences.[41] The shift had been preparing for several decades. The Romantic fascination with history, antiquarianism, and archaeological discovery had led some to advocate for an increased role for the sciences at Oxford in the early decades of the century. In 1868, the first tutor in natural sciences was appointed at Magdalen College, and between 1870 and 1875 the Royal Commission on Scientific Instruction and the Advancement of Science was publicly engaged in efforts to revitalize scientific education at Oxford and Cambridge. But it Heinrich Schliemann's 1876 discoveries at Mycenae (the site of ancient Troy where he famously uncovered the Mask of Agamemnon) that inspired at Oxford an interest in a more direct and scientific study of the ancient past.[42] As Iain Ross notes, Wilde's mentor and travel companion, J.P. Mahaffy, was acquainted with and responsive to Schliemann's findings, though it remains open to question whether Wilde and Mahaffy actually met Schliemann during their 1877 travels through Greece.[43] What is clear is that Wilde found himself at Oxford at a crucial turning point in the university's treatment of scientific thought.

The university was, after all, a key player in the organization of scientific knowledge in the nineteenth century. As John R. Gibbons observes, university dons wielded an enormous amount of control over the curriculum, so that the methodological interventions of individual thinkers often could have a broadly institutional impact. If Wilde was influenced by his father's speculative approach to historical study, as well as his wariness of stark empiricism, he also found Oxford divided between scholars who believed in textual study and those who favored the examination of material artifacts. The question at the time was, as it has been more recently, a controversial one: are scientific methods viable tools for humanistic study? Benjamin Jowett, Master of Balliol College (whose editions of Plato extensively informed Wilde's understanding of the classics), was a vocal opponent of empirical methods. According to biographers Evelyn Abbot and Leslie Campbell: "He was not attracted by antiquarian or archaeological researches, and would often dwell on the uncertainty of the results derived from them."[44] While this did not prevent him from endorsing the establishment of the Ashmolean as an archaeological museum, he would argue in "On Inscriptions" (1881) that artifacts constitute merely fragments of the past—"an accidental and multifarious kind of knowledge"—in most cases removed from their original locations and contexts. He goes on to reflect that ancient inscriptions, often preserving only a few scant words, are hardly of scientific value:

> To be busy on Greek soil, under the light of the blue heaven, amid the scenes of ancient glory, in reading inscriptions, or putting together fragments of stone or marble, has a charm of another kind than that which is to be found in the language of ancient authors. Yet even to appreciate truly the value of such remains, it is to the higher study of the mind of Hellas and of her great men that we must return, finding some little pleasure by the way (like that of looking at an autograph) in deciphering the handwriting of her children amid the dust of her ruins.[45]

Jowett repeatedly advocated for the vital importance of studying "the mind of Hellas" rather than dwelling upon the relics that constituted its mere skeleton. If Wilde found a certain charm in archaeological study, he seems to have shared Jowett's preference for reflecting on ancient ideas and methods.

Wilde makes occasional references to archaeological research in his Oxford notebook, remarking at one point upon Jacques Boucher de Perthes's discovery of flint tools in the "Drift valleys of the Somme," which had demonstrated that "man was coeval with the Stone Age · the mammoth and wooly rhinoceros ·."[46] Wilde's selection of Boucher de Perthes is suggestive. At the time of his excavations in 1830, many of Boucher de Perthes's findings were questioned on the grounds that he had failed to provide sufficient stratigraphical evidence for the dating of artifacts, something that was not accomplished until Charles Lyell published *Geological Evidences of the Antiquity of Man* in 1863. In Wilde's estimation, however, the work of Boucher de Perthes was part of a continuous history that reached back to Lucretius, whom he invokes in the next line of text: "Lucretius v.1281· quite accurate."[47] The excerpt from *De Natura Rerum* to which Wilde refers describes the use of tools by ancient man, hypothesizing that the age of iron followed man's use of stone implements:

> The first weapons of *mankind* were the hands, nails, and teeth; also stones, and branches of *trees*, the fragments of the woods: then flame and fire *were used*, as soon as they were known; and lastly was discovered the strength of iron and brass.[48]

By tracking the findings of late nineteenth-century science back to Lucretius, Wilde proposes that science does not stand apart from history, objectively charting the movements of time and space: science is itself subject to the shifting forces of history. Generations of scholars had posited that mankind lived alongside the mammoth, and yet it was not classified as scientific fact until the latter half of the nineteenth century. In other words, Wilde's history of scientific development does not merely track incremental progress over time; instead, he suggests that the cosmogonies of the ancients stand on equal footing with the scientific theses of the present. What distinguishes Lucretius from Lyell is not the scientific knowledge they convey but rather their manner of accessing and articulating it. Wilde would note only a short time later that the "early Greeks had mystic anticipations of nearly all great modern scientific truths."[49]

Lady Wilde too seems to have treated scientific inquiry less as a mode of discovering new knowledge than as a lexicon capable of deciphering the mysteries of the natural world. In *Driftwood from Scandinavia* (1884), she recalls fondly her encounters with Danish antiquarian Christian Jürgensen Thomsen, who shared her husband's enthusiasm for bringing the distant past to life:

> [...] we traversed all ages of humanity, from stone to iron, and all regions of the globe, from the shores of the Caspian to the snows of Lapland; across two oceans to far distant islands and remote lands, still tracing the progress of the human race from instinct to intellect, through the indestructible symbols which science has interpreted into words. Thus the exhaustless stores of the professor's knowledge added interest to every object, and his lucid interpretations seemed to reveal hidden mysteries.[50]

For Lady Wilde, Thomsen was a kind of hierophant who could decode the "indestructible symbols" of nature, rendering them into more or less comprehensible "stores" of knowledge. She uses the same language to describe the Lapland Museum, presenting it as "a great ethnological book written with objects in place of letters," so that "every object takes its place as a living link in human history, like the letters of an alphabet, which science alone can form into intelligible words."[51] More poet than scientist, it is perhaps natural that Lady Wilde should regard the work of Thomsen and her husband in these philological terms. Nevertheless, her claims also dovetail with William Wilde's longstanding interest in combatting a materialist approach to scientific inquiry with more narrative and even speculative methods. As we shall see, it was an approach that also attracted her son.

Infinitesimal Atoms

In his Oxford notebook, Wilde records the following unattributed quotation: "We have only five senses, but science has added largely to what nature has given us in the microscope, telescope, machines for the weighing and measures of infinitesimal atoms."[52] Acting as a kind of "sixth sense," science becomes here a visionary force, making it possible to reimagine—if not actually to comprehend—the universe and man's place within it. Science was, in a word, not distinct from but rather continuous with a more speculative, humanistic view of the world. As the epigraph to this chapter suggests, Wilde was at this time not comforted but rather stymied by the possibility that something so mechanical as "molecular action" could explain the fine gradations of human belief and emotion.[53] Accordingly, Wilde paid close attention to the efforts of his contemporaries to draw explicit links between scientific thought and the mysteries of feeling, social behavior, and metaphysical scrutiny. He would prove to be both a sympathetic and resistant reader.

Without question, Wilde would have witnessed such a fusion of scientific and aesthetic precepts in the work of his Oxford mentor, Walter Pater. As Kanarakis Yannis has demonstrated, Pater drew extensively from scientific literature in his aesthetic writings, establishing a "structural kinship between the two world views" by using chemical and biological processes as analogues for the aesthetic experience.[54] In his famous "Conclusion" to *Studies in the History of the Renaissance* (1873), for instance, Pater argues that everything—the physical world, our bodies, and even our thoughts—is in constant motion. Affording a sort of molecular basis for his claim that "experience alone is the end" of life, Pater leverages a quick succession of scientific analogies:

> What is the whole physical life in that moment but a combination of natural elements to which science gives their names? But these elements, phosphorus and lime and delicate fibres, are present not in the human body alone: we detect them in places most remote from it. Our physical life is a perpetual motion of them—the passage of blood, the wasting and repairing of the lenses of the eye, the modification of the tissues of the brain by every ray of light and sounds—processes which science reduces to simpler and more elementary forces.[55]

For Pater, the molecular structure of the universe provides a model for consciousness, which he views as a series of vibrations and variations. Like the physical world, the mind is in a constant state of flux, and this is a propensity to be actively engaged and welcomed.[56] If all phenomena are determined by physical laws that resist stasis, then life itself becomes little more than a kinetic string of experiences. In Pater's view, this is a liberating idea: no longer tethered to a fixed identity or way of life, the individual is free to experiment with a range of stimuli, experiences, and even identities.

Wilde read, admired, and often quoted the "Conclusion" to Pater's *Renaissance*, and he undoubtedly shared Pater's interest in exploring possible connections between the autonomous self and scientific laws. Yet if Pater's views would seem to coincide with Wilde's investment in an organic and mobile process of self-development (a subject treated at length in Chap. 2), Wilde does not merely replicate this analogy between science and art in his own work. So far from conceding that science distills the physical universe into "simpler and more elementary forces," Wilde would continue to interrogate underlying science of this analogy. Indeed, at another point in the Commonplace Book, Wilde revisits this question, noting that the laws of physics fail adequately to explain the origins of human behavior or desire. He reflects:

> It is impossible it is said to comprehend the nature of matter and force: we are obliged to postulate as the basis of life an indivisible inert mass—called an atom—from which forces emanate: the second incomprehensible is consciousness even in its lowest form the sensation of desire and aversion.
>
> It is incomprehensible how to a mass of nitrogen, oxygen, carbon, phosphorus and so on it can be otherwise than indifferent how they lie and move[57]:

Wilde's ruminations on the nature of atomic force, written only shortly after Anglo-Irish physicist George Stoney had developed the concept of the "electron," are far less animated and assured than those of Pater.[58] The principles of atomic motion are, for Wilde, strictly theoretical; even they were incontrovertible, they failed to explain the nature of consciousness. Because "a mass of nitrogen, oxygen, carbon, phosphorus and so on" lacks either desire or will, it becomes nearly impossible to reconcile scientific laws with a worldview that celebrates the value of experience and individual agency. So far, scientific inquiry had proven inadequate as a tool for excavating the groundwork of human thought and feeling.

For Wilde, a vital touchstone on this question was Herbert Spencer, who sought to clarify the connections between natural and social phenomena.[59] In *Social Statics* (1851), Spencer presents a provocative analogy between the laws of science and the laws of society: "[…] every social phenomenon must have its origin in some property of the individual. And just as the attractions and affinities which are latent in separate atoms, become visible when those atoms are approximated; so the forces that are dormant in the isolated man, are rendered active by juxtaposition with his fellows."[60] Where Pater saw a physical and intellectual universe characterized by shifting arrangements, Spencer instead focused on the scientific principles that helped to guide these arrangements, laws that might help us to see an apparently chaotic universe as coherent. Spencer claimed that knowledge, like the natural world itself, always evolving into more complex and diversified forms. Nevertheless, he was reluctant to place too much faith in any system of organizing knowledge and rejected outright the idea that the sciences could be "rationally arranged in serial order," as Auguste Comte had proposed.[61] Spencer's wariness of scientific discourse—including the products of his own research—suggests that he, like William Wilde, regarded scientific thought as contingent upon factors not easily accounted for by the laws of science. Indeed, even his own system of classification is presented with some reservation, offered merely as the best way of "grouping together the like and separating the unlike."[62] For Spencer, the project of outlining the relations among different branches of scientific study was not merely pedantic. He freely confessed that his schema was "still but imperfectly represented," for the relations among the scientific disciplines "cannot be truly shown on a plane, but only in space of three dimensions."[63] Wilde would confirm Spencer's view, noting: "Not a single branch of enquiry can be pursued successfully alone: there is a continual enlarging of boundaries, and an absorption of the results as well as the methods of other sciences."[64] Like Spencer, and like his father, Wilde treated scientific thought as part of a larger system of knowledge—not a separate field but rather a *lexicon* capable of bringing old ideas into new combinations.

Spencer elaborated on this model of organizing scientific knowledge in his 1871 essay "The Classification of the Sciences," which is invoked several times across Wilde's notebooks. In this piece, Spencer arranges the sciences into three categories: the abstract, the concrete, and the abstract-concrete. The abstract sciences (theoretical sciences like logic and mathematics) treat "the forms in which phenomena are known to us" and seek to reveal the relations of time, space, and sequence. The concrete sciences (astronomy, geology, or biology, for example) consider "the phenomena themselves [...] in their totalities"—that is, they consider phenomena as they manifest in nature. Finally, the abstract-concrete sciences (physics, chemistry, and mechanics) describe phenomena "in their elements"—in other words, they consider the physical laws that constitute and determine all natural occurrences.[65] In a fragment from the Commonplace Book entitled "The Sciences in their Educational aspect as forming habits of mind," Wilde offers a gloss on Spencer's system of classification that again highlights the dangers of setting too much stock on scientific "fact":

> From the abstract sciences we gain the perception of the necessity of relation, the absoluteness of uniformities: it's [sic] danger is that mathematicians are apt to simplify their problems too much and are bad reasoners on contingent matter.
>   From the (abstract) sciences we gain conception
>   (concrete)
>   of cause and effects · it's danger is that it makes us too analytical
>   From the concrete sciences we gain ideas of continuity · complexity · and contingency · and from the concrete · organic · sciences that of the fructification of causes ·[66]

If the notebook entry initially seems to offer a mere summation of Spencer's system, it also appraises the role each field of knowledge plays in our understanding of the world. The problem with the abstract sciences is that logic and mathematics cannot account for "contingent matter," those unpredictable and often irrational events that characterize social life. Both the abstract and concrete sciences afford a clear understanding of causal relationships but at the expense of becoming "too analytical" and detached from the real world. Science was, as Wilde had learned from his father, a complex amalgam of observable facts, theoretical knowledge, experience, and imagination. Seen this way, it is both suggestive and fitting that Wilde often expresses a preference for concrete sciences like medicine and geology, fields of which he had direct and personal knowledge through William Wilde. It is, for Wilde, chiefly in the concrete sciences that it becomes possible to evaluate the physical laws of the universe in combination with the "complexity and contingency" of social life. Indeed, early in his Commonplace Book Wilde notes that "all science is not exact science." As he goes on to assert, "in no concrete science is there absolute repetition · Even in astronomy the repetitions are only approximate ·"[67] By this logic, it would seem that Wilde remained unconvinced that even the ostensibly universal laws of physics were either stable or predictable.

If Wilde resisted aligning science with predictable patterns of repetition, it is perhaps unsurprising that he was keenly interested in biological theories of development that privileged the notion of change over consistency. Both John Wilson Foster and Michael Wainwright have made persuasive cases for regarding Wilde as a supporter of developmental theory, positing that he treated cultural progress as constituted less through repetitions than through productive deviations and developments.[68] As Wilson puts it, Wilde drew consistently upon evolutionary thought in his understanding of art, history, and society: "Life, he thought, imitates previous life as surely as it imitates art."[69] Without question, Wilde was familiar with the work of developmental thinkers like George Cuvier, Thomas Huxley, and Charles Darwin.[70] Perhaps intrigued by his attention to psychology, Wilde was also captivated by the work of William K. Clifford, whose *Lectures and Essays* (1879) he had eagerly devoured at Oxford. Following Darwin's developmental hypothesis, Clifford speculated that the moral sense was itself an evolutionary concept that developed in order to secure the survival of the "tribe." Wilde glosses Clifford's "On the Scientific Basis of Morals" at length in the Oxford notebook: "it is the Tribal self wh. is the first mainspring of action, and canon of right and wrong: a savage is not only hurt when a man treads on his own foot, but when the foot of the tribe is trodden on."[71] Moral and social choices are, by this logic, matters of collective survival: the biological is indistinguishable from the social instinct.[72] By treating morality as a biological impulse rather than a spiritual or philosophical practice, Clifford helped Wilde to understand social behaviors as part of a much longer evolutionary narrative. Some have speculated that Wilde used Clifford's theory to challenge the existence of universal standards of right and wrong and to rationalize his subversion of moral systems in his published work.[73] If moral precepts are linked to a "tribal instinct," then one might well argue that moral standards vary widely according to time and circumstance.

Herbert Spencer likewise provided a powerful model for Wilde in his study of developmental theory. Spencer's *First Principles* (1862) contends that the "principle of continuity" guided all phenomena in the natural world. According to Spencer, organisms are intrinsically unstable and tend to move from less to more differentiated forms over time:

> From the lowest living forms upwards, the degree of development is marked by the degree in which the several parts constitute a co-operative assemblage—are integrated into a group of organs that live for and by another. [...] And the same thing holds true of social products, as, for instance, of Science; which has become highly integrated not only in the sense that each division is made up of dependent propositions, but in the sense that the several divisions cannot carry on their respective investigations without aid from one another.[74]

In the same way that more evolved organisms demonstrate a greater complexity and heterogeneity of form, so too does science gradually develop into a more complex and heterogeneous endeavor, aggregating the knowledge of generations and diverse fields of inquiry. Adopting a similar analogy, Wilde describes scientific progress in these terms:

Just as the human embryo passes through all the stages of evolution from the lowest to the highest organism during the progress of its perfection, so the human mind must pass through all the stages which have been already taken in the progress of the intellectual world: neither in the world of thought or in that of matter is the past ever annihilated: progress in both must be made by slowly graduated stages from simple sensations, and formless protoplasms, to the highest differentiated organism and the purest abstractions of thought[75]:

In this passage, Wilde articulates an understanding of history that is shaped by evolutionary discourse, tracking a movement toward "perfection" and the "highest differentiated" structures of thought. He would reiterate his belief in developmental theory many times over during this period, remarking on one occasion, for instance, that "in history what we are to look for are not revolutions, but evolutions."[76] Such utterances would seem to suggest, again, that the history of science is evolutionary but hardly teleological. In the history of ideas, as in living organisms, the past is never "annihilated": vestiges of bygone eras remain, and the scientist who wishes to perceive the slow movement of things must adopt a view that is speculative and historical, rather than linear and progressive.

Such an argument would seem to align the methods of the scientist with the aesthetic discourses Wilde prized. In an 1887 letter to Frank Granger who had recently published *Notes on the Psychological Basis of Fine Art* (1887), for instance, Wilde appealed to scientific thought as the only sure way to encourage independent aesthetic judgment. Wilde writes:

If people would study art from the psychological and physiological point of view, as you do, there would be far less prejudice in aesthetic matters, and far more understanding. After all, preferences in art are very valueless, what is needed is to understand the conditions of each art, and to be, as Goethe said, ready for the reception of impressions.[77]

At first glance, the passage would seem to recommend a move away from the subjective view of art Wilde cultivated under the tutelage of Pater. If adopting a "psychological and physiological point of view" is the best technique for eradicating "prejudice" from aesthetic judgment, we might presume that Wilde expresses here a simple preference for critical objectivity. Yet Granger's scientific approach surprisingly affords more room for a subjective experience of art than earlier methods had. Whereas Herbert Spencer had claimed that "the simulation of useful activities is the cause of pleasure," implicitly linking aesthetic experience to man's survival instinct, Granger understood all human experience to be rooted in physiological causes.[78] For Granger, the pleasure acquired through aesthetic experience had little to do with its ability to mirror actions in the "real world" that might prove useful or productive; on the contrary, the aesthetic sense is valuable precisely because it helps to condition the mind to encounter new stimuli. "Just as play gives pleasure to the active side of mind," Granger observes, "so the fine arts give pleasure to the receptive side of mind."[79] Rather than treating aesthetic preferences as reflecting biological impulses, Granger proposes that aesthetic experience is necessary because it prepares the mind to engage with new knowledge. A scientific view of art, he argues, should move beyond matters of personal "preference" to consider how art works upon the human mind and body. His view is scientific, in other words, not because it claims to define *what* is beautiful but rather because it asks *why* and *how* we seek out beautiful things in the first place.

Wilde did not, then, regard even evolution as an entirely schematic or teleological process. The idea is echoed in Wilde's allusion to a chapter on science in Johann Wolfgang von Goethe's posthumously published. *Maxims and Reflections* (1833) where he writes: "In the sphere of natural science let us remember that we have always to deal with an insoluble problem. Let us prove keen and honest in attending to anything which is in any way brought to our notice, most of all when it does not fit in with our previous ideas. For it is only thereby that we perceive the problem, which does indeed lie in nature, but still more in man."[80] The "insoluble problem" Goethe highlights in this passage is one that colored Wilde's own scientific inquiries: how can humanity present a comprehensive and objective view of a natural world of which it constitutes a part? Man is always an experimental subject of the very study he claims to oversee. Faced with such a paradox, the scientist's quandary becomes akin to that of the artist or aesthetic critic. The scientist too is subject to the limits of his own perception and must, accordingly, attend to what deviates from natural laws—those phenomena that somehow seem to escape scientific explanation. For Wilde, the only truly scientific method is therefore one that remains open to its own fallibility, recognizing that a natural "law" is merely one possible way of expressing how human beings apprehend the world.

William K. Clifford too treated the mind in strictly physiological terms, tracking how neurological processes help to explain the body's actions and reactions to stimuli, as well as how those actions become codified as "taste" or "character." Hence, even the scientific treatment of the mind was subjected to the contingencies of individual experience. Although this might seem to preclude the possibility of spirit or will, Clifford insists that a material basis for life actually reinforces human agency:

> If we consider, for example, a machine such as Frankenstein made, and imagine
> ourselves to have been put together as that fearful machine was put together by
> a German student, the conception naturally strikes us with horror; but if we
> consider the actual fact, we shall see that our own case is not an analogous one.
> For, as a matter of fact, we were not made by any Frankenstein, but we made
> ourselves. I do not mean that every individual has made the whole of his own
> character, but that the human race as a whole has made itself during the process
> of ages. The action of the whole race at any given time determined what the
> character of the race shall be in the future[...][81]

If every individual is a product of predictable physiological processes, those processes transpire against the backdrop of unique environmental pressures and personal encounters. Thus, while his belief in biological determinism would seem to deny the existence of either Creator or individual will, Clifford claims that a shared biological experience and survival instinct prompts human beings to play an active role in constructing their own world: if we are driven by base needs and impulses, we continually make and remake a world within which the attainment of these needs becomes possible. Like his father, Wilde resisted treating the history of ideas as a teleology. His passion for the archaeological excursions of his father had fostered in him an appreciation for the vestiges of earlier forms of life—forms perhaps not perfect or even useful, yet all the more revealing for their obsolescence. Neither in biology nor in the history of scientific thought, Wilde observes, "is the past ever annihilated."[82] These unexplained and seemingly insignificant fragments of the past, as we shall see, would play an important role in Wilde's understanding of the scientific imagination.

New Methods

Wilde came to Oxford only two months following Tyndall's "Inaugural Address" to the British Association in August 1874. In this landmark address, Tyndall would track the history of scientific thought from the time of Lucretius to the present, highlighting the striking correlations between ancient cosmogonies and scientific truth. Tyndall repeatedly insisted that the history of scientific thought had never been linear and that the true man of science cultivates a recursive relationship to the past, returning again and again to the work of his progenitors. The history of science, by this logic, becomes a "history of errors—the error, in great part, consisting in ascribing fixity to that which is fluent, which varies as we vary, being gross when we are gross, and becoming, as our capacities widen, more abstract and sublime."[83] If Tyndall's address was widely perceived as championing science over feeling, it is worth noting that he adamantly defended the role of historical scrutiny and imaginative recollection in all scientific endeavors. Indeed, he unexpectedly concluded the lecture with a selection from William Wordsworth's "Lines Written a Few Miles Above Tintern Abbey," suggesting that the scientist, like the poet of Nature, must be attuned to the value of recollection and the limitations of human understanding. Only then can he begin to chart the hidden laws of the physical universe: "A motion and a spirit, that impels / All thinking things, all objects of all thought, / And rolls through all things."[84]

Wilde would come to share this view of scientific progress and echoes Tyndall at several points in the Oxford notebook, for instance when he speculates that the work of the poets have always dovetailed with the work of scientists:

> In early civilizations science is found intimately blended with poetry. Cf. the cosmologies: and the religious worship of the universality of number · in the Pythagoreans ·
> And in modern science, the fourth dimension of space, infinity, eternity, &c are poetical conceptions ·[85]

If Wilde sometimes disparages the acquisition of concrete facts, then, it is not because he rejects scientific principles or methods. It is because he privileges a scientific process that embraces and engages with contingency—those "abstract-concrete" sciences that do not foreclose so much as amplify the wonders of Nature. Poets are, Wilde insists, the "original men of science," for their questions are motivated by a desire to know the world in its material forms.[86] Poets are scientists, and scientists are, in a manner of speaking, poets.

Wilde's insistence upon the link between scientific and metaphysical thought was doubtless informed by his reading of Auguste Comte and Henry Thomas Buckle (both of whom are also discussed in Chap. 5). Comte had proposed that empirical inquiry alone revealed the laws of historical transformation, rejecting any form of metaphysical speculation as an affront to the laws of reason. Wilde assuredly read Comte's work, which he invokes at several points over the course of his notebooks, commenting on one occasion: "Modern Positivists are as men who while they deny the existence of the sun yet worship the sunlight on the Earth, who acknowledge that the fruit is sweet to eat, and the flower goodly for sight yet insist that the root is rotten, and the soil barren."[87] At this point in time at least, Wilde seems to have regarded Comte, with his rejection of metaphysical or theistic insight, as blind to realities that are plain to view, if unverifiable by empirical methods. As Joseph Bristow observes, Wilde was especially intrigued by John Elliott Cairnes's 1870 essay "M. Comte and Political Economy," which pointedly assailed Positivism on the grounds that all laws were ultimately abstract and meta-physical in nature.[88] The question posed by Cairnes was a compelling one: is it possible to provide any authoritative account of human society when even the most rigorous systems must rest upon first principles that transcend the physical world? Henry Thomas Buckle provided a solution to this problem in his *History of Civilization in England* (1862) by proposing that although the laws governing society could not be logically derived, they could be delineated in a manner consistent with the natural sciences. If the natural world fre-quently appeals to us through the imagination—if there is, as he puts it, "incessant contact between man and the external world"—then it is no sur-prise that the best scientists have often been regarded as "mere theorists, idle visionaries," whose hypotheses seemed to bear little relation to observable fact.[89] By the same token, Buckle avers, the modern historian must reject the "unnatural separation of the two great departments of inquiry, the study of the internal and that of the external," attempting instead to approach the laws of human society as a kind of science that cannot but inhere a degree of specu-lation and contingency.[90]

Harnessing this power of imagination is, Wilde goes on to explain, essential to any successful scientific venture. It was, he avers, a tendency to reject the imagination in favor of mere empiricism that hampered scientific progress in his own time:

> The elaborate researches of Mr. Tylor and Sir John Lubbock have done little more than verify the theories put forward in the PROMETHEUS BOUND and the DE NATURA RERUM; yet neither Aeschylus nor Lucretius followed in the modern path, but rather attained to truth by a certain almost mystic power of creative imagination, such as we now seek to banish from science as a dangerous power, through to it science seems to owe many of its most splendid generalities.[91]

Wilde's choice of touchstones in this passage is telling. Edward Burnett Tylor was an anthropologist, whose *Primitive Culture* (1871) exemplified the kind of cultural evolution Wilde had already encountered in the work of Spencer, Clifford, and others. Sir John Lubbock was an archaeologist, a supporter of Thomas Huxley at the 1860 Oxford evolution debate, whose findings in *The Origin of Civilization and the Primitive Condition of Man* (1870) helped to reinforce and popularize Darwinian theory. Tylor and Lubbock were, in short, proponents of the developmental hypothesis that Wilde found latent in the work of the Greeks. The difference was that modern science sought to suppress the "power of creative imagination," where the ancients celebrated that ideal. Just as William Wilde had warned against the empirics and their inability to account for what remains beyond the scope of observation, his son would argue that all men who failed to balance experience and imagination ran the risk of stunting scientific progress.

Wilde does not, however, claim that scientific inquiry can simply be translated into or replaced by poetic effusions. As if to reinforce the point, Wilde would provide an unlikely foil for his argument—the very touchstone Tyndall had invoked in his figuration of the scientist, William Wordsworth. In his "Preface to the Lyrical Ballads" (1802), Wordsworth speaks of poetry as "the impassioned expression which is in the countenance of all Science," a phrase that seems to stress the affective power of poetry; his suggestion that poetry might help to transform science into "a form of flesh and blood" implies that science had hitherto been synthetic, objective, and void of emotion.[92] For Wilde, though, it was precisely in history that one was to find models for the proper uses of the scientific imagination. In "The English Renaissance of Art" (1882), he clearly distinguishes his own approach from "that more obvious influence about which Wordsworth was thinking when he said very nobly that poetry was merely the impassioned expression in the face of science."[93] The value of the "artistic spirit," Wilde observes, is its effort in "preserving that close observation and the sense of limitation as well as of clearness of vision."[94] Turning again to the ancients, he notes that the Greeks had wondered at the marvels of the physical universe and expressed their hypotheses through mythologies and poetic utterances. If Wilde elsewhere presents the work of scientists as visionary, here he presents the work of the poet as one of close, incisive, and systematic study.

Wilde further developed this notion of the scientist as hierophant in "The Truth of Masks" (1885), returning to the archaeological excursions of his youth. The essay commences by remarking upon Edward Bulwer-Lytton's 1884 essay "Miss Anderson's Juliet." Loosely paraphrasing from Lytton's essay, Wilde ascribes to him the belief that "archaeology is entirely out of place in the presentation of any of Shakespeare's plays, and the attempt to introduce it one of the stupidest pedantries of an age of prigs."[95] The essay proceeds to celebrate not merely the value of costume and performance but the value of archaeology in cultivating a proper aesthetic effect on stage. To the people of the Renaissance, Wilde announces, archaeology "was not a mere science for the antiquarian; it was a means by which they could touch the dry dust of antiquity into the very breath and beauty of life, and fill with the new wine of romanticism forms that else had been old and outworn."[96] Here, Wilde holds poetry to be superior to archaeology, noting that the sonnets of John Keats rank higher than the philology of Friedrich Max Müller—that it is "Better to take pleasure in a rose than to put its root under a microscope."[97] The remark is strongly reminiscent of Wilde's 1885 cautions against "digging up Parnassus." Nevertheless, he insists on treating archaeology as more than an empirical process. He reflects:

> I can understand archaeology being attacked on the ground of its excessive realism, but to attack it as pedantic seems to be very much beside the mark. However, to attack it for any reason is foolish; one might just as well speak disrespectfully of the equator. For archaeology, being a science, is neither good nor bad, but a fact simply. Its value depends entirely on how it is used, and only an artist can use it. We look to the archaeologist for the materials, to the artist for the method.[98]

Initially, Wilde seems to adopt a somewhat detached view, presenting archaeological knowledge as "mere fact." Yet his attention to "how it is used" suggests that he does not regard archaeology as entirely devoid of imagination. The value of archaeology, like any science, depends upon two factors: the materials (that is, the subject matter itself) and the method (which must be *artistic*). The poet's "method," as Wilde carefully establishes, involves far more than translating the scientist's observations into affective verse. The poet provides, instead, a sense of clarity and proportion, helping us to accommodate scientific principles into our understanding and veneration of Nature.

This apparently optimistic view of science might well seem to chafe against perhaps the most famous of Wilde's ruminations on science—his delineation of Lord Henry Wotton in *The Picture of Dorian Gray*. Lord Henry famously remarks: "The advantage of the emotions is that they lead us astray, and the advantage of science is that it is not emotional."[99] Such a remark would seem to present science as objective and dispassionate: the very antithesis of the aesthetic spirit Wilde publicly embodied. Without question, Lord Henry presents science as an escape from the often confusing arena of human social interactions. Emotion breeds chaos; science is sober, objective, and tranquil. Traditionally, readers have seen this turn to science as a sign of Lord Henry's moral depravity. Treating Dorian Gray as little more than an experimental subject, he poses a stark contrast to the sympathetic artist, Basil Hallward. As Heather Seagrott puts it, the novel thus insists that art is always "a more appropriate means of representing the range and mutability of the human mind than any scientific discourse."[100]

In the context of Wilde's wider speculations on the cultural function of the scientist, however, it is worth reappraising the role of scientific thought in Wilde's only novel. Consider, as a point of comparison, Alan Campbell. If Campell is the most conventionally scientific man featured in all of Wilde's *oeuvre*, it is worth noting that his life and work are presented in terms that are strikingly parallel to Wilde's own. Initially, he is described as a brilliant and devoted student of chemistry:

> His dominant intellectual passion was for science. At Cambridge he had spent a great deal of his time working in the Laboratory, and had taken a good class in the Natural Science tripos of his year. Indeed, he was still devoted to the study of chemistry, and had a laboratory of his own, in which he used to shut himself up all day long, greatly to the annoyance of his mother, who had set her heart on his standing for Parliament and had a vague idea that a chemist was a person who made up prescriptions.[101]

Campbell's knowledge of chemistry is a useful plot device, for it is Campbell who provides the gruesome means by which Dorian is able to dispose of Basil Hallward's corpse. What is most striking about this description, however, is Wilde's attention to science as a form of inquiry that closely resembled his own narrative of humanistic study at Oxford. Wilde carefully presents Campbell's occupations as an all-consuming "passion," a form of "devotion" that sustains him even after Dorian Gray has, through unspecified means, depleted his spirit and abolished his love of music. As a man of science, Campbell is anything but heartless, as we perceive through his reluctance to assist Dorian and visceral disgust at what is demanded of him.

Lord Henry too considers himself to be a man of science—one might even say (to adopt a favorite term of Wilde's) that he *poses* as such. To be "scientific" in Lord Henry's view, is to focus purely on the material elements of existence, leaving aside questions of feeling, sympathy, or ethics. Taking issue with Lord Henry's cynical comments on matrimony, the Duchess of Monmouth remarks: "Our host is rather horrid this evening [...] I believe he thinks that Monmouth married me on purely *scientific* principles as the best specimen he could find of a modern butterfly."[102] Here, as elsewhere, Lord Henry is thought to align "scientific principles" with objectivity and detachment, and this in many ways reinforces John Wilson Foster's claim that Lord Henry treats science as essentially "amoral."[103] It was in precisely this spirit that Lionel Johnson reportedly ascribed to Wilde a "cold scientific intellect," citing the spirit of dominance and exaltation he sometimes exerted at social gatherings.[104]

Yet there is an important distinction to be drawn here between the value of scientific knowledge on the one hand and the moral qualities of the scientist himself. Reflecting on his own scientific experiments, Lord Henry famously remarks: "He had been always enthralled by the methods of natural science, but the ordinary subject-matter of that science had seemed to him trivial and of no import. And so he had begun by vivisecting himself, as he had ended by vivisecting others. Human life—that appeared to him the one thing worth investigating."[105] Lord Henry mistakes science as a form of detachment, a kind of vivisection that is devoid of any emotional investment or sympathy. Of course, Lord Henry's remarks on the vivisection of self and others prove more revealing than the narrator acknowledges. In the end, Lord Henry's methods reveal less about the nature of scientific knowledge than his own nature—the results of his own vivisection lay bear the distinction between the visionary scientist and the clinical practitioner.

Findings

While it is true that Wilde regarded the intellect as immune to the dictates of moral law, he by no means regards the mental life as devoid of passion or imagination. As he observes in "The Critic as Artist," "Action is limited and relative. Unlimited and absolute is the vision of him who sits at ease and watches, who walks in loneliness and dreams."[106] To observe and reflect upon the natural world is indeed to operate beyond the sphere of social action and the moral judgment it entails. But intellectual distance also makes possible a more critical, imaginative, and passionate quest for truth. Lord Henry's efforts to determine whether we could "ever make psychology so absolute a science that each little spring of life would be revealed to us," thus lack the vital element of scientific scrutiny: imagination.[107] Although Lord Henry views the "experimental method" as "the only method by which one can arrive at any scientific analysis of the passions," both Lord Henry and Dorian Gray remain too detached from their experiments to engage in a productive assessment of man's emotional life.[108] As Dorian moves systematically through the study of perfumes, music, jewels, and embroidery, he remains always at a distance from these objects, wary of falling into "the error of arresting his intellectual development by any formal acceptance of creed or system, or of mistaking, for a house in which to live, an inn that is but suitable for the sojourn of a night."[109]

Strikingly, Wilde confers upon Dorian his own fascination with developmental theory and anatomy. The nature and outcome of his inquiries, however, proves to be quite different. Dorian delves "for a season" into the "materialistic doctrines of the *Darwinismus* movement in Germany, and found a curious pleasure in tracing the thoughts and passions of men to some pearly cell in the brain, or some white nerve in the body, delighting in the conception of the absolute dependence of the spirit on certain physical conditions, morbid or healthy, normal or diseased."[110] Where Wilde's scientific inquiries were manifestly reflective, comparative, and even interdisciplinary, there is no real evolution in Dorian's mental life. Privileging repetition above development, he immerses himself in scientific thought "for a season," delighting in its potential to justify acts of moral depravity, and just as quickly dispenses with it, never permitting it to coalesce or collide with other modes of thought. Despite his immersion in the things of this world, Dorian remains apart from it, and his studies are guided less by his own imagination than by a desire to replicate the experiences of the hero he encounters in that curious yellow book lent to him by Lord Henry—the "wonderful young Parisian in whom the romantic and the scientific temperaments were so strangely blended."[111] Dorian cannot replicate these experiments because he does not actually, in his own person, blend the scientific temperament with the poetic imagination. If the tools for excavating his biological and psychological composition lay ready to hand, he lacks the qualities that Wilde, like his father before him, regarded as indispensable to the man of science: a vision at once narrative, experimental, and visionary.

When Dorian contemplates "the portrait with a feeling of almost scientific interest," then, he adopts a detached view, reflecting upon it as an experiment that bears little direct relation to himself. His thoughts are appropriately conveyed in scientific terms: "Was there some subtle affinity between the chemical atoms that shaped themselves into form and colour on the canvas and the soul that was within him? Could it be that what that soul thought, they realized?—that what it dreamed, they made true? Or was there some other, more terrible reason? He shuddered, and felt afraid, and, going back to the couch, lay there, gazing at the picture in sickened horror."[112] If Dorian himself understands his "scientific" proclivities as evidence of objectivity and indifference, they actually operate to very different ends. As Dorian adopts a more "scientific" lexicon, his thoughts become more speculative and less decisive. Wilde does not, then, present science as a viable alternative to moral, religious, or creative reflection; truly scientific inquiry provides a distinct and yet complementary way of reflecting on metaphysical truth. A similar occurrence transpires toward the end of the novel, when Dorian's thoughts again assume a scientific turn:

Had it indeed been prayer that had produced the substitution? Might there not be some curious scientific reason for it all? If thought could exercise its influence upon a living organism, might not thought exercise an influence upon dead and inorganic things? Nay, without thought or conscious desire, might not things external to ourselves vibrate in unison with our moods and passions, atom calling to atom in secret love or strange affinity? But the reason was of no importance. He would never again tempt by a prayer any terrible power. If the picture was to alter, it was to alter. That was all. Why inquire too closely into it?[113]

For a brief moment, Dorian's thoughts move seamlessly between the vocabularies of physical and metaphysical speculation as he inquires into the physical origins of the portrait's (and his own) transformation. Here, again, it is the scientific impulse as much as the moral one that prompts Dorian to reflect on his behavior. His refusal to adopt a more speculative view is precisely what makes it impossible to classify him as a true man of science; his espousal of a detached view is, correspondingly, a decisive factor in his undoing.

A successful scientific study, we are often told, culminates in the presentation of new findings—declamations of fact professing objectivity and validated by the scientific method. Wilde would have us think otherwise. In one of the more decisive passages from the Oxford notebook, he writes:

and primarily rem[ember] that man must use all his faculties in the search for truth: in this age we are so inductive that our facts are outstripping our knowledge—there is so much observation, experiment, analysis—so few wide conceptions: we want more ideas and less facts: the magnificent generalizations of [Isaac] Newton and [William] Harvey cd. Never have completed [sic] in this mod. age where eyes are turned to earth and particulars [114]

These lines resonate powerfully with Wilde's later indictments against utility and realism, for instance, in "The Critic as Artist," where Gilbert declares his disdain for the "dim dull abyss of facts" celebrated by his contemporaries.[115] Still, Wilde does not deny the importance of acquiring concrete knowledge of the natural world. The essential thing, for Wilde, is that an attention to this world be complemented by the methods his contemporaries often reserved for the poet: imagination, sympathy, and wonder. Wilde speculated in 1879:

The splendor and grace of swift limbs, the grave beauty of girlish foreheads, the physical ecstasy of sensuous life—do we love these things less because the germ of man is to be found in the formless protoplasm of the deep seas, or in the hideous sluggishness of the Lower Amoebae—as in the physical so it is in the moral life—we turn our eyes not to the deeper depths from which we may have sprung, but to the higher heights to which we can rise.[116]

To have one's eyes "turned to the earth," as his father had done, was no small matter, provided that the pursuit was treated as contingent and speculative. It was not evading the "deeper depths" that Wilde recommended, and despite his reluctance to "dig up Parnassus," he did not necessarily reject the value of what one might find "below ground."[117] In the natural world, as in the world of human relationships, it was necessary to look to the earth and to the heavens alike.

Notes

1. Oscar Wilde, "A Bevy of Poets," in *Journalism 1*, ed. John Stokes and Mark Turner, vol. 6 of *The Complete Works of Oscar Wilde* (Oxford: Oxford University Press, 201): 44–47, 46.
2. Mark Raffalovich, "The Root of the Matter," *Pall Mall Gazette* (30 March, 1885), 5.
3. Oscar Wilde, *Complete Letters of Oscar Wilde*, ed. Merlin Holland and Rupert Hart-Davis (New York: Henry Holt and Company, 2000), 256.
4. Frank Harris, *Oscar Wilde: His Life and Confessions* (New York, 1916), 22.
5. Harris, 27.
6. See Giles Whiteley, "Oscar Wilde's Reading of *Popular Science Monthly*," *Notes and Queries* 64.1 (March 2017), 142–44. Whiteley carefully compares passages from Wilde's college notebooks to passages from: Emil du Bois-Reymond, "Limits of our Knowledge of Nature," *Popular Science Monthly*, 5 (May 1874); G. J. Allman, "Protoplasm and Life," *Popular Science Monthly*, 15 (October 1879), 721; Eduard Oscar Schmidt, *The Doctrine of Darwinism and Descent* (London, 1875); Thomas Martin Herbert, *The Realistic Assumptions of Modern Science Examined* (London, 1879); and Henry Maudsley, *Body and Mind* (London, [1870] 1873).
7. A good example of this can be found in the work of Philip Smith II and Michael Helfand, whose discussion of the Oxford notebooks presents the work of Friedrich Hegel, William K. Clifford, Immanuel Kant, and Herbert Spencer as at once philosophical and scientific in scope. To be sure, the procedural concerns of philosophy and science frequently overlapped in the nineteenth century. Still, treating philosophical subjects (logic, causation, and epistemology) as distinct from scientific *disciplines* (like biology, physics, or chemistry) yields quite a different understanding of Wilde's intellectual range. See Oscar Wilde, *Oscar Wilde's Oxford Notebooks: A Portrait of Mind*

in the Making, ed. Philip E. Smith II and Michael Helfand (Oxford: Oxford University Press, 1989).

8. N.A. Rupke, "Oxford's scientific awakening and the role of geology," in vol. 6 of *The History of the University of Oxford*, ed. M.G. Brock and M.C. Curthoys (Oxford, Clarendon Press, 1997): 543–562, 545.

9. The *Novum Organon* stood chiefly as a point of comparison to Aristotle's *Logic*, to which it makes explicit reference. Montagu Burrows, *Pass and Class: An Oxford Guidebook* (Oxford: Parker, 1860), 146–7.

10. See Smith and Helfand, "The Context of the Text," in *Oscar Wilde's Oxford Notebooks: A Portrait of Mind in the Making*, ed. Philip E. Smith and Michael S. Helfand (New York: Oxford University Press, 1989): 5–34.

11. Suzanne Raitt, "Immoral Science in *The Picture of Dorian Gray*," *Strange Science: Investigating the Limits of Knowledge in the Victorian Age*, ed. Lara Karpenko and Shalyn Clagett (Ann Arbor: University of Michigan Press, 2016): 164–80, 166.

12. Carolyn Lesjak has made a striking argument for regarding Wilde's investment in scientific thought as inseparable from his aesthetic sensibilities. Wilde was, she avers, committed to no single way of viewing the world, and his reader must therefore attend to the "proximate" relations between different modes of thought, seeing them as simultaneously in competition and collusion. Lesjak notes that "the politics that emerge out of Wilde's ecumenical aesthetic practice draw their energy from the complex interplay of different notions of affinity, influence, and transmutation, some of which are richly congruent with scientific thinking of the time." See Carolyn Lesjak, "Oscar Wilde and the Art/Work of Atoms," *Studies in the Literary Imagination* 43.1 (2010): 1–26, 5.

13. By juxtaposing scientific discourse to more speculative forms of thought, Lesjak argues, Wilde could erase, symbolically and methodologically, the boundaries between matter and spirit: "Within the multiple lines of influence that call on Wilde and vice versa," Lesjak continues, "science holds a special place given its myth of sheer empiricism. It marks one side of the mind/matter divide and hence becomes an exemplary 'given' with which to think about matter—not in order to supplant it but rather to put in relation to 'mind' or thought" (Lesjak, 13).

14. Oscar Wilde, Commonplace Book, in *Oscar Wilde's Oxford Notebooks: A Portrait of Mind in the Making*, ed. Philip E. Smith II and Michael Helfand (Oxford: Oxford University Press, 1989): 107–152, 126 [93]. For all references to Wilde's Notebook Kept at Oxford and Commonplace Book, I have included the pagination from Smith and Helfand's edition, followed by the manuscript pagination in brackets (as shown).

15. John Pickstone, "Science in Nineteenth Century England: Plural Configurations and Singular Politics," in *The Organisation of Knowledge in*

Victorian Britain, ed. Martin Daunton (Oxford: Oxford University Press, 2005): 29–60, 32.

16. See Michael Wainwright, "Oscar Wilde, the Science of Heredity, and *The Picture of Dorian Gray*," *English Literature in Transition* 54.4 (2011): 494–522. See also Chara Ferrari, "Subversive Aims: Science and Contamination in Oscar Wilde's Dorian Gray," *Nineteenth-Century Prose* 44.1 (2017): 67–86.

17. William Wilde was extraordinarily prolific. His writings also include: "Medical Epidemics: Glaucoma and Iridectomy," *Dublin Quarterly Journal of Medical Science* (August, 1860), 68–90; *Austria: its literary, scientific, and medical institutions* (Dublin: William Curry, Jun. and Company, 1843); and countless other articles, reviews, and volumes on subjects as far-reaching as surgical procedures, archaeological relics, and Irish folklore.

18. William R. Wilde, "Medical Epidemics," 69; William R. Wilde, *Irish Popular Superstitions* (Dublin: James McGlashan, 1852), 30. In *Practical Observations*, he likewise observes: "above all, I have labored to divest this branch of medicine of that shroud of quackery, medical as well as popular, with which, until lately, it has been encompassed." William R. Wilde, *Practical Observations on aural surgery: and the nature and treatment of diseases of the ear* (Philadelphia: Branchard and Lea, 1853), 18.

19. William R. Wilde, *Practical Observations*, 22.

20. William R. Wilde, *Practical Observations*, 22.

21. Craig Ashley Hanson, *The English Virtuoso: Art, Medicine, and Antiquarianism in the Age of Empiricism* (Chicago: University of Chicago Press, 2009), 9. See also Hanson, 9–13. Samuel Johnson's *English Dictionary* had defined "empiricism" as "dependence on experience without knowledge or art," and this sense of the term persisted through the nineteenth century, as illustrated in an 1853 volume, which relentlessly satirizes quackery by focusing on "the false and destructive venom of empiricism." Samuel Johnson, *English Dictionary* (Boston: Nathan Hale, 1835), 234; *Sophistry of Empiricism* (Dublin: James McGlashan, 1853), 73.

22. Alex Warwick, "Margins and Centres," *Repositioning Victorian Sciences: Shifting Centres in Nineteenth-Century Scientific Thinking*, ed. David Clifford, Elisabeth Wadge, Alex Warwick, and Martin Willis (London: Anthem Press, 2006): 1–16, 3.

23. Jonathan Smith, *Fact and Feeling: Baconian Science and the Nineteenth-Century Literary Imagination* (Madison: The University of Wisconsin Press, 1994), 4.

24. John Tyndall, "Scientific Use of the Imagination," *Essays on the Use and Limit of the Imagination in Science* (London: Longmans, Green, and Co., 1870): 13–51, 16.

25. James McGeachie, "'Normal' Development in an 'Abnormal' Place: Sir William Wilde and the Irish School of Medicine," in Medicine, *Disease and*

the State in Ireland, 1650–1940, ed. Greta Jones and Elizabeth Malcolm (Cork: Cork University Press, 1999): 85–101, 85.

26. McGeachie, 86.
27. *Practical Observations*, 18.
28. *Practical Observations*, 234.
29. *Practical Observations*, 234–9.
30. William R. Wilde, *An Essay on the Malformations and Congenital Diseases of the Organs of Sight* (Dublin: Fannin & Company, 1862), 88.
31. William R. Wilde, *Malformations*, 88.
32. See T.G. Wilson, *Victorian Doctor: Being the Life of Sir William Wilde* (New York: L.B. Fischer, 1946); Terence de Vere White, *The Parents of Oscar Wilde: Sir William and Lady Wilde* (London: Hodder and Stoughton, 1967).
33. Lambert, 145.
34. William R. Wilde, *Narrative*, 255.
35. William R. Wilde, *Narrative*, 256.
36. Wilde, "Historical Criticism," in *Criticism*, ed. Josephine M. Guy, vol. 4 of *Complete Works of Oscar Wilde* (Oxford: Oxford University Press, 2007):1–67, 52.
37. Lady Jane Speranza Wilde, *Ancient legends, mystic charms and superstitions of Ireland* (London: Chattto and Windus, 1919), 3.
38. Lady Wilde, *Ancient Legends*, 3.
39. Iain Ross, *Oscar Wilde and Ancient Greece* (Cambridge: Cambridge University Press, 2012), 18.
40. Wilde, *Complete Letters*, 85.
41. Rupke, "Oxford's scientific awakening," 568.
42. Iain Ross includes a comprehensive discussion of the debates between empirical and textual study at Oxford in *Oscar Wilde and Ancient Greece*, 35–49.
43. See Iain Ross, *Oscar Wilde and Ancient Greece*, 50–1.
44. Evelyn Abbot and Lewis Campbell, eds., vol. 2 of *The Life and Letters of Benjamin Jowett* (New York: E.P. Dutton and Company, 1897), 145.
45. Benjamin Jowett, "On Inscriptions of the Age of Thucydides," in vol. 2 of *Thucydides* (Oxford: Clarendon Press, 1881), cii.
46. Oscar Wilde, Notebook Kept at Oxford, in *Oscar Wilde's Oxford Notebooks: A Portrait of Mind in the Making*, ed. Philip E. Smith II and Michael Helfand (Oxford: Oxford University Press, 1989): 153–74,154 [5]. Lady Wilde too would mention Boucher de Perthes's findings in "Sketches of the Irish Past" (*Ancient Legends*, 264).
47. Wilde, Notebook Kept at Oxford, 154 [5].
48. Lucretius, *De Rerum Natura* (London: Bell and Daldy, 1870), 239.
49. Wilde, Notebook Kept at Oxford, 162 [43].

50. Lady Wilde, *Driftwood from Scandinavia* (London: Richard Bentley and Company, 1884), 100.

51. Lady Wilde, *Driftwood from Scandinavia*, 115.

52. Wilde, Notebook Kept at Oxford, 159 [31]. No scholar has, to my knowledge, been able to locate an attribution for this source. The passage is formatted as a quotation in the notebook, though it is also possible (and has been suggested) that the words are Wilde's own. It curiously seems to anticipate the words of theologian Charles Woodruff Shields, who would write in *The Order of the Sciences* (1882): "In chemical science we have penetrated through solids, liquids and gases, among infinitesimal atoms, so definite that they can be mathematically weighed and measured, and yet so indefinite that no microscope will ever deter them; now grouped as solid spheres, cubes or rings, and non clustered as mere spaceless centers of force." See Charles Woodruff Shields, *The Order of the Sciences* (New York: Charles Scribner's Sons, 1882), 82–3. The concept of "infinitesimal atoms," of course, was also one Wilde would have encountered in the work of Democritus. See for instance, C.C.W. Taylor, *The Atomists: Leucippus and Democritus. Fragments, A Text and Translation with Commentary* (Toronto: University of Toronto Press, 1999).

53. Wilde, Commonplace Book, 164 [56].

54. Kanarakis Yannis, "The Aesthete as Scientist: Walter Pater and Nineteenth-Century Science," *Victorian Network* 2.1 (2010): 88–105, 103.

55. Walter Pater, *The Renaissance* (London: Macmillan, 1873), 207–208.

56. In his lecture "The Doctrine of Motion" (1893), Pater likewise reflects: "Our terrestrial planet is in constant increase by meteoric dust, moving to it through endless time out of infinite space. [...] The granite kernel of the earth it is said, is ever changing in its very substance, its molecular constitution, by the passage through it of electric currents" (20). If Darwin had established that living organisms are in a constant state of evolution, Pater suggests here that this precept applies to all matter, including the mind itself: "[...]as for philosophy—mobility, versatility, the habit of thought that can most adequately follow the subtle movement of things, that, surely, were the secret of wisdom, of the true knowledge of them. It means susceptibility, sympathetic intelligence, capacity, in short" (22). See Walter Pater, "The Doctrine of Motion," *The Works of Walter Pater: Plato and Platonism* (Cambridge: Cambridge University Press, 2011): 5–26.

57. Wilde, Commonplace Book, 126 [93]. As Smith and Helfand rightly point out, Wilde was likely responding to John Tyndall's "Professor Virchow and Evolution" (1878), *Fragments of Science: A Series of Detached Essays, Addresses, and Reviews*, 2 vols. (New York: D. Appleton and Company, 1900), 2: 407.

58. George Stoney first related the concept of the electron (which at the time he referred to as the "Electrine") at an 1874 meeting of the British Association for the Advancement of Science.

59. Interestingly, Wilde and Spencer were in New York at the same time during Wilde's 1881 tour of America. Rumors circulated that Spencer had denounced the young aesthete, though Spencer insisted: "I have expressed no opinion whatever concerning Mr. Oscar Wilde. Naturally, those who put in circulation fictions of this kind may be expected to mix much fiction with what fact they report." Edward Livingston Youmans, *Herbert Spencer on the Americans and the Americans on Herbert Spencer* (New York: D. Appleton and Company, 1883), 10.

60. Herbert Spencer, *Social Statics* (New York: D. Appleton and Company, 1873), 29.

61. Herbert Spencer, "The Classification of the Sciences," *Recent Discussions of Science, Philosophy, and Morals* (New York: D. Appleton and Company, 1871): 62–86, 62. It is worth noting that Spencer suggests here that challenging the serial arrangement of the sciences was the object of his 1854 essay "The Genesis of Science." Wilde similarly grapples with Spencer's system in his "Notebook on Philosophy," 1876–8, "Oscar Wilde and His Literary Circle Collection," MS W6721 M3 N9113, William Andrews Clark Memorial Library (Los Angeles, CA): 0201–2.

62. Spencer, "Classification," 62.

63. Spencer, "Classification," 86.

64. Wilde, Notebook Kept at Oxford, 171 [97]. Such a comment sounds strikingly akin to the words of Lady Wilde in "The Divinity of Humanity," where she remarks that "science goes but a short way along the shrouded path of infinite mystery, and can affirm only with a hesitating asseverance what may be afterwards overthrown by wider views and more perfect knowledge of the physical world." Lady Jane Wilde, "The Divinity of Humanity," *The Dublin University Magazine* (May 1877): 627–639, 633.

65. Spencer, "Classification," 66.

66. Wilde, Commonplace Book, 110 [13].

67. Wilde, Commonplace Book, 108 [4].

68. Michael Wainwright does an excellent job of tracing some of Wilde's most noteworthy scientific influences. His reading of the novel rests upon the notion that the relationship between Dorian Gray and the painting is akin to the relationship embryologist August Weisman posits between *soma* and germ. Dorian ultimately remains static, undeveloped, and unproductive because he defies a critical law of biological reproduction. See also John Foster Wilson, "Against Nature?: Science and Oscar Wilde," *University Toronto Quarterly* 63.2 (Winter 1993/40): 328–46. Wilson emphasizes Wilde's special fixation on evolution, noting his thematization of "flawed heredity" in both *Dorian Gray* and *De Profundis* (338). Moreover, Wilson articulates in clear terms the relationship between developmental theory and Wilde's understanding of the self: "It was by his Oxford reading that Wilde discovered the evolutionary foundation of his belief in individuality, thereafter lifelong" (336).

69. Wilson, "Against Nature?," 340.

70. Wilde would have had at least a passing exposure to the work of George Cuvier, who was central to his father's work in *A Voyage to Madeira*. He alludes to work by Huxley and Darwin in Commonplace Book, 134 [139], 151 [214], 127 [22]; Notebook Kept at Oxford, 163–4 [49–55], 165 [57–61]; and Wilde, *Complete Letters*, 388.

71. Wilde, Commonplace Book, 129–30 [119].

72. In such a remark, we might well detect a harbinger of Wilde's "The Ballad of Reading Gaol," a poem in which the speaker, a prisoner awaiting the execution of a fellow inmate, is able actually to feel the guilt of a crime he has not committed:" Alas! it is a fearful thing / To feel another's guilt! / For, right within, the sword of Sin / Pierced to its poisoned hilt, / And as molten lead were the tears we shed / For the blood we had not spilt." The collective guilt of the inmates, who do not merely understand but actually share the guilt of their fellow prisoner, reflects Wilde's enduring interest in the possibility that scientific precepts might be linked to the moral or imaginative faculty. Oscar Wilde, "The Ballad of Reading Gaol," in *Poetry and Poems in Prose*, ed. Bobby Fong and Karl Beckson, vol. 1 of *The Complete Works* (Oxford: Oxford University Press, 2000): 195–216, 203 [line 265].

73. See for instance Smith and Helfand's treatment of the subject in "The Context of the Text," 29–32.

74. Herbert Spencer, *First Principles* [1862] (New York: D. Appleton and Company, 1898), 338.

75. Wilde, Commonplace Book, 125 [83].

76. Wilde, Commonplace Book, 154 [2].

77. Wilde, *Complete Letters*, 335.

78. Frank Granger, *Notes on the Psychological Basis of Fine Art* (Nottingham: James Bell, 1887), 10.

79. Granger, *Notes*, 10.

80. Johann Wolfgang von Goethe, *Maxims and Reflections* (London: Macmillan 1906), 183.

81. William K. Clifford, *Lectures and Essays* (London: Macmillan, 1879), 58.

82. Wilde, Commonplace Book, 125 [83].

83. John Tyndall, "Inaugural Address Before the British Association," *Popular Science Monthly* 5 (October 1874), 652–86, 655.

84. Tyndall, "Inaugural Address," 686.

85. Wilde, Notebook Kept at Oxford, 162. Smith and Helfand suggest that this passage invokes the words of Henry Thomas Buckle in *The History of Civilization* (1862).

86. Wilde, Notebook Kept at Oxford, 172 [101].

87. Wilde, Commonplace Book, 125 [89].

88. See Bristow, "Wilde's Abstractions."

89. Buckle, 307.

90. Buckle, 31.

91. Wilde, "Historical Criticism," 27.

92. William Wordsworth, "Observations [Preface to the Lyrical Ballads]," *Complete Poetical Works of William Wordsworth* (Paris: A. and W. Galignani and Co.): 251–9, 255.

93. Oscar Wilde, "The English Renaissance of Art," *Miscellanies*, ed. Robert Ross (London: Methuen and Company, 1908): 241–77, 247.

94. Wilde, "The English Renaissance of Art," 247.

95. Wilde, "The Truth of Masks," in Criticism, ed. Josephine M. Guy, vol. 4 of *The Complete Works of Oscar Wilde*, (Oxford: Oxford University Press, 2007): 208–28, 208. Wilde's remark is a close paraphrase of a footnote included in Lytton's essay: "The attempt to archaeologize the Shakespearean drama is one of the stupidest pedantries of this age of prigs. Archaeology would not be more out of place in a fairy tale than it is in a play of Shakespeare. This scene is beautiful and animated, and that is all that is wanted." Edward Robert Bulwer Lytton, "Miss Anderson's Juliet," *The Nineteenth Century* (December 1884), 886.

96. Wilde, "The Truth of Masks," 215.

97. Wilde, "The Truth of Masks," 215.

98. Wilde, "The Truth of Masks," 218.

99. Oscar Wilde, *The Picture of Dorian Gray* (1891), in *The Picture of Dorian Gray: The 1890 and 1891 Texts*, ed. Joseph Bristow, vol. 3 of *The Complete Works of Oscar Wilde* (Oxford: Oxford University Press, 2005), 28.

100. Heather Seagroatt, "Hard Science, Soft Psychology, and Amorphous Art in The Picture of Dorian Gray," *Studies in English Literature* 38.4 (Autumn 1998), 741–59, 742.

101. Wilde, *Dorian Gray*, 306.

102. Wilde, *Dorian Gray* 336. Emphasis added.

103. See Wilson, "Against Nature?," 331, 334.

104. W.B. Yeats, "More Memories," *The Dial* 73 (September 1922): 133–58, 135.

105. Wilde, *Dorian Gray*, 47.

106. Wilde, "The Critic as Artist," 175.

107. Wilde, *Dorian Gray*, 219.

108. Wilde, *Dorian Gray*, 49.

109. Wilde, *Dorian Gray*, 111.

110. Wilde, *Dorian Gray*, 111.

111. Wilde, *Dorian Gray*, 105.

112. Wilde, *Dorian Gray*, 249.

113. Wilde, *Dorian Gray*, 83.

114. Wilde, Notebook Kept at Oxford, 162 [43].

115. Wilde, "The Critic as Artist," 142.

116. Wilde, Commonplace Book, 125 [87].
117. Wilde, *Complete Letters*, 256.

Bibliography

Abbot, Evelyn, and Lewis Campbell, eds. 1897. *The Life and Letters of Benjamin Jowett*. Vol. 2. New York: E.P. Dutton and Company.

Bristow, Joseph. 2018. Wilde's Abstractions: Notes on *Literae Humaniores, 1876–1878*. In *Oscar Wilde and Classical Antiquity*, ed. Kathleen Riley, Alastair Blanchard, and Maria Manny, 69–90. Oxford: Oxford University Press.

Buckle, Henry Thomas. 1864. *The History of Civilization in England*. Vol. 2. London: Longman, Green, Longman, Roberts, and Green.

Burrows, Montagu. 1860. *Pass and Class: An Oxford Guidebook*. Oxford: Parker.

Clifford, William K. 1879. *Lectures and Essays*. London: Macmillan.

Ferrari, Chara. 2017. Subversive Aims: Science and Contamination in Oscar Wilde's Dorian Gray. *Nineteenth-Century Prose* 44 (1): 67–86.

Granger, Frank. 1887. *Notes on the Psychological Basis of Fine Art*. Nottingham: James Bell.

Hanson, Craig Ashley. 2009. *The English Virtuoso: Art, Medicine, and Antiquarianism in the Age of Empiricism*. Chicago: University of Chicago Press.

Johnson, Samuel. 1835. *English Dictionary*. Boston: Nathan Hale.

Jowett, Benjamin. 1881. On Inscriptions of the Age of Thucydides. In Vol. 2 of *Thucydides*. Oxford: Clarendon Press.

Lesjak, Carolyn. 2010. Oscar Wilde and the Art/Work of Atoms. *Studies in the Literary Imagination* 43 (1): 1–26.

Lucretius. 1870. *De Rerum Natura*. London: Bell and Daldy.

Lytton, Edward Robert Bulwer. 1884. Miss Anderson's Juliet. *The Nineteenth Century* (December): 886.

McGeachie, James. 1999. 'Normal' Development in an 'Abnormal' Place: Sir William Wilde and the Irish School of Medicine. In *Medicine, Disease and the State in Ireland, 1650–1940*, ed. Greta Jones and Elizabeth Malcolm, 85–101. Cork: Cork University Press.

Pater, Walter. 1873. *Studies in the History of the Renaissance*. London: Macmillan.

———. 2011. The Doctrine of Motion. In *The Works of Walter Pater: Plato and Platonism*, 5–26. Cambridge: Cambridge University Press.

Pickstone, John. 2005. Science in Nineteenth Century England: Plural Configurations and Singular Politics. In *The Organisation of Knowledge in Victorian Britain*, ed. Martin Daunton, 29–60. Oxford: Oxford University Press.

Raffalovich, Mark. 1885. The Root of the Matter. *Pall Mall Gazette*, March 30, 5.

Raitt, Suzanne. 2016. Immoral Science in *The Picture of Dorian Gray*. In *Strange Science: Investigating the Limits of Knowledge in the Victorian Age*, ed. Lara Karpenko and Shalyn Clagett, 164–180. Ann Arbor: University of Michigan Press.

Rupke, N.A. 1997. Oxford's Scientific Awakening and the Role of Geology. In Vol. 6 of *The History of the University of Oxford*. Ed. M.G. Brock and M.C. Curthoys. Oxford: Clarendon Press.

Seagroatt, Heather. 1998. Hard Science, Soft Psychology, and Amorphous Art in *The Picture of Dorian Gray*. *Studies in English Literature* 38 (4/Autumn): 741–759.

Shields, Charles Woodruff. 1882. *The Order of the Sciences*. New York: Charles Scribner's Sons.

Smith, Jonathan. 1994. *Fact and Feeling: Baconian Science and the Nineteenth-Century Literary Imagination*. Madison: The University of Wisconsin Press.

Sophistry of Empiricism. 1853. Dublin: James McGlashan.

Spencer, Herbert. 1871. The Classification of the Sciences. In *Recent Discussions of Science, Philosophy, and Morals*, 62–86. New York: D. Appleton and Company.

———. 1873. *Social Statics*. New York: D. Appleton and Company.

———. 1898. *First Principles*. New York: D. Appleton and Company.

Taylor, C.C.W. 1999. *The Atomists: Leucippus and Democritus. Fragments, a Text and Translation with Commentary*. Toronto: University of Toronto Press.

Tyndall, John. 1870. Scientific Use of the Imagination. In *Essays on the Use and Limit of the Imagination in Science*, 13–51. London: Longmans, Green, and Co.

———. 1874. Inaugural Address Before the British Association. *Popular Science Monthly* 5 (October): 652–686.

———. 1900. Professor Virchow and Evolution (1878). In *Fragments of Science: A Series of Detached Essays, Addresses, and Reviews*. New York: D. Appleton and Company.

von Goethe, Johann Wolfgang. 1906. *Maxims and Reflections*. London: Macmillan.

Wainwright, Michael. 2011. Oscar Wilde, the Science of Heredity, and *The Picture of Dorian Gray*. *English Literature in Transition* 54 (4): 494–522.

Warwick, Alex. 2006. Margins and Centres. In *Repositioning Victorian Sciences: Shifting Centres in Nineteenth-Century Scientific Thinking*, ed. David Clifford, Elisabeth Wadge, Alex Warwick, and Martin Willis, 1–16. London: Anthem Press.

White, Terence de Vere. 1967. *The Parents of Oscar Wilde: Sir William and Lady Wilde*. London: Hodder and Stoughton.

Whiteley, Giles. 2017. Oscar Wilde's Reading of *Popular Science Monthly*. *Notes and Queries* 64 (1): 142–144.

Wilde, William. 1843. *Austria: Its Literary, Scientific, and Medical Institutions*. Dublin: William Curry, Jun. and Company.

Wilde, Oscar. 1852. *Irish Popular Superstitions*. Dublin: James McGlashan.

———. 1853. *Practical Observations on Aural Surgery: And the Nature and Treatment of Diseases of the Ear*. Philadelphia: Branchard and Lea.

———. 1860. Medical Epidemics: Glaucoma and Iridectomy. *Dublin Quarterly Journal of Medical Science* (August): 68–90.

———. 1862. *An Essay on the Malformations and Congenital Diseases of the Organs of Sight*. Dublin: Fannin.

Wilde, Lady Jane Francesca. 1884. *Driftwood from Scandinavia*. London: Richard Bentley.

————. 1888. *Ancient Legends, Mystic Charms, and Superstitions of Ireland*. London: Ward and Downey.

Wilde, Oscar. 1908. The English Renaissance of Art. In *Miscellanies*, ed. Robert Ross, 241–277. London: Methuen and Company.

Wilde, Lady Jane Francesca. 1909. Divinity of Humanity. In *Essays and Stories*. Boston: C.T. Brainard.

Wilde, Oscar. 1989a. Commonplace Book. In *Oscar Wilde's Oxford Notebooks: A Portrait of Mind in the Making*, ed. Philip E. Smith II and Michael Helfand, 107–152. Oxford: Oxford University Press.

————. 1989b. Notebook Kept at Oxford. In *Oscar Wilde's Oxford Notebooks: A Portrait of Mind in the Making*, ed. Philip E. Smith II and Michael Helfand, 153–174. Oxford: Oxford University Press.

————. 2000. The Ballad of Reading Gaol. In *Poems and Poems in Prose*, ed. Bobby Fong and Karl Beckson, 195–216. Vol. 1 of *The Complete Works of Oscar Wilde*. Oxford: Oxford University Press.

————. 2005. *The Picture of Dorian Gray* (1891). In *The Picture of Dorian Gray: The 1890 and 1891 Texts*, ed. Joseph Bristow. Vol. 3 of *The Complete Works of Oscar Wilde*. Oxford: Oxford University Press.

————. 2007a. "The Critic as Artist." In *Criticism*, ed. Josephine M. Guy, 123–206. Vol. 4 of *The Complete Works of Oscar Wilde*. Oxford: Oxford University Press.

————. 2007b. The Rise of Historical Criticism. In *Criticism*, ed. Josephine Guy, 1–67. Vol. 4 of *The Complete Works of Oscar Wilde*. Oxford: Oxford University Press.

————. 2007c. The Truth of Masks. In *Criticism*, ed. Josephine M. Guy, 208–228. Vol. 4 of *The Complete Works of Oscar Wilde*. Oxford: Oxford University Press.

————. 2013. A Bevy of Poets. In *Journalism 1*, ed. John Stokes and Mark Turner, 44–47. Vol. 6 of *The Complete Works of Oscar Wilde*. Oxford: Oxford University Press.

Wilson, T.G. 1946. *Victorian Doctor: Being the Life of Sir William Wilde*. New York: L.B. Fischer.

Wilson, John Foster. 1993/1940. Against Nature? Science and Oscar Wilde. *University Toronto Quarterly* 63 (2): 328–346.

Wordsworth, William. 1828. Observations [Preface to the Lyrical Ballads]. In *Complete Poetical Works of William Wordsworth*, 251–259. Paris: A. and W. Galignani and Company.

Yannis, Kanarakis. 2010. The Aesthete as Scientist: Walter Pater and Nineteenth-Century Science. *Victorian Network* 2 (1): 88–105.

Yeats, W.B. 1922. More Memories. *The Dial* 73 (September): 133–158.

Youmans, Edward Livingston. 1883. *Herbert Spencer on the Americans and the Americans on Herbert Spencer*. New York: D. Appleton and Company.

5

The Philosopher

Ay! I can bear the ills of other men,
Which is philosophy.
Oscar Wilde, *The Duchess of Padua*

In "The Nightingale and the Rose," a story published in Wilde's 1888 collection *The Happy Prince and Other Tales*, a philosophy student finds himself distracted by love: "'She said that she would dance with me if I brought her red roses,' cried the young Student; 'but in all my garden there is no red rose.'" A true believer in love, the nightingale punctures her breast and dyes a white rose with her own blood, sacrificing her life in the process. When the princess later rejects the student's offering, he turns away from love altogether:

> "What a silly thing love is!" said the student as he walked away. "It is not half as useful as logic, for it does not prove anything, and it is always telling one of things that are not going to happen, and making one believe things that are not true. In fact, it is quite unpractical, and, as in this age to be practical is everything, I shall go back to philosophy and study metaphysics."[1]

Here, philosophy serves as an escape from affective bonds and the pain that sometimes accompanies them. The student who returns to his dusty books will presumably forsake human attachments and the example of the nightingale in favor of philosophy, which is comparatively docile, predictable, and pragmatic. Philosophy, it would seem, is the province of the dull and doctrinaire. As Wilde had noted only a few years earlier in his Commonplace Book:

© The Author(s) 2019
K. J. Stern, *Oscar Wilde*, Literary Lives,
https://doi.org/10.1007/978-3-030-24604-4_5

"Philosophy began with assertions about physical science and seems likely to end in the laboratory."[2]

If such utterances might seem to suit a man known for celebrating levity and wit, they are also somewhat peculiar, for Wilde studied philosophy quite extensively. It constituted the very foundation of his education at Oxford, and prominent philosophers and schools of thought make regular appearances across his published and unpublished writings, where we encounter copious references to Plato, Spinoza, Anaxagoras, Pythagoras, Democritus, Heraclitus, Cassius Longinus, René Descartes, Gottfried Wilhelm Leibniz, Voltaire, John Locke, Gotthold Ephraim Lessing, Johann Gottlieb Fichte, George Berkeley, David Hume, Immanuel Kant, Friedrich Hegel, Auguste Comte, William Lecky, John Stuart Mill, and countless others. The philosophical subjects Wilde studied are equally varied, encompassing inquiries into causation, epistemology, utility, positivism, logic, ethics, dialectics, empiricism, and more. Given the amount of time and effort Wilde put into his own philosophical inquiries, it hardly seems likely that he deemed philosophy to be detached, dogmatic, or unfeeling. How then are we to reconcile Wilde's student of philosophy, who devotes himself to the study of a "great dusty book," with his depiction, for example, of Lord Henry Wotton in *The Picture of Dorian Gray* (1890/1), whose philosophy dances wildly, "like a Bacchante over the hills of life"?[3] Is philosophy, for Wilde, something exacting and cerebral, or is it sprightly and elusive?

Scholars have long been divided on the question of Wilde's philosophical temperament. Some claim that Wilde's intellectual trajectory was progressive and methodical, ultimately yielding a system of thought one might well regard as a complete philosophy of life. In *Cosmopolitan Criticism: Oscar Wilde's Philosophy of Art* (1997), Julia Prewitt Brown situates Wilde within "a European tradition of thought that stretches from Kant and [Friedrich] Schiller, through [Søren] Kierkegaard and [Friedrich] Nietzsche, to the pre-eminent cosmopolitan artist-critics of [the twentieth century], [Walter] Benjamin and [Theodor] Adorno."[4] Wilde's seriousness as a philosopher, in Brown's view, is confirmed through his cultivation of a capacious theory of aesthetics—one that culminates in a belief that art is the only means of resisting the materialism of modern life. Of course, as Brown herself readily acknowledges, several of the writings she uses to contextualize Wilde's work—for instance, Kierkegaard's *Either/Or* (1843) or Nietzsche's *On the Genealogy of Morals* (1887)—were not translated into English until the twentieth century, and although Wilde could read German there is little evidence to suggest that he encountered these works even indirectly.[5] Certainly, Brown's understanding of Wilde is astute and generative, and the comparisons she draws are compelling. Nevertheless, her stated aim is to place Wilde within an established canon of influential thinkers that reaches well beyond his own lifetime, rather than to clarify his immediate intellectual context. Seeking to assert the coherence and contemporary relevance of Wilde's "philosophy," Brown understandably accords less attention to ideas and thinkers that do not contribute to this larger narrative.[6]

Philip E. Smith and Michael S. Helfand likewise argue that Wilde's treatment of philosophy was both coherent and systematic, proposing that Wilde's journals reflect the emergence of "an idealist interpretation of evolution" that would unite the work of developmental theorists with that of the German idealists.[7] Seen this way, the notebooks serve as a kind of map, allowing us not only to discern Wilde's interest in dialectical thinkers like Hegel but actually to look on as he puts such a dialectical process into practice. There are impediments even to such an approach as this one. Josephine Guy and Ian Small rightly caution against treating Wilde's notebooks as a systematic effort at intellectual synthesis, noting that the entries often constitute mere transcriptions or summaries of ideas he would have encountered in his readings or Oxford lectures. Any reference to a philosophical work in the notebooks, then, does not necessarily indicate that Wilde read that work in its entirety or that he endorsed the ideas therein contained. The "striking absence in the notebooks of sustained argument, detailed exposition, and of logical summary" presents a significant obstacle to scholars seeking to decipher in them a coherent worldview.[8]

For some, however, this lack of coherence is itself a marker of serious intellectual study. Simon Reader proposes that we can appreciate Wilde's writings for their intellectual acuity without lamenting a lack of consistency. In this spirit, he treats Wilde's Notebook on Philosophy, kept between 1876 and 1878 while attending Oxford, "not as evidence for a unified field theory of Wilde's writings, but simply as a notebook, a tentative assemblage of short writings that do not necessarily reveal a systematic program."[9] To resist imposing closure and coherence upon Wilde's writings certainly seems in keeping with his tendency to celebrate dissonance and subjectivity in his later works. In "Phrases and Philosophies for Use of the Young," a series of aphorisms published in *The Chameleon* in 1894, Wilde would famously contend: "The well-bred contradict other people. The wise contradict themselves."[10] In the same document, he broadens this claim to suggest not only that contradiction is a mark of true understanding but that consensus is dangerous: "A truth ceases to be true when more than one person believes in it."[11] In such utterances, Wilde seems to reject all philosophical systems, arguing for an unsystematic, even anarchic approach to metaphysical problems. Accordingly, scholars like Guy Willoughby have persuasively argued that Wilde anticipates the work of post-structuralism, reflecting the futility of finding meaning either in empirical observation of the world or in larger structures of meaning.[12]

My object in this chapter is neither to establish a clear vision of Wilde's philosophy, nor to claim that he embraced a deliberately subversive approach to philosophical questions. Like Reader, I do not presume that Wilde's remarks on philosophy denote the emergence of a coherent worldview. Yet I do think it is possible for us to draw some conclusions about *how* Wilde engaged philosophy as a field of study. It is impossible to survey all of Wilde's philosophical investments, or all extant discussions of the subject, in a single chapter. Readers seeking more background on the philosophical movements of the period will find much to satisfy their curiosity in the "Further Reading" provided at the end of this volume. In the space available to me here, I seek to clarify Wilde's general view of philosophy as a constitutive element of our humanity, albeit one that is too often hampered by the formal strictures of language, logic, and abstraction. Wilde was attracted by the claims of Immanuel Kant, Friedrich Hegel, Arthur Schopenhauer, and others; yet his understanding of these thinkers took shape within a specific intellectual milieu, which did not categorically accept or reject their work. In the end, Wilde was profoundly critical of philosophical systems, for they are predicated on principles that are themselves open to metaphysical speculation. As a field of study, philosophy encompassed the questions Wilde regarded as most vital; yet by systematizing and asserting their ability to access certain knowledge, individual schools of thought often risked undermining the very idea of philosophy. As we shall see, Wilde's view of philosophy was neither synthetic nor purely ludic. Over the course of his life, he would treat philosophy as systematic but never static, synthetic but never linear, playful but never capricious.

The Idealist

There are, to be sure, certain impediments to tracking Wilde's encounters with philosophy. As I have indicated, we cannot always verify how extensively Wilde engaged with any particular thinker, and his tendency to combine concepts from different philosophical schools might seem to imply a lack of fidelity to or intimate knowledge of their work. These are fair and reasonable concerns. My own method has been to identify the source material Wilde encountered in a variety of ways and which he invokes directly in his writings. I do not claim that Wilde's encounters with these ideas was always exhaustive, direct, or systematic; I do, however, think we can work toward understanding how Wilde engaged these philosophical arguments, as well as what they might reveal about his intellectual outlook more broadly.

One example—Wilde's interest in Immanuel Kant—should serve as a useful illustration. Philip Smith notes that although Wilde likely read some of Kant's work, it is by no means clear that he was familiar with his entire *oeuvre*, nor is it clear that he would have read Kant in the original German.[13] It is, however, clear that he was familiar with Kant's systems of moral and aesthetic philosophy, for he frequently invokes Kantian precepts in his college notebooks. It is possible that he gleaned some of this insight from his Trinity College tutor J.P. Mahaffy, who translated Kuno Fischer's *Commentary on Kant's Critique of Pure Reason* in 1866. The volume includes an introduction and annotations that, as William Stanford and Robert McDowell put it, "not only put Fischer right on some points but vigorously challenged [John Stuart] Mill and G.H. Lewes, then well established leaders of British philosophic thought."[14] Owing to the overwhelming success of the *Commentary*, which sold out within only a few years, Mahaffy undertook a three-volume commentary on Kant's *Analytic* and *Dialectic* (1872–1874), which would be published together as Kant's *Critical Philosophy for English Readers* in 1889. Mahaffy's *Commentary* was a required text for the Classics course Wilde completed at Trinity, and Mahaffy was working on his *Critical Philosophy* during the period of his greatest intimacy with Wilde. But while it is plausible that Wilde and Mahaffy would have discussed Kant's philosophy, no record of such an exchange remains to verify this line of influence.

We do know that Wilde purchased works by two celebrated scholars of Kant at Shrimpton's bookshop in 1877–78: William Wallace's *Logic of Hegel* (1873) and T.H. Green's *Introduction* (1874) to the works of David Hume. Wilde clearly derived much insight into Kant's philosophy from Wallace's volume, the 1874 edition of which included an illuminating *Prolegomena* that is invoked frequently across Wilde's notes from the period. Of particular interest for Wilde was Kant's contention that the "thing-in-itself" (*ding en sich*)—that is, an object understood independent of human observation—was unknowable. Such a contention potentially rendered the pursuit of knowledge and therefore all metaphysical inquiry futile. In his Commonplace Book, Wilde seems to reiterate this claim: "Kant annihilated metaphysics: but he acted on the hypothesis that man in his individual capacity is all in all."[15] The passage reflects not only the substance but also the language of Wallace, who writes in his *Prolegomena*:

Kant dealt a deadly blow, as it seemed, to the dogmatic Metaphysics, and the Deism of his time. Hume had shaken the certainty of Metaphysics and thrown doubt upon Theology: but Kant apparently made an end of metaphysics, and annihilated Deistic theology.[16]

Wilde was indebted to Wallace's volume—and perhaps, to a lesser extent, Edward Caird's *Hegel* (1883)—for his insights into Kant. But even if we presume that Wilde encountered Kant in more diluted, homeopathic doses, this is not to diminish the importance of Kantian principles in his intellectual life.[17] It is, rather, to highlight that German philosophy was so prevalent at Trinity and Oxford at this time that one could easily absorb these ideas from a wide range of sources. In short, Wilde's understanding of specific thinkers was almost certainly informed by his cumulative reading of philosophical works across the 1870s and 1880s, as well as his exposure (through lectures, tutorials, and social encounters) to major philosophical thinkers of the day. Whether or not Wilde ever read Kant in the original, then, seems of less importance than the fact that he was reflecting upon Kantian precepts and assigned it a crucial place in his evolving understanding of Western philosophy. In attending to Wilde's transcriptions of thinkers like Plato, Kant, Hegel, and others, we must attend not simply to whether or not Wilde comprehends their philosophies in their entirety; it is at least equally important to take note of the ideas that Wilde records and recapitulates, though they may be taken out of context, seen through the eyes of other thinkers, or even misconstrued.

I have commenced with the example of Kant deliberately, for any understanding of Wilde's relationship to philosophy must take seriously his interest in the German idealists. Moreover, it helps to highlight the extent to which Wilde's understanding of specific philosophers was not always acquired firsthand; it was also filtered through the insights of his teachers, who offered unique critical assessments of these works. To grasp Wilde's relationship to philosophy as a field of study, then, we must also interrogate the many different and often layered approaches to the philosophical schools Wilde encountered during the period of his closest engagement with them. To some extent, this layering effect limits my ability to fully explicate some of the passages that follow. When Wilde invokes the "contemplative life," he may well be drawing on Aristotle's concept of *bios theoretikos*, Arthur Schopenhauer's notion of "pure contemplation," or even the "whole life of intelligence" described by Matthew Arnold in "The Function of Criticism at the Present Time."[18] Although I have done much to clarify both the substance and context for Wilde's reflections on these thinkers, to offer a comprehensive discussion of how they converge and combine in Wilde's work must remain a project for another time. In this chapter, I seek simply to highlight a few unexpected ways in which Wilde responds to the thinkers he admires. Seen this way, the difficulty of placing Wilde within any single philosophical tradition can be understood less as a sign of intellectual caprice or singularity; instead, we might discern in this process a deliberate interrogation of philosophy and its limitations.

Philosophy was, in many ways, the very cornerstone of the Literae Humaniores program when Wilde was an undergraduate at Oxford. In addition to the standard composition exercises and historical works, class men were expected to produce a paper on logic demonstrating some knowledge of Aristotle's *Organon* (his six works on logic) and Francis Bacon; a paper on moral philosophy "with especial reference to Aristotle's *Ethics*, Plato's *Republic*, and [Bishop Joseph] Butler"; a paper on political philosophy treating Aristotle's *Politics* and Plato's *Republic*; and finally a paper on general philosophy, which was to reflect a knowledge of both ancient and modern works in the field.[19] Although the set readings favored the ancient Greek and Roman philosophers, there was at this time a burgeoning interest in what was known as *speculative* philosophy—that is, philosophy that privileged reason over empirical observation—and even the classics were sometimes presented through the lens of German idealists like Kant or Hegel.[20] Smith and Helfand have treated Wilde as a product of this atmosphere, congenially absorbing and deploying Hegelian precepts in his critical writing.[21] But Iain Ross and others have proposed that "Wilde's thought was not nearly so systematic as they suggest."[22] Indeed, if we are to treat Wilde's ruminations on philosophy seriously, we would do well to attend as much to his criticism of idealist thought as to his admiration for it. In the pages that follow, I want to suggest that it was in large part Wilde's education—and the specific context in which he first studied German idealism—that shaped his approach to philosophy as a discipline. From the time of his first encounters with it, Wilde both approved and resisted the lure of idealism.

Benjamin Jowett, Master of Balliol College during Wilde's time at university, played a significant role in the rise of German idealism at Oxford. Jowett had been inspired by a journey to Germany in 1844, and the following year met Hegel's former roommate, friend, and rival Friedrich Schelling. Several men who would become leading members of the British idealist movement—Wallace, Green, and Caird—studied Plato under Jowett's tutelage. Indeed, it was through Jowett's teaching of Plato and his Introductions to Plato's *Dialogues* (1871), overflowing as they do with references to Hegel, that German idealism truly set down roots at Oxford. Perhaps the most illuminating instance of this occurs in the introduction to the *Republic*, where Jowett observes:

> The nearest approach in modern philosophy to the universal science of Plato, is to be found in the Hegelian 'succession of moments in the unity of the idea.' Plato and Hegel alike seem to have conceived the world as the correlation of abstractions; and not impossibly they would have understood one another better than any of their commentators understand them [...][23]

Jowett's comparison of Plato and Hegel is certainly apt. Plato has often been touted as the first idealist, chiefly owing to his Theory of Forms. According to Plato, eternal truth does not exist in the material world, which only ever constitutes a reflection or *shadow* of reality.[24] The only real truth exists in the realm of ideas. In a general sense, then, Plato articulates a key tenet of idealism: the notion that reality is constituted primarily through the mind rather than through the observation of the material world.

Hegel too felt that empiricism was limited in its ability to avail universal truths, precisely because any phenomenon observed in the world was subject to the contingencies of time and place. Abstract philosophy, by the same token, failed to account adequately for human experience and social behavior. Hegel accordingly proposed that only through speculative reason could one attain to anything approximating real knowledge of the world. Truth exists, for Hegel, only in the reflective mind; hence, it can only be perceived through a harmony among thoughts, rather than through any objective correlation between thought and material reality. Truth must be pursued through a dialectic that allows for the reconciliation of opposites, a theory that would naturally attract Wilde. As Wilde himself puts it, paraphrasing again from William Wallace's *Prolegomena*:

> [...] it remained for Hegel to show men that the Absolute and the Infinite were not unknowable as Kant would have it, and yet that man does not as [Friedrich Heinrich] Jacobi thought naturally by faith and intuition know the secrets of God: to him the road to true knowledge passed from the onesided identification of the understanding, to the disintegrating method of the free dialectic, till the contradictions of thoughts are unraveled, and the absolute knowledge of absolute Being, the Idea of pure thought is ultimately reached.[25]

Building upon the work of Aristotle, Hegel proposed that resolving the philosophical contradictions of this world required a dialectical approach. Put simply, the collision of two ideas—thesis and antithesis—generates under the right intellectual conditions a synthesis, a new thesis that can in turn be subjected to the same dialectical process.[26] Over time, such an approach promises to disclose what Hegel terms the Absolute Idea—the metaphysical truth that underlies all existence.

Of course, all human endeavors are also subject to the contingencies of time and place. In Hegel's view, the attainment of the Absolute Idea thus depends implicitly upon the development of human society, which is itself subject to an historical dialectic, whereby the present always develops out of and resists the claims of the past. In Jowett's view, it is this historical consciousness that finally distinguishes Hegel from Plato. He writes of the two great idealists:

> There is, however, a difference between them: for whereas Hegel is thinking of all the minds of men as one mind, which develops the stages of the idea in different countries or at different times in the same country, with Plato these gradations are regarded only as an order of thought or ideas; the history of the human mind had not yet dawned upon him.[27]

Hegel's treatment of truth-seeking as an endeavor that takes place across time and space naturally held some appeal for Wilde who, as I note in Chap. 3, shared his father's interest in historical inquiry. As Giles Whitely and others have established, Wilde's essay "The Rise of Historical Criticism," produced for (though not awarded) the Chancellor's English Essay Prize at Oxford in 1879, demonstrates a keen affinity for Hegelian thought, seeking to place the tradition of historical criticism itself within a recognizable historical dialectic.[28] Yet for Wilde, the history of ideas was also recursive. Even in "The Rise of Historical Criticism," Wilde notes that Plato was perhaps not entirely blind to the "history of the human mind." He writes: "Now just as the earliest account of the nature of the progress of humanity is to be found in Plato, so in him too we find the first explicit attempt to found a universal philosophy of History upon wide rational grounds."[29] To be sure, Plato's impulse is "to create history by the deductive method, and to proceed from a priori psychological principles" in order to identify the laws of human development—an "order of thought or ideas," as Jowett would have it.[30] To this extent, Wilde seems to approve Jowett's assertion that Plato had attended more to the general principles of historical development than to the evolution of thought. Also like Jowett, Wilde's understanding of intellectual history is not restricted to a linear, dialectical principle. On the contrary, Wilde seems equally attracted by an historical vision in which the cyclical reiteration of old ideas plays a significant role. My point is not to suggest simply that Wilde attenuated the claims of Hegel, for this work has already been ably accomplished by other scholars. Instead, I want to stress that even at moments when Wilde seems most attracted to a particular philosophical method, his understanding of it is often colored by multiple overlapping and even conflicting sources. Although

Wilde concurred with Hegel regarding the value of dialectic and the primacy of individual perception, it is by no means clear that he endorsed this methodology wholeheartedly.

Jowett, one of Wilde's principal sources of insight into idealism, was hardly an unwavering disciple. If he conferred "immeasurable respect" upon the idealist philosophy of Schelling, Jowett would also prove a critical audience of his *Naturphilosophie*: "All his systems of philosophy were the creation of a man of genius, and showed a great deal of thought and insight, but they had no definite relation to history or fact. All of them claimed to be based on first principles and eternal truth. In a few years they were no longer remembered."[31] Of Hegel too Jowett expressed some reservations, and these reservations would reach a peak in the later part of his life. While admiring Hegel as a "critic of philosophy," Jowett proclaimed in 1885 that he was himself "not a Hegelian," citing especially his concerns that the Hegelian dialectic did not accord with historical reality.[32] At times, Jowett seems to have resisted the notion that thought resolves in a neat synthesis of ideas. Edward Caird noted that Jowett's own intellectual process actively resisted a linear dialectic: "His treatment of great questions never took the form of an attempt to think them out consecutively but of a series of glances at truth from various points of view somewhat inconsistent with each other [...] Hence what was for him a satisfactory expression of his conviction might seem to others like a collection of aporias or conflicting views that want for reconciliation."[33] If Hegel provided an illuminating model for understanding how ideas converge and combine over generations, it was not a model that corresponded to lived experience. The evolution of ideas, for Jowett, was hardly ever so systematic or progressive.

This view was shared by Friedrich Max Müller, the Oxford philologist whom Wilde encountered during his first year at the university. Müller had studied the work of Hegel under Christian Weisse at the University of Leipzig and remarked that in his youth to "be a Hegelian was considered a sine quâ non, not only among philosophers, but quite as much among theologians, men of science, lawyers, artists, in fact, in every branch of human knowledge, at least in Prussia. If Christianity in its Protestant form was the state-religion of the kingdom, Hegelianism was its state philosophy."[34] Weisse had taught Müller to revere but also to be wary of Hegel's system, noting that historical facts did not always bear out his vision of progress, particularly with respect to the "growth of religious thought."[35] In his 1856 essay "Comparative Mythologies," Müller would argue against "the idea of a humanity emerging slowly from the depths of an animal brutality," reflecting: "We still speak the language of the first ancestors of our race; and this language, with its wonderful structure, bears witness against such gratuitous imputations."[36] As in the case of Jowett, it was this conflict between Hegel's historiography and historical reality that unsettled Müller's "belief in the correctness of Hegel's fundamental principles."[37] In his own scholarship, which would focus especially on Eastern religion, Müller adopted a developmental approach but consistently refused to assign to history a logical or linear dialectic.[38] This is, it would seem, an important detail, for it suggests that Wilde was exposed, from the moment of his arrival at Oxford, to varied and often critical interpretations of idealist precepts.

It was likely Müller who introduced Wilde to Zhuangzi (transcribed by Wilde as Chuang Tsŭ and by Müller as Kwang-ze), for he had included his multivolume tome *The Sacred Books of the East* (1879), referring to him as "the Tâoist sage."[39] Zhuangzi would become the subject of Wilde's 1889 essay "A Chinese Sage," which draws compelling parallels between Daoist philosophy and nineteenth-century aestheticism. As Jerusha McCormack has persuasively established, many of the aphorisms so often attributed to Wilde seem in fact to be rough paraphrases of Zhuangzi's work.[40] Tellingly, Wilde describes the Chinese philosopher as a man who "spent his life in preaching the great creed of Inaction, and in pointing out the uselessness of all useful things."[41] Although Wilde's appeal to material luxury seems to directly contravene the precepts of Daoism, Wilde too would aver that utility all too often undermines man's quest after higher ideas; under the playful guise of the dandy (as discussed in Chap. 2) he too would claim that inaction provided much needed time and space for the cultivation of thought.[42]

More importantly, however, "A Chinese Sage" offers a direct appraisal of the philosophical methods current at Oxford in the 1880s. The essay commences: "An eminent Oxford theologian once remarked that his only objection to modern progress was that it progressed forward instead of backward."[43] Whether the term "Oxford theologian" was a playful moniker for Müller must remain a matter of speculation; assuredly, however, the remark recalls Wilde's tutelage under Müller, who resisted Hegel's notion of a progressive and dialectical history on the grounds that it was unsupported by historical reality. It is perhaps unsurprising, then, that Wilde's treatment of Zhuangzi resolutely resists the notion of dialectical progress. Instead, he locates the sage as a forebear to a longer continuum of Western philosophy, which has unknowingly and repeatedly circled back to the insights of ancient China:

> To resolve action into thought, and thought into abstraction, was his wicked transcendental aim. Like the obscure philosopher of early Greek speculation, he believed in the identity of contraries; like Plato, he was an idealist, and had all the idealist's contempt for utilitarian systems; he was a mystic like Dionysius,

and Scotus Erigena, and Jacob Böhme, and held, with them and with Philo, that the object of life was to get rid of self-consciousness, and to become the unconscious vehicle of a higher illumination. In fact, Chuang Tzu may be said to have summed up in himself almost every mood of European metaphysical or mystical thought, from Heraclitus down to Hegel.[44]

Over the course of this passage, Wilde tracks a philosophical tradition from ancient Greece (Plato and Heraclitus) to first-century Athens (Dionysius of Areopagite), to seventh-century Ireland (Scotus Erigena), to sixteenth-century Germany (Jakob Böhme), and back to ancient Alexandria (Philo). For Wilde, modern thinkers were not necessarily more astute than the ancients—the difference was the manner in which they accessed and articulated knowledge. Accordingly, Zhuangzi anticipates centuries of Western thought while adopting a style that seems to elude the linear, systematic logic that had dogged modern philosophy. As Wilde puts it succinctly, it was in the works of Zhuangzi that he encountered "the most caustic criticism of modern life [he had] met with for some time."[45] In such an utterance, Wilde seems to suggest that philosophy is a discipline at once subject and resistant to historical pressures.

Wilde cultivated this idea, in part, through his close study of Henry Thomas Buckle, whose *History of Civilization in England* (1857) served as an important source text for "The Rise of Historical Criticism," as Philip Smith has noted.[46] Buckle had argued that human history unfolds according to scientific laws that are as consistent as those that inform Nature, noting that "while most moral inquiries have depended on some theological or metaphysical hypothesis, the investigation to which I allude are exclusively inductive."[47] In this spirit, Wilde records in his Oxford notebook: "For a scientific conception of History the first requisite is the doctrine of uniform sequence · in other words that certain events having happened, certain other events corresponding to them will happen: that the past is the key of the future:"[48] Smith and Helfand cite Buckle's volume as a verified source for this passage, and the ideas reflected upon here certainly correspond to his outlook. Importantly, however, Wilde's excerpts do not merely paraphrase Buckle's text. Wilde seems to have skipped widely across Buckle's *History*, and the resulting synthesis would eventually appear in a slightly altered form in "The Rise of Historical Criticism," where it serves to highlight a singular concept: the scientific and sequential unfolding of historical events.[49]

As I discuss in Chap. 4, Wilde understood science as a form of speculative thought, albeit one that was grounded in examinations of the natural world. With this in mind, it is perhaps appropriate that Buckle's argument in favor of a "scientific" approach to history does not amount, in Wilde's view, to an empirical or systematic understanding of the past. Indeed, the passage just quoted is followed immediately by another short paragraph: "In the character of a nation inconsistency is impossible: in the <u>moral</u> world as in the physical nothing is anomalous: yet while we have now a natural science in the sphere of history the theological doctrine of irregularity still holds place:"[50] By definition, nothing can occur in Nature that is unnatural. To this extent, Wilde seems to concede Buckle's claims that "in the mineral kingdom, there is, properly speaking, no irregularity," since even apparent deviations from the norm can be explained by an appeal to "higher truth." The final clause of this passage, however, suggests a perspective that is perhaps more detached. If history is to be studied through a scientific lens, Wilde interposes, such a view does not necessarily confirm a progressive view of human civilization; according to the "doctrine of irregularity," deviations, accidents, and hindrances are all part of the natural course of things. If Buckle promotes a progressive and systematic view of history, then, it is also a view that accounts for the contingencies of social life and the errors of human perception. The human mind and nature, Buckle remarks, work in reciprocal relation to one another, so that "all the vicissitudes of the human race, their progress or their decay, their happiness or their misery, must be the fruit of a double action; an action of external phenomena upon the mind, and another action of the mind upon the phenomena."[51] To this extent, Buckle sought to unite the empirical and idealist view of history, acknowledging the role the mind plays in shaping and writing history even as he insisted that one might divine in the past predictable patterns of behavior.

For Wilde, then, history might be regarded as both the product of the mind perceiving it and the force acting upon that mind.[52] "History," he writes, "may be looked on either as a work of art—whose τέλος [telos] is in the maker—or an organism, evolving its own τέλος [telos]."[53] In the context of the present discussion, what is most striking about these words is the fact that Wilde seems to stand precisely on the line between an idealist and a materialist view of history. Although Wilde was attracted by the principles of dialectic and idealism, this should not necessarily lead us to conclude that he was a devoted practitioner of either. From the 1870s on Wilde cultivated a view of history as a recursive project, wherein every generation of thinkers revisits the same ideas using different tools and vocabularies. It was in that spirit that Wilde remarked that the "early Greeks had mystic anticipations of nearly all great modern scientific truths."[54] In the history of ideas, too, Wilde found that intellectual development did not always follow a straight line. He would, for instance, trace Hegelian thought not to Plato, as Jowett had done, but to Parmenides, the pre-Socratic philosopher who first speculated on the nature of being: "Founder of Idealism and of dialectic, of metaphysics and logic [...]".[55] In a later entry in the Commonplace Book, Wilde turns to Francis Bacon's *Novum Organum* as a source of critical insight:

> Against Hegels Philosophy of History Bacon says (ref. to Arabs & Schoolmen)
>   "Sunt enim non minus temporum quam regionum eremi et vastitates" [*In times no less than in regions there are wastes and deserts*]
>   Limit to investigation of Nature "subtilitas naturae subiltilitatem [*sic*] sensus et intellectis multis partibus superat" [*The subtlety of nature is greater many times over than the subtlety of the senses and understanding*]
>   Scientia et potentia humana in idem coincidunt: [*Human knowledge and human power meet in one*]
>   ipissimae res veritas et utilitas. [*Truth therefore and utility are here the very same things*][56]

Wilde studied the *Novum Organum* closely during his time at Oxford, as I note in Chap. 4.[57] In this entry, Wilde does not merely transcribe a series of excerpts from Bacon: together, these excerpts reflect an argument "Against Hegel's Philosophy of History," which posits that humanity's capacity to access higher knowledge is subject to the contingencies of time and nature: history too has its "wastes and deserts." Excerpted thus, Bacon seems to treat eras of human progress as the exception, not the rule. If a dialectical process is in place, it is continually disrupted by moments of destruction and stasis. In part, this is because the human "senses and understanding" are always subject to natural laws, a claim that both Jowett and Müller had endorsed. As Bacon puts it: "Man, being the servant and interpreter of Nature, can do and understand so much and so much only as he has observed in fact or in thought of the course of nature: beyond this he neither knows anything nor can do anything."[58] It is the very problem Wilde had tackled in relation to the concrete sciences: how can man ever understand or govern a system to which he is himself confined?

If we consider the final excerpt Wilde takes from Bacon—and if we place it within its original context—a more sweeping indictment on philosophical thinking comes into view. Contemplative acts are, Bacon avers, only ever made possible and informed by one's movements within the natural world:

> But I say that those foolish and apish images of worlds which the fancies of men have created in philosophical systems, must be utterly scattered to the winds. Be it known then how vast a difference there is (as I said above) between the Idols of the human mind and the Ideas of the divine. The former are nothing more

than arbitrary abstractions; the latter are the creator's own stamp upon creation, impressed and defined in matter by true and exquisite lines. Truth therefore and utility are here the very same things [...][59]

If philosophy seeks to clarify the meanings and structures of this world, it must do so by drawing on the limited knowledge available to a philosopher who is likewise subject to the limits of time, space, and human cognition. In his illuminating discussion of Wilde's inquiries into "abstraction," Joseph Bristow notes that Bacon "encouraged Wilde to remember that abstraction may well involve creating forms that bear no relation to the mutable complexities of matter."[60] Even speculative reason must admit its limits. In Wilde's excerpts from Bacon, the evidence for a world that exists beyond human perception—perhaps even one of divine origin—is to be found in nature alone. Human perception is "arbitrary" and abstract; nature is concrete and bears the "stamp" of the divine. To this extent, metaphysical truth is utterly dependent upon empirical observation and the claims of "utility." Paradox though it may seem, Wilde's excerpts suggest that empirical thought underlies idealism, just as idealist principles seem to underlie empiricism.

This is not to suggest that Wilde regarded philosophy as a futile exercise, one destined to undermine its own premises. On the contrary, Wilde's interest in these warring perspectives—and his tendency to shift from one side to the other—implies a wariness of philosophical argument, paired with a mounting interest in the real stuff of metaphysical *inquiry*. While Wilde's notebook offers no further gloss on Bacon's argument, it is suggestive that he draws Bacon into dialogue with Hegel, seeing in Bacon a legitimate challenge to the work of the German philosopher who would succeed him several generations later. Attracted by Hegel's attempt to reconcile opposites through the work of dialectic, Wilde remained unconvinced that either human thought or human society could be relegated to such a linear or progressive system.[61]

The Pessimist

In *An Ideal Husband* (1895), the scheming adventuress Mrs. Cheveley presents Sir Robert Chiltern with the following dilemma: "But may I ask, at heart, are you an optimist or a pessimist? Those seem to be the only two fashionable religions left to us nowadays."[62] Mrs. Cheveley's query promises to organize English society tidily into two classes: idealists and cynics. Her casual remark, however, is quickly jettisoned by Chiltern's response. "Oh, I'm neither," he replies. "Optimism begins in a broad grin, and Pessimism ends with blue spectacles. They are both of them merely poses."[63] Characteristically, Wilde refuses a system of classification that would make one's choice of philosophy akin to the selection of a buttonhole or cravat. Robert Chiltern's refusal to identify himself as either a pessimist or an optimist seems at first to dismiss such philosophical distinctions out of hand. But as we have seen, Wilde is often less concerned with assuming a resolute stance on specific schools of thought than in querying the forms of philosophical discourse. To align oneself with a fixed methodology is to adopt a decidedly *unphilosophical* method—one that has a clear "beginning" and "end," and resolves in a statuesque "pose." If Wilde prized philosophy chiefly as a process, then to "pose" as either optimist or pessimist is actually to forsake the love of wisdom for a more static existence.

Hence, while Chiltern's remarks would at first seem to cast the pessimist as a mere curmudgeon who luxuriates in his own suffering, they assume a slightly different connotation in the context of Wilde's longstanding interest in the study of philosophy. Wilde admired the underlying principles of idealism but remained wary of adopting any single system that claimed to resolve the problem of metaphysical truth. At times, he would indulge in dialectical experiments, as Smith and Helfand have established; but at other times he would refuse such a dialectic outright, preferring instead to view all knowledge as elusive. By way of elucidating Wilde's complicated relationship to dialectic, I want to trace here his engagement with an outlook that adamantly resists the notion of progress, teleology, or even productive truth-seeking: namely, the philosophical pessimism of Arthur Schopenhauer. If Wilde celebrated the value of conversation and dialectical exchange, he often seems equally committed to a philosophical posture that celebrates the *failures* of dialectic.

While we cannot definitively establish that Wilde read Schopenhauer, there is good reason to believe that he at least encountered his work indirectly through conversations with his mother and others in his immediate circle. Jean Pierrot has noted that Schopenhauer's influence was so extensive in the 1880s that his ideas might be ranked as "one of the commonplaces of the day," as much a part of living in the world as knowledge of Darwin, and several scholars have noted the compelling conceptual and syntactical similarities between Wilde's aesthetic utterances and those of Schopenhauer.[64] Irrespective of how Wilde encountered Schopenhauer's work, it is almost certain that he did encounter and reflect upon it, for his writings from the 1870s on bear traces of its influence. In an 1876 letter to William Ward, Wilde remarked upon his mother's passion for philosophy:

Her last pessimist, Schopenhauer, says the whole human race ought on a given day, after a strong remonstrance firmly but respectfully urged on God, to walk into the sea and leave the world tenantless, but of course some skulking wretches would hide and be left behind to people the world again I am afraid.[65]

While his tone here suggests mocking aversion to Schopenhauer's bleak view of the future, Wilde's refusal to accept that the world could ever be free of people or their vices situates him as a perfect pessimist. Wilde's response to this prophecy is appropriately despairing, and he fears that even Schopenhauer's prediction of a world devoid of human presence may be too hopeful. Some "skulking wretches" would doubtless mar the peace and serenity such a vision promises.

Yet Schopenhauer was not, as Wilde assuredly knew, a mere fatalist. He was an inveterate critic of Hegel, referring to him at one time as "that pernicious person, who completely disorganized and ruined the minds of a whole generation."[66] Like some of his contemporaries—much like Wilde himself—Schopenhauer felt that Hegel's disciples had gone too far in uncritically espousing his ideas. Hegel's influence was so profound, in short, that he had "paralyzed mentally a whole generation of scholars," who were fluent in the terms of his philosophy but unable to interrogate its first principles.[67] Schopenhauer accordingly returned to the work of Immanuel Kant, taking as his first premise the separation between the human mind and what Kant termed the "thing in itself." According to Schopenhauer, the world is characterized by a fissure between the material reality we perceive as external to ourselves (Representation) and the hidden truth that undergirds it (the Will or Idea). Human suffering originates in our desire to perceive this hidden truth, which always remains beyond our comprehension. Desire, then, is only ever an awareness of what we lack. Everything we might regard as a positive good becomes, paradoxically, a wellspring of pain.

If this seems a somewhat hopeless condition, Schopenhauer actually assigns pain a productive role in individual and social life. For Schopenhauer, pain is an unavoidable and even welcome fact of existence, precisely because it cultivates action and experience: "I know of no greater absurdity than that propounded by most systems of philosophy in declaring evil to be negative in its character. Evil is just what is positive; it makes its own existence felt."[68] By this logic, happiness and pleasure connote not merely the absence of pain but the cessation of all action. "A certain amount of care or pain or trouble," he further notes, "is necessary for man at all times. A ship without a ballast is unstable and will not go straight."[69] The very motion of life depends on some form of resistance. When that resistance is removed, life itself ceases to have meaning—so far from being a positive good, happiness paradoxically under-mines the generative quality of life itself. "Certain it is" he writes "that *work, worry, labor* and *trouble,* form the lot of almost all men their whole life long. But if all wishes were fulfilled as soon as they arose, how would men occupy their lives? what would they do with their time? If the world were a paradise of luxury and ease […] men would either die of boredom or hang themselves […]"[70] Lady Wilde herself echoes this idea in her 1877 essay "The Destiny of Humanity": "In such pain, however, there is no misery; rather, as Schopenhauer has remarked, the intensest consciousness of life. Without it life would be mere passivity—a dull negation, where the upward striving of the soul would be annihilated."[71] Schopenhauer's pessimism thus rejects those binaries (good and evil, pain and pleasure) that his society took for granted. Material luxury is both bad, because it stimulates man's insatiable appetite for pleasure, and good, because even the most agonizing pangs of desire prompt us to engage actively with the world. Certainly this rhetorical move—the inversion of accepted binaries—is also quite typical of Wilde.

The strongest kinship between these thinkers, however, is to be found in their treatment of the aesthetic experience as an anodyne to the sufferings of this world. As Wilde notes in "The Critic as Artist," "the mission of the aes-thetic movement is to lure people to contemplate" and thus to inhabit a world where radical ideas, impressions, and experiences become possible.[72] The plas-ticity of aesthetic expression allows one to leave aside the real world to access the world as it might be. To that end, the aesthete "rejects those obvious modes of art that have but one message to deliver […] and seeks rather for such modes as suggest reverie and mood, and by their imaginative beauty make all interpre-tations true, and no interpretation final."[73] Wilde's vision of aestheticism is tinged throughout by idealism. Art provides more than a mere respite from the suffering of this world; cultivating the individual's capacity for perception, reflection, and interpretation, it allows one to reimagine and recreate reality upon entirely new foundations. Such a theory of art bears a strong resemblance to Schopenhauer's outlook. For Schopenhauer, art provides us with a way of escaping the suffering of material existence, for the contemplation of beauty allows us to experience the world not merely as a reality external to oneself but as a reality that is forged through and in turn helps to constitute the self. As "the whole consciousness is filled and occupied with one single sensuous pic-ture," Schopenhauer writes, man submits simultaneously to a sensory experi-ence of the world and to a transcendent unity with it.[74] The process of aesthetic contemplation, in that moment, takes precedence over the ontological quest for truth and affords an escape from desire. In the end, then, Schopenhauer treats material pleasure as a profound, if necessary and desirable, source of pain that can be only momentarily eluded through the contemplation of an aesthetic object.

Wilde seems to have found much to admire in Schopenhauer's aesthetic vision, for he would invoke it explicitly at several points over the course of his career. In "The Decay of Lying," Vivian remarks: "Schopenhauer has analysed the pessimism that characterizes modern thought, but Hamlet invented it."[75] At first glance, the remark would seem to be an off-hand allusion to Schopenhauer's despairing view of existence, meant chiefly to underscore the primacy of all art in constructing the world in which we live: it is not philosophy but fiction that shapes reality. Still, Vivian's remark does not casually pass over Schopenhauer's criticism of modern life. After all, his very argument echoes Schopenhauer's claim that lies actually constitute reality and determine our conduct. "Many undoubtedly owe their good fortune," Schopenhauer writes, "to the circumstance that they possess a pleasing smile with which they win hearts. Yet these hearts would do better to beware and to learn from Hamlet's tables that one may smile, and smile, and be a villain."[76] Later on in the same work, Schopenhauer would go further, noting (much like Vivian) that art should not imitate but rather should forge our vision of the world. He writes:

> One would suppose that art achieved the beautiful by imitating nature. But how is the artist to recognize the perfect work which is to be imitated, and distinguish it from the failures, if he does not anticipate the beautiful before experience? […] That we all recognize human beauty when we see it, but that in the true artist this takes place with such clearness that he shows it as he has never seen it, and surpasses nature in his representation; this is only possible because *we ourselves are* the will whose adequate objectification at its highest grade is here to be judged and discovered.[77]

With good reason, scholars tend to cite Plato as the primary inspiration for "The Decay of Lying," noting the connections between Wilde's essay and those famous passages from the *Republic* that treat representational art as a form of untruth.[78] Without overstating the scope of Schopenhauer's influence, however, it is worth attending to Wilde's suggestive echoing of his work in this passage. Like Schopenhauer, Wilde would claim that true artists should not reproduce what they see in nature but must instead capture the unseen beauty that they alone perceive. Put simply: "No great artist ever sees things as they really are. If he did, he would cease to be an artist."[79]

My object is not merely to identify Schopenhauer as an unlikely source text for "The Decay of Lying." On the contrary, attending to this seemingly casual reference illuminates why and how Wilde seems to at once embrace and recoil from formal philosophical methods. If Vivian's invocation of Schopenhauer seems fleeting and dismissive, Wilde's appraisal of pessimism was neither of these things. Indeed, he strategically purveys some of Schopenhauer's central ideas while seeming to dismiss the author, terms, and forms usually attributed to them. In this way, he could divest Schopenhauer's philosophy of its formal trappings and more effectively set his ideas in motion. To systematically seek out metaphysical truth is, in Schopenhauer's view, to condemn oneself to a life of disappointment and despair; accordingly, Wilde abandons such an approach in favor of one that calls our attention to art—the one thing, as the pessimist would have it, that can offer solace.

Of course, Wilde's rhetorical strategy in this passage also reflects an important point of departure from Schopenhauer. Whereas the pessimist presents art as an escape from this state of suffering, Wilde suggests that art is a site of transformation and movement. For Wilde, the Platonic distinction between being and becoming is fundamental: to exist in perpetual movement and to continually evolve is, for Wilde, a state to be positively embraced:

> the contemplative life, the life that has for its aim not *doing* but *being*, and not *being* merely, but *becoming*—that is what the critical spirit can give us. [...] From the high tower of Thought we can look oumt at the world. Calm, and self-centred, and complete, the aesthetic critic contemplates life, and no arrow drawn at a venture can pierce between the joints of his harness. He at least is safe. He has discovered how to live.[80]

Like Schopenhauer, Wilde insists that the aesthetic realm—the "world as representation"—is uniquely illuminating because it is liberated from the constraints of material existence. It is the mobility afforded by art that provides the most potent mode of becoming. Through aesthetic contemplation, one finds the freedom to engage and evolve, while remaining safe from the practical risks of the material world.[81]

It is thus unsurprising that this shared investment in the distinction between "being" and "becoming"—a distinction first articulated by Plato—informed both Schopenhauer's and Wilde's understanding of identity itself. Consider Wilde's proclamation at the end of his essay "The Truth of Masks":

> Not that I agree with everything that I have said in this essay. There is much with which I entirely disagree. The essay simply represents an artistic standpoint, and in aesthetic criticism attitude is everything. For in art there is no such thing as a universal truth. A Truth in art is that whose contradictory is also true.

And just as it is only in art-criticism, and through it, that we can apprehend the Platonic theory of ideas, so it is only in art-criticism, and through it, that we can realise Hegel's system of contraries. The truths of metaphysics are the truths of masks.[82]

As Giles Whiteley rightly points out, generations of scholars have treated this passage as a clear expression of Wilde's philosophy of art. On the face of it, Wilde would seem here to be an outspoken advocate for philosophical idealism and Hegelian dialectics.[83] Whiteley goes on, however, to highlight important differences between Wilde and the philosophers who are typically described as his chief influences, finally proposing that critics have been too quick to label Wilde as an idealist. In Whiteley's view, it would be more accurate to understand Wilde as breaking radically from his precursors, treating him instead as a forerunner to poststructuralists like Gilles Deleuze and Jean Baudrillard, whose concept of the "simulacrum" Wilde's work seems at times to anticipate. The "truth of masks," according to Whiteley, points to Wilde's overarching belief in the power of illusion and an investment in "images which are no longer referential to anything other than themselves."[84] In other words, Wilde regards truth as always existing within a system of references that are themselves open to scrutiny, so that the only truth is the one that resists the very concept of the Absolute Idea. Seen this way, Wilde does not recommend Hegel's "system of contraries" as a method for attaining truth; indeed, Wilde seeks to supplant that system with one in which we recognize reality as being continually constructed and reconstructed through the seductive gaze of the mask.[85]

For Schopenhauer, knowledge of oneself is similarly elusive. "The real meaning of *persona* is *a mask*," he writes, "such as actors were accustomed to wear on the ancient stage; and it is quite true that no one shows himself as he is, but wears his mask and plays his part. Indeed, the whole of our social arrangements may be likened to a perpetual comedy; and this is why a man who is worth anything finds society so insipid, while a blockhead is quite at home in it."[86] Such a remark finds countless echoes in the work of Wilde, who would recast the sentiment in his approach to British aestheticism. On the surface, the British aesthete was a modern dandy, preoccupied with luxury, beauty, and idleness—a fashionable young man dressed in outlandish costume and professing a passion for poetry and the decorative arts. For Wilde, however, the aesthete was no mere a lover of fashion: he was a man who had discovered how to fully realize himself through a direct engagement with beauty. In "The Critic as Artist" (1891), Wilde would describe the aesthete as a modern philosopher who attains revelation through the contemplation of art: "Calm, and self-centred, and complete."[87]

Whiteley's claim that Wilde regards the mask as a vehicle for truth is a compelling one, and Wilde certainly calls attention to the relativity and even inaccessibility of knowledge in many of his published writings. Yet Wilde's words suggest more than a categorical rejection of absolute truth. Where Jean Baudrillard might propose that postmodern culture can no longer differentiate between nature and artifice (the simulacrum), for Wilde the highest form of beauty was always, by nature, practically indistinguishable from truth. The true aesthetic experience does not avail a reflection of reality that remains hidden from view; it instantiates, as we have seen, a generative process of metaphysical inquiry. If that process allows the individual to forge meaning and to see this world anew (thus generating new simulacra), my argument here is that Wilde treats the experience of aesthetic contemplation, and not its object, as the nearest thing to metaphysical truth. Like Jowett, Wilde may have preferred to engage knowledge as a "collection of aporias or conflicting views that want for reconciliation."[88] If Hegelian idealism is typically aligned with the synthesis of discrete postulations, Wilde values it less for the promise of new knowledge than for the philosophical process it instantiates.

For Wilde, then, intellectual synthesis is far less important than the prospect of accepting the coexistence of opposed views. Metaphysical truth—in an absolute sense—remains elusive, yet its very elusiveness is precisely what motivates the process of *becoming* that informs so much of Wilde's thought. In his Commonplace Book, he would paraphrase from Wallace's *Prolegomena*: "The opposition between Idealism and Realism is a shallow one belonging to the onesided [sic] method of the understanding: Every true philosophy must be both idealist and realist: for without realism a philosophy would be void of substance and matter. Without idealism it wd. [would] be void of form and truth."[89] Although Wilde adopts Wallace's terms throughout this passage, his words go far beyond mere paraphrase. Wallace had proposed that dialectic may well have, "in opposition to the one-sided products of understanding, the look of a destructive agent," for it is by nature concerned with transcending a postulated truth.[90] Yet because it wholly embraces the "rational or speculative" spirit, seeking to generate rather than abolish thought, dialectic becomes far more the mere skepticism.

Hence, Wallace too would contend that the methods of nineteenth-century philosophy were all too often relegated to rigid and misleading categories. Discussing the "new idealism" of Hegel and Kant, Wallace observes:

But, as perhaps may have been apparent, to call this way of thought idealism need not keep us from acknowledging that the same philosophy is also realism. If it insists, so to say, on the idealism of—what we sometimes call material— nature, it no less insists on the realism of—what is supposed immaterial—mind. The mental or spiritual world loses its unsubstantial intangibleness, its mere supposedness, its 'ideal' or *merely*-ideal character.[91]

It was important to Wallace that philosophical endeavors abandon a fidelity to such rigid terms, submitting itself to an ongoing process of scrutiny and forever eluding such binary thinking. Without merely transcribing Wallace's words, Wilde suggestively collapses his treatment of dialectic and philosophical idealism, insinuating that the most generative dialectic challenges man to navigate between the unknowability of abstract knowledge and the practical demands of language, action, and the material world.

Wilde's pessimism is, then, of a curiously optimistic bent: the inaccessibility of desire is, for Wilde, a good to be embraced, for it is the process of philosophical speculation and not its resolution that constitutes meaning. It is in this spirit, perhaps, that Lane, the worldly butler in *The Importance of Being Earnest* (1895), embraces his role as pessimist:

Algernon: I hope tomorrow will be a fine day, Lane.
Lane: It never is.
Algernon: Lane, you're a perfect pessimist.
Lane: I do my best to give satisfaction, sir.[92]

At such a moment, Lane proves himself to be every bit as much a philosopher as his shrewd master. In this case, after all, to give satisfaction is to despair of attaining the ideal. Pessimism and perfection may coexist, Lane suggests, and one may accept this fact without seeking recourse in the relativity of truth. Indeed, he seems to forego the resolution promised by dialectical engagement and, rather than resolving the paradox, freely embraces it. If paradox is, as I suggest in Chap. 2, a hermeneutic loop—a stylized mobility of thought— then Lane seems to recommend embracing that mobility as a way of engaging (without necessarily validating) two very different schools of thought. For Wilde, critiquing philosophical systems did not necessarily amount to the construction of his own philosophy of art or life. It had far more to do with escaping the epistemological certainty that such systems promised.

The Student of Philosophy

"Are you a Pessimist?" Lady Chiltern asks of the provocative Lord Goring in *An Ideal Husband*. "What will the other dandies say? They will all have to go into mourning." Lord Goring's reply is revealing: "No, Lady Chiltern, I am not a Pessimist. Indeed I am not sure that I quite know what Pessimism really means. All I do know is that life cannot be understood without much charity, cannot be lived without much charity. It is love, and not German philosophy, that is the true explanation of this world, whatever may be the explanation of the next."[93] Lord Goring proposes that it is sympathy—not philosophy—that underlies our reality. To this extent, he presents a direct counterpoint to the love-sick philosophy student in "The Nightingale and the Rose." Where the student forsakes love in pursuit of metaphysical truth, Lord Goring embraces love and denounces the formal terms of philosophy. His refusal to assert a clear philosophical stance brings us back to the question with which this chapter commenced. Was Wilde a serious philosopher with a unique world-view he wished to impart? Or was he a desultory student of philosophy, who merely skimmed the surface of those works? Was philosophy his passion—one he undertook with seriousness and purpose—or a mere pose?[94]

For the remainder of this chapter, I want to suggest that Wilde's slighting references to philosophy in some of his published work constitute less a rejection of philosophy than a recognition that philosophical systems are themselves of limited value in pursuing metaphysical truth. When the love-sick student in "The Nightingale and the Rose" abandons love in favor of metaphysics, one gets the distinct sense that his quest will not end in true philosophy. Although he may eagerly devour philosophical precepts, his disavowal of human bonds runs contrary to the spirit of metaphysical inquiry, which probes the first principles of existence—causation, knowledge, and experience. The hermetic student remains too detached to undertake such a quest in earnest. By contrast, Lord Goring emerges as the unlikely hero of *An Ideal Husband*, a ludic figure whose very refusal to take a side proves most empowering. It may well be in this spirit that Lord Goring, the astute and quietly sympathetic dandy of *An Ideal Husband* is described as the "first well-dressed philosopher in the history of thought."[95]

While it would be misleading to suggest that Goring embodies in any direct way Wilde's own philosophical tenets, there is good reason for describing Wilde as a reluctant philosopher—a man who was drawn to philosophical inquiry but repelled by the forms it so often assumed. He may well have gleaned some of this impulse from his Oxford mentor Walter Pater, who turned to philosophy for justification of his radically idealist (one might even say protean) vision of aesthetics. In his Commonplace Book, Wilde loosely transcribes the following line from Walter Pater's essay "Winckelmann":

> "We must renounce metaphysics if we would mould our lives to artistic perfection [.]
>
> For Philosophy serves culture not by the fancied gift of absolute or transcendental knowledge but by suggesting questions which help one to detect the passion and strangeness and dramatic contrasts of Life"[96]

In this passage, Pater seems to reject the value of philosophical systems, which he views as detached from the real movement and volatility of lived experience. Pater was indebted to Hegel in certain respects, and "Winckelmann" commences with a nod to Hegel's 1826 *Introductory Lectures on Aesthetics*, which he had read in the original German in 1863.[97] As Kate Hext observes, Hegel's belief in teleology and synthesis—and in the mutual dependence of individual and social identity—all ran contrary to Pater's investment in mobility, irresolution, and subjectivity.[98] Hence, Pater's idealism might be more closely aligned with the work of George Berkeley, who suggested that individual perception was the locus of all perceived reality.[99] Pater's idealism, read a certain way, recommended that the individual's experience of the world was the *only* form of knowledge worth cultivating.

If Pater's words would seem to buttress Wilde's aversion to philosophical systems, however, Wilde's brief commentary upon the excerpt recommends a slight departure from his Oxford mentor. As Wilde writes in the Commonplace Book: "Yet surely he who sees in colour no mere delightful quality of natural things but a spirit dwelling in things is in a way a metaphysician."[100] It is not metaphysics itself that proves limiting, Wilde suggests, but rather our understanding of what constitutes metaphysical inquiry. To be a metaphysician is not perforce to restrict oneself to the world of abstraction: it is merely to probe into the meaning and nature of existence, and this is an endeavor that may be as effectively pursued through speculation as through art or experience. The real problem, then, is that our understanding of what constitutes metaphysical inquiry is all too limited, leading some to become lost in its labyrinths and others to flee from it altogether. Seen this way, metaphysics becomes a tool rather than what Wilde acknowledged it to be—a process of inquiry that is essential to being human:

> Like the Sphinx . Those who do not try to answer her questions are annihilated—and often he who solves her riddle comes to no good end—for he

dwells apart from men in the colourless abstractions of a spiritual world, in the
vacuity of an infinite which has no contents [.]

The danger of metaphysics is that men are often turning nomina into numina[101]

Like Pater, Wilde expresses some concern about the metaphysician who exists
only in a world of "colourless abstractions," detached from the investments of
this world. Such a philosopher risks continually mistaking mere *terms*
(nomina) for spiritual *laws* (numina). If Wilde shared Pater's wariness of philosophical systems, it was not because he valued experience above metaphysical speculation. On the contrary, it was because he regarded metaphysical
speculation as essential to any substantive experience of art, nature, or
social life.

At several points in his notebooks, Wilde reflects upon the nineteenth-
century turn to empiricism, and his remarks often imply a desire to defend
metaphysical speculation before its critics. He turns, for instance, to Jowett on
the subject, excerpting from his introductions to "Sophist" and "Parmenides":

> it is really not a question between ~~good~~ emploing [sic] metaphysics, or not, but
> between emploing [sic] good or bad metaphysics:
>   There are more metaphysics (i.e., more a priori assumption) in an unmeta-
> physical age than in any other . <u>We do not consider how much metaphysics</u> are
> required to place us <u>above</u> metaphysics—see (Jowett Plato. 4. 155) [.] We talk
> about facts when we are really resting on ideas:[102]

Noting Plato's careful interrogation of metaphysical terms, Jowett suggests
that one of the greatest hindrances to philosophy was for centuries a lack of
"inquiry into the relation of language and thought," hence breeding debates
that rested upon little more than semantic differences. Jowett notes that the
same principle might well be applied to nineteenth-century social and scientific discourses, "while similar words, such as development, evolution, law,
and the like, are constantly put in the place of facts, even by writers who profess to base truth entirely upon fact."[103] Jowett's claim, as paraphrased and
interpreted by Wilde in his notebook, is that our understanding of the world
can only ever be mediated through words that represent what we *believe*
to be true.

All facts, then, rest upon ideas. Only by inquiring into the relation between
things and words—only through metaphysical speculation—can we give cre-
dence to empirical observations. In this spirit, Wilde, inscribes the following
note opposite to the excerpt from Jowett: "So even David Hume the precursor of the modern phenomenistic empirical school of thought said 'We

must cultivate ∧true metaphysics with some care, in order to destroy the false and adulterated'"—[104] Wilde seems here to regard metaphysics as a vital part of all intellectual inquiry; it is confining vocabularies and strictures, he reflects, rather than the actual aims of metaphysical study that arouse the rancor of critics. Shortly after the selection from Jowett's introductions, Wilde returns to the question, noting: "Those who object to Metaphysics often mean no more than this that all our knowledge must be expressed in terms of the means by which knowledge is acquired, that is in terms ultimately reducible to statements about our sensations therefore strictly relative·".[105]

If Wilde sometimes seems to be critical of philosophy, then, it is by no means because he did not value or understand it. The problem was less philosophy or metaphysics as a mode of thought than the languages and systems were are used to express them. A signature instance of this problem, in Wilde's view, was to be found in the Positivist movement. The Positivists argued that the basis for all knowledge was sensory data, which could be interpreted through reason in order to divine the underlying laws of experience. Auguste Comte had argued in *A General View of Positivism* (1848) that such a method must ultimately replace metaphysics in order for human society to attain its most enlightened state. For Wilde, Positivism exemplified a fundamental misunderstanding about speculative philosophy, for it presupposed that metaphysics was a closed system of thought that excluded experience, rather than understanding it more broadly as a mode of inquiry into the very nature of experience. As his earlier notes indicate, Wilde concurred with Jowett's assertion that speculative reason underlies even the most rigorous of empirical systems. Hence, Positivism was in Wilde's view little more than "dogmatism without criticism."[106] Every philosophical method, including Positivism itself, must turn to metaphysical speculation—inquiries into the basic concepts of experience, being, and knowing—if they are to be internally coherent. Invoking George Grote's words from an 1865 essay in the *North British Review*, Wilde writes in his unpublished Philosophy Notebook: "Philosophy passes into religion because it cannot answer its own questions."[107]

Wilde would perhaps overcorrect for this anti-empirical stance in his assertion that "Nothing that actually occurs is of the smallest importance."[108] Elsewhere, Wilde seems to have acknowledged the challenges of operating entirely in the world of abstraction, noting of Plato that the "problems of idealism and realism, as he sets them forth, may seem to many to be somewhat barren of result in the metaphysical sphere of abstract being in which he places them."[109] Hence, while we can discern in Wilde's notebooks a defense of metaphysics, he was clearly aware of its limitations. It is perhaps on this basis that Wilde would turn to art as a possible middle ground between the ideal and the real, between thought and experience. Metaphysical precepts may seem detached from the things of this world, but "transfer them to the sphere of art," Wilde advises us, "and you will find that they are still vital and full of meaning."[110]

Synthesis

Paradoxically, Wilde's metaphysical leanings left him vulnerable to being misunderstood as a materialist, Epicurean, or worse—an unqualified hedonist. When the Marquess of Queensberry was arrested and tried for libelling Wilde in 1895, Edward Carson sought to use Wilde's "Phrases and Philosophies" as a foundation for the charge that he lacked a respect for conventional mores. In quick sequence, Carson reads from the text as Wilde fires back responses:

Carson: "If one tells the truth, one is sure, sooner or later, to be found out"?
Wilde: That is a pleasing paradox, but I do not set very high store on it as an axiom.
Carson: Is it good for the young?
Wilde: Anything is good that stimulates thought in whatever age.
Carson: Whether moral or immoral?
Wilde: There is no such thing as morality or immorality in thought. There is immoral emotion.
Carson: "Pleasure is the only thing one should live for"?
Wilde: I think that the realization of oneself is the prime aim of life, and to realize oneself through pleasure is finer than to do so through pain. I am, on that point, entirely on the side of the ancients—the Greeks. It is a pagan idea.
Carson: "A truth ceases to be true when more than one person believes in it"?
Wilde: Perfectly. That would be my metaphysical definition of truth; something so personal that the same truth could never be appreciated by two minds.[111]

It is true that the conditions of the courtroom placed Wilde in a precarious position, rhetorically speaking. It may well be that his turns of phrase were meant simply to rebut Carson's claims—claims intended to malign Wilde's moral character and confirm that he willfully "corrupted" young men into acts of sexual depravity. Yet these rebuttals, as other scholars have demonstrated, hardly constituted an effective defense.[112] If anything, they seemed to muddy the waters, introducing matters of metaphysical speculation into a space governed by logic and empirical evidence. Assuredly, Wilde felt that to discuss metaphysical truth was always to negotiate, speculate, and even argue with others. To this extent, Wilde might be more aptly aligned with thinkers like Heraclitus, who rather than viewing opposition as a foundation for new truths found truth in opposition itself: "the way upward and downward are one and the same."[113] Concepts that seem to be irreconcilable are, to be sure, distinct and opposed; yet they need not be treated as mutually exclusive.

Wilde acknowledged that such an understanding of truth had deep historical roots. In his Commonplace Book, Wilde reflects upon the Platonic dialogue, *Parmenides*, in which Plato's Theory of Forms is challenged by the pre-Socratic philosopher Parmenides, often credited as the first thinker to reflect upon the nature of reality. Parmenides had proposed in *On Nature*—a work that, appropriately, remains to us only in tantalizing fragments—that existence was eternal, static, and coherent. In Plato's dialogue, Parmenides must confront Socrates's claim that reality, if broken down into material (sensible) and ideal (mental) forms, may be seen as a plurality in which different elements appear simultaneously as like and unlike. In other words, the many different components of existence can participate in a unified order while also maintaining distinct qualities. To this extent, opposites are not necessarily opposed to one another, and contradictions are not necessarily unsound. Wilde writes:

> In the <u>Parmenides</u> we have an anticipation of the Spinozistic omnis determinatio est negatio[:] "ideas are not absolute atoms but relative and cannot be apprehended without relation to contraries.["] In <u>Sophist</u>: Hegelian conception of not-being as equally essential To being[:] "the nature of a thing is only sum of it's relations to what it is not" [.][114]

I do not want to suggest that this passage provides us with access to Wilde's final "philosophy" but I do think it reveals something compelling about his manner of engaging with philosophy. Spinoza's principle of "omnis determinatio est negatio," translates roughly as "determination is negation."[115] Hegel himself would adopt this dictum as the foundation for his own law of contradiction: we only ever know what something is, Hegel would claim, by knowing what it is *not*.[116] If this is true, then every idea remains unknowable and can only be understood in relative terms, through comparison, contrast, or juxtaposition with other ideas. To some extent, this recalls Carolyn Lesjak's persuasive claim that Wilde always conceives of material and metaphysical truth as existing in tension. For Lesjak, Wilde invokes scientific discourse in order to develop a kind of "chemical philosophy" that treats the distinction between material and metaphysical reality "less in dualistic terms than along a continuum."[117]

Wilde adopts this principle of "proximate relations" not only in his treatment of material and social reality but in his understanding of all intellectual problems.[118] Philosophy demands by its very nature conversation and even disagreement. The chief difference between Wilde and Hegel would seem to be that contradictions are, for Hegel, the building blocks of knowledge: the union of thesis and antithesis brings us ever closer to truth. For Wilde, however, the real value of contradiction is that it prompts contemplation. The pursuit of ideas is, as the Greeks would have it, prompted by the love (*philos*) of wisdom (*sophia*). It is perhaps in this spirit that in *The Importance of Being Earnest*, when Jack charges Algernon with wanting to "argue about things," his friend suggestively retorts: "That is exactly what things were originally made for."

Notes

1. Oscar Wilde, "The Nightingale and the Rose," *House of Pomegranates, The Happy Prince, and Other Tales* (London: Methuen and Company, 1908): 187–200, 197. A similar moment appears in Wilde's "The Remarkable Rocket," a story in which an egoistic firecracker who has been unluckily discarded in a pool of water reflects upon the many attainments to which he can still lay claim:

   > I like hearing myself talk. It is one of my greatest pleasures. I often have long conversations all by myself, and I am so clever that sometimes I don't understand a single word of what I am saying.

   > "Then you should certainly lecture on philosophy," said the dragonfly, and he spread a pair of lovely gauze wings and soared away into the sky. (Oscar Wilde, "The Remarkable Rocket," *A House of Pomegranates, The Happy Prince, and Other Tales*. London: Methuen and Company, 1908: 233–54, 251)

2. Oscar Wilde, *Commonplace Book. Oscar Wilde's Oxford Notebooks: A Portrait of Mind in the Making*, ed. Philip E. Smith II and Michael Helfand (Oxford: Oxford University Press, 1989): 107–152, 135 [145]. For all references to Wilde's Notebook Kept at Oxford and Commonplace Book, I have included the pagination from Smith and Helfand's edition, followed by the manuscript pagination in brackets (as shown).

3. Wilde, "Nightingale and the Rose," 197; Wilde, *The Picture of Dorian Gray* (1891), *The Picture of Dorian Gray: The 1890 and 1891 Texts*, ed. Joseph Bristow, vol. 3 of *The Complete Works of Oscar Wilde* (Oxford: Oxford University Press, 2005), 204.

4. Julia Prewitt Brown, *Cosmopolitan Criticism: Oscar Wilde's Philosophy of Art* (Charlottesville: University of Virginia Press, 1997), xviii.

5. Philip Smith details the limitations of Brown's source base in "Philosophical Approaches to Interpretation of Oscar Wilde" in *Palgrave Advances in Oscar Wilde Studies*, ed. Frederick S. Roden (New York: Palgrave, 2004): 143–66.

6. Regina Gagnier and Lawrence Danson alike have noted that Brown's deliberate turn away from Wilde's immediate intellectual and social contexts renders the account somewhat abstract, making it more difficult to discern how his varied literary output "amounts to *a* philosophy" (Danson, 187). See Regina Gagnier, "Wilde Lite," *English Literature in Transition* 41.4 (1998): 472–75; Lawrence Danson, "Cosmopolitan Criticism: Oscar Wilde's Philosophy of Art," *Victorian Studies* 42.1 (1998): 185–87.

7. Philip E. Smith and Michael S. Helfand, "The Context of the Text," *Oscar Wilde's Oxford Notebooks: A Portrait of Mind in the Making*, ed. Philip E. Smith and Michael S. Helfand (New York: Oxford University Press, 1989): 5–34, 34.

8. Josephine Guy and Ian Small, *Oscar Wilde's Profession: Writing and the Culture Industry* (Oxford: Oxford University Press, 2000), 258.

9. Simon Reader, "Wilde at Oxford: A Truce with Facts," *Philosophy and Oscar Wilde*, ed. Michael Bennett (New York: Palgrave, 2017): 9–27, 14. Giles Whiteley points out, in like spirit: "The notebooks constitute a kind of creative testing of the philosophical water, rather than a fully fledged 'system.' This aspect of the notebooks has been ignored by Wilde studies in favor of a kind of name-checking: the gravitas of the proper name Hegel is supposed to rehabilitate Wilde as a serious thinker, as though such a rehabilitation were necessary in the first place." Giles Whiteley, *Oscar Wilde and the Simulacrum: The Truth of Masks* (Cambridge: Cambridge University Press, 2013), 8–9.

10. Oscar Wilde, "Phrases and Philosophies for Use of the Young," in *The Major Works*, ed. Isobel Murray (New York: Oxford University Press, 2000): 572–73, 572.

11. Wilde, "Phrases and Philosophies for Use of the Young," 572.

12. See Guy Willoughby, "Oscar Wilde and Post-Structuralism," *Philosophy and Literature* 13.2 (October 1989): 316–24. Bruce Bashford and Michael Y. Bennett have likewise proposed that Wilde in many ways anticipates the work of twentieth-century philosophy, from Henry Johnstone's treatment of "cooperative argument" in *Philosophy and Argument* (1959) to Bertrand Russell's challenge to British Idealism in "On Denoting" (1905), respectively. See Bruce Bashford, "'Even Things That Are True Can Be Proved':

Oscar Wilde on Argument," in *Philosophy and Oscar Wilde*, ed. Michael Y. Bennett (New York: Palgrave, 2017): 53–72; Michael Y. Bennett, "Wilde Thoughts on Philosophical Reference in *An Ideal Husband*: 'An Ideal' Versus 'The Ideal' Husband," in *Philosophy and Oscar Wilde*, ed. Michael Y. Bennett (New York: Palgrave, 2017): 151–166.

13. Smith, "Philosophical Approaches," 156.

14. William Stanford and Robert McDowell, *Mahaffy: Biography of an Anglo-Irishman* (New York: Routledge, 1971), 150.

15. Wilde, *Commonplace Book*, 148 [199].

16. William Wallace, *The Logic of Hegel with Prolegomena* (Oxford: Clarendon Press, 1874), lii. Smith and Helfand do not note the close correspondence between Wilde's remarks upon Kant and those contained in Wallace's volume, though they have scrupulously documented Wilde's transcriptions from Wallace elsewhere in the notebooks.

17. Giles Whiteley has persuasively established that Wilde consulted Edward Caird's volume in "Some Unnoted Sources in Oscar Wilde's Commonplace Book," 64.4 (2017): 628–34.

18. Aristotle, *The Nicomachean Ethics*, ed. Lesley Brown (New York: Oxford, 2009), 10.6–8; Arthur Schopenhauer, *The World as Will and Idea*, vol. 1 (London: Trübner and Company, 1883), 239–41; Matthew Arnold, "The Function of Criticism at the Present Time," *Essays in Criticism* (London: Macmillan and Co., 1865): 1–41,16.

19. Montagu Burrows, *Pass and Class: An Oxford Guidebook* (Oxford: Parker, 1860), 19.

20. In 1863, Lady Wilde translated Wilhelmine Canz's *Eritis Secut Deus*, a German novel in three volumes, which translates literally as "Ye Shall Be as Gods," though it was published under the more provocative title *The First Temptation*. The novel tracks the progress of Robert Schartel, a gifted professor of philosophy who "has all the gifts and qualities that could make a life noble, except faith in God" (63). Anticipating Friedrich Nietzsche's vision of the *übermensch* (superman), Schartel believes that man might "make a world of beauty and harmony of his own will and power by culture and knowledge," but despairs of this dream as "every evil act committed by his followers is flung back to him as a consequence of his own teaching, a deduction from his own philosophy" (64). "The First Temptation by Lady Wilde," *Duffy's Hibernian Magazine* 4 (July 1863): 63–70. In this case, the accusations prove to be true, and only his wife, sustained by the religion of her upbringing, is able to withstand the lure of sensual pleasures. As William Hamilton would note in 1882: "the hero is an Hegelian Philosopher, whose religion is the cultures of Beauty, and perhaps the English publisher may have feared that such a theory would school the faith or morals of his readers, but in any case nearly the whole edition was burnt, accidentally as was supposed, and the work is now very scarce in consequence." William

Hamilton, *The Aesthetic Movement in England* (London: Reeves and Turner, 1882), 97. While we do not have any evidence that Wilde himself read or engaged with his mother's translation, we do know that he conferred with her about the German Rationalists at some length. Lady Wilde was an avid consumer of German philosophy, routinely invoking the work of Hegel, Kant, Schelling, Fichte, and Schopenhauer in her essays. She ensured that he was tutored in both French and German from an early age.

21. See Smith and Helfand, "The Context of the Text."
22. Iain Ross, *Oscar Wilde and Ancient Greece* (Cambridge: Cambridge University Press, 2012), 34.
23. Benjamin Jowett, Introduction to *The Republic* in vol. 2 of *The Dialogues of Plato* (New York: Scribner, Armstrong, and Company, 1873), 142.
24. See especially Plato, *The Republic* Book III: 402–403 and Book V: 472–483.
25. Wilde, *Commonplace Book*, 128 [109]. Wilde alludes here to Jacobi's 1787 *On Faith, or Idealism and Realism*, which contended that although the "thing-in-itself" of which Kant speaks—that is, the existence of an object independent of its perception—cannot be directly known but must instead be accepted on the basis of faith.
26. Aristotle highlights the relationship between rhetoric and dialectic in *Topics* 1.10–13. See Aristotle, *Organon*, ed. Octavius Friere Owen (London: Henry G. John, 1853), 370–74.
27. Jowett, Introduction to the *Republic*, 142.
28. Whiteley, *Oscar Wilde and the Simulacrum*, 57–8.
29. Oscar Wilde, "The Rise of Historical Criticism," *Complete Works of Oscar Wilde*, IV, ed. Josephine Guy (Oxford: Oxford University Press, 2007):1–67, 30.
30. Wilde, "The Rise of Historical Criticism," 30.
31. Benjamin Jowett, "Sermon VII: Heb. Xi.4, in Arthur Penrhyn Stanley," *Sermons Biographical and Miscellaneous* (London: John Murray, 1899), 130–151, 142.
32. Evelyn Abbott and Lewis Campbell, eds., *The Life and Letters of Benjamin Jowett*, vol. 2 (New York: E.P. Dutton and Company, 1897), 169.
33. Qtd. in Arthur Quinn, *The Confidence of British Philosophers: An Essay in Historical Narrative* (Leiden: E.J. Brille, 1977), 163.
34. F. Max Müller, *My Autobiography: A Fragment* (New York: Charles Scribner's Sons, 1901), 130.
35. Müller, *Autobiography*, 142.
36. Friedrich Max Müller, "Comparative Mythology," *Essays on Mythology, Traditions, and Customs* (London: Longmans, Green, and Company, 1867): 1–143, 8.
37. Müller, *Autobiography*, 142.

38. For further discussion of Müller's treatment of history in relation to Hegel, see Jon R. Stone, Introduction, *The Essential Max Müller on Language, Mythology, and Religion* (New York: Palgrave, 2002): 1–24. The only extensive discussion of Müller's influence on Wilde appears in Smith and Helfand's "Context of the Text," where he features as yet another mentor who would encourage Wilde's inexorable turn to Hegelian philosophy (8–10). While Smith and Helfand note Müller's wariness of adopting a strictly Darwinian approach to history, they do not remark upon Müller's critique of Hegel.

39. F. Max Müller, *The Sacred Books of the East* 39 (Oxford: Clarendon, 1891), 24.

40. Jerusha McCormack, "Oscar Wilde: As Daoist Sage," *Philosophy and Oscar Wilde*, ed. Michael Bennett (New York: Palgrave, 2018): 73–104.

41. Oscar Wilde, "A Chinese Sage," in *Journalism* II, vol. 7 of *The Complete Works of Oscar Wilde* VII (Oxford: Oxford University Press, 2013), 237–43, 238.

42. One might turn, for an additional example, to Wilde's 1895 trial. On that occasion, Edward Carson asked Wilde to comment on one of his "philosophies": "The condition of perfection is idleness: the aim of perfection is youth"? Wilde retorted: "Oh, yes; I think so. Half of it is true. The life of contemplation is the highest life, and so recognized by the philosopher." Merlin Holland, ed., *The Real Trial of Oscar Wilde* (New York: Harper, 2004), 76. The remark bears a striking resemblance to Wilde's famous dictum on utility: "We can forgive a man for making a useful thing as long as he does not admire it" (Wilde, *Dorian Gray*, 68).

43. Wilde, "A Chinese Sage," 237.

44. Wilde, "A Chinese Sage," 238.

45. Wilde, "A Chinese Sage," 237.

46. See Philip E. Smith, "Oscar Wilde's Philosophy of History" in *Oscar Wilde and Philosophy*, ed. Michael Y. Bennett (New York: Palgrave, 2018): 29–52.

47. Henry Thomas Buckle, *The History of Civilization in England* (London: Parker, Son, and Bourn, 1861), 19–20.

48. Oscar Wilde, Notebook Kept at Oxford, *Oscar Wilde's Oxford Notebooks: A Portrait of Mind in the Making*, ed. Philip E. Smith II and Michael Helfand (Oxford: Oxford University Press, 1989): 153–74, 159 [29].

49. Wilde, "Rise of Historical Criticism," 29.

50. Wilde, Notebook Kept at Oxford, 159 [29].

51. Buckle, 18.

52. It is an idea he would revisit in "The Rise of Historical Criticism": "History, no doubt, has splendid lessons for our instruction, just as all good art comes to us as the herald of the noblest truth. But, to set before either the painter or the historian the inculcation of moral lessons as an aim to be consciously pursued, is to miss entirely the true motive and characteristic both of art and history, which is in the one case the creation of beauty, in the other the discovery of the laws of the evolution of progress: Il ne faut demander de l'Art que l'Art, due passé que le passé" [translation: "One need ask of art nothing

but art, of the past nothing but the past"] (Wilde, "The Rise of Historical Criticism," 17).

53. Oscar Wilde, Notebook Kept at Oxford, 156 [21].

54. Wilde, Notebook Kept at Oxford 162 [43].

55. Wilde, Commonplace Book, 132 [131].

56. Wilde, Commonplace Book, 143 [177]. In the final line of this passage, Wilde abbreviates the quotation from Bacon; the translation provided reverts to Bacon's original Latin text. See Francis Bacon, *Novum Organum* in vol. 4 of *The Works of Francis Bacon* (London: Longmans and Company, 1875), 77, 51, 47, 110.

57. As Simon Reader observes, Wilde may well have been attracted by Bacon's stylistic use of the aphorism, taking it as "an example of open, unfettered inquiry that evades Aristotle's logical systems" (19).

58. Bacon, 47.

59. Bacon, 110.

60. Bristow's discussion pertains specifically to the Philosophy Notebook and Wilde's juxtaposition of Bacon and John Elliott Cairnes's critique of Auguste Darwin in *Essays in Political Economy* (1873); See Joseph Bristow, "Wilde's Abstractions: Notes on *Literae Humaniores*, 1876–1878," *Oscar Wilde and Classical Antiquity*, ed. Kathleen Riley, Alastair Blanchard, and Maria Manny (Oxford: Oxford University Press, 2018): 69–90, 86.

61. See, for example, Joseph Bristow, "Oscar Wilde's Poetic Traditions," *Oscar Wilde in Context*, ed. Kerry Powell and Peter Raby (Cambridge: Cambridge University Press, 2013): 73–87, 75–77. Chris Foss has suggested that Wilde is more easily reconciled to the "unresolved contradictions" of Romantic thinkers like John Keats or Friedrich Schlegel, who embraced a dialectical process that did not necessarily reconcile thesis and antithesis. While we know that Wilde was a great admirer of Keats, I have, to date, been unable to verify that Wilde ever encountered or remarked upon the philosophy of Schlegel. Still, the comparison is a tantalizing and generative one. Taking a cue from Foss, I propose that we place Wilde with the context of an altogether different strain of German Romanticism: one that, as we shall see, was just as invested in the failures as by the possibilities of dialectic. See Chris Foss, "Oscar Wilde and the Importance of Being Romantic," *Wilde Discoveries: Traditions, Histories, Archives*, ed. Joseph Bristow (Toronto: University of Toronto, 2013): 43–64.

62. Wilde, *An Ideal Husband*, in *The Major Works*, ed. Isobel Murray (New York: Oxford University Press, 2000): 389–476, 397.

63. Wilde, *An Ideal Husband*, 397.

64. See, for example, Michael S. Foldy, T*he Trials of Oscar Wilde: Deviance, Morality, and Late-Victorian Society* (New Haven: Yale University Press, 1997), 108–109; Whiteley, 283; and Joseph Pearce, *The Unmasking of Oscar Wilde* (San Francisco: Ignatius Press, 2000), 82–84.

65. Oscar Wilde, *Complete Letters of Oscar Wilde*, ed. Merlin Holland and Rupert Hart-Davis (New York: Henry Holt and Company, 2000), 25–6.

66. Arthur Schopenhauer, *Parerga and Paralipomena: Short Philosophical Essays* 1 (Oxford: Clarendon Press, 2000): 168.

67. Schopenhauer, *Parerga and Paralipomena*, 173.

68. Arthur Schopenhauer, *Studies in Pessimism: A Series of Essays* (London: Swan Sonnenschein and Company, 1892), 11.

69. Schopenhauer, *Studies in Pessimism*, 13.

70. Schopenhauer, *Studies in Pessimism*, 13.

71. Lady Wilde, "Divinity of Humanity," *Essays and Stories* (Boston: C.T. Brainard, 1909), 133.

72. Oscar Wilde, "The Critic as Artist," in *Criticism*, ed. Josephine M. Guy, vol. 4 of *The Complete Works of Oscar Wilde* (Oxford: Oxford University Press, 2007): 123–206, 193. The claim is reinforced by the dialogue's full title: "The Critic as Artist: with some remarks upon the importance of discussing everything" (267).

73. Oscar Wilde, "Critic as Artist," 161.

74. Arthur Schopenhauer, *The World as Will and Idea*, 231.

75. Wilde, "Decay of Lying," "The Decay of Lying," *Criticism*, ed. Josephine M. Guy, vol. 4 of *The Complete Works of Oscar Wilde* (Oxford: Oxford University Press, 2007): 72–103, 92.

76. Arthur Schopenhauer, *Studies in Pessimism*, 69. Schopenhauer appeals to Hamlet repeatedly over the course of *The World as Will and Idea*, noting on one occasion that the famous "mousetrap" scene is a precise illustration of how art should help to illuminate truth: "If the whole world as idea is only the visibility of will, the work of art is to render this visibility more distinct. It is the camera obscura which shows the objects more purely, and enables us to survey them and comprehend them better. It is the play within the play, the stage upon the stage in 'Hamlet'" (345). For Schopenhauer, then, the work of art should always function as it does in Shakespeare's play: it should reflect and sharpen one's perception of reality, while also spurring one on to contemplation, revelation, and action. In other words, art does not serve as a simple mirror of reality: it presents an opportunity to suspend one's suffering by creating, in effect, another reality.

77. Schopenhauer, *The World as Will and Idea*, 287.

78. See, for example, Josephine Guy's notes on the essay (Wilde, "The Decay of Lying," 366n and 407n).

79. Wilde, "Decay of Lying," 37.

80. Wilde, "The Critic as Artist," 179. Schopenhauer once wrote: "[…] in a world where all is unstable, and nought can endure, but is swept onwards at once in the hurrying whirlpool of change; where a man, if he is to keep erect at all, must always be advancing and moving, like an acrobat on a rope—in such a world, happiness is inconceivable. How can it dwell where, as Plato

says, *continual Becoming and never Being* is the sole form of existence?" (Schopenhauer, *Studies in Pessimism*, 35).

81. Indeed, Wilde's pessimism arguably becomes most apparent in his treatment of the material world. In "The Soul of Man Under Socialism," which I discuss at greater length in Chap. 6, Wilde wryly suggests that private property constitutes a source of corruption for the elite and the impoverished alike, leading men to equate their self-worth with material wealth: "For the recognition of private property has really harmed Individualism, and obscured it, by confusing a man with what he possesses. [...] The true perfection of man lies, not in what man has, but in what man is." Oscar Wilde, "The Soul of Man Under Socialism," in *Criticism*, ed. Josephine M. Guy, vol. 4 of *The Complete Works of Oscar Wilde* (Oxford: Oxford University Press, 2007): 231–68, 237.

82. Oscar Wilde, "The Truth of Masks," in vol. 4 of *The Complete Works of Oscar Wilde*, ed. Josephine Guy (Oxford: Oxford University Press, 2007): 208–228, 228.

83. Whiteley, *Oscar Wilde and the Simulacrum*, 5.

84. Whiteley, *Oscar Wilde and the Simulacrum*, 16.

85. "The simulacrum is never that which conceals the truth," as Jean Baudrillard puts it, "it is the truth which conceals that there is none." The citation from Ecclesiastes serves as the epigraph to Jean Baudrillard's *Simulacra and Simulation* (Ann Arbor: University of Michigan, 1994), 1.

86. Schopenhauer, *Studies*, 61.

87. Wilde, "The Critic as Artist," 278.

88. Qtd. in Quinn, *The Confidence of British Philosophers*, 163.

89. Wilde, Commonplace Book, 127 [101].

90. William Wallace, *Prolegomena to the Study of Hegel's Philosophy* (Oxford: Clarendon Press, 1894), 354.

91. Wallace, *Prolegomena*, 190.

92. Wilde, *The Importance of Being Earnest, The Major Works*, ed. Isobel Murray (New York: Oxford University Press, 2000): 477–538, 499.

93. Wilde, *An Ideal Husband*, 427.

94. Michael Y. Bennett examines Wilde's critique of idealism by positioning him as an antecedent to Bertrand Russell in his essay "Wilde Thoughts on Philosophical Reference in *An Ideal Husband*": "An Ideal" versus "The Ideal" Husband, *Oscar Wilde and Philosophy*, ed. Michael Y. Bennett (New York: Palgrave, 2018): 151–66.

95. Wilde, *An Ideal Husband*, 440.

96. Wilde, *Commonplace Book*, 141 [169].

97. Pater writes: "Hegel, in his Lectures on the Philosophy of Art, estimating the work of his predecessors, has also passed a remarkable judgment on Johann Joachim Winckelmann's writings. 'Winckelmann by contemplation of the ideal works of the ancients received a sort of inspiration through which he

opened a new sense for the study of art. He is to be regarded as one of those who in the sphere of art have known how to initiate a new organ for the human spirit.' That it has given a new sense, that it has laid open a new organ, is the highest that can be said of any critical effort" (147). For astute explorations of Pater's relationship to Hegel see, for instance, Giles Whiteley, *Aestheticism and the Philosophy of Death: Walter Pater and Post-Hegelianism* (Oxford: Legenda, 2010); Kit Andrews, "Walter Pater as Oxford Hegelian: Plato and Platonism and T.H. Green's Prolegomena to Ethics," *Journal of the History of Ideas* 72.3 (July 2011): 437–59.

98. See Kate Hext, *Walter Pater: Individualism and Aesthetic Philosophy* (Edinburgh: Edinburgh University Press, 2013).

99. Wilde remarked in his Notebook Kept at Oxford that "the Berkeleyan hypothesis of abolishing the substance of matter altogether" was troubling, for the "same argument however wd justify the abolition of the soul" (165 [59]).

100. Wilde, *Commonplace Book*, 141 [169].

101. Wilde, *Commonplace Book*, 140–141 [168].

102. Wilde, *Commonplace Book*, 133 [133].

103. Benjamin Jowett, Introduction to *Parmenides* in vol. 4 of *The Dialogues of Plato* (Oxford: Clarendon, 1875): 121–58, 155.

104. Wilde, *Commonplace Book*, 133 [132].

105. Wilde, *Commonplace Book*, 136 [151].

106. Wilde, *Commonplace Book*, 151 [214].

107. Oscar Wilde, "Notebook on Philosophy," 1876–8, "Oscar Wilde and His Literary Circle Collection," MS W6721M3 N9113, William Andrews Clark Memorial Library, Los Angeles, CA. The original line appears in George Grote, "Plato and the Companions of Socrates," *The North British Review* 43 (1865): 351–84, 373.

108. Wilde, "Phrases and Philosophies," 142.

109. Wilde, "The Critic as Artist," 140.

110. Wilde, "The Critic as Artist," 140.

111. Montgomery Hyde. *The Trials of Oscar Wilde* (London: W. Hodge, 1949), 123.

112. Wilde's appeal to aesthetic and literary dialogue in the courtroom was in Merlin Holland's words "insanely quixotic" and almost certainly precipitated his undoing (xliii).

113. Heraclitus, *The Fragments of the Works of Heraclitus of Ephesus on Nature* (Baltimore: M. Murray, 1889), 101.

114. Wilde, *Commonplace Book*, 147 [195].

115. The concept was originally expressed in a 1674 letter to his friend Jarig Jelles. Spinoza, *The Letters*, trans. Samuel Shirley (Indianapolis: Hackett Publishing, 1995), 260.

116. Hegel writes: "That true and positive meaning of the antinomies is this: that every actual thing involves a coexistence of opposed elements. Consequently

to know, or, in other words, to comprehend an object is equivalent to being conscious of it as a concrete unity of opposed determinations. The old metaphysic, as we have already seen, when it studied the objects of which it sought a metaphysical knowledge, went to work by applying categories abstractly and to the exclusion of their opposites." George Friedrich Hegel, *The Logic of Hegel*, ed. William Wallace (London: Oxford University Press, 1892), 100.

117. Carolyn Lesjak, "Oscar Wilde and the Art/Work of Atoms," *Studies in the Literary Imagination* 43.1 (2010), 1–26, 3.

118. Lesjak, 2.

Bibliography

Abbott, Evelyn, and Lewis Campbell, eds. 1897. *The Life and Letters of Benjamin Jowett*. New York: E.P. Dutton and Company.

Andrews, Kit. 2011. Walter Pater as Oxford Hegelian: Plato and Platonism and T.H. Green's Prolegomena to Ethics. *Journal of the History of Ideas* 72 (3/ July): 437–459.

Aristotle. 1853. *Organon*, ed. Octavius Friere Owen. London: Henry G. John.

———. 2009. *The Nicomachean Ethics*, ed. Lesley Brown. New York: Oxford.

Arnold, Matthew. 1865. The Function of Criticism at the Present Time. In *Essays in Criticism*, 1–41. London: Macmillan and Co.

Bacon, Francis. 1875. *Novum* Organum. In Vol. 4 of *The Works of Francis Bacon*. London: Longmans and Company.

Bashford, Bruce. 2017. 'Even Things That Are True Can Be Proved': Oscar Wilde on Argument. In *Philosophy and Oscar Wilde*, ed. Michael Y. Bennett, 53–72. New York: Palgrave.

Baudrillard, Jean. 1994. *Simulacra and Simulation*. Ann Arbor: University of Michigan.

Bennett, Michael Y. 2017. Wilde Thoughts on Philosophical Reference in *An Ideal Husband*: 'An Ideal' Versus 'The Ideal' Husband. In *Philosophy and Oscar Wilde*, ed. Michael Y. Bennett, 151–166. New York: Palgrave.

Bristow, Joseph. 2013. Oscar Wilde's Poetic Traditions. In *Oscar Wilde in Context*, ed. Kerry Powell and Peter Raby, 73–87. Cambridge: Cambridge University Press.

———. 2018. Wilde's Abstractions: Notes on *Literae Humaniores*, 1876–1878. In *Oscar Wilde and Classical Antiquity*, ed. Kathleen Riley, Alastair Blanchard, and Maria Manny, 69–90. Oxford: Oxford University Press.

Brown, Julia Prewitt. 1997. *Cosmopolitan Criticism: Oscar Wilde's Philosophy of Art*. Charlottesville: University of Virginia Press.

Buckle, Henry Thomas. 1861. *The History of Civilization in England*, 19–20. London: Parker, Son, and Bourn.

Burrows, Montagu. 1860. *Pass and Class: An Oxford Guidebook*. Oxford: Parker.

Danson, Lawrence. 1998. Cosmopolitan Criticism: Oscar Wilde's Philosophy of Art. *Victorian Studies* 42 (1): 185–187.

Foldy, Michael S. 1997. *The Trials of Oscar Wilde: Deviance, Morality, and Late-Victorian Society*. New Haven: Yale University Press.

Foss, Chris. 2013. Oscar Wilde and the Importance of Being Romantic. In *Wilde Discoveries: Traditions, Histories, Archives*, ed. Joseph Bristow, 43–64. Toronto: University of Toronto.

Gagnier, Regina. 1998. Wilde Lite. *English Literature in Transition* 41 (4): 472–475.

Grote, George. 1865. Plato and the Companions of Socrates. *The North British Review* 43: 351–384.

Guy, Josephine M., and Ian Small. 2000. *Oscar Wilde's Profession: Writing and the Culture Industry*. Oxford: Oxford University Press.

Hamilton, William. 1882. *The Aesthetic Movement in England*. London: Reeves and Turner.

Hegel, George Friedrich. 1892. *The Logic of Hegel*, ed. William Wallace. London: Oxford University Press.

Heraclitus. 1889. *The Fragments of the Works of Heraclitus of Ephesus on Nature*. Baltimore: M. Murray.

Hext, Kate. 2013. *Walter Pater: Individualism and Aesthetic Philosophy*. Edinburgh: Edinburgh University Press.

Holland, Merlin, ed. 2004. *The Real Trial of Oscar Wilde*. New York: Harper.

Hyde, Montgomery. 1949. *The Trials of Oscar Wilde*. London: W. Hodge, 123.

Jowett, Benjamin. 1873. Introduction to *The Republic*. In Vol. 2 of *The Dialogues of Plato*. New York: Scribner, Armstrong, and Company.

———. 1875. Introduction to *Parmenides*. In Vol. 4 of *The Dialogues of Plato*. Oxford: Clarendon, 121–58.

Lesjak, Carolyn. 2010. Oscar Wilde and the Art/Work of Atoms. *Studies in the Literary Imagination* 43 (1): 1–26.

McCormack, Jerusha. 2018. Oscar Wilde: As Daoist Sage. In *Philosophy and Oscar Wilde*, ed. Michael Bennett, 73–104. New York: Palgrave.

Müller, F. Max. 1867. Comparative Mythology. In *Essays on Mythology, Traditions, and Customs*, 1–143. London: Longmans, Green, and Company.

Müller, F. 1891. *The Sacred Books of the East*. Oxford: Clarendon.

———. 1901. *My Autobiography: A Fragment*. New York: Charles Scribner's Sons.

Pearce, Joseph. 2000. *The Unmasking of Oscar Wilde*. San Francisco: Ignatius Press.

Quinn, Arthur. 1977. *The Confidence of British Philosophers: An Essay in Historical Narrative*. Leiden: E.J. Brille.

Reader, Simon. 2017. Wilde at Oxford: A Truce with Facts. In *Philosophy and Oscar Wilde*, ed. Michael Bennett, 9–27. New York: Palgrave.

Ross, Iain. 2012. *Oscar Wilde and Ancient Greece*. Cambridge: Cambridge University Press.

Schopenhauer, Arthur. 1883. *The World as Will and Idea*. London: Trübner.

————. 1892. *Studies in Pessimism: A Series of Essays*. London: Swan Sonnenschein.

————. 2000. *Parerga and Paralipomena: Short Philosophical Essays*. Oxford: Clarendon Press.

Smith, Philip E. 2004. Philosophical Approaches to Interpretation of Oscar Wilde. In *Palgrave Advances in Oscar Wilde Studies*, ed. Frederick S. Roden, 143–166. New York: Palgrave.

————. 2018. Oscar Wilde's Philosophy of History. In *Oscar Wilde and Philosophy*, ed. Michael Y. Bennett, 29–52. New York: Palgrave.

Smith, Philip E., and Michael S. Helfand. 1989. The Context of the Text. In *Oscar Wilde's Oxford Notebooks: A Portrait of Mind in the Making*, ed. Philip E. Smith and Michael S. Helfand, 5–34. New York: Oxford University Press.

Spinoza. 1995. *The Letters*. Trans. Samuel Shirley. Indianapolis: Hackett Publishing.

Stanford, William, and Robert McDowell. 1971. *Mahaffy: Biography of an Anglo-Irishman*. New York: Routledge.

Stanley, Arthur Penrhyn. 1899. *Sermons Biographical and Miscellaneous*, 130–151. London: John Murray.

Stone, Jon R. 2002. Introduction. In *The Essential Max Müller on Language, Mythology, and Religion*, 1–24. New York: Palgrave.

The First Temptation by Lady Wilde. 1863. *Duffy's Hibernian Magazine* 4 (July): 63–70.

Wallace, William. 1874. *The Logic of Hegel with Prolegomena*. Oxford: Clarendon Press.

————. 1894. *Prolegomena to the Study of Hegel's Philosophy*. Oxford: Clarendon Press.

Whiteley, Giles. 2010. *Aestheticism and the Philosophy of Death: Walter Pater and Post-Hegelianism*. Oxford: Legenda.

————. 2013. *Oscar Wilde and the Simulacrum: The Truth of Masks*. Cambridge: Cambridge University Press.

————. 2017. Some Unnoted Sources in Oscar Wilde's Commonplace Book. *Notes and Queries* 64 (4): 628–634.

Wilde, Oscar. 1876–8. Notebook on Philosophy. In *Oscar Wilde and His Literary Circle Collection*, MS W6721M3 N9113. Los Angeles: William Andrews Clark Memorial Library.

————. 1908a. The Nightingale and the Rose. In *A House of Pomegranates, the Happy Prince, and Other Tales*, 187–200. London: Methuen and Company.

————. 1908b. The Remarkable Rocket. In *A House of Pomegranates, the Happy Prince, and Other Tales*, 233–254. London: Methuen and Company.

Wilde, Lady Jane Francesca. 1909. Divinity of Humanity. In *Essays and Stories*. Boston: C.T. Brainard.

Wilde, Oscar. 1989a. Commonplace Book. In *Oscar Wilde's Oxford Notebooks: A Portrait of Mind in the Making*, ed. Philip E. Smith II and Michael Helfand, 107–152. Oxford: Oxford University Press.

————. 1989b. Notebook Kept at Oxford. In *Oscar Wilde's Oxford Notebooks: A Portrait of Mind in the Making*, ed. Philip E. Smith II and Michael Helfand, 153–174. Oxford: Oxford University Press.

———. 2000a. *Complete Letters of Oscar Wilde*, ed. Merlin Holland and Rupert Hart-Davis. New York: Henry Holt and Company.

———. 2000b. *An Ideal Husband*. In *The Major Works*, ed. Isobel Murray, 389–476. New York: Oxford University Press.

———. 2000c. *The Importance of Being Earnest*. In *The Major Works*, ed. Isobel Murray, 477–538. New York: Oxford University Press.

———. 2000d. Phrases and Philosophies for Use by the Young. In *The Major Works*, ed. Isobel Murray, 572–573. New York: Oxford University Press.

———. 2005. *The Picture of Dorian Gray*. In *The Picture of Dorian Gray: The 1890 and 1891 Texts*, ed. Joseph Bristow. Vol. 3 of *The Complete Works of Oscar Wilde*. Oxford: Oxford University Press.

———. 2007a. The Rise of Historical Criticism. In *Criticism*, ed. Josephine M. Guy, 1–67. Vol. 4 of *The Complete Works of Oscar Wilde* IV. Oxford: Oxford University Press.

———. 2007b. The Critic as Artist. In *Criticism*, ed. Josephine M. Guy, 123–206. Vol. 4 of *The Complete Works of Oscar Wilde*. Oxford: Oxford University Press.

———. 2007c. The Soul of Man Under Socialism. In *Criticism*, ed. Josephine M. Guy, 231–268. Vol. 4 of *The Complete Works of Oscar Wilde*. Oxford: Oxford University Press.

———. 2007d. The Truth of Masks. In *Criticism*, ed. Josephine M. Guy, 208–228. Vol. 4 of *The Complete Works of Oscar Wilde*. Oxford: Oxford University Press.

———. 2013. A Chinese Sage. In *Journalism II*, ed. John Stokes and Mark Turner, 237–243. Vol. 7 of *The Complete Works of Oscar Wilde*. Oxford: Oxford University Press.

Willoughby, Guy. 1989. Oscar Wilde and Post-Structuralism. *Philosophy and Literature* 13 (2): 316–324.

6

The Reformer

First Burgher. What is this "reform"! What means it, eh?
Second Burgher. Faith! It mean this, to let all be as 'tis.
I would have somewhat else.
Oscar Wilde, *The Duchess of Padua*

At the beginning of this volume, I invoked Wilde's passion for the contemplative life. For Gilbert, the provocateur who gives voice to this ideal in "The Critic as Artist" (1891), those who would live such a life must prize thoughts above deeds, giving themselves over to a world in which anything and everything is possible: "Action is limited and relative. Unlimited and absolute is the vision of him who sits at ease and watches, who walks in loneliness and dreams."[1] The basis of all action is "lack of imagination," as Gilbert goes on to explain, for to act is to limit oneself to a specific course, abandoning the multiple and often conflicting possibilities that exist in the realm of thought. In the end, Gilbert avers, it is best to stand apart from the business of everyday life: "in the sphere of action a conscious aim is a delusion," for to act is to catapult oneself into a world "limited by accident, and ignorant of its direction."[2] Thought is expansive and liberating; action is final and often dangerous.

One might presume on the basis of such remarks that Wilde had little interest in the prospect of social reform. Edouard Roditi, one of the first critics to engage Wilde's politics in a serious way, notes that even his early writings betray marks of "the Romantic-liberal esthete's [sic] curiously ambivalent politics"—a marked tension between a passion for liberty and detachment from worldly things.[3] By the 1890s, Roditi observes, Wilde had thus developed a "non-political politics of the citizen who is perfect as a man" and has

© The Author(s) 2019
K. J. Stern, *Oscar Wilde*, Literary Lives,
https://doi.org/10.1007/978-3-030-24604-4_6

little need for government of any kind.[4] Patricia Behrendt likewise suggests that Wilde's commitment to the better world promised by art ultimately led him to ignore stark political and social realities. Wilde's "political naïveté" was most apparent, she observes, when he was charged with acts of gross indecency in 1895 and presumed that "the poetic language of the artist on the witness stand could prevail against the language of the law."[5] Seen this way, Wilde refused to adopt the pragmatic model of political actor or social reformer either in his work, which often chafes against pragmatism and utility, or in his life.

Josephine Guy notes that even in works where Wilde seems anything but naïve—for instance, in his most overtly political essay "The Soul of Man Under Socialism"—his detachment from the world of politics is apparent in his casual deployment of ideological concepts that are irreconcilable.[6] By this logic, Wilde's relationship to socialism, individualism, nationalism, or the emerging women's movement should be regarded less as original attempts at political activism than as a mirroring of ideas already circulating in contemporary journals.[7] Guy's close attention to publication history and the circulation of text is compelling, and the caution that we should not always treat Wilde as a systematic political thinker is well taken. Wilde assuredly did not acquire knowledge of the world solely through deep study, and cursory or even superficial encounters with political thought may well have led him to occlude important nuances. Yet as Jarlath Killeen rightly observes, Wilde's contradictions may well reflect an instability of political language that was typical of the period. For Killeen, Wilde's desultory engagement with political and social reform can be better explained if we acknowledge that the ideas he invoked were themselves in historical flux and subject to the vicissitudes of an evolving Irish political landscape.[8] While perhaps reflecting the limits of his knowledge of or fidelity to any particular social movement, it is precisely because his knowledge was evolving, multiform, and sometimes disinterested that Wilde's treatment of reform warrants further scrutiny.

In the final pages of this volume, I do not provide a systematic account of Wilde's political and social views. This task lies beyond the purview of an intellectual biography that seeks to illuminate not what but *how* Wilde thought. It is, moreover, a subject that has been ably essayed and much debated by the scholars just mentioned.[9] Instead, this chapter will explore how Wilde understood the very concept of reform, defined as a deliberate endeavor to translate ideas into the realm of politics, economics, and social movements. The reader should thus treat this chapter in the light of a conclusion, which seeks less to provide a history of Wilde's social ideas than to speculate more broadly on why he sometimes struggled—perhaps even demurred—to translate those ideas into the real world. Although Wilde's views on Irish nationalism, labor, or prison reform constitute important touchstones in the discussion that follows, I am far more concerned with exploring Wilde's treatment of reform as a concept. If Wilde's treatment of political and social reality at times seems to be unsystematic or detached, I want to suggest that this is owing to his understanding of reform as a cultural idea. Wilde's textual referents do not always seek to authorize or articulate a social platform; frequently, they help to illuminate the challenges of translating thought into social action. Wilde reveals, that is to say, the pathways rather than the endpoints of his social consciousness. It is my hope that illuminating these pathways will put readers in a stronger position to evaluate some of the seeming inconsistencies in Wilde's political allusions and to better comprehend precisely what, if any, relation the contemplative life bears to the world in which we live.

The Unreformed

In his important 1976 book *Keywords*, Raymond Williams notes that the term "reform" may be construed in two very distinct ways: etymologically speaking, to reform means either to "restore [something] to its original form" or "to make [it] into a new form."[10] On the face of it, the two meanings would seem to be irreconcilable, for one cannot at once return to an idyllic past and embark upon an uncharted future. It is perhaps unsurprising, then, that the term has been hotly contested since its very origins. According to Arthur Burns and Joanna Innes, the semantic currency of reform reached its acme in the nineteenth century, in part owing to a growing belief that "men were made good or bad by the socio-political framework in which they operated," so that legal and institutional change came to be seen as a powerful tool for transforming moral behavior.[11] Whereas "reform" had constituted a kind of "bogey word" in the wake of the French Revolution, by the middle of the century its alliance with institutional culture and moral progress resulted in its becoming "largely naturalized and tamed."[12] After the 1830s—a period marked by the debates over the First Reform Act of 1832, the Slavery Abolition Act of 1833, the 1838 publication of the People's Charter, and the Factory Acts—the term "reform" "passed into more general currency" and was deployed by divergent political and social groups.[13] Hence reform, which had hitherto operated chiefly as a "noun of process," came more commonly to denote a specific measure intended to bring about social or moral improvement.[14] Although the nineteenth century is often referred to as the "Age of Reform," then, the term was a charged one through-out the period. By the 1870s, reform had arguably become a byword of English culture. Where reform had once signified a gradual change, by Wilde's lifetime it often signified an *action*. If reform was regarded in the opening decades of the century as something remarkable, perhaps even dan-gerous, by the closing decades of the century it was a fact routinely acknowl-edged in contemporary journals and parliamentary reports. It is against this backdrop—a landscape in which announcements of reform had become habitual and even formulaic—that we must evaluate Wilde's relationship to social activism.

In preceding chapters, I have deliberately focused on Wilde's contemplative life, avoiding wherever possible assigning to him definitive political or social views. But it is important and perhaps inescapable that we should at last come to the vital question: how did Wilde's contemplative life translate into the world of real social action and interaction? To date, scholars have been under-standably divided regarding Wilde's ideological sympathies, and some have been reluctant to assign him a distinct political profile at all. In part, this tendency finds its roots in Wilde's relationship to utility in general. Gilbert enlightens us upon this point:

> We live in the age of the overworked, and the undereducated; the age in which people are so industrious that they become absolutely stupid. And, harsh though it may sound, I cannot help saying that such people deserve their doom. The sure way of knowing nothing about life is to try to make oneself useful.[15]

To commit oneself to a life of action and utility is, by this logic, to abandon the life of speculation. "All art is quite useless," as Wilde puts it in the Preface to *The Picture of Dorian Gray* (1890/1), not because we do not value it but rather because art transcends the utility of this world and, refusing to be deployed in the service of specific ends, becomes a source of inspiration and intellectual clarity.[16] Wilde would echo Gilbert's words in an 1891 letter to Ernest Bernulf Clegg: "If the contemplation of a work of art is followed by an activity of any kind, the work is either of a very second-rate order, or the spec-tator has failed to realize the complete artistic impression."[17] To be "useless" is, in short, to exist apart from the world of mere things. It is meant to prompt feeling, thought, or speculation: it should never recommend a course of action or social outlook.

Over the course of his career, Wilde would accordingly treat social move-ments as belonging to the sphere of action. He critiques reform, that is to say, in its proper mid-nineteenth century sense—as an action that seeks to reshape existing structures, rather than as a process that takes place naturally and over time. To some extent, Wilde avers, it is a forgivable state. Gilbert notes that the "brawling social reformer" must, as such, be "blinded by the sufferings of that unimportant section of the community among whom he has cast his lot"; committed to his platform and plan of action, he cannot adopt a more stereoscopic view on the subject.[18] That Gilbert describes the object of this reformer's efforts as "unimportant" underscores, in this case, how relative social and political commitments can be. If the plight of the Irish laborer is important to one, it may be comparatively "unimportant" to the priest who seeks to save one's soul. To join a social movement may be laudable in spirit, but it also means foreclosing the possibilities afforded by opposing viewpoints. Reform cannot, in other words, be regarded as an absolute good but must instead be placed within its immediate social context—a context in which pursuing one clearly defined end may well mean abandoning others.

Wilde's first play *Vera* (1880), which closed after only 1 week during its initial 1882 run in New York, is specially concerned with challenging the definition, scope, and efficacy of social reform. Set in nineteenth-century Russia, the play (which Wilde once called his "first attack on Tyranny") follows the story of Vera, a young barmaid who is persuaded by her imprisoned brother to fight against the Czar, a despotic ruler whose policies only exacerbate the sufferings of the working class[19] Vera follows his advice, becoming an assassin for the Nihilists and eventually falling in love with fellow radical Alexis, who later reveals that he is the heir to the Russian throne. After the assassination of the Czar, Vera must choose between her devotion to Alexis and her fidelity to the Nihilists, who have tasked her with his assassination, convinced that only a political coup will make possible the founding of a true republic. In the end, she chooses to kill herself, rather than kill the man she loves—and who loves the Russian people. Initially, reform is treated as little more than an empty gesture. Michael, one of Vera's fellow Nihilists, tellingly remarks that "nothing is impossible in Russia but reform," to which Baron Raff adds: "What have we always done in Russia when a Czar suggests reform?—nothing. You forget we are diplomatists. Men of thought should have nothing to do with action. Reforms in Russia are very tragic, but they always end in a farce."[20] Wilde's use of the theatrical idiom is compelling: under the Czar's rule, reform constitutes a kind of burlesque, characterized by exaggerated and mocking gestures that only reveal its difference from real social change. The travesty of reform becomes its tragedy. In *Vera*, reform is treated as a vacuous concept precisely because reformers are by nature idealists and thus ill-equipped to translate their ambitions into the real world. Elsewhere in the play, however, the term "reform" is treated more explicitly as a decoy for real social change. Michael predicts that the Czar will "throw some sop of reform to the people" in order to forestall the founding of a true Republic.[21] The remark implies that reform is little more than a palliative that deludes people into feeling as though meaningful change has occurred. Moreover, Michael suggests that even seemingly positive reforms may serve ethically questionable ends, precisely because they are limited to discrete actions and fail to address more systemic problems. The theory is confirmed when Professor Marfa, also a Nihilist, presents the scheme to overthrow the government in starkly ideological terms: "assassination considered as a method of political reform."[22]

But suggestively, reform is not always a vapid term in *Vera*, nor is it always limited to the sphere of action. When General Kotemkin, Baron Raff, and other members of the court confer regarding Alexis after the death of the Czar, they note that the new leader is "really too romantic," because he opposes monopolies, denounces lavish spending at court, sympathizes with the plight of the impoverished, favors the founding of a representative Parliament, and "threatens a complete reform in the public service on the ground that the people are too heavily taxed."[23] In this case, reform does not seem to stand in for empty gestures, for it is aligned with a ruler who is thoughtful and "romantic"—one who seeks to bring beautiful things into the world. To this extent, the idealistic and rebellious Alexis, who threatens the reign of tyranny seems to anticipate Wilde's later reflections on the value of the visionary critic, who transforms the world by seeing it anew. In *Vera*, then, Wilde treats reform as a contestable term, distinguishing carefully between the actions people call reforms, which are often ineffective and short-sighted, and real social change, which remains somewhat elusive.

In subsequent years, Wilde would continue to treat reform as a hollow concept, meant to present the appearance—but not the reality—of social transformation. The idea is explicitly lampooned in his fable "The Remarkable Rocket" (1888), in which a duck reflects upon his own dreams of social change: "I had thoughts of entering public life once myself. [...] there are so many things that need reforming. Indeed, I took the chair at a meeting some time ago, and we passed resolutions condemning everything that we did not like. However, they did not seem to have much effect."[24] Here, the impulse to bring about social change contrasts sharply with actual reform efforts. In this case, the passing of resolutions does little more than convey the indignation of those whose political views are already fixed and accordingly do "not seem to have much effect." Resolving a question through the adoption of a clear platform, such resolutions resist what makes the contemplative life so powerful: its capacity for evolution and nuance. They fail precisely because they represent thought entering into the realm of action.

In like spirit, Lady Hunstanton remarks in *A Woman of No Importance* (1893) that the roguish Lord Illingworth "is quite hopeless [...] I have given up trying to reform him. It would take a Public Company with a Board of Directors and a paid Secretary to do that."[25] If Lady Hunstanton's comment suggests that reforming Lord Illingworth requires an effort as great as those committees devoted to large-scale philanthropic work, it also insinuates that such a reform might be brought about by entirely formal measures: a reallocation of private funds or legal resolutions. In reality, the reform of Lord Illingworth, like the reform of a society, requires much more. Wilde would revisit this idea in *The Importance of Being Earnest* (1895), in which the reprobate Algernon coyly suggests that Cecily make it her "mission" to reform him. The resulting dialogue lampoons the presumption that to articulate a reformatory impulse is to see it accomplished:

Cecily: I'm afraid I've no time, this afternoon.
Algernon: Well, would you mind my reforming myself this afternoon?
Cecily: It is rather Quixotic of you. But I think you should try.
Algernon: I will. I feel better already.[26]

Of course, Algernon has not been reformed by his—or Cecily's—romantic aspirations, though his claim that he feels "better already" reinforces Wilde's belief that reform often constitutes a kind of superficial make-over, a reshaping of reality that fails to question its underlying tenets.

Wilde's apparent opposition to reform, then, seems to have revolved around two chief principles. On the one hand, to commit oneself to any course of action carries teleological challenges. As I note in Chap. 5, Wilde was intrigued by Hegelian dialectics, with its promise to guide human knowledge incrementally closer to absolute truth; yet in much of his life and work Wilde seems to have favored the coexistence of warring ideas to the kind of rhetorical synthesis sometimes advocated by his favorite philosophers. In contrast to the sphere of politics and social reform, the contemplative life permitted one to entertain irreconcilable views; it alone permitted one to be, as Wilde wrote in 1880, "simultaneously, brilliant and unreasonable, speculative and well-informed."[27] On the other hand, Wilde worried that to reform was merely to reshape society from the outside without altering its underlying nature. To this extent, he was in league with thinkers like Matthew Arnold, whose 1865 essay "The Function of Criticism at the Present Time" served as a key textual impetus for "The Critic as Artist." Here, Arnold offers his famous appraisal of English culture as governed by "practical" men who pursue knowledge as "a social, practical, pleasurable affair, almost requiring a chairman, a secretary, and advertisements; [...] in general, plenty of bustle and very little thought."[28] The connection to Wilde in this passage is especially apparent, for Wilde too laments that the intellectual life—and the social ideals it fosters—must always be treated as a knowable system that yields decided outcomes and courses of action. In his Notebook on Philosophy, Wilde would write:

> popular views are one-sided: not so blind as one-sided: the public see every side of a question but unite contradictory views: yet to picture the great ideas that philosophy could apprehend: (such as creation) the philosopher must be "συνοπτικος" [*synoptikos*; seeing the whole together][29]

The term συνοπτικος (*synoptikos*) is delineated in Henry George Liddell and Robert Scott's *Greek-English Lexicon* (1843) as "seeing the whole together; taking a comprehensive view."[30] At the very least, Wilde seems here to share Arnold's view of the critic as one who is able to assume a detached view, rising above partisan interests and pursuing dialectic as a means of attaining to higher truth.

But it is arguably Arnold's view of reform, rather than his approach to English culture more generally, that establishes the strongest kinship between his work and that of Wilde. Arnold categorically rejects the tendency to translate theory into action, famously citing the French Revolution as an event that was noble in spirit but misguided in execution. Like Wilde, he contends that the truly enlightened critic will remain disinterested, considering all views on a matter rather than acting (or writing) on behalf of a fixed agenda. Arnold saw such efforts as ineffectual because they contradicted the natural course of social evolution. He recalls a "man of thought and energy" dejected at the contrast between the present generation and early nineteenth-century reform efforts:

> "What reformers we were then!" he exclaimed; "What a zeal we had! how we canvassed every institution in Church and State, and were prepared to remodel them all on first principles!" He was inclined to regret, as a spiritual flagging, the lull which he saw. I am disposed rather to regard it as a pause in which the turn to a new mode of spiritual progress is being accomplished. [...] Let us think of quietly enlarging our stock of true and fresh ideas, and not, as soon as we get an idea or half an idea, be running out with it into the street, and trying to make it rule there.[31]

As discussed in Chap. 2, the cultivation of a student's intellectual faculties was, for Wilde, preferable to the passive consumption of established wisdom.

The Platonic model of education was to be celebrated because it nurtured the natural development of a student's aesthetic and moral instincts. At least one of the problems with Dorian Gray's education, such as it is, is that he absorbs knowledge rather than seeking it out for himself. In like manner, Wilde would repeatedly suggest that society must evolve according to the dictates of nature, rather than implementing the edicts of reformers. To this extent, Wilde seems to echo Arnold's wariness of programmatic social change, preferring to allow the world to be cultivated anew through the free exchange of ideas.[32]

As Julia Prewitt Brown has suggested, however, there are important differences between the two thinkers as well. In Wilde's view, one cannot be at once a disinterested thinker and a progressive reformer, for to truly engage in the free play of ideas is to remain unmoored to any kind of political program. Accordingly, Wilde "never declares that such disinterestedness is intended to accomplish certain ends, though he is not without hope that it will."[33] Brown rightly underscores Wilde's investment in balancing social consciousness against a desire to maintain critical detachment. In what follows, I want to propose that Wilde's emphasis on Arnoldian detachment constitutes the foundation—rather than the annulment—of his political sensibility. If Wilde's political stances often appear to be muddled, desultory, or even self-defeating, these inconsistencies strangely help to clarify his politics—a politics that is less concerned with the advancement of specific political doctrines than with reimagining how social bodies operate.

Political Animals

Before proceeding further, we would do well to clarify a few of Wilde's chief political influences and inclinations. As previous chapters have established, Wilde emerged from a politically engaged household. Although Lady Wilde's family was avowedly Unionist, she declared her nationalist sympathies at the age of twenty-five when she began writing for *The Nation*. As the periodical outlet of Young Ireland, a movement that had agitated for independent Irish rule from the 1830s, *The Nation* was outspokenly radical in its views. Lady Wilde contributed thirty-nine poems to the paper before its life was cut short by the publication of her essay "Jacta Alea Est" (1848). Enraged by the government's treatment of the Irish people, and especially its failure to alleviate the sufferings wrought by the Great Famine, Lady Wilde purveyed a grim fantasy of revolt against Dublin Castle:

Oh! For a hundred thousand muskets glittering brightly in the light of heaven, and the monumental barricades stretching across each of our noble streets, made desolate by England, circling round that doomed Castle, made infamous by England, where the foreign tyrant has held his council of treason and iniquity against our people and our country for seven hundred years.[34]

The editor of the *Nation*, Charles Gavin Duffy, was brought to trial. He refused to name the author, and the paper was permanently closed on the grounds of sedition. According to some reports, Lady Wilde attended the trial and revealed herself as the author of the controversial piece; accounts vary as to whether Lady Wilde was not heard or was simply ignored by the court.[35] What is certain is that her son would come to revere her as a cultural and political hero of the 1840s.

Practically without question, Wilde shared his mother's early sympathies with Irish nationalism and most forms of political tyranny.[36] He referred to James Anthony Froude's *The Two Chiefs of Duboy* (1889), a novel that drew extensively on Irish cultural stereotypes, as "the record of one of the greatest tragedies of modern Europe," noting that "[i]f in the last century she tried to govern Ireland with an insolence that was intensified by race-hatred and religious prejudice, she has sought to rule her in this century with a stupidity that is aggravated by good intentions."[37] Wilde's own appraisal of the 1840s in his lecture "Irish Poets and Poetry of the Nineteenth Century," delivered in San Francisco in 1882, offers some insight into how his mother's political identity may have translated into his own experience:

> As regards these men of '48, I look on their work with peculiar reverence and love, for I was indeed trained by my mother to love and reverence them, as a Catholic child is the Saints of the Calendar, and I have seen so many of them also. The earliest hero of my childhood was Smith O'Brien, whom I remember well—tall and stately with the dignity of one who had fought for a noble idea and with the sadness of one who had failed; no, perhaps I should not use the word failed, such failures are at least often grander than a hundred victories.[38]

Wilde refers to William Smith O'Brien, a leader of the Young Ireland movement and Member of Parliament with strong nationalist leanings. O'Brien was sentenced to death for his role in the Rebellion of 1848, though he was ultimately deported to Tasmania (then Van Dieman's Land). To this extent, Wilde suggests that the heroes of his youth were those who openly resisted English rule of law. Over the course of his lecture, Wilde celebrated such Irish nationalist poets as John Mitchel, John Savage, Thomas Davis, James Clarence

Mangan, Michael Joseph Barry, and Denis Florence MacCarthy, among others, referring to them as "men who made their lives noble poems also, men who had not merely written about the sword but were ready to bear it; who not only could rhyme to Liberty but could die for her also, if need had so been."[39]

Wilde would come to emulate the example of these men and of his mother in the 1880s, producing a number of anti-imperial and Irish nationalist poems (including "Ave Imperatrix," "Italia," "Sonnet on the Massacre of the Christians at Bulgaria," and "Sonnet to Liberty," to mention only a few).[40] His poem "Quantum Mutata" (1881), for instance, takes its cue from John Milton's sonnet "On the Late Massacre in Piedmont," which denounced the violent massacre and forced Catholic conversion of the Waldensians in northern Italy in 1655. Recalling Oliver Cromwell's protest in support of the Waldensians, the speaker of Wilde's poem laments England's transformation from a "lion" fighting against the "oppressor" into a state power governed by more commercial aims:

> How comes it then that from such high estate
> We have thus fallen, save that Luxury
> With barren merchandise piles up the gate
> Where nobler thoughts and deeds should enter by [...].[41]

Wilde is hardly explicit in identifying a specific course of political action, though as Karl Beckson and Bobby Fong point out the most likely subject of this poem (and of "Theoretikos," which is discussed below) is the reluctance of the English government to intervene in support of Turkish revolutionaries in the Balkans.[42] Under Prime Minister Benjamin Disraeli, the government remained adamantly opposed to taking any action that might make the area vulnerable to Russian incursions, despite escalating state violence and suppression of individual freedoms, what William Gladstone referred to as the "Bulgarian Horrors." Wilde's political consciousness seems almost transparent in such a poem. The speaker is a defender of individual liberties, who curiously denounces England's pose of political detachment. Given Wilde's tendency to prefer thought over action, it is perhaps a surprisingly direct and even declamatory text.

Yet on the facing page in the original edition of *Poems*, the reader encounters a very different sentiment. In "Libertatis Sacra Fames" (1881) Wilde actually seems to resist the democratic spirit of his other work, observing: "Better the rule of One, whom all obey, / Than to let clamorous demagogues betray / Our freedom with the kiss of anarchy."[43] Reflecting upon the Nihilists' violent protests against Czar Alexander II, Wilde seems to suggest that the risk of violence does not justify political action, even in defense of democratic principles. Such a reading of the poem would seem to directly contradict the radical spirit of *Vera*, which was written just a year earlier. Within the same narrow time period—indeed, within the same volume of poems—Wilde seems to vacillate between a progressive impulse and a capitulation to the status quo, which at least forestalls the violent work of revolution and "Murder with his silent bloody feet."[44]

The seeming contradictions in Wilde's political outlook have been accounted for in various ways. John Sloan has observed that although "Republican in sympathy, Wilde, like his mother, was politically conservative by instinct," noting in particular his attachment to the monarchy.[45] In Sloan's view, Wilde was never as radical as contemporary readers expect him to be. Even Wilde's most outspoken claims on behalf of Irish nationalism, Sloan continues, emerged during his American tour and might well constitute "an expression of affinity [...] rather than of political commitment."[46] In like manner, Julie Buckler suggests that Wilde sometimes prioritized commercial or artistic aims above politics. Because Vera chooses love over radical social change, Buckler avers, even his most overtly political play ultimately devolves into apolitical melodrama.[47] Ruth Robbins too acknowledges the tensions between Wilde's commercial, aesthetic, and political objectives, noting that his first published volume, *Poems*, deliberately dabbles in different ideological perspectives. What was perhaps at first an experiment designed to test a range of public authorial personae, Robbins contends, ultimately reinforced the popular notion of Wilde as a poseur who retained little fidelity to either conservative or progressive worldviews.[48]

Such approaches to Wilde's political outlook are perfectly fair, though to an extent they rest on a presumption that political work must be authenticated by action. Although Wilde's Irish nationalism was expressed predominantly through words rather than active participation, I am not quite sure that this signifies a lack of commitment or unqualified conservatism on his part.[49] As we have seen, even the most earnest political sympathies do not always generate a clear and incontrovertible course of action. Even in Wilde's most radical poetry, then, political ideals often give rise to nagging uncertainties regarding how best to translate thought into action. It is suggestive that "Quanta Mutata" and "Libertatis Sacra Fames" appeared in the original 1881 edition of *Poems* on facing pages, a fact that invites the reader to appraise Wilde's call for a return to the reformatory spirit of seventeenth-century England alongside a caution that even his own preference for a "state republic / Where every man is Kinglike" bears with it certain dangers. This seems to be more than a "curiously ambivalent politics," as Roditi had suggested, the marker of a mind that is undecided in its course. On the contrary, we might discern here signs of a deliberate attempt to juxtapose ideas that seem to be in tension with one another—ideas that, if contemplated together, might expand the reader's knowledge and sympathy.

The poem "Theoretikos" provides ample justification for such a view. Robbins suggests that this poem recommends a "complete withdrawal from all political, ethical or religious commitment" and ultimately "praises a retreat into art as an alternative to political engagement or commitment."[50] To be sure, the speaker closes by observing that political agitation "mars my calm" and prompts him to seek out "dreams of Art / And loftiest culture."[51] Knowing that Wilde placed inordinate value upon the world of thought, we might well conclude that this is a salutary end. After all, the poem's title refers to Aristotle's concept of *bios theoretikos* (literally, the contemplative life), which Wilde would invoke again years later in "The Critic as Artist." The idea of the thinker who "stand[s] apart / Neither for God, nor for his enemies" is apolitical in the strictest sense of the word—he belongs to no party and professes no agenda.[52] Yet one of the most striking elements of this poem is Wilde's deliberate juxtaposition of the world of action—that "mighty empire" with its "feet of clay," which has become little more than a "vile traffic-house"—and the world of ideas.[53] If Britain once pursued loftier principles and could lay claim to its "crown of bay," such aspirations have now been subordinated to the values of a material culture, wherein "Wisdom and reverence are sold at mart."[54] In the context of this historical account, the speaker's retreat into art seems less celebratory than wistful and desperate. If Robbins is right to suggest that Wilde cherishes the contemplative life as a withdrawal from the world of political strife, the value of such an existence is not its occlusion of politics but rather the ability it confers upon the speaker to see beyond partisan disputes. It is *bios theoretikos* that makes possible his assessment of contemporary politics, which may be disinterested but is hardly indifferent.

We see evidence of the tension between Wilde's convictions and his philosophy of reform elsewhere in his political life. Consider, for instance, his views on the emerging women's movement. Barbara Caine's helpful essay on the subject acknowledges a certain ambivalence in his approach to women's issues, though she is careful to note that he personally seems to have favored the proto-feminist impulses of his mother. While Caine accentuates Wilde's progressive leanings, she notes that his published work often trades one social reform for another, so that in *An Ideal Husband* he seems to "raise feminist questions while undermining the idea that women can meaningfully influence or engage in political life."[55] Assuredly, the play's elision of femininity and domestic life—and Lady Chiltern's apparent detachment from her husband's political work—would seem to reinforce this view. Yet underlying this panorama of apolitical actors is a more systemic critique of social reform. Lord Goring, the unlikely hero of the play, remarks that he enjoys political parties, for they "are the only place left to us where people don't talk politics." The ensuing exchange would seem to suggest that even female enfranchisement cannot save a system that is so fundamentally flawed:

Lady Basildon: I delight in talking politics. I talk them all day long. But I can't bear listening to them. I don't know how the unfortunate men in the House stand these long debates.
Lord Goring: By never listening.[56]

The implication here is that politics is itself merely a matter of inflating one's own self-importance, rather than an earnest dialogue about social issues. Lady Chiltern attends a meeting of the regional Woman's Liberal Association but has little to say other than that her husband's name is greeted with approval.[57] For Lady Chiltern, as for most other characters in this play, politics is primarily a vehicle through which one can amplify her social standing. Reform hardly enters into the picture at all.

Wilde himself, as Caine likewise notes, was committed to providing women with a platform for discussing the intellectual, social, and political issues of the day in a frank and non-partisan manner. When he assumed the editorship of *Lady's World* in 1888, one of the first things he did was to rechristen it *Woman's World*, noting that the new name was more respectful and more likely to attract male and female contributors of the educated classes. Wilde was careful, however, to insist that the publication was less a political organ committed to advancing certain principles, than a mode through which individual writers might voice their own idiosyncratic views: "The magazine will have no political or artistic creed of its own—it will be merely the channel through which many streams will flow."[58] Observing that *Woman's World* should be concerned "not only with what women wear, but with what they think," Wilde seemed to have been less interested in promoting his own political views than in facilitating debate.[59] His editorship was defined, in other words, less by a wish to promote specific political measures than by a desire to prepare the groundwork for reform through engaged conversation.[60] What might be deemed a detached or apolitical stance, then, might also be regarded as a preeminently liberal approach to political dialogue, one that arguably shares in Arnold's commitment to the "free play of the mind."[61]

We would be relatively safe, then, to conclude that Wilde's political principles were of a broadly progressive scope, though he was by no means consistent in sustaining those principles. Wilde was an Irish landlord who admitted to abandoning his accent at Oxford and routinely faced charges of elitism; he was also an Irish nationalist who sympathized with the plight of the working man. He supported the advancement of women, though this hardly spared them from becoming the objects of satire in his written work. Such tensions, I think, are fairly accounted for by the distance between intellect and practice—at the very least, it is accounted for by the fact that human beings are seldom entirely consistent in the fulfillment of political and social ideals. Yet there is something especially troubling to readers about the inconsistencies in Wilde's political expression. Many have attempted to explain or justify them; some have proposed that it discloses Wilde's lack of seriousness as a political thinker. In some cases, however, it may well reveal Wilde's intellectual subtlety. As he had pointed out repeatedly, the world of thought was flexible enough to withstand contradiction and paradox—reality was not.

The Anti-Socialist

Perhaps the most visible instance of this tension is to be seen in Wilde's treatment of labor politics. Socialist critic and playwright Bernard Shaw knew Wilde from boyhood, when he regarded him simply as a "Dublin snob."[62] Although they would continue to have a sporadic and uneasy relationship over the years, Shaw's posthumous recollection of Wilde was more charitable. Wilde had been an unlikely supporter of the eight anarchists who were charged in the 1886 Haymarket Affair, a rally for worker's rights in Chicago that turned violent when a bomb was thrown at police. Shaw writes: "I tried to get some literary men in London, all heroic rebels and skeptics on paper, to sign a memorial asking for the reprieve of these unfortunate men. The only signature I got was Oscar's. It was a completely disinterested act on his part; and it secured my distinguished consideration for him for the rest of his life."[63] Although Shaw seems to have regarded Wilde's gesture as an essentially apolitical act, they would again cross paths when Wilde met him at "a meeting somewhere in Westminster at which I delivered an address on Socialism, and at which Oscar turned up and spoke."[64] Robert Ross later remarked to Shaw that this address was the origin of "The Soul of Man Under Socialism" (1891).[65]

Shaw's reluctance to regard Wilde as a political actor, despite encountering him in explicitly political contexts, has been mirrored in contemporary scholarship, where Wilde's commitment to aesthetic questions has often been read as a disavowal of social activism. Whereas some critics have sought to establish Wilde as a serious political thinker, others have preferred to treat his remarks on social questions as political posturing or, at best, as a creative synthesis of ideas already in circulation.[66] The debate regarding Wilde's political authenticity has often revolved around "The Soul of Man Under Socialism," where he contends provocatively: "Socialism itself will be of value simply because it will lead to Individualism."[67] Josephine Guy has persuasively established that Wilde's essay reflects political arguments that were far from original at the time of its publication.[68] Of particular note for Guy is Grant Allen's "Individualism and Socialism," an essay published in the *Contemporary Review* just a few months prior to the appearance of Wilde's piece.[69] It is unclear whether Wilde knew of Allen's essay at the time of writing "Soul of Man," but he assuredly knew Allen by reputation, and the connections between the two essays are compelling.[70] Indeed, "The Soul of Man Under Socialism" was published alongside another essay by Grant Allen ("The Celt in English Art") in *The Contemporary Review*, prompting the two writers to admire one another's work. They seem to have written to one another almost simultaneously, with Allen praising Wilde's "noble and beautiful essay" and noting: "I would have written every line of it myself—if only I had known how."[71] For Guy and others, the material and temporal proximity of Wilde's essay to that of Allen confirms that Wilde was hardly the first to propose a link between socialism and individualism.

Yet this is not to suggest that Wilde uncritically parroted contemporary source material on social reform. As I propose in the following pages, Wilde's interest in reconciling individualism and socialism underscores a concern that emerges across his readings and *oeuvre*: the calculated risks of bringing ideas into the world. In the nineteenth century, the term individualism did not merely connote a celebration of personal liberty; it encompassed a range of very specific political precepts, including a staunch resistance to government oversight. Following the work of Herbert Spencer, which Wilde studied at length during his time at Oxford, proponents of individualism treated society as a complex organism subject to slow evolutionary change. Any attempt at programmatic reform, by this logic, risked disrupting the natural course of historical development. I want to suggest here that Wilde's seeming aversion to social reform in "Soul of Man Under Socialism" invokes the claims of individualism not in order to originate or to advocate for a specific political platform but rather to highlight the difficulty of implementing social reform. Rather than asserting or defending Wilde's originality as a political thinker, I consider Wilde's remarks on socialism and labor as a testing ground for his evolving political consciousness—a consciousness that was troubled (and at times paralyzed) by the translation of thought into action. Wilde's interest in political questions was not occasional or idiosyncratic; it was marked and enduring, though not always pointed or transparent.

We can trace Wilde's investment in social reform back to Oxford, where he read widely in classical political history and theory. Importantly, Wilde recognized the limitations of political theory well before he ever came to write on the subject.[72] In his Notebook on Philosophy, written between 1876 and 1878 while still at Oxford, Wilde evinces a decidedly skeptical attitude toward the social sciences:

> The hypotheses of pol. econ. [political economy] are such as "labour circulates according to the demand" or that "wages fall wherever labour is attracted to a certain locality" [.] We must presuppose a country where labour can circulate and where men are at liberty to move: of course the ties of family and Poor Laws prevent men moving ·
>   also, "that a man will get the biggest price he can" which is really untrue:
>   also "that free competition is to be allowed" but the govt. of such a country must prevent στάσις [stasis] · The govt. [government] must be strong:
>   In fact the qualifications are so numerous they destroy the rules ·[73]

More than a decade prior to writing "The Soul of Man Under Socialism," Wilde expresses a wariness of treating society purely as an abstraction, noting that "the rules" only can be regarded as such if experience tends to validate them. If social reality repeatedly deviates from the fixed laws of political economy, then the soundness of those laws must surely be called into question. At the time of writing this passage, Wilde had been reading the work of John Elliott Cairnes, who treated political economy as a scientific system that must be understood apart from social life. In his *Essays in Political Economy* (1873), Cairnes takes issue with Auguste Comte's tendency to treat political economy as a philosophy that might be critiqued, rejected, or adapted to political ends.[74] Wilde saw a contradiction in the approaches of Comte and Cairnes, both of whom insisted upon the validity of social "rules" that failed to acknowledge the complex, illogical, and often unpredictable relationship between the individual and society at large.

It was an idea that he would cultivate as an attentive reader of Spencer, whose 1851 volume *Social Statics* is routinely cited in the Oxford notebooks. As I explain in Chap. 4, Spencer posited that human society, like an organism in the natural world, is utterly dependent upon the individuation of its parts. It is in this spirit that Wilde echoes Spencer in his Commonplace Book: "Progress is the assertion of individualism against authority, and progress in matter is the differentiation and specialization of function: those organisms which are entirely subject to external influences do not progress any more than a mind entirely subject to authority."[75] The idea would dovetail—and in Wilde's notebook appears literally alongside—William K. Clifford's discussion of the "tribal self" whose works of altruism were driven chiefly by necessity: "service done to a community by an individual who is part of that community."[76] Invoking at another point Theodor Mommsen's *History of Rome* (1854), Wilde writes: "Between the Tarquins and the Caesars, that long five hundred years of extraordinary deeds and ordinary men Appius Claudius Caecus is the great link: he was the incarnation of the idea of progress, neither an aristocrat or a democrat, but rather a political humanist."[77] As a "political humanist," Caecus connected disparate parts of a growing empire through the construction of roads—what would become "the network of the world"—while elevating "the Greek ideal of individualization."[78] If we cannot take this statement as a testimony of Wilde's beliefs, we can at least discern here his attraction to a political ethos that treated individualism as a positive asset to the most advanced and diversified community.

John Ruskin held a similar view, presenting art as a link between the inner life of the singular artist and the world of social action. Wilde carefully studied *The Stones of Venice* (1851), in which Ruskin would aver that thought and labor are not opposed but rather mutually sustaining impulses. Ruskin writes: "We are always in these days endeavoring to separate the two; we want one man to be always thinking, another to be always working, and we call one a gentleman, and the other an operative; whereas the workman ought often to be thinking, and the thinker often to be working, and both should be gentlemen, in the best sense."[79] For Ruskin, the contemplative life should never be divorced from the material world in which we live, for it is in this world that our thoughts assume the visible—original, creative, perhaps imperfect—form of the beautiful. Art is the visible expression of man's possibilities and imperfections; to this extent, it is a vehicle for both individual and social transformation. Although Wilde often seems to draw a stark line between the world of action and the world of thought, his views on art would eventually accommodate Ruskin's spiritualized vision of labor. In "Art and the Handicraftsman," a lecture written at the beginning of his tour of America, Wilde recalled how Ruskin intercepted Wilde and his friends as he was "going up to lecture in cap and gown":

> He seemed troubled and prayed us to go back with him to his lecture, which a few of us did, and there he spoke to us not on art this time but on life [...] He thought, he said, that we should be working at something that would do good

to other people, at something by which we might show that in all labour there was something noble. Well, we were a good deal moved, and said we would do anything he wished.[80]

Accordingly (as I note in Chap. 2), Ruskin arranged for the men to build a road connecting North and South Hinskey, which had long been kept apart by a "great swamp." The resulting thoroughfare was not merely to be a practical improvement; it would be a visible manifestation of the fellowship and virtue shared among the students. In a manner of speaking, their labor translated belief into action. Having worked on the road through the winter, the student workers eventually dispersed. Ruskin had departed for Venice, and without a leader their efforts proved aimless. By Wilde's account, however, this episode was the foundation of his own aesthetic movement, for it inspired in him the possibility that men might work—separately and yet collectively—toward some great effort:

> And I felt that if there was enough spirit amongst the young men to go out to such work as road-making for the sake of a noble ideal of life, I could from them create an artistic movement that might change, as it has changed, the face of England. So I sought them out—leader they would call me—but there was no leader: we were all searchers only and we were bound to each other by noble friendship and by noble art.[81]

For Wilde, as for Ruskin, there was positive value in the collective effort, which helped to facilitate the unfettered expression of the individual. Indeed, Wilde's articulation of this endeavor seems in many respects to anticipate the political impetus of "Soul of Man Under Socialism." Lacking any form of official oversight, the aesthetic movement would be composed of individual seekers, each pursuing a different métier and yet "bound to each other" by bonds of affection and beauty.

I do not mean to suggest here that Wilde's early writings openly endorse the precepts of individualism or socialism, as such; yet his engagement with Ruskin and with other thinkers of the time reflects a close attention to how the work of individuals might productively shape social reality. To be sure, this would seem to antedate Wilde's investment in the specific vision he offers in "The Soul of Man Under Socialism." More importantly, however, his manner of reflecting on the connection between the individual and social reform was firmly grounded, even in this early period, in a tendency to align political change with forms of aesthetic engagement. It was a subject to which Wilde recurred throughout his critical work in the 1880s. In 1888, he produced a series of essays responding to the lectures of the Arts and Crafts Exhibition Society. The term "Arts and Crafts" was first used at the exhibition to describe those who celebrated the decorative arts as a means of combatting industrialization through the celebration of traditional handicrafts and social reform. In the series of essays reporting on the exhibition, Wilde presents the principles of the movement as largely consonant with his own views on aesthetic labor. In "Mr. Morris on Tapestry," for instance, Wilde writes of William Morris's socialist aesthetic:

> Commercialism, with its vile god cheapness, its callous indifference to the worker, its innate vulgarity of temper, is our enemy. To gain anything good we must sacrifice something of our luxury—must think more of others, more of the State, the commonweal [...][82]

Wilde would reiterate his concerns about this "pet god, cheapness" only a few weeks later in an essay on "The Beauties of Bookbinding," noting this time his concerns about the worker who is "diminished to a machine" rather than elevated to the level of an artist.[83] In these pieces, Wilde reflects an enduring interest in linking the life of the artist to the world of labor. In an essay written in February 1889, only a few months later, Wilde more clearly delineates his intellectual investment in working-class politics. His review of Edward Carpenter's *Chants of Labour: A Song-Book of the People* (1889), "Poetical Socialists," lauds the diversity of authorship he sees at work in the volume:

> It shows that Socialism is not going to allow herself to be trammeled by any hard-and-fast creed, or to be stereotyped into an iron formula. She welcomes many and multiform natures. She rejects none, and has room for all. She has the attraction of a wonderful personality, and touches the heart of one and the brain of another, and draws the man by his hatred of injustice, and his neighbor by his faith in the future, and a third, it may be, by his love of art, or by his wild worship of a lost and buried past. And all of this is well. For to make men Socialists is nothing, but to make Socialism human is a great thing.[84]

Resisting the lure of "any hard-and-fast creed," socialism emerges here less as a political platform than as a philosophy seeking to maximize individual liberty through the support and diversity of a collective effort. Such an effort must remain aloof from doctrinal assertions: after all, to "make men Socialists" is merely to assign them a political designation. The real achievement, Wilde explains, would be to realize the values of Socialism without imposing "an iron formula," in a manner that facilitates free and natural sympathies among men. While it is by no means clear that Wilde was avowedly socialist at this time—or indeed at any other—it is clear that well before the publication of Grant Allen's "Individualism and Socialism" Wilde was attracted by a politics that treated individual expression and the collective good as mutually sustaining.

Even in his American lectures, Wilde had suggested that not merely aesthetic contemplation but aesthetic production might sow the seeds of reform. As I established in Chap. 2, Wilde proposed that the best means of cultivating a child's social and moral faculties was through exposure to art, handicrafts, building, and immersion in the natural world. Wilde was aware that it would strike some as incongruous that he, a man who disavowed utility and pragmatism, should speak about social reform:

> Perhaps you may be surprised at my talking of labour and the workman. You have heard of me, I fear, through the medium of your somewhat imaginative newspapers as, if not a 'Japanese young man,' at least a young man to whom the rush and clamour and reality of the modern world were distasteful, and whose greatest difficulty in life was the difficulty of living up to the level of his blue china—a paradox from which England has not yet recovered.[85]

But it was a paradox that Wilde was determined to sustain and, if possible, to perpetuate. The difficulty of living up to the level of art—whether it be blue china or a portrait—is that such an effort acknowledges the importance of pursuing the beautiful and the good, even when it might seem most out of reach. When art is treated as a consumable object rather than a source of contemplation, such an endeavor becomes impossible. Hence, Wilde would later recommend that "a workshop [be] attached to every school, and one hour a day [be] given up to the teaching of simple decorative arts."[86] In such a way, Wilde insisted that a tactile engagement with the real world would help to promote the aesthetic and social development of children, if not the inculcation of marketable skills. Wilde would note: "We must have, as Emerson said, a mechanical craft for our culture, a basis for our higher accomplishments in the work of our hands—the uselessness of most people's hands seems to me one of the most unpractical things."[87] Work, it would seem, might constitute both an aid to contemplation and a vehicle for translating thought into the material world.

The essay invoked here is, of course, Ralph Waldo Emerson's "Man the Reformer" (1842), originally presented as a lecture to the Mechanics' Apprentices Library Association in Boston. Wilde selectively quotes from Emerson's essay throughout "The Soul of Man Under Socialism," and there are clear affinities between his outlook at that of Wilde.[88] First and perhaps most importantly, Emerson regards the true reformer as a "mediator between the spiritual and the actual world," a "Re-maker of what man has made."[89] As such, he must operate quite apart from existing social reform movements, which he represents as selective, sporadic, and superficial. Emerson elaborates:

> I do not wish to be absurd and pedantic in reform. I do not wish to push my criticism on the state of things around me to that extravagant mark, that shall compel me to suicide, or to an absolute isolation from the advantages of civil society. If we suddenly plant our foot, and say,—I will neither eat nor drink nor wear nor touch any food or fabric which I do not know to be innocent, or deal with any person whose whole manner of life is not clear and rational, we shall stand still.[90]

So far from advocating programmatic social reform, Emerson highlights the transformative power of personality and the "contemplative life." "The power," he writes "which is at once spring and regulator in all efforts of reform, is the conviction that there is an infinite worthiness in man which will appear at the call of worth [...]"[91] For Emerson, then, it is less important to pursue a new political or social platform than to reform one's manner of seeing the world.

Such a wariness of reform efforts, as I have suggested, makes its most striking appearance in Wilde's "Soul of Man Under Socialism." Although it may strike the reader as peculiar that Wilde's most political essay seems to reject the efficacy of reform efforts, in the context of the intellectual history I trace here it becomes more intelligible. In Wilde's view, programs designed to alleviate the sufferings of the poor have proven almost universally ineffective: "with admirable though misdirected intentions, they very seriously and very sentimentally set themselves to the task of remedying the evils that they see. But their remedies do not cure the disease: they merely prolong it. Indeed, their remedies are part of the disease."[92] Social reform movements fail, in other words, by attending to material palliatives while overlooking the deeper causes of social iniquity. As he puts it, "Feeding and entertaining the poor is not a solution: The proper aim is to try and reconstruct society on such a that poverty will be impossible."[93] For some, such a remark might seem to underscore the limits of Wilde's capacity for serious political thought, since he seems to deliberately ignore the stark realities of this world: poverty may never be eliminated altogether. Lawrence Danson has proposed that the essay is not concerned with pragmatism at all: "Wilde's 'socialism' is ahistorical, or it exists after history's end, when ideology in no way mediates either individual existence or relationship between individuals."[94] In other words, Wilde does not concern himself with outlining the steps by which we might attain a society that has extinguished poverty. Instead, he confers upon us an imaginative vision of what that society might look like:

> It will be a marvelous thing—the true personality of man—when we see it. It will grow naturally and simply, flower-like, or as a tree grows. It will not beat discord. It will never argue or dispute. It will not prove things. It will know everything. […] It will not be always meddling with others, or asking them to be like itself. It will love them because they will be different. And yet, while it will not meddle with others, it will help all, as a beautiful thing helps us by being what it is.[95]

Reform itself—the attempt to "meddle" in the lives of others—is treated here as the enemy of true freedom and social transformation. "Selfishness is not living as one wishes to live," Wilde adds, "it is asking others to live as one wishes to live. And unselfishness is letting other people's lives alone, not interfering with them."[96] By this logic, reform constitutes yet another instance of the individual imposing upon the liberty of others. If change must be instituted through laws or resolutions, it is a sign that Nature has not yet prepared the way for such a change.

Given that Christianity had constituted a significant arm of social reform in the nineteenth century, it is perhaps fitting that Wilde turns to Christ as a refutation of conventional reform movements and as an exemplar of his own social vision.[97] As I note in Chap. 3, Wilde was attracted to Christian thought despite its institutional and doctrinal associations, which he sometimes sought deliberately to eschew. In this spirit, Wilde imagines Christ as a man who preached the value of self above the value of possessions, thus making possible the cultivation of beautiful impulses. On the one hand, Wilde's Christ urges precisely the turn from material to spiritual wealth that Wilde recommends:

> What Jesus meant, was this. He said to man, "You have a wonderful personality. Develop it. Be yourself. Don't imagine that your perfection lies in accumulating or possessing external things. Your affection is inside of you. If only you could realise that, you would not want to be rich. Ordinary riches can be stolen from a man. Real riches cannot. In the treasury-house of your soul, there are infinitely precious things, that may not be taken from you."[98]

Wilde does not merely disavow the value of worldly goods—after all, material and sensory experience might well bring one into closer relation with the divine. On the contrary, Wilde advocates here for a revaluation of material wealth and a renewed commitment to the contemplative life. Emerson had written: "Why needs any man be rich? Why must he have horses, fine garments, handsome apartments, access to public houses and places of amusement? Only for want of thought. Give his mind a new image, and he flees into a solitary garden or garret to enjoy it, and is richer with that dream, than the fee of a county could make him."[99] It was, indeed, in dreams and in visions that Wilde saw man's best chance at real reform.

Precisely such an idea is at work in Wilde's fairy tales, which as Jarlath Killeen notes, frequently broach the question of labor reform.[100] In "The Young King," for instance, Wilde pointedly demonstrates that the production of material goods is based on corruption. Although the story stops short of advancing a conventional moral, the king himself is reformed over time—not through a dogmatic program and change in policy but rather through a series of dreams that reveal to him the sufferings wrought by his material desires. His visions are crowded with "pale, sickly-looking children" working at the textile mills, women "seated at a table sewing" and suffocating in the "foul and heavy" air that surrounds them, and "a huge galley that was being rowed by a hundred slaves" who are severely whipped and give their lives diving for a pearl to ornament the king's scepter.[101] So grief-stricken is the king by these visions that he arrives at his coronation the next morning "appareled as a beggar," wearing a crown of twigs and holding a wooden staff. But as the king kneels in the church, he is visibly transformed before the eyes of the attendants:

> And lo! through the painted windows came the sunlight streaming upon him, and the sunbeams wove round him a tissued robe that was fairer than the robe that had been fashioned for his pleasure. The dead staff blossomed, and bare lilies that were whiter than pearls. The dry thorn blossomed, and bare roses that were redder than rubies. Whiter than fine pearls were the lilies, and their stems were of bright silver. Redder than male rubies were the roses, and their leaves were of beaten gold.[102]

If this would seem to be a tale of classic moral reform, it is worth noting that it is not the king but rather those who witness the spectacle that are most transformed. The Bishop, the guards, and the townspeople who wished to see their king slain rather than forego royal vestments, are persuaded otherwise, not by a homily but by the spectacle of beauty, as the king's inner virtue is made visible—so much so that they cannot look upon his face, "for it was like the face of an angel."[103] One thinks again of Wilde's words in "The English Renaissance of Art": "For the worker then, handicraftsman of whatever kind he is, art is no longer to be a purple robe woven by a slave and thrown over the whitened body of a leprous king to hide and to adorn the sin of his luxury, but rather the beautiful and noble expression of a life that has in it something beautiful and noble."[104] Reform, in this case, is not a matter of programmatic change and cannot be accomplished by *telling* the people what he has learned: the king attempts to explain his visions, but no one will heed his words. The only thing capable of bringing about real change is an aesthetic experience so elevated as to approximate spiritual revelation.

Loose Ends

But how precisely does such a revelation translate into reform? If we rely upon the power of ideas and art alone, then social reform would seem to be a dream perpetually deferred. As Wilde himself famously notes in "The Soul of Man Under Socialism": "A map of the world that does not include Utopia is not worth glancing at, for it leaves out the one country at which Humanity is always landing. And when Humanity lands there, it looks out, and, seeing a better country, sets sail. Progress is the realization of Utopias."[105] On the face of it, Wilde playfully observes that utopia—the etymology of which is, famously, "no place"—cannot be located clearly on a map, though it is perhaps more important to traverse than the earth beneath our feet.[106] One might well discern in Wilde's proclamation a call to seek out higher ideals, which are to be gradually implemented in the real world. Julia Prewitt Brown suggests that Wilde imagines here "a situation in which the individual himself is like a nation, secured with rights and acknowledging the rights of others."[107] To be sure, the map Wilde describes would seem to be a highly subjective one, for it is always shifting as time and space are passed over.

Yet if "Humanity" pursues collectively the quest for a "better country," then the search for utopia is never truly about discovering a perfect world—it is about continually seeing the world from new perspectives. Progress is made through movement itself, through an ongoing pursuit of new political vistas. Practical solutions have absolutely nothing to do with reform. "For," Wilde continues, "what is a practical scheme? A practical scheme is either a scheme that is already in existence, or a scheme that could be carried out under existing conditions. But it is exactly the existing conditions that one objects to; and any scheme that could accept these condition is wrong and foolish."[108] Such an insight recalls Wilde's remark in "A Chinese Sage," an essay he had written just a year earlier for *The Speaker*. In this piece, Wilde appraises the rhetorical efficacy of the fourth century Chinese philosopher Zhuangzi, whose work is distinguished by a refusal to endorse clear moral precepts. Zhuangzi positively refuses to sympathize with existing conditions:

It is the race itself that he objects to; and as for active sympathy, which has become the profession of so many worthy people in our own day, he things that trying to make others good is as silly an occupation as 'beating a drum in a forest in order to find a fugitive.' It is a mere waste of energy. That is all.[109]

To pass a law or set life to a new cadence is to enact superficial changes, leaving the underlying sentiments, habits, and affinities of society unaffected. The individual is merely bound by another doctrine that does not accord with his nature.

To some degree, this helps to clarify why Wilde, whose work seems to be inflected with social values, so often decried books that offered sound "morals." In his criticism, Wilde draws a clear line between good literature—books that bring about such transformative effects—and books that seek to "do good" by promoting a course of social reform. The late nineteenth century was, he observes, "an age in which all social reforms have been preceded and have been largely influenced by fiction."[110] Without question, Wilde refers here to the rise of the social problem novel, works that seek to illustrate the effects of a specific social ill (for instance, industrialism, class conflict, urban crime) upon individual characters.[111] Wilde had little patience for such works. He called Mary Humphrey Ward's *Robert Elsmere* (1888), which depicts the social work of an English clergyman, a "masterpiece of the genre ennuyeux,"[112] He was comparatively less tolerant of the popular novelists who "wish to reform the morals, rather than to portray the manners of their age. They have made the novel the mode of propaganda."[113] The dangers of such an approach are manifold. In the first place, as the preceding pages have suggested, Wilde regarded such prescriptive measures as ineffectual. Delineating a course of action rather than appealing to the reader's aesthetic sense, such efforts only provided temporary and often superficial remedies.

But following the material suffering of his own prison sentence, Wilde was more deliberate and prescriptive in his later reform efforts. He wrote two letters to the editor of the *Daily Chronicle* on prison reform: one treating the condition of children in prison (dated 27 May 1897) and the second discussing the Prisons Act (dated 23 March 1898), which promised to alleviate some of the hardships (the use of the treadmill, for instance, and extended periods of isolation) that Wilde himself had endured. In this letter, Wilde remarks upon the move to increase the number of prison inspections, one of the signature proposals of the Prisons Act. In Wilde's view, such measures were too beholden to the existing system:

Such a reform as this is entirely useless. The reason is extremely simple. The inspectors and justices of the peace that visit prisons come there for the purpose of seeing that the prison regulations are duly carried out. They come for no other purpose, nor have they any power, even if they had the desire, to alter a single clause in the regulations.[114]

Recognizing that material palliatives have real effects on the suffering body, Wilde carefully documents the physical conditions of prison life and insists upon the need for "adequate and wholesome" food, an end to the "punishment of insomnia," "entirely altered" sanitary practices, an "adequate supply of good books," and more.[115] These seemingly practical recommendations are coupled, however, with a recognition that procedural reform must be accompanied by spiritual and ethical change. Wilde observes, for instance, that it is not the moral sense but rather the law, which has determined that children may be confined to "a dimly lit cell, for twenty-three hours out of the twenty-four." Wilde goes further:

> If an individual, parent or guardian, did this to a child, he would be severely punished. The Society for the Prevention of Cruelty to Children would take the matter up at once. There would be on all hands the utmost detestation of whomsoever had been guilty of such cruelty. A heavy sentence would, undoubtedly, follow conviction. But our own actual society does worse itself [...][116]

For Wilde, then, at least one of the chief obstructions to real social reform was a tendency to differentiate between ethical and institutional culture. Child abuse is universally deemed abhorrent, until it comes to be enforced by that "strange abstract force" of law. In the end, Wilde values his procedural recommendations for prison reform as less vital than the renewal of human sympathy. As Wilde puts it: "But to make even these reforms effectual, much has to be done. And the first, and perhaps the most difficult task is to humanize the governors of prisons, to civilise the warders and to Christianise the chaplains."[117]

In *Lady Windermere's Fan*, the rakish Lord Darlington patently rejects the idea of adopting a different mode of life: "Ah! You are beginning to reform me. 'Tis a dangerous thing to reform any one, Lady Windermere."[118] As I said at the beginning of this chapter, my aim has not been to present a clear vision of Wilde's politics but rather to illuminate how he thought about reform, understood as the translation of ideas into the world of action. Wilde believed in social reform, though he did not—at least as a matter of principle—openly endorse social reform movements. For Wilde, any significant change in the real world was to take place first in the world of thought. This did not mean simply devising an inspired new vision of society, one founded on worshiping beauty and denouncing suffering. The true man of reform belonged to the contemplative life. I have deliberately avoided referring to this final chapter as a "conclusion," although it assuredly fulfills many of the functions of one. To conclude would be to suggest that Wilde's intellectual life ever had a clear origin or terminus. And we have seen in the preceding chapters that the world of thought he inhabited stretched back to the beginning of time and reaches out to us, here, at this very moment.

Notes

1. Wilde, "Critic as Artist," in *Criticism*, ed. Josephine M. Guy, vol. 4 of *The Complete Works of Oscar Wilde* (Oxford: Oxford University Press, 2007): 123–206, 175.
2. Wilde, "Critic as Artist," 147.
3. Edouard Roditi, *Oscar Wilde* (New York: New Directions, 1935), 104.
4. Roditi, *Oscar Wilde*, 113.
5. Patricia Behrendt, *Oscar Wilde: Eros and Aesthetics* (New York: Palgrave, 1991), 15. Although it is almost impossible to assess whether Wilde's conduct at trial was a matter of tragic naïvete or bravery, there is a great deal of sympathetic truth to Behrendt's assessment. Wilde's refusal to operate according to the rules of politics and social custom is at once exhilarating and agonizing to behold in the trial transcripts. See Merlin Holland, *The Real Trial of Oscar Wilde* (New York: Perennial, 2004).
6. See Josephine M. Guy, "Oscar Wilde and Socialism," in *Oscar Wilde in Context*, ed. Peter Raby and Kerry Powell (Cambridge: Cambridge University Press, 2013): 242–52. See also: Josephine M. Guy and Ian Small, *Oscar Wilde's Profession: Writing and the Culture Industry* (Oxford: Oxford University Press, 2000), 275–280.
7. Wilde's debt to writers like Peter Kropotkin, Bernard Shaw, Sidney Webb, William Morris, and others has been established, for instance, in George Woodcock, *Anarchism* (Harmondsworth: Penguin, 1963); J.D. Thomas, "The Soul of Man Under Socialism": An Essay in Context, *Rice University Studies* 51 (1965): 83–95; Isobel Murray (ed.), *Oscar Wilde: The Soul of Man and Prison Writings* (Oxford: Oxford University Press, 1990), vii–xviii; Laurence Davis, "Morris, Wilde, and Marx on the Social Preconditions of Individual Development," *Political Studies* 44.4 (1996): 719–32; and Ruth Livesy, "Morris, Carpenter, Wilde, and the Political Aesthetics of Labor," *Victorian Literature and Culture* 32.2 (2004): 601–16.
8. In particular, Killeen observes that the terms "anarchism," "socialism," and "Fenianism" were often used interchangeably at the time—and none of

these categories was organized around a clearly defined set of principles that would have been legible to the general reader. See Jarlath Killeen, *The Faiths of Oscar Wilde* (London: Palgrave, 2005), 110–115.

9. For instance, see also Sos Eltis, *Revising Wilde: Society and Subversion in the Plays of Oscar Wilde* (Oxford: Clarendon Press, 1996).

10. Raymond Williams, *Keywords* (Oxford: Oxford University Press, 2015), 202.

11. Joanna Innes, "'Reform' in English Public Life: The Fortunes of a Word," in *Rethinking the Age of Reform: Britain 1780–1850*, ed. Arthur Burns and Joanna Innes (Cambridge: Cambridge University Press, 2009): 71–97, 84.

12. Joanna Innes, Introduction to *Rethinking the Age of Reform: Britain 1780–1850*, ed. Arthur Burns and Joanna Innes (Cambridge: Cambridge University Press, 2009): 1–70, 62.

13. Innes, "Reform in English Public Life," 96.

14. Williams, *Keywords*, 203.

15. Wilde, "Critic as Artist," 180.

16. Oscar Wilde, *The Picture of Dorian Gray* (1891), in *The Picture of Dorian Gray: The 1890 and 1891 Texts*, ed. Joseph Bristow, vol. 3 of *The Complete Works of Oscar Wilde* (Oxford: Oxford University Press, 2005), 168.

17. Oscar Wilde, *Complete Letters of Oscar Wilde*, ed. Merlin Holland and Rupert Hart-Davis (New York: Henry Holt and Company, 2000), 478. In many sources (including the *Complete Letters*), the recipient has been presumed to be "R. Clegg," though the true recipient seems to have been Ernest Bernulf Clegg, whose handwriting was at times less than exemplary.

18. Wilde, "Critic as Artist," 179.

19. Wilde, *Complete Letters*, 117. An especially rich discussion of this often overlooked play is to be found in Elizabeth Carolyn Miller, "Reconsidering Wilde's *Vera; or, The Nihilists*," in *Wilde Discoveries: Traditions, Histories, Archives*, ed. Joseph Bristow (Toronto: University of Toronto Press, 2013): 65–84.

20. Oscar Wilde, *Vera*, in *Salome, A Florentine Tragedy, Vera* (Boston: John W. Luce, 1908), 115–261, 147, 244.

21. Wilde, *Vera*, 220.

22. Wilde, *Vera*, 144. Stuart Robertson has suggested that the play "offers the spectacle of the revolutionary as a scapegoat, one whose sacrifice highlights the logic of the systems of representation to which they belong" (154). The same approach, in Robertson's view, would inform Wilde's decision to become both spectacle and scapegoat following his 1895 arrest. See Stuart Robertson, "The Terrorist, the Artist, and the Citizen: Oscar Wilde and *Vera*," *Journal for Cultural Research* 18.2 (2014): 146–157.

23. Wilde, *Vera*, 240, 242.

24. Oscar Wilde, "The Remarkable Rocket," in *A House of Pomegranates, The Happy Prince, and Other Tales* (London: Methuen and Company, 1908): 233–54, 253.

25. Oscar Wilde, *A Woman of No Importance* in *The Importance of Being Earnest and Other Plays*, ed. Peter Raby (New York: Oxford University Press, 1995): 93–158, 104.

26. Wilde, *The Importance of Being Earnest in The Major Works*, ed. Isobel Murray (New York: Oxford University Press, 2000): 477–538, 504.

27. Wilde, *Complete Letters*, 102–103.

28. The line that follows could practically serve as an epigraph to "The Critic as Artist": "To act is so easy, as Goethe says; to think is so hard!" Matthew Arnold, "The Function of Criticism at the Present Time," *Essays in Criticism* (London: Macmillan and Co., 1893): 1–41, 28. Years earlier, Arnold had remarked in "To a Republican Friend" (1848): "Yet, when I muse on what life is, I seem / Rather to patience prompted, than that proud / Prospect of hope which France proclaims so loud." Matthew Arnold, *Poems* (New York: Macmillan, 1879), 6–7.

29. Oscar Wilde, "Notebook on Philosophy," 1876–8, "Oscar Wilde and His Literary Circle Collection," MS W6721 M3 N9113, William Andrews Clark Memorial Library (Los Angeles, CA), 0029.

30. Henry George Liddell and Robert Scott, *An Intermediate Greek-English Lexicon* (Oxford: Clarendon Press, 1869).

31. Matthew Arnold, "The Function of Criticism," 36. Walter Pater would note in his review of *The Picture of Dorian Gray* that Wilde "carries on, more perhaps than any other writer, the brilliant critical work of Matthew Arnold." He was speaking, most immediately, of Wilde's talent for "startling his 'countrymen,'" a tactic that would seem calculated to promote the free and fresh current of ideas Arnold so prized. Walter Pater, "A Novel by Mr. Oscar Wilde," *The Bookman* (November 1891): 50–60, 59.

32. Indeed, Arnold's language in *Culture and Anarchy* (1869) seems to dovetail everywhere with Wilde's later writings, especially on this point: "So that, here as elsewhere, the practical operations of our liberal friends, by which they set so much store, and in which they invite us to join them and to show what Mr. Bright calls a commendable interest, do not seem to us so practical for real good as they think; and our Liberal friends seem to us themselves to need to Hellenise, as we say, a little,—that is, to examine into the nature of real good, and to listen to what their consciousness tells them about it,— rather than to pursue with such heat and confidence their present practical operations." Matthew Arnold, *Culture and Anarchy* (New York: Macmillan, 1896), 192.

33. Julia Prewitt-Brown, *Cosmopolitan Criticism: Oscar Wilde's Philosophy of Art* (Charlottesville: University of Virginia Press, 1997), 67.

34. Lady Wilde, "Jacta Alia Est," in *The Complete Works of Oscar Wilde, together with Essays and Stories by Lady Wilde* (Boston: The Aldine Publishing Company, 1910): 20–30, 20.

35. Both Karen Sasha Tipper and Joy Melville remark upon rumors that Lady Wilde proclaimed herself to be "the culprit, if culprit there be," though no contemporary transcripts verify this account (Melville, 39). See Karen Sasha Anthony Tipper, *A Critical Biography of Lady Jane Wilde, 1821?–1896, Irish Revolutionist, Humanist, Scholar and Poet* (Lewiston: The Edwin Mellen Press, 2002), 224; and Joy Melville, *Mother of Oscar* (London: John Murray, 1994), 38–9.

36. See Melville and Tipper.

37. Oscar Wilde, "Mr Froude's Blue-Book," in *Journalism 2*, ed. John Stokes and Mark Turner, vol. 7 of *The Complete Works of Oscar Wilde* (Oxford: Oxford University Press, 2013), 203–206.

38. M.J. O'Neill, "Irish Poets of the Nineteenth Century. Unpublished Lecture Notes of Oscar Wilde," *University Review* 1.4 (1955) 29–32, 29.

39. O'Neill, "Irish Poets," 30.

40. Bobby Fong and Karl Beckson have scrupulously annotated Wilde's political allusions in these poems, though noting that the limited recognition the poems garnered upon publication "may have been responsible for Wilde's decision to limit the thematic range of his later work to mainly classical, pastoral, and Decadent subjects" (xxv). It is, of course, difficult to assess to any degree of certainty whether Wilde's movement away from political verse may have been motivated by the market, but his political leanings certainly assumed a different form from this time forward, taking for instance a more abstract and speculative form in the fairy tales. One especially illuminating discussion of Wilde's political poetry is to be found in Nicholas Frankel, "'Ave Imperatrix': Oscar Wilde and the Poetry of Englishness," *Victorian Poetry* 35.2 (1997): 117–37.

41. Oscar Wilde, "Quantum Mutata," in *Poems and Poems in Prose*, ed. Bobby Fong and Karl Beckson, vol. 1 of *The Complete Works of Oscar Wilde* (Oxford: Oxford University Press, 2000): 40 [lines 10–13]. The poem also calls to mind Ford Madox Brown's painting "Cromwell, Protector of the Vaudois" (1877), which features Cromwell in conversation with Milton over the massacre. The painting was first exhibited in Manchester, where it remains still, and I have thus far been unable to find concrete evidence of Wilde's encounter with the painting.

42. See Oscar Wilde, *Poems and Poems in Prose*, ed. Bobby Fong and Karl Beckson, vol. 1 of *The Complete Works of Oscar Wilde* (Oxford: Oxford University Press, 2000): 237–38, 245.

43. Oscar Wilde, "Libertatis Sacra Fames," in *Poems and Poems in Prose*, ed. Bobby Fong and Karl Beckson, vol. 1 of *The Complete Works of Oscar Wilde* (Oxford: Oxford University Press, 2000): 148 [lines 6–8].

44. Wilde, "Libertatis Sacra Fames," 148 [lines 14].

45. John Sloan, *Authors in Context: Oscar Wilde* (Oxford: Oxford University Press, 2003), 100. The implication is that both Wilde and his mother,

despite their avowed sympathies for nationalism and labor, nevertheless aspired to and celebrated a decidedly English form of aristocracy in practice.

46. Sloan, *Oscar Wilde*, 100.
47. Julia A. Buckler, "Melodramatizing Russia: Nineteenth-Century Views from the West," in *Imitations of Life: Two Centuries of Melodrama in Russia*, eds. Louise McReynolds and Joan Neuberger (Durham: Duke University Press, 2002).
48. Ruth Robbins, *Oscar Wilde* (London: Continuum, 2011), 24–26.
49. Jarlath Killeen has established, many times over, that Irish culture was an enduring rather than an occasional influence on Wilde's work. See *The Faiths of Oscar Wilde* and *The Fairy Tales of Oscar Wilde* (New York: Routledge, 2016). See also Jerusha McCormack, *Wilde the Irishman* (New Haven: Yale University Press, 1998) and Davis Coakley, *Oscar Wilde: The Importance of Being Irish* (Dublin: Town House, 1994).
50. Robbins, *Oscar Wilde*, 26.
51. Oscar Wilde, "Theoretikos," in *Poems and Poems in Prose*, ed. Bobby Fong and Karl Beckson, vol. 1 of *The Complete Works of Oscar Wilde* (Oxford: Oxford University Press, 2000): 44–5, 44.
52. Wilde, "Theoretikos," 45.
53. Wilde, "Theoretikos," 44.
54. Wilde, "Theoretikos," 44.
55. Barbara Caine, "Feminism," in *Oscar Wilde in Context*, ed. Kerry Powell and Peter Raby (Cambridge: Cambridge University Press, 2013): 289–96, 291.
56. Wilde, *An Ideal Husband*, in *The Major Works*, ed. Isobel Murray (New York: Oxford University Press, 2000): 389–476, 401.
57. In *An Ideal Husband*, Lady Chiltern enters the stage announcing: "I have just come from the Woman's Liberal Association, where, by the way, Robert, your name was received with loud applause […]" (197).
58. Wilde, *Complete Letters*, 311.
59. Wilde, *Complete Letters*, 297.
60. For more context regarding Wilde's editing of *Woman's World*, see Diana Maltz, "Wilde's *The Woman's World* and the Culture of Aesthetic Philanthropy," in *Wilde Writings: Contextual Conditions*, ed. Joseph Bristow (Toronto: University of Toronto Press, 2003): 186–211; Molly Youngkin, "The Aesthetic Character of Oscar Wilde's *The Woman's World*," in *Wilde Discoveries: Traditions, Histories, Archives* (Toronto: University of Toronto Press, 2013): 121–42.
61. Matthew Arnold, "The Function of Criticism at the Present Time," 18, 19, 21, 22.
62. Bernard Shaw, *Shaw: An Autobiography, 1856–1898* (New York: Weybright and Talley, 1969), 251.
63. Shaw, 251.

64. Shaw, 248.
65. Shaw, 248.
66. For an examination of Wilde as a political thinker, see for instance: Sos Eltis, *Revising Wilde*.
67. Wilde, "Soul of Man," 233.
68. Josephine M. Guy, "'The Soul of Man Under Socialism': A (Con) Textual History," in *Wilde Writings: Contextual Conditions*, ed. Joseph Bristow (Toronto: University of Toronto Press, 2003): 59–85.
69. Grant Allen, "Individualism and Socialism," *Contemporary Review* 55 (1889): 730–34.
70. Dan Bivona has recently been at work establishing new and provocative links between Wilde and Allen in a piece soon to be published, though the connection has also been explored in Lindsay Wilhelm, "Sex in Utopia: The Evolutionary Hedonism of Grant Allen and Oscar Wilde," *Victorian Literature and Culture* 46.2 (2018): 403–424.
71. Wilde, *Complete Letters*, 470n.
72. Edward Sullivan reported: "He never entertained any pronounced views on social, religious or political questions while in College." Qtd. in Frank Harris, *Oscar Wilde: His Life and Confessions* (New York, 1916), 38. Sullivan's account is, of course, a subjective one, and Wilde certainly seems to have offered direct commentaries on political ideas, especially in *Poems*. Nevertheless, personal convictions are always difficult to verify, and Wilde's political views do seem to vacillate a great deal, as his early poetry would seem to indicate.
73. Oscar Wilde, "Notebook on Philosophy," 1876–8, "Oscar Wilde and His Literary Circle Collection," MS W6721 M3 N9113, William Andrews Clark Memorial Library (Los Angeles, CA): 0013.
74. This at least is the source Wilde mentions in the notebook. Cairnes's critique of Comte first appeared in an 1870 essay for the *Fortnightly Review*, entitled "M. Compte and Political Economy."
75. Oscar Wilde, *Commonplace Book*, in *Oscar Wilde's Oxford Notebooks: A Portrait of Mind in the Making*, ed. Philip E. Smith II and Michael Helfand (Oxford: Oxford University Press, 1989): 107–152. 121 [69]. For all references to Wilde's Notebook Kept at Oxford and Commonplace Book, I have included the pagination from Smith and Helfand's edition, followed by the manuscript pagination in brackets (as shown).
76. Wilde, Commonplace Book, 130 [121].
77. Wilde, Commonplace Book, 116 [43].
78. Wilde, Commonplace Book, 116 [43].
79. John Ruskin, *Stones of Venice* (London: Smith, Elder, and Company, 1853), 169–70.
80. Oscar Wilde "Art and the Handicraftsman," in *Miscellanies*. Ed. Robert Ross. London: Methuen and Company, 1908. 291–308, 307.

81. Wilde, "Art and the Handicraftsman," 307.

82. Oscar Wilde, "Mr. Morris on Tapestry," in *Journalism 2*, ed. John Stokes and Mark Turner, vol. 7 of *The Complete Works of Oscar Wilde* (Oxford: Oxford University Press, 2003), 96–98.

83. Oscar Wilde, "The Beauties of Bookbinding," in *Journalism 2*, ed. John Stokes and Mark Turner, vol. 7 of *The Complete Works of Oscar Wilde* (Oxford: Oxford University Press, 2003), 104–106. A similar sentiment is conveyed by Wilde the following week in "The Close of the 'Arts and Crafts'": "In old days the craftsman was a designer, he had his prentice days of quiet study, and even the painter began by grinding colours. Some little old ornament still lingers here and there, on the brass rosettes of cart-horses, in the common milk-cans of Antwerp, in the water-vessels of Italy. But even this is disappearing. 'The tourist passes by,' and creates a demand that commerce satisfies in an unsatisfactory manner. We have not yet arrived at a healthy state of things. [...] Art depends on Life. We cannot get it from machines. And yet machines are bad only when they are our masters." Oscar Wilde, "The Close of the 'Arts and Crafts'," in *Journalism 2*, ed. John Stokes and Mark Turner, vol. 7 of *The Complete Works of Oscar Wilde* (Oxford: Oxford University Press, 2003), 106–108. To be sure, Wilde goes on to remark somewhat doubtfully on classifying bookbinding as a mode of individual expression; articulating "its own beauty, its own wonder," Wilde remains reluctant to align it with painting or literature ("Beauties of Bookbinding," 106). In later years, Wilde would take great care in selecting the binding for many of his own works, suggesting at least that such considerations helped to augment the effect of his own writing.

84. Oscar Wilde, "Poetical Socialists," in *Journalism 2*, ed. John Stokes and Mark Turner, vol. 7 of *The Complete Works of Oscar Wilde* (Oxford: Oxford University Press, 2003), 170–72, 171.

85. Wilde, "Art and the Handicraftsman," in *Miscellanies* (London: Methuen and Company, 1908): 291–308, 305.

86. Wilde, *House Decoration*, in *Miscellanies*, ed. Robert Ross. London: Methuen and Company, 1908. 279–90, 288–89.

87. Wilde, "Art and the Handicraftsman," 208.

88. Isobel Murray is especially attuned to Emerson's influence on Wilde. See her notes to Oscar Wilde, "The Soul of Man Under Socialism," *Soul of Man, De Profundis, The Ballad of Reading Gaol*, ed. Isobel Murray (Oxford: Oxford University Press, 1999): 1–37, 200, 201, 206.

89. Ralph Waldo Emerson, "Man the Reformer," in *Representative Men, Nature, Addresses, and Lectures* (Boston: Houghton Mifflin, 1860): 215–44, 236.

90. Emerson, "Man the Reformer," 235.

91. Emerson, "Man the Reformer," 237.

92. Wilde, "Soul of Man," 232.

93. Wilde, "Soul of Man," 232.

94. Lawrence Danson, *Wilde's Intentions: The Artist in his Criticism* (Oxford: Clarendon Press, 1997), 167.
95. Wilde, "Soul of Man," 240.
96. Wilde, "Soul of Man," 264.
97. The Christian Socialists constitute a relevant instance of this tendency. See, for example: Edward R. Norman, *The Victorian Christian Socialists* (Cambridge: Cambridge University Press, 2002).
98. Wilde, "Soul of Man," 241.
99. Emerson, 232.
100. See Jarlath Killeen, *The Fairy Tales of Oscar Wilde.*
101. Oscar Wilde, "The Young King," *The Complete Shorter Fiction* (Oxford: Oxford University Press, 1979): 171–84, 175.
102. Wilde, "The Young King," 183.
103. Wilde, "The Young King," 184.
104. Oscar Wilde, "The English Renaissance of Art," in *Miscellanies*, ed. Robert Ross (London: Methuen and Company, 1908): 241–77, 275.
105. Wilde, "Soul of Man," 247.
106. See Thomas More, *Utopia* (New York: Columbian Publishing Company, 1891).
107. Brown, *Cosmopolitan Criticism*, 32.
108. Wilde, "Soul of Man," 262.
109. Oscar Wilde, "A Chinese Sage," in *Journalism 2*, ed. John Stokes and Mark Turner, vol. 7 of *The Complete Works of Oscar Wilde* (Oxford: Oxford University Press, 2003): 237–43, 238. As Jerusha McCormack has astutely noted, Wilde's rhetoric throughout the 1890s resembles and sometimes even seems to paraphrase that of Zhuangzi. See Jerusha McCormack, "Oscar Wilde: A Daoist Sage," in *Philosophy and Oscar Wilde*, ed. Michael Bennett (New York: Palgrave, 2018): 73–104.
110. Oscar Wilde, "Literary and Other Notes," in *Journalism 2*, ed. John Stokes and Mark Turner, vol. 7 of *The Complete Works of Oscar Wilde* (Oxford: Oxford University Press, 2003): 1–11. 1.
111. For a detailed and illuminating treatment of the social problem novel, see Josephine M. Guy, *The Victorian Social-Problem Novel: The Market, the Individual, and Communal Life* (London: Macmillan, 1996).
112. Wilde, "Decay of Lying" in *Criticism*, ed. Josephine M. Guy, vol. 4 of *The Complete Works of Oscar Wilde* (Oxford: Oxford University Press, 2007): 72–103, 78.
113. Oscar Wilde, "Some Literary Notes," in *Journalism 2*, ed. John Stokes and Mark Turner, vol. 7 of *The Complete Works of Oscar Wilde* (Oxford: Oxford University Press, 2003), 175–84, 180.
114. Wilde, *Complete Letters*, 1045.
115. Wilde, *Complete Letters*, 1046–47.
116. Wilde, *Complete Letters*, 849.

117. Wilde, *Complete Letters*, 1045–1049.
118. Oscar Wilde, *Lady Windermere's Fan* in *Major Works*, ed. Isobel Murray (New York: Oxford University Press, 2000), 331–88, 12.

Bibliography

Allen, Grant. 1889. Individualism and Socialism. *Contemporary Review* 55: 730–734.

Arnold, Matthew. 1865. The Function of Criticism at the Present Time. In *Essays in Criticism*, 1–41. London: Macmillan and Co.

———. 1879. To a Republican Friend. In *Poems*, 6–7. New York: Macmillan.

———. 1896. *Culture and Anarchy*. New York: Macmillan.

Behrendt, Patricia. 1991. *Oscar Wilde: Eros and Aesthetics*. New York: Palgrave.

Brown, Julia Prewitt. 1997. *Cosmopolitan Criticism: Oscar Wilde's Philosophy of Art*. Charlottesville: University of Virginia Press.

Buckler, Julia A. 2002. Melodramatizing Russia: Nineteenth-Century Views from the West. In *Imitations of Life: Two Centuries of Melodrama in Russia*, ed. Louise McReynolds and Joan Neuberger. Durham: Duke University Press.

Caine, Barbara. 2013. Feminism. In *Oscar Wilde in Context*, ed. Kerry Powell and Peter Raby, 289–296. Cambridge: Cambridge University Press.

Coakley, Davis. 1994. *Oscar Wilde: The Importance of Being Irish*. Dublin: Town House.

Danson, Lawrence. 1997. *Wilde's Intentions: The Artist in his Criticism*. Oxford: Clarendon Press.

Davis, Laurence. 1996. Morris, Wilde, and Marx on the Social Preconditions of Individual Development. *Political Studies* 44 (4): 719–732.

Eltis, Sos. 1996. *Revising Wilde: Society and Subversion in the Plays of Oscar Wilde*. Oxford: Clarendon Press.

Emerson, Ralph Waldo. 1860. Man the Reformer. In *Representative Men, Nature, Addresses, and Lectures*, 215–244. Boston: Houghton Mifflin.

Frankel, Nicholas. 1997. Ave Imperatrix': Oscar Wilde and the Poetry of Englishness. *Victorian Poetry* 35 (2): 117–137.

Guy, Josephine M. 1996. *The Victorian Social-Problem Novel: The Market, the Individual, and Communal Life*. London: Macmillan.

———. 2003. 'The Soul of Man Under Socialism': A (Con) Textual History. In *Wilde Writings: Contextual Conditions*, ed. Joseph Bristow, 59–85. Toronto: University of Toronto Press.

———. 2013. Oscar Wilde and Socialism. In *Oscar Wilde in Context*, ed. Peter Raby and Kerry Powell, 242–252. Cambridge: Cambridge University Press.

Guy, Josephine M., and Ian Small. 2000. *Oscar Wilde's Profession: Writing and the Culture Industry*, 275–280. Oxford: Oxford University Press.

Harris, Frank. 1916. *Oscar Wilde: His Life and Confessions*. New York.

Holland, Merlin, ed. 2004. *The Real Trial of Oscar Wilde*. New York: Perennial.

Innes, Joanna. 2009a. Introduction. In *Rethinking the Age of Reform: Britain 1780–1850*, ed. Arthur Burns and Joanna Innes, 1–70. Cambridge: Cambridge University Press.

———. 2009b. 'Reform' in English Public Life: The Fortunes of a Word. In *Rethinking the Age of Reform: Britain 1780–1850*, ed. Arthur Burns and Joanna Innes, 71–97. Cambridge: Cambridge University Press.

Killeen, Jarlath. 2005. *The Faiths of Oscar Wilde: Catholicism, Folklore, and Ireland*. London: Palgrave.

———. 2016. *The Fairy Tales of Oscar Wilde*. London: Routledge.

Livesy, Ruth. 2004. Morris, Carpenter, Wilde, and the Political Aesthetics of Labor. *Victorian Literature and Culture* 32 (2): 601–616.

Maltz, Diana. 2003. Wilde's *The Woman's World* and the Culture of Aesthetic Philanthropy. In *Wilde Writings: Contextual Conditions*, ed. Joseph Bristow, 186–211. Toronto: University of Toronto Press.

McCormack, Jerusha, ed. 1998. *Wilde the Irishman*. New Haven: Yale University Press.

———. 2018. Oscar Wilde: As Daoist Sage. In *Philosophy and Oscar Wilde*, ed. Michael Bennett, 73–104. New York: Palgrave.

Melville, Joy. 1994. *Mother of Oscar*. London: John Murray.

Miller, Elizabeth Carolyn. 2013. Reconsidering Wilde's *Vera; or, The Nihilists*. In *Wilde Discoveries: Traditions, Histories, Archives*, ed. Joseph Bristow, 65–84. Toronto: University of Toronto Press.

More, Thomas. 1891. *Utopia*. New York: Columbian Publishing.

Murray, Isobel, ed. 1990. *Oscar Wilde: The Soul of Man and Prison Writings*. Oxford: Oxford University Press.

Norman, Edward R. 2002. *The Victorian Christian Socialists*. Cambridge: Cambridge University Press.

O'Neill, M.J. 1955. Irish Poets of the Nineteenth Century. Unpublished Lecture Notes of Oscar Wilde. *University Review* 1 (4): 29–32.

Pater, Walter. 1891. A Novel by Mr. Oscar Wilde. *The Bookman* (November): 50–60.

Robertson, Stuart. 2014. The Terrorist, the Artist, and the Citizen: Oscar Wilde and *Vera*. *Journal for Cultural Research* 18 (2): 146–157.

Roditi, Edouard. 1935. *Oscar Wilde*. New York: New Directions.

Ruskin, John. 1853. *Stones of Venice*. London: Smith, Elder, and Company.

Shaw, Bernard. 1969. *Shaw: An Autobiography, 1856–1898*. New York: Weybright and Talley.

Sloan, John. 2003. *Authors in Context: Oscar Wilde*. Oxford: Oxford University Press.

Thomas, J.D. 1965. 'The Soul of Man Under Socialism': An Essay in Context. *Rice University Studies* 51.

Tipper, Karen Sasha Anthony. 2002. *A Critical Biography of Lady Jane Wilde, 1821?–1896, Irish Revolutionist, Humanist, Scholar and Poet*. Lewiston: The Edwin Mellen Press.

Wilde, Oscar. 1876–8. Notebook on Philosophy. In *Oscar Wilde and His Literary Circle Collection*, MS W6721M3 N9113. Los Angeles: William Andrews Clark Memorial Library.

————. 1908a. Art and the Handicraftsman. In *Miscellanies*, ed. Robert Ross, 291–308. London: Methuen.

————. 1908b. The English Renaissance of Art. In *Miscellanies*, ed. Robert Ross, 241–277. London: Methuen.

————. 1908c. The Remarkable Rocket. In *A House of Pomegranates, the Happy Prince, and Other Tales*, 233–254. London: Methuen.

————. 1908d. Vera. In *Salome, a Florentine Tragedy, Vera*, 115–261. Boston: John W. Luce.

Wilde, Lady Jane Francesca. 1910. Jacta Alia Est. In *The Complete Works of Oscar Wilde, Together with Essays and Stories by Lady Wilde*, 20–30. Boston: The Aldine Publishing.

Wilde, Oscar. 1979. The Young King. In *The Complete Shorter Fiction*, 171–184. Oxford: Oxford University Press.

————. 1995. In *A Woman of No Importance. The Importance of Being Earnest and Other Plays*, ed. Peter Raby, 93–158. New York: Oxford University Press.

————. 2000a. *Complete Letters of Oscar Wilde*, ed. Merlin Holland and Rupert Hart-Davis. New York: Henry Holt and Company.

————. 2000b. An Ideal Husband. In *The Major Works*, ed. Isobel Murray, 389–476. New York: Oxford University Press.

————. 2000c. The Importance of Being Earnest. In *The Major Works*, ed. Isobel Murray, 477–538. New York: Oxford University Press.

————. 2000d. Lady Windermere's Fan. In *The Major Works*, ed. Isobel Murray, 331–388. New York: Oxford University Press.

————. 2000e. Libertatis Sacra Fames. In *Poems and Poems in Prose*, ed. Bobby Fong and Karl Beckson, 148. Vol. 1 of *The Complete Works of Oscar Wilde*. Oxford: Oxford University Press.

————. 2000f. Quantum Mutata. In *Poems and Poems in Prose*, ed. Bobby Fong and Karl Beckson, 40. Vol. 1 of *The Complete Works of Oscar Wilde*. Oxford: Oxford University Press.

————. 2000g. Theoretikos. In *Poems and Poems in Prose*, ed. Bobby Fong and Karl Beckson, 44–45. Vol. 1 of *The Complete Works of Oscar Wilde I*. Oxford: Oxford University Press.

————. 2005. *The Picture of Dorian Gray* (1891). In *The Picture of Dorian Gray: The 1890 and 1891 Texts*, ed. Joseph Bristow. Vol. 3 of *The Complete Works of Oscar Wilde*. Oxford: Oxford University Press.

————. 2007a. The Critic as Artist. In *Criticism*, ed. Josephine M. Guy, 123–206. Vol. 4 of *The Complete Works of Oscar Wilde*. Oxford: Oxford University Press.

————. 2007b. The Decay of Lying. In *Criticism*, ed. Josephine M. Guy, 72–103. Vol. 4 of *The Complete Works of Oscar Wilde*. Oxford: Oxford University Press.

————. 2007c. The Soul of Man Under Socialism. In *Criticism*, ed. Josephine M. Guy, 231–268. In Vol. 4 of *The Complete Works of Oscar Wilde*. Oxford: Oxford University Press.

————. 2013a. The Beauties of Bookbinding. In *Journalism II*, ed. John Stokes and Mark Turner, 104–106. Vol. 7 of *The Complete Works of Oscar Wilde*. Oxford: Oxford University Press.

————. 2013b. A Chinese Sage. In *Journalism II*, ed. John Stokes and Mark Turner, 237–243. Vol. 7 of *The Complete Works of Oscar Wilde*. Oxford: Oxford University Press.

————. 2013c. The Close of the 'Arts and Crafts'. In *Journalism II*, ed. John Stokes and Mark Turner, 106–108. Vol. 7 of *The Complete Works of Oscar Wilde*. Oxford: Oxford University Press.

————. 2013d. Literary and Other Notes. In *Journalism II*, ed. John Stokes and Mark Turner, 1–11. Vol. 7 of *The Complete Works of Oscar Wilde*. Oxford: Oxford University Press.

————. 2013e. Mr Froude's Blue-Book. In *Journalism II*, ed. John Stokes and Mark Turner, 203–206. Vol. 7 of *The Complete Works of Oscar Wilde*. Oxford: Oxford University Press.

————. 2013f. Mr. Morris on Tapestry. In *Journalism II*, ed. John Stokes and Mark Turner, 96–98. Vol. 7 of *The Complete Works of Oscar Wilde*. Oxford: Oxford University Press.

————. 2013g. Poetical Socialists. In *Journalism II*, ed. John Stokes and Mark Turner, 170–172. Vol. 7 of *The Complete Works of Oscar Wilde*. Oxford: Oxford University Press.

————. 2013h. Some Literary Notes. In *Journalism II*, ed. John Stokes and Mark Turner, 175–184. Vol. 7 of *The Complete Works of Oscar Wilde*. Oxford: Oxford University Press.

Wilhelm, Lindsay. 2018. Sex in Utopia: The Evolutionary Hedonism of Grant Allen and Oscar Wilde. *Victorian Literature and Culture* 46 (2): 403–424.

Williams, Raymond. 2015. *Keywords*. Oxford: Oxford University Press.

Woodcock, George. 1963. *Anarchism*. Harmondsworth: Penguin.

Youngkin, Molly. 2013. The Aesthetic Character of Oscar Wilde's *The Woman's World*. In *Wilde Discoveries: Traditions, Histories, Archives*, 121–142. Toronto: University of Toronto Press.

Further Reading[1]

Education

Birch, Dinah. 2008. *Our Victorian Education*. Oxford: Blackwell.

Daunton, Martin, ed. 2005. *The Organisation of Knowledge in Victorian Britain*. Oxford: Oxford University Press.

Dowling, Linda. 2014. *Hellenism and Homosexuality in Victorian Oxford*. Ithaca: Cornell University Press.

Rauch, Alan. 2001. *Useful Knowledge: The Victorians, Morality, and the March of Intellect*. Durham: Duke University Press.

Scott, Patrick, and Pauline Fletcher, eds. 1990. *Culture and Education in Victorian England*. Lewisburg: Bucknell University Press.

Religion

Fraser, Hilary. 1986. *Beauty and Belief: Aesthetics and Religion in Victorian Literature*. Cambridge: Cambridge University Press.

Hanson, Ellis. 1997. *Decadence and Catholicism*. Cambridge: Harvard University Press.

Knight, Frances. 2016. *Victorian Christianity at the Fin de Siècle: The Culture of Religion in a Decadent Age*. London: I.B. Tauris.

Knight, Mark, and Emma Mason, eds. 2006. *Nineteenth-Century Religion and Literature: An Introduction*. Oxford: Oxford University Press.

Larsen, Timothy. 2006. *Crisis of Doubt: Honest Faith in Nineteenth-Century England*. Oxford: Oxford University Press.

© The Author(s) 2019
K. J. Stern, *Oscar Wilde*, Literary Lives,
https://doi.org/10.1007/978-3-030-24604-4

Science

Holmes, John, and Sharon Ruston, eds. 2017. *The Routledge Research Companion to Nineteenth-Century British Literature and Science*. New York: Routledge.

Lightman, Bernard. 2008. *Victorian Science in Context*. Chicago: University of Chicago Press.

Olson, Richard. 2008. *Science and Scientism in Nineteenth-Century Europe*. Urbana: University of Illinois Press.

Secord, James. 2015. *Visions of Science: Books and Readers and the Dawn of the Victorian Age*. Chicago: University of Chicago Press.

Philosophy

Dunham, Jeremy, Iain Hamilton Grant, and Sean Watson. 2011. *Idealism: The History of a Philosophy*. London: Routledge.

Guyer, Paul. 2018. *A History of Modern Aesthetics: The Nineteenth Century*. Cambridge: Cambridge University Press.

Mander, W.J. 2014. *The Oxford Handbook of British Philosophy in the Nineteenth Century*. Oxford: Oxford University Press.

Moyar, Dean, ed. 2010. *The Routledge Companion to Nineteenth Century Philosophy*. London: Routledge.

Politics and Reform

Burns, Arthur, and Joanna Innes, eds. 2003. *Rethinking the Age of Reform: Britain 1780–1850*. Cambridge: Cambridge University Press.

Craig, D., and J. Thompson. 2013. *The Languages of Politics in Nineteenth-Century Britain*. New York: Springer.

Dennis, Barbara, and David Skilton. 2016. *Reform and Intellectual Debate in Victorian England*. London: Routledge.

Steinbach, Susie L. 2016. *Understanding the Victorians: Politics, Culture and Society in Nineteenth-Century Britain*. London: Routledge.

Note

1. It is impossible to survey in a single volume the range of ideas and institutions circulating during Oscar Wilde's lifetime. The reader wishing to delve further into Oscar Wilde's treatment of specific subjects and thinkers will find much to

satisfy their curiosity in the notes provided at the end of each chapter. For the reader who wishes to bring into focus broader historical contexts, however, I offer this brief list of resources, which provides a starting point for understanding nineteenth-century attitudes toward education, religion, science, philosophy, and reform.

Index[1]

---

[1] Note: Page numbers followed by 'n' refer to notes.

© The Author(s) 2019
K. J. Stern, *Oscar Wilde*, Literary Lives,
https://doi.org/10.1007/978-3-030-24604-4